Antoinette

Children's Illustrated Dictionary

John McIlwain

DK

DORLING KINDERSLEY

Contents

DK

LONDON, NEW YORK,
MELBOURNE, MUNICH, AND DELHI

Senior Editors Nicola Tuxworth,
Susan Peach
Senior Art Editor Rowena Alsey
Project Editor Lee Simmons
Art Editor Marcus James
Editor Claire Watts
Designers Cheryl Telfer, Diane Clouting
Managing Editor Jane Yorke
Managing Art Editor Chris Scollen
Production Jayne Wood

Photography by Andy Crawford,
Steve Gorton, Susanna Price,
and Tim Ridley
Illustrated by Grahame Corbett,
Peter Dennis, Bill Le Fever,
Nicholas Heweteson, Louis Mackay,
Roger Stewart, and Jolyon Webb
Language Consultants The Centre for Literacy
in Primary Education, London
Pronunciation Consultant Sheila Dignen

2014 Edition:

DK UK

Project Editor Ashwin Khurana
Senior Art Editor Jim Green
Editor Helen Abramson
Managing Editor Linda Esposito
Managing Art Editor Diane Peyton Jones
Publisher Andrew Macintyre
Pre-production Producer Adam Stoneham
Producer Gemma Sharpe
Jacket Editor Manisha Majithia
Jacket Designer Laura Brim
Jacket Development Manager Sophia MTT
Geography Consultant Simon Mumford
Publishing Director Jonathan Metcalf
Associate Publishing Director Liz Wheeler
Art Director Phil Ormerod

DK India

Senior Editors Samira Sood, Neha Gupta
Editor Esha Banerjee
Art Editors Mahipal Singh, Vikas Chauhan
Assistant Editor Deeksha Saikia
Assistant Art Editor Honlung Zach Ragui
DTP Designers Syed Md Farhan,
Vishal Bhatia
Picture Researcher Surya Sankash Sarangi
Illustrator Arun Pottirayil
Deputy Managing Editor Kingshuk Ghoshal
Deputy Managing Art Editor Govind Mittal
Pre-production Manager Balwant Singh
Production Manager Pankaj Sharma

First published in Great Britain in 1994.
This revised edition published in 2014 by
Dorling Kindersley Limited,
80 Strand, London, WC2 ORL

Copyright © 1994, 2009, 2014
Dorling Kindersley Limited
A Penguin Company
2 4 6 8 10 9 7 5 3 1
001 – 187514 – 07/14

A CIP catalogue record for this book
is available from the British Library.

ISBN 978-1-4093-3702-7

Colour reproduction by Alta Images, UK
Printed and bound by South China Printing
Co Ltd, China

Discover more at
www.dk.com

Introduction

The Dorling Kindersley Children's Illustrated Dictionary is specifically aimed at children of seven years and up, an age when children are becoming increasingly independent readers and writers, and when a dictionary can be a valuable companion.

Words and pictures

Unlike many other dictionaries, *The Children's Illustrated Dictionary* is not just about words – it also contains pictures. Children today are used to information being presented in a visual form through television, film, and computers, and are skilled readers of images. As a result, they require books to be increasingly visually sophisticated.

The colourful photographs and illustrations in this dictionary are fresh, exciting, and highly relevant to children's interests and concerns. These images will help to draw young readers into the book, and also work with the text to give clear and concise definitions.

Vital skills for readers and writers

Using a dictionary can teach children many useful skills. One of the most important is the ability to locate information that is organized in alphabetical order. Once acquired, this skill will enable them to use many other reference books, from telephone directories to encyclopedias, which are organized along the same principle. The clear design and layout of this dictionary make it easy for children to learn how to look things up.

The Children's Illustrated Dictionary can also help to widen vocabulary and improve spelling. Young readers and writers can find out for themselves what an unfamiliar word means, or check any spellings about which they are unsure.

In addition, this book will help children develop their awareness of words and the relationships between them. An introductory section explains the concept of parts of speech, such as nouns and verbs, which are also listed under each entry in the dictionary, while the end section looks at word beginnings and endings, spelling patterns, and common abbreviations.

A dictionary with a difference

A unique feature of this dictionary is the 26 full-page entries, where words and pictures are grouped by

theme. Browsing through these word collections, on subjects as diverse as costume and time, children will enjoy recognizing known words and concepts, and discovering new vocabulary and information. These pages offer many opportunities for discussion and provide the basis for further exploration of a wide range of topics and themes.

A lasting work of reference

The Children's Illustrated Dictionary combines a core of common vocabulary with words that have a high interest level for children of this age group. It provides them with both a rich source of information about the world and an important resource for developing their reading and writing skills.

The Centre for Literacy in Primary Education, London

All about words

In every sentence that we speak or write, there are several types of word. They are called "parts of speech". Each of them has its own name and its own job to do in the sentence. In this dictionary, each word entry has its part of speech printed below it in *italic* type. The parts of speech that are labelled in the dictionary (verbs, adverbs, adjectives, interjections, prepositions, and nouns) are explained on these two pages.

Verbs

Verbs are sometimes called "action words" because they are words that describe what a person or a thing is doing. **Sit**, **think**, **sleep**, **sing**, and **climb** are all verbs. A sentence must contain a verb to make sense. There are a few special kinds of verb, such as "being" and "helping" verbs, that do slightly different jobs in a sentence.

*He **runs** for an hour every morning.*

*The dog often **lies** on the floor.*

*They **were** both very angry.*

Being verbs

Being words, such as **am**, **is**, **are**, **was**, and **were** all come from the verb **to be**. They link someone or something with the words that describe them.

Helping verbs

Verbs such as **have**, **be**, **will**, **must**, **may**, and **do**, are sometimes used with other verbs in a sentence. They show how possible or necessary it is that an action takes place. Helping verbs can also show a verb's tense.

*It **may rain** tomorrow.*

*I **do like** sandwiches!*

Verb tenses

The form of a verb shows whether the action it describes takes place in the present, the past, or the future. This is called the verb's tense. When a verb, such as **hang**, appears in this dictionary, the entry looks like this:

hang
hangs hanging hung
verb

The second line of the entry shows how the verb is written in three different tenses – the present, the continuous present, and the past tense. These tenses are used like this:

Present tense:
*She **hangs** up her T-shirt.*

Continuous present tense:
*She **is hanging** up her T-shirt.*

Past tense:
*She **hung** up her T-shirt.*

Adverbs

An adverb is a word that gives more information about a verb, an adjective, or another adverb. Adverbs can tell us how, when, where, how often, or how much. **Slowly**, **yesterday**, **upwards**, and **very** are all adverbs. Many adverbs end with the letters "ly".

*These newspapers are all published **daily**.*

*They played **happily** with the ball.*

Nouns

A noun is a word that names a thing, a person, or a place. **Cat**, **teacher**, **spoon**, and **city** are all nouns. Nouns do not have to be things that you can see – words such as **truth** and **geography** are also nouns.

*They often went to the **café** for a **snack**.*

*The **present** came in a big **box**, tied with **ribbon**.*

Adjectives

An adjective is a word that is used to describe a noun. **Fat**, **yellow**, **sticky**, **dark**, and **hairy** are all adjectives.

*The car was **green** and **shiny**.*

*a **tall**, **green**, **prickly** cactus*

Interjections

Interjections are words such as **hello** and **goodbye** which can be used on their own, without being part of a full sentence. Exclamations, such as **Oh**! and **Ouch**!, are also interjections.

Conjunctions

Conjunctions are words such as **and**, **but**, and **or**, which are used to join parts of sentences together.

Prepositions

Prepositions, such as **in**, **with**, **behind**, and **on**, show how one person or thing relates to another.

*She held the ball **above** her head.*

Comparatives and superlatives

If you want to compare a person or thing with another, you often use an adjective in the comparative or superlative form. **Taller**, **easier**, **better**, and **quicker** are comparatives. **Tallest**, **easiest**, **best**, and **quickest** are superlatives. Comparatives either end with the letters "-er", or include the word "more". Superlatives either end with the letters "-est" or include the word "most".

Adjective:
*This ball is **big**.*

Comparative:
*This ball is **bigger**.*

Superlative:
*This ball is the **biggest**.*

a b c d e f g h i j k l m n o p q r s t u v w x y z

How to use this dictionary

Read the information on these two pages to find out how to get the most from your dictionary. Most pages in the book look like the double page from the letter **R** section shown below. There are also 26 full-page entries in the dictionary, which provide a whole page of pictures and vocabulary on a theme. The page shown here is about cars.

What's on a page

Guide word

Use the guide word at the top of the page to help you find the page a word is on. The left-hand guide word, **rabbi**, tells you that this is the first word on the page.

Headword

This is the word you are looking up. The headword is printed in heavy, grey letters at the start of the entry. The definition underneath explains what the headword means.

Guide word

The right-hand guide word, **rate**, tells you that this is the last word on this page.

New letter section

Each new letter section starts with a big letter, like this **R**.

Pictures

The photos and illustrations show you exactly what things look like and help to define the headwords.

Alphabet

Use the alphabet running down the side of the page to help you find your place in the dictionary. The highlighted letter tells you that you are in the **R** section.

Word box

Families of linked words are enclosed in a box. All the words in this box start with the same word, **rain**.

Full-page entries

All the pictures and labels on a full-page entry are linked to the main headword. This page shows types of car, with their various parts labelled.

Alphabetical order

The headwords in this dictionary are listed in alphabetical order – the same order as the letters of the alphabet. Words that begin with **A** are grouped at the start of the dictionary, followed by **B** words, and so on up to **Z**. Where several words start with the same letter, the second letters of the words are used to decide which comes first. So **cat** comes before **cot**, because **A** comes before **O** in the alphabet. If words start with the same two letters, then the third letter decides the order. So **radius** comes before **raft**, because **D** comes before **F**.

How the entries work

Headword
The headword is printed at the start of the entry. This shows you how to spell the word.

Plural
This tells you how to write a noun when there is more than one of the thing it is referring to. Here, **rams** is the plural of the headword **ram**.

Definition
This part of the entry explains what the headword means. If a word has more than one meaning, the first meaning given is normally the one that is most common. Other meanings are listed below.

ram
rams *noun*
1 a male sheep.

2 a device for pushing against something with force.

*They used the log as a **ram** to break down the door.*
ram *verb*

Part of speech
This shows whether the word is a noun, verb, adjective, interjection, adverb, or preposition. Find out more about parts of speech on pages 4–5.

Tenses of verbs
These three forms of the verb **share** show how it is written in the present, continuous present, and past tenses. These tenses are explained on page 4.

share
shares sharing shared *verb*
1 to have or use together.
2 to divide something into parts to give to others.

*They **shared** the melon.*

Sample sentence
The sentence that follows the definition gives you an example of how the headword is used. In the sample sentence the headword is always written in heavy, black type like this: ***shared***.

Comparisons
The two forms of an adjective that are shown here are called the comparative and superlative. They are explained on page 5. **Rarer** means "more rare" and **rarest** means "the most rare".

rare
adjective
unusual or not common.
*a **rare** blue morpho butterfly*
■ comparisons **rarer rarest**
■ opposite **common**

Opposite
This tells you the word that is the opposite of the headword. For example, **common** is the opposite of the headword **rare**.

Pronunciation guide
This guide helps you to pronounce difficult words. It respells the word so that you can sound out the letters. Part of the guide is in heavy, black type. This shows you which part of the word to stress, or say more loudly.

communicate
communicates communicating communicated *verb*
to talk, write, or send a message to someone else.

communicating by telephone
■ say kom-**yoo**-ni-kate
communication *noun*

Related words
Other words that are related to the headword are listed here. This related word, **communication**, is the noun that comes from the headword **communicate**.

a
b
c
d
e
f
g
h
i
j
k
l
m
n
o
p
q
r
s
t
u
v
w
x
y
z

Dictionary games

See if you can solve these word puzzles, using your dictionary to help you. The games will help you learn how to use the dictionary quickly and easily. You can play all of the games on your own, but you could also play with a friend. Try giving a point for each correct answer and then see which of you gets the highest score. The answers to all the puzzles are somewhere in this dictionary. Have fun!

Alphabetical birds

How quickly can you arrange these 12 bird names in alphabetical order? You could use the alphabet at the side of the page to help you to sort them out. For more help, turn to page 6, where alphabetical order is explained in detail.

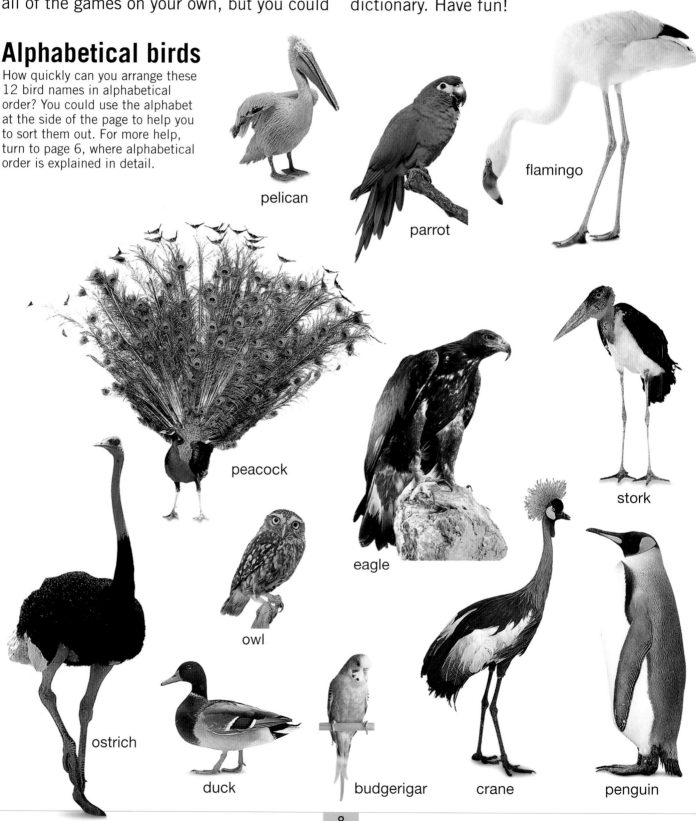

pelican

parrot

flamingo

peacock

stork

eagle

owl

ostrich

duck

budgerigar

crane

penguin

True or false?

Here are some word definitions for you to read. Can you tell which are true and which are false? Remember to check every part of the definition before you decide whether it is true. You can find out whether you were right by looking up the words in the dictionary.

An **elephant** is a huge mammal that lives in Europe and North America.

A **microscope** is an instrument that magnifies very tiny things so that they can be seen in detail.

A **harp** is a musical instrument that you hit with sticks or your hands to make a noise.

A **stethoscope** is an instrument that is used by doctors for looking in your ears.

An **iguana** is a large lizard found mainly in Central and South America.

A **mosaic** is a picture or pattern made of small squares of coloured stone.

A **plumber** is a person who repairs the glass in broken windows.

An **amphibian** is an animal that can live in water and on land.

Sound alikes

Below are some pairs of pictures. The two words that go with each pair sound the same but are spelt differently. Can you work out what they are? The first letter of each answer is shown as a clue.

Here's an example to help you:

hair

h

hare

s

f

r

p

Sound unlikes

This is the opposite of the game above. The two words that go with these pairs of pictures are spelt the same, but sound different. Can you work out what the words are? The first letter of each answer is given as a clue.

b

t

w

Odd word out

If you look carefully at these pictures of animals and objects, you will see that in each group there is an "odd word out". Which is it and why? If you get stuck, the special full-page entries in the dictionary will help you.

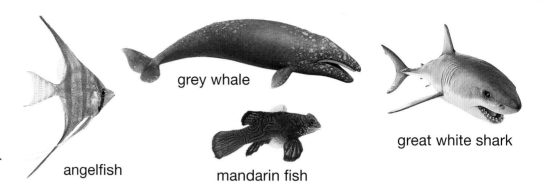

angelfish

grey whale

mandarin fish

great white shark

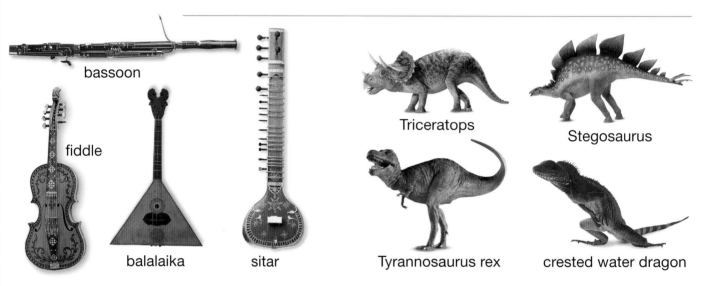

bassoon

fiddle

balalaika

sitar

Triceratops

Stegosaurus

Tyrannosaurus rex

crested water dragon

Action words

The people in these pictures are all doing something. The words in the list are all "action words", or verbs. Can you match the right verb to each of the pictures? There are more verbs than pictures, so choose carefully. Check your answers by looking up the words in the dictionary.

juggle
kneel
climb
throw
hit
crouch
bend
stretch
drum
explore

Word detective

Be a detective and follow the clues to answer these questions. The answers are all in the dictionary.

◆ Which mammal gnaws down trees to build dams in rivers?
Look for a word beginning with b.

◆ What are emeralds, sapphires, and rubies?
Look for a page of sparkly things.

◆ Which word connects an egg, a nut, and a crab?
Look on page 183.

◆ What is the opposite of few?
Check on page 125.

◆ What is the name of a planet and also the name of the silver-coloured metal used in thermometers?
Look for a word beginning with m on page 229.

◆ Which animal has withers, hocks, and a forelock?
Look for a page of large, plant-eating mammals.

◆ Where would you find a sprit, a main sheet, and a daggerboard?
Look for a page of vessels that travel on water.

Guess the word

Some words have more than one meaning. Each of these groups of pictures illustrates three different meanings of the same word. Can you work out what it is? Check in the dictionary to see if you are right.

Here's an example to help you:

| A drink of **punch**... | ...giving a **punch**... | ...and a hole **punch**. |

Rhyming words

This is a game where you have to spot the "odd word out". The words that go with each of these groups of pictures all rhyme except one. Which one is it?

The first letter of each word is there to give you a clue. Remember that there can be lots of different ways of spelling the same sound.

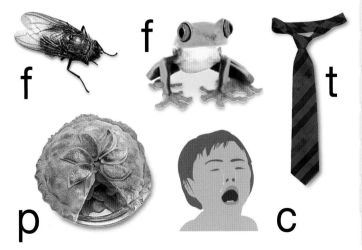

A
B C D E F G H I J K L M N O P Q R S T U V W X Y Z

abacus
abacuses *noun*
a frame with sliding beads, used for counting.

abbreviation
abbreviations *noun*
a short way of writing a word or a group of words.
*Ave is an **abbreviation** of avenue.*
■ say a-bree-vee-**ay**-shun

abdomen
abdomens *noun*
the part of an animal's or a person's body that contains the intestines and stomach (see **insect** on page 108 and **sea life** on page 178).
■ say **ab**-do-men

ability
abilities *noun*
a talent for doing something.
*He had a natural **ability** at high jump.*

about
preposition
1 on the subject of.
*We talked **about** the play.*
2 around.
*The baby crawled **about** the room.*

about
adverb
more or less.
*There were **about** 300 people at the circus.*

above
preposition
over, or higher than something.

*She held the ball **above** her head.*
■ opposite
below

abroad
adverb
in or to another country.
*She went **abroad** for her holiday.*

absent
adjective
not there, or away.
*He was **absent** from school because he had a cold.*
■ opposite **present**

absorb
absorbs absorbing absorbed *verb*
to soak up.

*A sponge **absorbs** liquid.*
absorbent *adjective*

absurd
adjective
silly or ridiculous.
*She looked **absurd** leaving for school in her pyjamas.*

accent
accents *noun*
1 the way people say words.
*She had a foreign **accent**.*
2 a mark on a letter showing you how to pronounce it.
Café is pronounced kafay.

accept
accepts accepting accepted *verb*
to take something that is offered to you.

accident
accidents *noun*
something that goes wrong by chance.
*He spilt his milk, but it was an **accident**.*

accordion
accordions *noun*
a musical instrument that you squeeze to make a sound.

accurate
adjective
exactly right.
*A stopwatch gives **accurate** time.*
■ say **ak**-yoo-rut

accuse
accuses accusing accused *verb*
to say someone has done something wrong.
*She **accused** him of lying.*
■ say a-**kyooz**

ace
aces *noun*
a playing card that has one main symbol in the centre.

ache
aches aching ached *verb*
to feel a steady pain.

*His stomach **ached**.*
■ rhymes with **cake**

acid
acids *noun*
a sharp-tasting, sour liquid.
*Some **acids** can burn you.*

acorn
acorns *noun*
the seed of
an oak tree.

acrobat
acrobats *noun*
a person who performs
gymnastics on a stage
or in a circus.

across
preposition
from one
side to
the other.

across
the bridge

act
acts acting acted *verb*
1 to behave in a certain way.
*He was **acting** very strangely.*
2 to take part in a play,
a film, or a television
programme.

action
actions *noun*
anything that somebody does.
*His quick **action** put out
the fire.*

activity
activities *noun*
1 energetic movement.
2 something that has been
planned for you to do.
active *adjective*

adapt
adapts adapting adapted *verb*
to change something to
suit a special purpose.

add
adds adding added *verb*
1 to put one thing
with another.

***Add** cherries to the mixture.*
2 to find the sum of two
or more numbers.

21+54=75

*Twenty-one **added** to fifty-four
equals seventy-five.*
addition *noun*

addict
addicts *noun*
someone who cannot give
up a habit that they have.

address
addresses *noun*
the building and area where
someone lives or works.

Jane Horne
1 Highrise flats
Bristol
BS43 1PQ

adjective
adjectives *noun*
a word that is used to
describe a noun.

adjust
adjusts
adjusting
adjusted *verb*
to make
a small
change to
something.

*She **adjusted** her belt.*

admire
**admires admiring
admired** *verb*
to think that something is
nice or good.

*She **admired** herself in
the mirror.*

admit
admits admitting admitted
verb
1 to say reluctantly that
something is true.
2 to allow someone to enter.
*A ticket **admits** you to
the cinema.*

adopt
adopts adopting adopted *verb*
to take a child into your home
as part of your family.

adult
adults *noun*
a grown-up person.
■ opposite **child**

advantage
advantages *noun*
something
that is useful
to have.

*Her long legs gave her
an **advantage**.*
■ opposite
disadvantage

adventure
adventures *noun*
something you do that
is exciting and new.
*Exploring the river was
a real **adventure**.*
adventurous *adjective*

adverb
adverbs *noun*
a word that describes a verb,
adjective, or another adverb.
*The tortoise moved **slowly**.*

advertisement
advertisements *noun*
words or pictures that try to
persuade you to buy or to do
something. Advertisement can
be shortened to advert or ad.

■ say ad-**ver**-tiss-ment

advice
noun
suggestions to help you decide
what you should do.
*Follow your dentist's **advice**
on brushing your teeth.*
advise *verb*

a b c d e f g h i j k l m n o p q r s t u v w x y z

B
C
D
E
F
G
H
I
J
K
L
M
N
O
P
Q
R
S
T
U
V
W
X
Y
Z

aerial
aerials *noun*
a device for receiving radio and television signals (see **car** on page 39).

aerial
adjective
in the air.
*An **aerial** photograph.*
■ say air-ee-al

aerobics
noun
energetic physical exercises that are done in time to music.

■ say air-**roh**-biks

aerosol
aerosols *noun*
a can that forces out liquid in a fine spray.
■ say air-**roh**-sol

affect
affects affecting affected *verb*
to make something or someone different.
*The drought badly **affected** the harvest.*

affection
noun
the feeling that you like someone very much.
affectionate *adjective*

afford
affords affording afforded *verb*
to have enough money to buy something.
*We can **afford** to go away on holiday this year.*

afraid
adjective
scared.
*He was **afraid** of spiders.*

after
preposition
1 later than.

*It is **after** 8 o'clock.*
2 behind.
*He was **after** me in the queue.*
3 following.
*The cat ran **after** the mouse.*

afternoon
afternoons *noun*
the period of time between midday and evening.

again
adverb
once more.
*The fans cheered when their team scored **again**.*

against
preposition
1 opposed to, or not on the same side.
*She was **against** the decision.*
2 next to something, touching it.

__against__ the wall

age
noun
1 how old someone or something is.

*The number of rings in a tree's trunk shows its **age**.*
2 a period in history.
*The Iron **Age**.*

aggressive
adjective
ready to attack.

*Cats can be **aggressive** if they are frightened.*
aggressively *adverb*

agony
agonies *noun*
extreme pain.
*The footballer was in **agony** when he broke his leg.*

agree
agrees agreeing agreed *verb*
to think the same as someone else.
■ opposite **disagree**

agriculture
noun
farming.

*One kind of **agriculture** in Thailand is rice growing.*
agricultural *adjective*

aground
adverb
stranded on rocks or sand, or in shallow water.
*The ship ran **aground** in the storm.*

ahead
adverb
in front.

*He moved **ahead** of the other cyclist.*

aid
noun
1 help.
*The helicopter came to the **aid** of the stranded walkers.*
2 a machine or a device that helps you do something.

hearing **aid**

aim
aims aiming aimed *verb*
1 to point an object at someone or something.

__aiming__ at the target

2 to try to do something.
*We **aim** to please.*
aim *noun*

air

air
noun
the mixture of gases that plants and animals breathe.
A layer of air surrounds Earth.

aircraft
noun
any vehicle that can fly.

aircraft-carrier
aircraft-carriers *noun*
a ship for aircraft to take off from and land on.

airline
airlines *noun*
a company that owns and flies aircraft.

airmail
noun
post that is carried by aeroplane.

airport
airports *noun*
a place where people go to travel by aeroplane.

ajar
adjective
slightly open.

The door is ajar.

alarm
noun
1 a loud noise that warns you of something.

alarm clock

2 a feeling of fear.

album
albums *noun*
a blank book for displaying pictures and other items.
A photograph album.

alcohol
noun
a strong drink, such as wine or beer.
■ say **al**-ka-hol

alert
adjective
watching and listening very carefully.

The dog looked very alert.

alien
aliens *noun*
something that seems strange or foreign.
■ say **ay**-lee-en
alien *adjective*

alike
adjective
very similar.

These sisters look alike.

alive
adjective
living.

Flowers need water to stay alive.
■ opposite **dead**

all
adjective
every part of, or everyone.
He ate all the cake himself.

allergy
allergies *noun*
an unpleasant reaction to something that doesn't affect most people.
She has an allergy to cats.

allergic *adjective*

alligator
alligators *noun*
a large reptile that lives in swamps and rivers. Alligators eat fish and other animals that come close to the water's edge.

allow
allows allowing allowed *verb*
to let someone do something.
Her parents allowed her to stay up and watch the programme.
■ opposite **forbid**

almost
adverb
nearly.

The bottle is almost empty.

alone
adjective
by yourself, without anyone else.

He was fishing alone.

along
preposition
from one end to another.
We walked along the beach.

aloud
adverb
so that it can be heard.
He read the letter aloud.

a b c d e f g h i j k l m n o p q r s t u v w x y z

alphabet
alphabets noun
a series of letters or symbols, written in a particular order, which people use to write words.
alphabetical adjective

ABCDEFGHIJKLMNOPQRSTUVWXYZ
abcdefghijklmnopqrstuvwxyz

Roman alphabet

aeiou — *letters* — bcdfghjklmnpqrstvwxyz

vowels   *consonants*

ΑΒΓΔΕΖΗΘΙΚΛΜΝΞΟΠΡΣΤΥΦΧΨΩ
αβγδεζηθικλμνξοπρστυφχψω

Greek alphabet

АБВГДЕЁЖЗИЙКЛМНОПРСТУФХЦЧШЩЪЫЬЭЮЯ
абвгдеёжзийклмнопрстуфхцчшщъыьэюя

Cyrillic alphabet

א ב ג ד ה ו ז ח ט י כ ל מ נ ס ע פ צ ק ר ש ת

Hebrew alphabet

أ ب ت ث ج ح خ د ذ ر ز س ش ص ض ط ظ ع غ ف ق ك ل م ن ه و

Arabic alphabet

Gujarati alphabet

あいうえおかきくけこさしすせそたちつてとなにぬ
ねのはひふへほまみむめもやゆよらりるれろわをん

Japanese alphabet

All of these messages say "Happy Birthday" in different alphabets.

Happy Birthday
Roman

Χρονια πολλά
Greek

с днем рождения
Cyrillic

Hebrew

Arabic

Gujarati

お誕生日 おめでとう ございます。
Japanese

already
adverb
by this time.
*She was **already** eating breakfast when he woke up.*

also
adverb
as well.
*Sue is **also** coming with us.*

alter
alters altering altered *verb*
to change something.
*I have **altered** my story to give it a happy ending.*

altogether
adverb
including everyone or everything.

*There are eight apples **altogether**.*

aluminium
noun
a silvery-white metal that is light but strong.

aluminium container

■ say al-yoo-**min**-ee-um

always
adverb
1 very often.
*He is **always** playing loud music.*
2 forever.
*I will **always** remember our holiday.*
■ opposite **never**

amazing
adjective
very surprising or out of the ordinary.

*an **amazing** photograph of the Sistine Chapel*
amaze *verb*

ambition
ambitions *noun*
what you want to be or do.
*Her **ambition** is to travel to the Moon.*

ambulance
ambulances *noun*
a vehicle for taking sick or injured people to and from hospital.

ambush
ambushes ambushing ambushed *verb*
to hide and wait for someone, then attack them by surprise when they come along.

among
preposition
in the middle of.

*There is a pen **among** the pencils.*

amount
amounts *noun*
how much there is of something.

*twice the **amount** of flour as brown sugar*

amphibian
amphibians *noun*
an animal that can live in water and on land.

■ say am-**fib**-ee-an
amphibious *adjective*

amplifier
amplifiers *noun*
a piece of equipment to make music sound louder.

amuse
amuses amusing amused *verb*
to make someone smile or laugh.
*The cartoon **amused** them.*

anaesthetic
anaesthetics *noun*
a medicine given to patients so that they don't feel pain during an operation.
■ say an-us-**thet**-ik

ancestor
ancestors *noun*
a relative from a previous generation.

*Homo habilis is an **ancestor** of man.*
■ say **an**-ses-tor

anchor
anchors *noun*
a large, heavy, metal hook that digs into the seabed to stop a ship from drifting away.

■ say **an**-ker

ancient
adjective
very old.

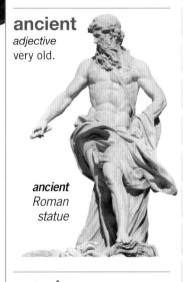

ancient Roman statue

angel
angels *noun*
a messenger from a god or God.

anger
noun
a strong feeling of annoyance.
angry *adjective*

angle
angles noun
a corner where two lines or surfaces meet.

right **angle** *(90°)*

animal
animals noun
any living thing that breathes and moves about. Insects, fish, birds, mammals, and reptiles are all types of animal.

bird

fish

insect

mammal

reptile

animation
animations noun
still pictures, often in cartoon form, which appear to move.

ankle
ankles noun
the joint between your leg and your foot.

anniversary
anniversaries noun
a special event that is remembered every year on the same date.
Wedding **anniversary**.

announce
announces announcing announced verb
to say something for everyone to hear.
"I'm going," he **announced**.

annoy
annoys annoying annoyed verb
to make someone cross.

The sound **annoyed** *her.*
annoyance noun

annual
adjective
happening every year.
Wimbledon is an **annual** *tennis competition.*
annually adverb

annual
noun
a book or a magazine published once every year.

anonymous
adjective
without a name.
An **anonymous** *letter.*
■ say a-**non**-ee-mus

another
adjective
1 different.
Have you got **another** *pen? I think this one is broken.*
2 one more.
Do you want **another** *biscuit?*

answer
answers answering answered verb
to reply to a question.
answer noun

ant
ants noun
an insect that lives in large, organized groups. The males and egg-laying females have wings.

wood **ant**

antelope
antelopes noun
a mammal that is found on dry plains in Africa and Asia. Antelopes eat grass and other plants.

A Nyala is a kind of **antelope**.

antenna
antennae or **antennas** noun
1 a long, thin part on certain animals' heads that is used for feeling (see **insect** on page 108 and **sea life** on page 178).
2 an aerial (see **universe** on page 229).

antibiotic
antibiotics noun
a medicine that kills bacteria.

antiseptic
antiseptics noun
a substance put on cuts and grazes to prevent infection.

anxious
adjective
worried or nervous.
■ say **ank**-shus

any
adjective
some or every.
■ **Any**body can do that, it's easy!
■ *She didn't tell* **any**one *what she had seen.*
■ *I'm going out, and you can't do* **any**thing *to stop me!*
■ *It might be cloudy, but we could go for a picnic* **any**way.
■ *Have you seen my pet mouse* **any**where?

apart
adverb
away from each other, or separate.

standing with feet **apart**

apartment
apartments noun
a home that is made up of a set of rooms inside a larger building.

ape
apes noun
a mammal that lives in forests in warm regions, and feeds on insects and fruit. Apes have no tails and can walk on two legs.

apologize
apologizes apologizing apologized verb
to say you are sorry.

app
apps noun
a specialized program that usually can be downloaded onto mobile phones and tablets.

apparatus
noun
the equipment you need
for a particular task.

scientific **apparatus**

appear
**appears appearing
appeared** *verb*
to come into view.
*The Sun **appeared** from
behind the clouds.*
- opposite **disappear**

appendix
appendices or **appendixes**
noun
a very small part of your
lower intestines.

stomach
appendix | intestines

appetite
appetites *noun*
a desire for food.

*He has
a huge
appetite.*

applause
noun
clapping and cheering.
*The **applause** rang out as the
team ran onto the pitch.*

apple
apples *noun*
an edible fruit
with a smooth
skin and crisp flesh.

application
applications *noun*
1 a written request, usually for
employment or membership.
2 something that can be used
for a particular purpose.

appointment
appointments *noun*
a meeting at a certain time.
*A dental **appointment**.*

appreciate
**appreciates appreciating
appreciated** *verb*
to be grateful for something.
*She **appreciated** the flowers
that her daughter sent her.*
- say a-**pree**-shee-ate

approach
**approaches approaching
approached** *verb*
to come near to something.
*The train slowed down as it
approached the station.*

approve
**approves approving
approved** *verb*
to think that something is
right or good.
*Does your mum **approve** of
your new shoes?*

approximate
adjective
almost accurate,
or not exact.

*The **approximate** number of
marbles in the jar is 50.*
approximately *adverb*

apricot
apricots *noun*
an edible fruit with soft flesh
and a stone at
its centre.

aquarium
aquariums or **aquaria** *noun*
a glass tank
in which to keep
fish and other
water animals
and plants.

arch
arches *noun*
a curved part of a building
or bridge.

architect
architects *noun*
a person who
designs buildings.
- say **ar**-kee-tekt

area
areas *noun*
1 a certain piece of ground or
space, or part of a surface.
*This is a play **area**.*
2 the amount of space
something covers.
*The wood covers a large **area**.*

argue
argues arguing argued *verb*
to talk angrily with someone
because you disagree
with them.
argument *noun*

arithmetic
noun
the adding, subtracting,
multiplying, and dividing
of numbers.

$25+17=42$
adding

$36-25=11$
subtracting

$14\times7=98$
multiplying

$28\div2=14$
dividing

arm   armpit

arm
arms *noun*
the part of your
body between
your shoulder
and your hand.

armadillo
armadillos *noun*
a nocturnal mammal that lives
in North and South America,
and eats insects, snakes, and
frogs. The armadillo's body
is protected by hard,
bony plates.

a b c d e f g h i j k l m n o p q r s t u v w x y z

armchair
armchairs *noun*
a soft, padded chair with arms.

armour
noun
a suit of thick metal plates worn long ago to protect knights in battle.

army
armies *noun*
a group of people and machines that fight on land.

around
adverb
1 nearby.
*I left my bag **around** here.*
2 in every direction.
*For miles **around**.*

around
preposition
1 from place to place.
*We walked **around** the city.*
2 on all sides.
*We sat **around** the table.*

arrange
arranges arranging arranged *verb*
1 to plan something.
*She **arranged** to meet me at 10 o'clock.*
2 to place something in a special order.

arrest
arrests arresting arrested *verb*
to catch hold of someone and officially accuse them of breaking the law.

arrive
arrives arriving arrived *verb*
to come to a place.
*The plane **arrived** at the airport.*
arrival *noun*

arrow
arrows *noun*
1 a pointed piece of metal that is shot from a bow.

2 a pointed shape that shows you which way to go or look.

art
noun
the creation of something, often through drawing, painting, sculpture, or design.

artery
arteries
noun
one of the tubes that carries blood from the heart to the rest of the body.

 artery

artificial
adjective
something false that is made to look like the real thing.

*an **artificial** flower*
■ say ar-tee-**fish**-al

artist
artists *noun*
someone who creates pictures, sculptures, music, or other creative things.

artistic *adjective*

ash
ashes *noun*
1 the grey powder that is left behind after something has been burnt.

*wood **ash***

2 a deciduous, broad-leaved tree, with spreading branches that grow in pairs. The female ash produces "winged" seeds. The wood is hard and strong.

ash leaves

ashamed
adjective
feeling guilty about something you have done.
*She felt **ashamed** about teasing her little brother.*

ask
asks asking asked *verb*
to try to find something out from someone.
***Ask** your dad if you can come with us.*

asleep
adjective
resting the whole body and mind with the eyes closed.
sleep *verb*

aspirin
aspirins *noun*
a type of medicine taken as a pill, used for relieving pain and fever.

assemble
assembles assembling assembled *verb*
1 to put something together.
*I **assembled** a model boat.*
2 to meet together.
*They **assembled** in the hall.*
assembly *noun*

assist
assists assisting assisted *verb*
to help somebody.
*He **assisted** the customer with his coat.*
assistance *noun*

assortment
assortments *noun*
a collection of different types of the same thing.

*an **assortment** of buttons*

asthma
noun
an illness or allergy that can make breathing difficult.
■ say **as**-ma
asthmatic *adjective*

astonish
astonishes astonishing astonished *verb*
to amaze someone very much.
*She **astonished** the crowd by winning the race.*

astronaut
astronauts *noun*
a person who is trained to travel into space.

astronomy
noun
the scientific study of stars and planets.

ate
*from the verb **to eat***
*I **ate** a whole loaf of bread yesterday.*

athlete
athletes *noun*
a person who takes part in races or sports competitions.
athletics *noun*

atlas
atlases *noun*
a book of maps.

atmosphere
noun
1 the layer of air that surrounds Earth.
2 the feeling in a room or a place.
*The dark room had a gloomy **atmosphere**.*

atom
atoms *noun*
a very tiny part of any substance.

*model of an **atom***

attach
attaches attaching attached *verb*
to fasten.

attached *with a paperclip*

attack
attacks attacking attacked *verb*
to try to hurt a person or an animal.
*The wild dog **attacked** the flock of geese.*

attempt
attempts attempting attempted *verb*
to try to do something.
*They **attempted** to climb the wall, but had to give up.*

attend
attends attending attended *verb*
to go to an event, or to go somewhere regularly.
*I **attended** school for 11 years.*

attention
noun
1 listening carefully.
*Pay **attention**!*
2 standing stiff and straight.
*Stand to **attention**.*

attic
attics *noun*
a room at the top of a house, usually in the space under the roof.

attract
attracts attracting attracted *verb*
1 to interest.
*The museum **attracts** many visitors.*
2 to make something come closer.

*Magnets **attract** iron filings.*

attractive
adjective
pleasing to the eye, mind, and senses.

audience
audiences *noun*
the people who come to watch a show or concert.

aunt
aunts *noun*
the sister of someone's parent, or their uncle's wife.

author
authors *noun*
a person who writes books, poems, or plays.

autograph
autographs *noun*
a signature, usually of a famous person.
■ say **au**-toe-grarf

automatic
adjective
1 without thinking.
*Blinking is **automatic**.*
2 working by itself, without any assistance.
***Automatic** doors.*

automobile
automobiles *noun*
another name for a car. Cars are often called automobiles in America.

*vintage **automobile***

autumn
autumns *noun*
one of the four seasons. Autumn follows summer and comes before winter. It is the time when the leaves on some trees change colour and fall to the ground.

a b c d e f g h i j k l m n o p q r s t u v w x y z

avalanche
avalanches *noun*
a large amount of snow, rocks, and ice that suddenly slides down a mountain.

avenue
avenues *noun*
a type of street. It is often wide and sometimes has a line of trees down each side.

average
adjective
ordinary.
*He was of **average** height for his age.*

average
averages *noun*
1 a usual amount.
*My marks were above **average**.*
2 a number of things spread out equally.
*He eats 14 apples a week, an **average** of two a day.*

avocado
avocados *noun*
a green, pear-shaped tree fruit with a leathery skin and smooth, creamy flesh.

avoid
avoids avoiding avoided *verb*
to keep away from something.
*The car swerved to **avoid** the dog.*

awake
adjective
not asleep.
*I stayed **awake** all night.*

award
awards *noun*
a prize.
*A rosette is an **award**.*
award *verb*

aware
adjective
knowing something.
*He became **aware** that someone was watching him.*

away
adverb
1 not here.
*The teacher was **away** today.*
2 to another place.
*I put all my games **away**.*

awful
adjective
very bad.
*I had an **awful** day at school.*

awkward
adjective
1 difficult to use or inconvenient.
2 clumsy.

*A new-born foal looks **awkward** on its feet.*
awkwardly *adverb*

axe
axes *noun*
a tool that is used to chop wood.

Bb

baboon
baboons *noun*
a large monkey that is found all over Africa. Baboons live on the ground and eat plants and small animals.

baby
babies *noun*
a very young child (see **growth** on page 94).

back
adverb
returning.
*I am going to the shops. I'll be **back** later.*

back
backs *noun*
1 the part of your body that is opposite your chest, and between your neck and your bottom.

backpack
backpacks *noun*
a large bag with shoulder straps, often worn by walkers to hold clothes and equipment.

backwards
adverb
moving towards the back.
*I fell **backwards** into a prickly bush.*

bacon
noun
salted meat from the back or side of a pig.

bacteria
noun
very small organisms. Some cause disease, while others help your body.
*Some **bacteria** help break down food in your stomach.*
■ say bak-**tee**-ree-a

2 the part opposite the front.
back *adjective*

back of a clock

back

bad
adjective
1 wrong.
*Stealing is very **bad**.*
2 serious.
*I've got a **bad** earache.*
3 rotten, or faulty.
*The food had gone **bad**.*
■ comparisons **worse worst**

badge
badges *noun*
a decoration that
can be pinned
or sewn onto
clothes.

*sheriff's **badge***

badminton
noun
an indoor game played by
two or four people on a court.
Each player uses a racket
to hit a shuttlecock over
a net (see **sport** on page 197).

baffle
baffles baffling baffled *verb*
to confuse someone or make
a person puzzled.
*The quiz completely
baffled him.*

bag
bags *noun*
a container that you can carry
things in, usually made of
material, plastic, or paper.

baggy
adjective
fitting loosely.
*He likes
wearing
baggy trousers.*

*baggy
trousers*

bake
bakes baking baked *verb*
to cook in an oven or fire. Pies,
cakes, and bread are baked.

*She **baked** with her mother.*

balance
**balances balancing
balanced** *verb*
to keep steady so you do not
fall over.
*The tightrope walker **balanced**
on the high wire.*

balcony
balconies *noun*
a platform for standing on that
is attached to the wall of a
building above the ground.

bald
adjective
without any hair.
*A **bald** head.*

ball
balls *noun*
1 a rounded object used to
play many games and sports.

2 a big, grand party where
there is dancing.
*A summer **ball**.*

ballet
ballets *noun*
a performance on stage
that tells a story
through music
and dance.
■ say **bal**-lay

balloon
balloons *noun*
a bag of rubber or other
material filled with air or
another gas.

*hot-air
balloon*

bamboo
noun
a tall, tropical grass with
hard, hollow stems.
Bamboo can be used
to make garden
poles and
furniture.

***bamboo**
poles*

ban
bans banning banned *verb*
to forbid people to
do something.
*Smoking is **banned** on
public transport.*

banana
bananas *noun*
a tree fruit with a
smooth, thick outer
skin and a soft, edible
centre. Bananas grow
in hot, damp regions.

band
bands *noun*
1 a group of people who play
music together.

2 a strip of material such as
fabric, elastic, or metal, that
holds things together.

*elastic **band***

bandage
bandages *noun*
a strip of material that is used
to wrap around a wound to
keep it clean.

a
b
c
d
e
f
g
h
i
j
k
l
m
n
o
p
q
r
s
t
u
v
w
x
y
z

bang
bangs *noun*
a sudden, loud noise.
*The firework went off with a loud **bang**.*

bank
banks *noun*
1 a sloping piece of ground, often on the side of a river.

2 a company that looks after people's money and also lends money.

banner
banners *noun*
a large flag or piece of cloth that has a picture or a message on it.

*weight-lifting **bar***

bar
bars *noun*
1 a long, narrow piece of metal.

2 a counter or a room where drinks or snacks are sold.

barbecue
barbecues *noun*
1 a grill over an open fire that is lit outdoors and used for cooking meat, fish, or vegetables.

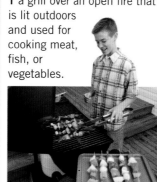

2 a party or special meal where food is cooked on a barbecue.
■ say **bar**-bi-kew

bare
adjective
without any covering.

__bare__ feet

bargain
bargains *noun*
something bought cheaply.
*My shoes were a real **bargain** in the sale.*

bark
noun
the rough wood on the outside of a tree trunk.

bark
barks barking barked *verb*
to make a rough, loud noise like a dog.
bark *noun*

barley
noun
a type of cereal grown on farms to make food and beer.

barn
barns *noun*
a large farm building used as a store or for keeping animals in.

barrel
barrels *noun*
a large, rounded, wooden or metal container for storing beer and other liquids.

barrier
barriers *noun*
a structure built to stop someone or something from passing through.
*The police placed a **barrier** across the road.*

base
bases *noun*
the bottom of something.

*lamp **base***

baseball
noun
a game for two teams of nine players, which started in the USA. The winning team is the one that scores the highest number of runs around the pitch (see **sport** on page 197).

basement
basements *noun*
a floor in a building that is partly or completely below ground level.

basin
basins *noun*
a bowl-shaped container. A wash-basin is used for washing in, and a pudding-basin is used for cooking in.

basket
baskets *noun*
a container for carrying things in, usually made of cane, twigs, or straw.

basketball
noun
a team game with five players on each side. Points are scored by throwing a ball through a raised hoop called the basket (see **sport** on page 197).

bat
bats *noun*
1 a stick, often made of wood or metal, that is used to hit a ball (see **sport** on page 197).

*softball **bat***

2 a nocturnal mammal with wings. Bats live in caves and dark places, and eat insects, fruit, or small animals. They rest hanging upside-down (see **mammal** on page 124).

*long-eared **bat***

bath
baths *noun*
a large tub for washing the whole of your body.

baton
batons *noun*
a thin piece of wood or metal. Conductors of orchestras and band leaders use different types of batons to keep time.

battery
batteries *noun*
a closed container of chemicals that makes and stores small amounts of electricity.

*watch **battery***

battle
battles *noun*
a fight between two armies that are at war.

bawl
bawls bawling bawled *verb*
to shout or cry very loudly.

bay
bays *noun*
a deep, inward curve in a coastline or the edge of a lake.

beach
beaches *noun*
land at the edge of a sea or lake, usually covered in pebbles or sand.

bead
beads *noun*
a small piece of wood, stone, or glass that can be threaded onto string.

beak
beaks *noun*
the hard, bony mouth of a bird or dinosaur (see **dinosaur** on page 61).

*toucan's **beak***

beam
beams *noun*
1 a long, narrow ray of light.

2 a long, strong piece of wood or metal, often used in buildings to hold up the roof.

bean
beans *noun*
a seed or pod that is eaten as a vegetable.

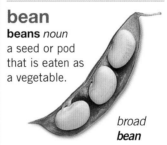

*broad **bean***

bear
bears *noun*
a large mammal with thick fur that usually lives in forests. All bears eat meat, but some also eat honey, roots, plant buds, and fruit.

bear
bears bearing bore born or **borne** *verb*
1 to produce or give birth to. *This plant **bears** red berries.*
2 to carry or support. *Can that branch **bear** your weight?*
3 to put up with. *I can't **bear** to think about it.*

beard
beards *noun*
the hair that grows on the lower part of a man's face if he does not shave.

beat
beats beating beat beaten *verb*
1 to defeat someone. *My friend **beat** me at chess.*
2 to hit or stir repeatedly. *She **beat** the eggs.*
3 to make a repeated movement, or noise. *My heart is **beating** loudly.*

beat
beats *noun*
a steady stroke or sound. *A metronome ticks with a steady **beat**.*

beautiful
adjective
very pleasant to look at. *What a **beautiful** view!*
■ say **byoo**-te-ful

beaver
beavers *noun*
a large rodent that gnaws down trees to build dams and island homes, called lodges, in rivers. Beavers eat bark, roots, and twigs.

a b c d e f g h i j k l m n o p q r s t u v w x y z

A B C D E F G H I J K L M N O P Q R S T U V W X Y Z

beckon
beckons beckoning beckoned *verb*
to make a sign that tells someone to come to you.

become
becomes becoming became *verb*
to change or grow into.
*A tadpole **becomes** a frog.*

bed
beds *noun*
1 a piece of furniture that you sleep on.
2 the bottom of a river, lake, or sea.

bee
bees *noun*
a flying insect that usually lives in large, well-organized groups. Bees feed on pollen, nectar, and the honey they make from nectar.

beech
beeches *noun*
a deciduous forest tree with smooth, grey bark and spreading branches (see **tree** on page 223).

beech leaf

beef
noun
the meat from a cow or bull.

beehive
beehives *noun*
a type of box that people keep bees in. They collect the honey that the bees make.

beer
beers *noun*
an alcoholic drink made from cereal grains.

beetle
beetles *noun*
an insect with hard, often brightly coloured, wing cases. Some beetles eat small insects; others eat wood and plants.

*jewel **beetle***

beetroot
beetroots *noun*
the hard, red root of the beet plant, which is eaten as a vegetable (see **vegetable** on page 233).

before
preposition
earlier than.

*I woke up just **before** four o'clock.*

before
adverb
in the past.
*I've heard that story **before**.*

beg
begs begging begged *verb*
to ask for something very strongly.

*The dog **begged** for a piece of meat.*

begin
begins beginning began begun *verb*
to start something.
*The story **begins** in a castle.*
beginning *noun*

behave
behaves behaving behaved *verb*
to act in a particular way in front of other people.
*Our class **behaved** well at the zoo.*
behaviour *noun*

behind
preposition
at the back of.

*She stood **behind** her friend.*
behind *adverb*

being
beings *noun*
someone or something that exists.

believe
believes believing believed *verb*
to feel strongly that something is true.

bell
bells *noun*
a cup-shaped piece of metal that makes a ringing sound when it is struck.

belong
belongs belonging belonged *verb*
to be someone's possession or property.
*That book **belongs** to me.*

below
preposition
lower than.

***below** her waist*
■ opposite **above**

belt
belts *noun*
a narrow strip of fabric or leather that you wear around your waist.

bench
benches *noun*
1 a long, wooden seat.

*park **bench***

2 a work table.

bend
**bends bending
bent** *verb*
to change
something
straight into
a curved
shape.

*She **bent** over
to touch her toes.*

bend
bends *noun*
a curve.

*a **bend** in the road*

benefit
benefits benefiting benefited
verb
to receive help from someone
or something.
*The school would **benefit**
from having new computers.*
benefit *noun*

beret
berets *noun*
a soft, flat hat.

■ say **ber**-ray

berry
berries *noun*
a small, round
juicy fruit with
seeds inside.

*blue**berries***

beside
preposition
at the side of.

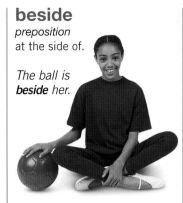

*The ball is
beside her.*

best
*from the adjective **good***
better than any other.

bet
bets betting bet *verb*
to believe that something
is going to happen.
*I **bet** it's going to rain later.*

better
*from the adjective **good***
1 more able or of
a superior quality.
*You are good at science
but he is **better**.*
2 well again.
*I'm feeling **better**, thanks.*

between
preposition
in the
middle of.

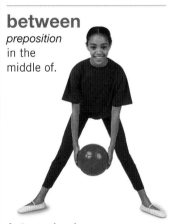

***between** her knees*

beware
verb
to be careful of something.
***Beware** of the dog!*

beyond
preposition
further away than.
*The hills lay
beyond the river.*

bicycle
bicycles *noun*
a vehicle with two wheels
that you ride by
turning the pedals
with your feet.
Bicycle can be
shortened
to bike.

big
adjective
large in
width
or size.

*The helmet
and boots
are too **big**
for him.*
■ comparisons
bigger biggest

bikini
bikinis *noun*
a swimming
costume with
two pieces,
worn by
girls and
women.

bill
bills *noun*
1 the hard, bony mouth of a bird.
2 a piece of paper that shows
you how much you have to
pay for something.
*The waiter brought
us the **bill** at the
end of our meal.*
3 a plan for a new law
that must be voted on by
a country's government.
*The new education **bill** will be
discussed in Parliament today.*

bill

billow
billows billowing billowed *verb*
to spread out and be blown
about in the wind.
*Smoke **billowed** out from
the chimneys.*

bin
bins *noun*
a container for things you want
to throw away.

binoculars
noun
two small telescopes
joined together that
make things that
are far away
look closer.

biodegradable
adjective
able to be broken down
by bacteria.
*Most paper is **biodegradable**.*
■ say by-oh-dee-**gray**-da-bul

a b c d e f g h i j k l m n o p q r s t u v w x y z

A
B
C
D
E
F
G
H
I
J
K
L
M
N
O
P
Q
R
S
T
U
V
W
X
Y
Z

bird

birds *noun*
an animal that has warm blood,
feathers on its body, and wings
(see **skeleton** on page 188).

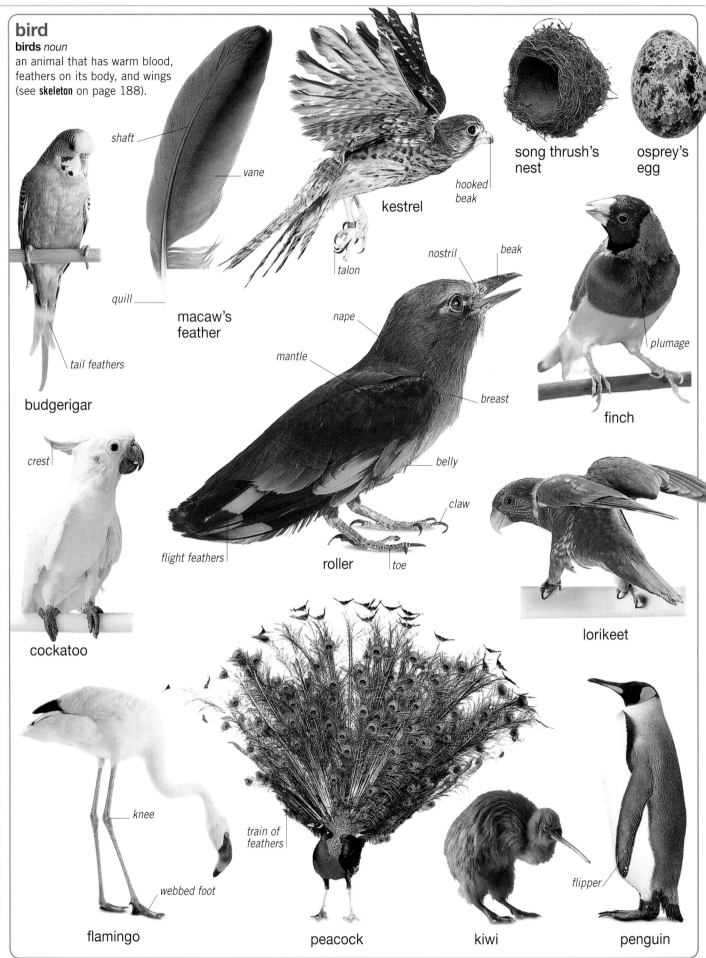

shaft

vane

hooked beak

kestrel

song thrush's nest

osprey's egg

nostril *beak*

nape

mantle

breast

plumage

finch

quill

macaw's feather

tail feathers

budgerigar

crest

belly

claw

flight feathers

roller

toe

lorikeet

cockatoo

knee

train of feathers

webbed foot

flamingo

peacock

kiwi

flipper

penguin

birthday

birthday
birthdays *noun*
the anniversary of the day you were born.

birthday cake
birthday cakes *noun*
a special cake with candles on top that is baked for your birthday.

birthday card
birthday cards *noun*
a card that people send to you on your birthday, to congratulate you on being a year older.

birthday party
birthday parties *noun*
a party to celebrate someone's birthday.

birthday present
birthday presents *noun*
a gift that you give to someone on their birthday.

biscuit
biscuits *noun*
a small, flat, crisp type of cake made from dough.
■ say **bis**-kit

bit
bits *noun*
a small piece of something.
*The mouse nibbled a **bit** of cheese.*

bite
bites biting bit bitten *verb*
to use your teeth in a cutting action, usually with food.

bite *noun*

bitter
adjective
having a sour, sharp taste.
*Strong coffee can taste **bitter**.*

black
noun
1 a colour.

2 very dark.
*She saw a faint glow in the **black** of the night.*

blackberry
blackberries *noun*
a black or dark purple fruit that grows on prickly stems called brambles.

blackbird
blackbirds *noun*
a bird that lives in gardens and fields, and eats insects and seeds. The male has black feathers and the female has brown feathers.

blackboard
blackboards *noun*
a board that has been painted black. Blackboards can be written on with chalk.

blade
blades *noun*
1 the flat, sharp, metal part of a knife or a sword.

knife **blade**

2 a stem of grass.

blade

blame
blames blaming blamed *verb*
to think or say that someone has done something wrong.
*She always **blames** me for letting the toast burn.*

blank
blanks *noun*
an empty space.
*This page has been left **blank**.*

blank *adjective*

blackbird → blanket

blanket
blankets *noun*
a soft covering, usually made of wool, that is used to keep people or animals warm.

blast
blasts *noun*
a powerful explosion or gust of wind.
*A **blast** of cold air came in through the window.*

blaze
blazes blazing blazed *verb*
to burn very brightly.

*The fire **blazed** through the old building.*
blaze *noun*

blazer
blazers *noun*
a jacket that is often worn as part of a uniform.

bleach
noun
a very powerful chemical that removes colour. Bleach can burn your skin.

A B C D E F G H I J K L M N O P Q R S T U V W X Y Z

bleed
bleeds bleeding bled *verb*
to lose blood.
*My nose started to **bleed**
when I fell over.*

blind
adjective
unable
to see.

*Some **blind** people have
guide dogs.*

blink
blinks blinking blinked *verb*
to open and shut your
eyes quickly.
*The bright light made
me **blink**.*

blister
blisters *noun*
a bubble of watery liquid that
forms under your skin when it
has been burnt or rubbed.
*Tight shoes give me **blisters**.*

blizzard
blizzards *noun*
a very heavy snowstorm.

blob
blobs *noun*
a small lump of something
with no shape.

*a **blob** of face cream*

block
blocks *noun*
1 a solid shape, such as
a block of wood.
2 a very big building or
a group of buildings.

block
blocks blocking blocked *verb*
to be in the way.
*The road was **blocked**
by the fallen tree.*

blond / blonde
adjective
having light-coloured hair.
Blond is used for boys and
men, and blonde is used for
girls and women.

blond boy

blonde girl

blood
noun
the red liquid that flows
around our body through
veins and arteries. Blood
carries nutrients and oxygen
to our skin and muscles.

bloom
**blooms blooming
bloomed** *verb*
to produce flowers.
*Fruit trees **bloom** in
the spring.*

blossom
blossoms *noun*
the flowers on a tree
that appear before
the fruit.

*hawthorn **blossom***

blot
blots *noun*
a stain on paper, usually
made by ink or paint that
has been spilt.

blouse
blouses *noun*
a type of shirt usually worn
by girls or women.

blow
blows blowing blew blown
verb
1 to move in air, or be moved
in air.
2 to force air out of your nose
or mouth.

*She **blew** up the balloon.*

blue
noun
a colour.

bluff
bluffs bluffing bluffed *verb*
to trick someone into
believing something.
*She pretended to be brave,
but she was **bluffing**.*

blunt
adjective
having a rounded end or edge.

■ opposite **sharp**

blur
blurs blurring blurred *verb*
to make something unclear
and difficult to see.
*The view through the window
was **blurred** by rain.*

blush
blushes blushing blushed *verb*
to turn red because you are
embarrassed or shy.

board
boards *noun*
a flat piece of wood, or
very stiff paper.

boast
boasts boasting boasted *verb*
to tell people about something
in a proud and annoying way.
*He **boasted** about his money.*

boat

boats *noun*
a small open vessel that carries goods and people across water.

sprit

sail

boom

tiller

mast

stern

main sheet

rudder

bow

daggerboard

dinghy

anchor

hull

junk

blade

lifebuoy

propeller

prow

fishing **boat**

cockpit

reed **boat**

paddle

cabin

thwart

yard

keel

coble (fishing **boat**)

rudder

stay

powerboat

propeller

narrowboat

deck

sailing **boat**

A
B
C
D
E
F
G
H
I
J
K
L
M
N
O
P
Q
R
S
T
U
V
W
X
Y
Z

body
bodies noun
all the physical parts that make up an animal or person.

boil
boils boiling boiled verb
to heat a liquid until it starts to bubble and steam rises from it.

bold
adjective
brave and fearless.
*The **bold** knight marched up to the dragon's cave.*

bolt
bolts noun
1 a metal rod that is used to fasten things together.

2 a sliding metal bar that is used for fastening a door.

bomb
bombs noun
an exploding weapon that can cause damage to anything around it.
■ say **bom**

bone
bones noun
the hard parts of an animal's or person's body that make up the skeleton.

*femur (upper leg **bone**)*
bony adjective

bonfire
bonfires noun
a large outdoor fire.

book
books noun
printed pieces of paper joined together inside a cover.

boom
booms booming boomed verb
to make a deep, loud sound.
*His voice **boomed** out through the loudspeaker.*

boomerang
boomerangs noun
a curved piece of wood that comes back to you when you throw it. Boomerangs were used in the past as a weapon by Australian Aboriginals.

boot
boots noun
a type of shoe that covers your foot and part of your leg.

*wellington **boot***

border
borders noun
1 the boundary between two countries.

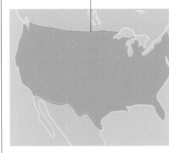

*country **border***

2 a strip around the edge of something.

*blue **border***

bore
bores boring bored verb
1 to be very uninteresting.
*She **bored** us for weeks by telling the same joke.*
2 to make a round hole in something.
*They **bored** a hole in the ground in search of oil.*

bore
from the verb **to bear**
1 *She **bore** 10 children.*
2 *Luckily, the bridge **bore** the truck's weight.*

born
from the verb **to bear**
*I was **born** 10 years ago, so I am 10 years old.*

borrow
borrows borrowing borrowed verb
to take something for a while and then return it.
*I **borrowed** my friend's pen.*
■ opposite **lend**

boss
bosses noun
the person who is in charge at work.

both
adjective
not just one thing, but two.

***Both** bowls contain rice.*

bother
bothers bothering bothered verb
to worry or annoy someone.

bottle
bottles noun
a container for liquids, usually made of glass or plastic.

bottom
bottoms noun
1 the lowest part of something.

*The turtle was at the **bottom** of the sea.*
■ opposite **top**
2 the part of your body that you sit on.

bought
from the verb **to buy**
I **bought** *a present for my friend yesterday.*
■ say **bort**

bounce
bounces bouncing bounced *verb*
to spring up and down.

bounce
noun

boundary
boundaries *noun*
the edge of a piece of land.

bouquet
bouquets *noun*
a bunch of flowers that has been specially arranged and wrapped.

■ say
bo-**kay**

bow
bows bowing bowed *verb*
to bend from the waist as a greeting or a sign of respect.

■ rhymes
with **now**

bow
bows *noun*
the front of a ship.
■ rhymes with **now**

bow
bows *noun*
1 a knot with two loops.

2 a curved piece of wood with a string attached to each end, used for shooting arrows.

3 a wooden stick with horse hair attached at each end, used for playing musical instruments.

violin **bow**

■ rhymes with **go**

bowl
bowls *noun*
a curved, open container, usually used for food.

bowl
bowls bowling bowled *verb*
1 to throw a ball for someone to hit.
2 to roll a ball in the game of lawn bowls.
3 to roll a ball in tenpin bowling.

tenpin **bowling**

box
boxes *noun*
a container to store things in.

cardboard box

boy
boys *noun*
a young male person.

brace
braces *noun*
a piece of wire that is fitted over your teeth to help straighten them.

bracelet
bracelets *noun*
a decorative band or chain that is worn around your wrist. Bracelets are usually made of metal or beads.

braille
noun
a type of writing in which letters are represented by raised dots. People who are blind read the dots by feeling them with their fingertips.

■ say **brayl**

brain
brains *noun*
the part of your body inside your head that controls how you think and move.

brake
brakes *noun*
a part of a vehicle that slows it down or stops it.

brake
brakes braking braked *verb*
to slow down or stop a vehicle by using the brakes.

branch
branches *noun*
the part of a tree that grows out of the trunk.

trunk / **branch**

brass
noun
a hard, yellow-coloured metal made from a mixture of copper and zinc.

brass door knocker

brave
adjective
willing to do something even though you are afraid.
The **brave** *girl dived into the lake to rescue her brother.*
■ comparisons **braver bravest bravery** *noun*

a b c d e f g h i j k l m n o p q r s t u v w x y z

33

A
B
C
D
E
F
G
H
I
J
K
L
M
N
O
P
Q
R
S
T
U
V
W
X
Y
Z

bread
noun
a food made from flour and baked in an oven.

break
breaks breaking broke broken *verb*
to damage something so that it cannot be used.

The cat is always **breaking** *things.*

break
breaks *noun*
a period of rest.

breakfast
breakfasts *noun*
the first meal of the day, eaten in the morning.

breathe
breathes breathing breathed *verb*
to take air in and out of your lungs, through your nose or mouth.
breath *noun*

breathless
adjective
having difficulty in breathing.
Running for the bus made the old man **breathless**.

breed
breeds breeding bred *verb*
to keep animals so that they produce young.
She **breeds** *racehorses.*

breed
breeds *noun*
a particular type of animal.

A dalmatian is a **breed** *of dog.*

breeze
breezes *noun*
a gentle wind.

bribe
bribes bribing bribed *verb*
to pay someone secretly to do something that they shouldn't do.
The prisoner **bribed** *the guard to set him free.*

brick
bricks *noun*
a block used for building, made out of baked clay.

bride
brides *noun*
a woman on the day she gets married.

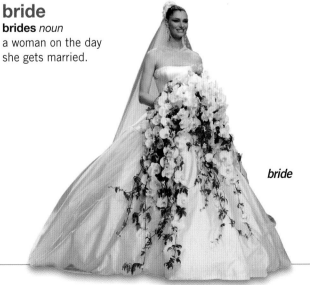

bride

bridge
bridges *noun*
a structure that is built over an obstacle such as a railway line or a river.

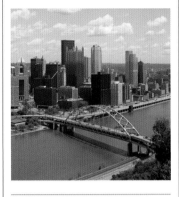

brief
adjective
short in time.
He made a **brief** *speech, lasting only five minutes.*

bright
adjective
1 giving off a lot of light.
A car has **bright** *headlights.*
2 clever.
The **bright** *pupil knew all the answers.*
■ comparisons **brighter brightest**
brightly *adverb*

brilliant
adjective
1 very clever indeed.
The inventor had a **brilliant** *idea.*
2 very bright.
Diamonds are **brilliant**.

brim
brims *noun*
1 the edge of a hat.

brim

2 the top of a container, such as a glass or a cup.

full to the **brim**

bring
brings bringing brought *verb*
to take something or someone with you when you go somewhere.
Can I **bring** *my friend along?*

bristle
bristles *noun*
stiff hairs, usually on an animal or a brush.

bristles

nail-brush

brittle
adjective
easily broken.
Icicles are very **brittle**.

broad
adjective
very wide.

The river is **broad** *at its mouth.*
■ comparisons **broader broadest**

broadcast
broadcasts broadcasting broadcast *verb*
to send sound or pictures by radio or television.
The Olympic Games are **broadcast** *all over the world.*

broccoli
noun
a vegetable with edible green or purple buds.
Broccoli is related to the cauliflower.

brochure

brochures *noun*
a small book that
contains information.
■ say **broh**-sher

broke

from the verb **to break**
I **broke** *my pencil in half.*

bronze

noun
a brown-coloured metal made
from a mixture of
copper and tin.

*an ornament made
of* **bronze**

brooch

brooches *noun*
a piece of jewellery that is
usually pinned onto clothes.
■ say **broach**

broom

brooms *noun*
a stiff, long-handled brush
that is used for sweeping.

brother

brothers *noun*
a male person who has the
same mother and father as
someone else.

brought

from the verb **to bring**
I **brought** *my dog with me.*
■ say **brort**

brown

noun
a colour.

brush

brushes brushing brushed
verb
1 to sweep.
2 to touch something lightly as
you pass by it.
The woman **brushed** *past me
in the street.*

brush

brushes *noun*
a tool with a handle
and bristles.

animal **brush**

bubble

bubbles *noun*
a light ball of liquid
with air inside.

bubble *verb*

bucket

buckets *noun*
a large container with a
handle, usually used for
carrying liquids.

buckle

buckles *noun*
an object for fastening two
ends of a belt or strap.

bud

buds *noun*
a small
swelling on
a plant, containing
young leaves or
flowers (see **tree**
on page 223).

tree **bud**

Buddhist

Buddhists *noun*
a person who follows
the teachings of Buddha,
a religious teacher who lived
about 2,500 years ago.
■ say **buh**-dist

buffalo

buffaloes *noun*
a large mammal that lives on
open plains and eats grass.

bugle

bugles *noun*
a brass musical instrument
that you blow through to
produce sound.

build

builds building built *verb*
to join things together to
make a structure.
The bird **built** *a nest out
of twigs.*

building

buildings *noun*
a structure, usually with walls
and a roof, for sheltering
people or objects.

bulb

bulbs *noun*
1 the glass
part of an
electric light.

light **bulb**

2 the rounded
part of some
plants that grows
underground.

daffodil
bulb

bulge

bulges bulging bulged *verb*
to swell or be lumpy.
Her pockets **bulged** *with food.*

bull

bulls *noun*
1 a male mammal of
the cattle family.
2 the male of some large
animals, such as elephants,
whales, and seals.

bulldozer

bulldozers *noun*
a machine with a large, metal
blade at the front for moving
earth and rocks.

bullet

bullets *noun*
a pointed metal object fired
from a gun.

bully

bullies *noun*
an unpleasant person who
frightens others.
bully *verb*

a b c d e f g h i j k l m n o p q r s t u v w x y z

A B C D E F G H I J K L M N O P Q R S T U V W X Y Z

bump
bumps bumping bumped *verb*
to knock into something.

bump
bumps *noun*
a rounded shape on a smooth surface.
It was difficult to ride my bike over the **bumps.**
bumpy *adjective*

bunch
bunches *noun*
a group of things together.

***bunch** of carrots*

bundle
bundles *noun*
a group of things that are loosely joined together.

***bundle** of twigs*

bungalow
bungalows *noun*
a house with all its rooms on one level.

bunk bed
bunk beds *noun*
a pair of beds, with one bed placed on top of the other.

buoy
buoys *noun*
an object that is tied to an anchor and floats on water. Buoys are used as a warning or guide for ships and boats.

■ say **boy**

burglar
burglars *noun*
a person who steals things from people's houses.

burn
burns burning burnt or **burned** *verb*
to damage or destroy by fire.

burrow
burrows *noun*
an animal's underground home.

*rabbit **burrow***

burst
bursts bursting burst *verb*
to split open.
*The water-pipe **burst** and flooded the kitchen.*

bury
buries burying buried *verb*
to put something in the ground and cover it over.
*The dog **buried** its bone.*
■ say **ber**-ree

bus
buses *noun*
a road vehicle for carrying a large number of passengers.

bush
bushes *noun*
1 a large plant with a rounded shape. Bushes are smaller than trees, and have many branches low to the ground.

2 the wild countryside in Australia, New Zealand, and Africa.

business
businesses *noun*
1 an organization that sells products or services.
2 the things that only you should know about and look after.
*Mind your own **business**.*
■ say **biz**-nis

busy
adjective
doing lots of things.
■ say **bizzy**

butcher
butchers *noun*
a person who prepares and sells meat.

butter
noun
a soft, yellow food made from cream.

buttercup
buttercups *noun*
a small, wild flower.

butterfly
butterflies *noun*
an insect with wings covered in very fine, coloured scales. Butterflies begin life as caterpillars. Most butterflies eat plants (see **growth** on page 94).

birdwing
butterfly

button
buttons *noun*
1 a small object used to fasten two parts of a piece of clothing together.

2 a switch to activate an electronic device.

buy
buys buying bought *verb*
to pay for something.
*I'm going to **buy** a book with my pocket money.*

buzz
buzzes buzzing buzzed *verb*
to make a low, humming noise.
*The bees **buzzed** in the hive.*

byte
bytes *noun*
a piece of information that a computer stores in its memory.

Cc

cabbage
cabbages *noun*
a vegetable with a short stem and tightly wrapped layers of broad leaves.

cabin
cabins *noun*
1 a hut, often made of logs.

2 a room for passengers or crew on an aeroplane or ship.

cable
cables *noun*
1 a very strong rope or chain.

2 a bundle of wires for carrying electrical power or signals, often laid underground.

electric cable

cactus
cacti or
cactuses *noun*
a plant that grows in hot deserts. Cacti store water in their stems, and have prickly spines that protect them from animals.

café
cafés *noun*
a place where people buy and eat meals, snacks, and drinks.
■ say **kaf**-ay

cage
cages *noun*
a container with metal bars for keeping animals or birds in.

cake
cakes *noun*
a sweet food that is usually made from flour, sugar, eggs, and butter and baked in an oven.

calculator
calculators *noun*
a small electronic machine for doing maths quickly.

■ say **kal**-kew-late-or

calendar
calendars *noun*
a chart of all the days, weeks, and months of the year.

calf
calves *noun*
1 a young cow or bull.
2 some young mammals, such as elephants or whales.

3 the back of your leg below the knee.

calf

calf

call
calls calling called *verb*
1 to shout out.
*They **called** for help.*
2 to give something a name.
*I **called** my dog Spot.*
3 to phone or visit somebody.
*My cousin **called** to see me.*

calligraphy
noun
beautiful handwriting, using ink or paint.

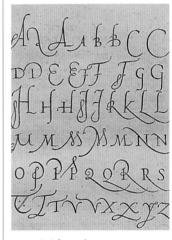

■ say kal-**ig**-ra-fee

calm
adjective
1 still and quiet.
*The sea was **calm** after the storm had passed.*
2 peaceful.
*Yoga makes her feel **calm**.*
■ say **karm**
■ comparisons **calmer calmest**

came
from the verb **to come**
*He **came** with us yesterday.*

a b c d e f g h i j k l m n o p q r s t u v w x y z

A B **C** D E F G H I J K L M N O P Q R S T U V W X Y Z

camel
camels *noun*
a mammal with one or two humps on its back that lives in hot deserts. Camels store fat in their humps to help them go without water or food for long periods of time.

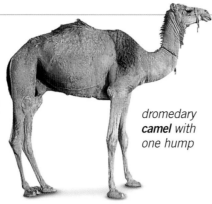

dromedary **camel** *with one hump*

camera
cameras *noun*
a piece of equipment used for taking photographs, or for making videos or films.

digital **camera**

camouflage
camouflages *noun*
a disguise that helps to hide an animal or person.

leaf insect

■ say **kam**-o-flarj
camouflage *verb*

camp
camps camping camped *verb*
to stay in a tent outdoors.

camping *noun*

campaign
campaigns *noun*
a series of events organized for the same aim.
She led a **campaign** *to stop the new motorway.*
■ say kam-**pain**

can
can could *verb*
to be able to or to know how to do something.
She **can** *touch her toes.*
■ opposite **cannot** or **can't**
■ always used with another verb

can
cans *noun*
a metal container used for preserving food or drink.

canal
canals *noun*
a water channel that has been built across land for boats and ships to travel on.

canary
canaries *noun*
a yellow bird that is often kept as a pet because it sings. Wild canaries are green.

cancel
cancels cancelling cancelled *verb*
to stop something that has been planned.
We **cancelled** *our trip.*
■ say **kan**-sel
cancellation *noun*

cancer
cancers *noun*
a serious disease in which harmful cells spread through the body.
■ say **kan**-ser

candidate
candidates *noun*
someone who enters an exam, or someone who tries to be elected or to get a job.
Presidential **candidate***.*

candle
candles *noun*
a stick of wax with a string called a wick running through it. Candles are burnt to give light.

candy
candies *noun*
a type of sweet food.

cane
canes *noun*
1 a walking stick.
2 the thick, hollow stem of some plants.

sugar **cane**

canoe
canoes *noun*
a light, narrow boat. A paddle is used to move the canoe along.

canyon
canyons *noun*
a steep-sided, rocky valley.

capable
adjective
having the ability or skill to do something.
They are both **capable** *cooks.*

capacity
capacities *noun*
the amount that something will hold.

These jars have different **capacities***.*

capital
capitals *noun*
1 a city where a country has its government offices and parliament.
Moscow is the **capital** *of Russia.*
2 a large letter of the alphabet used to start a sentence or a special name.

capture
captures capturing captured *verb*
to catch and hold on to someone or something.

car

cars *noun*
a type of road vehicle with wheels that is moved by an engine, and used to carry people from place to place.

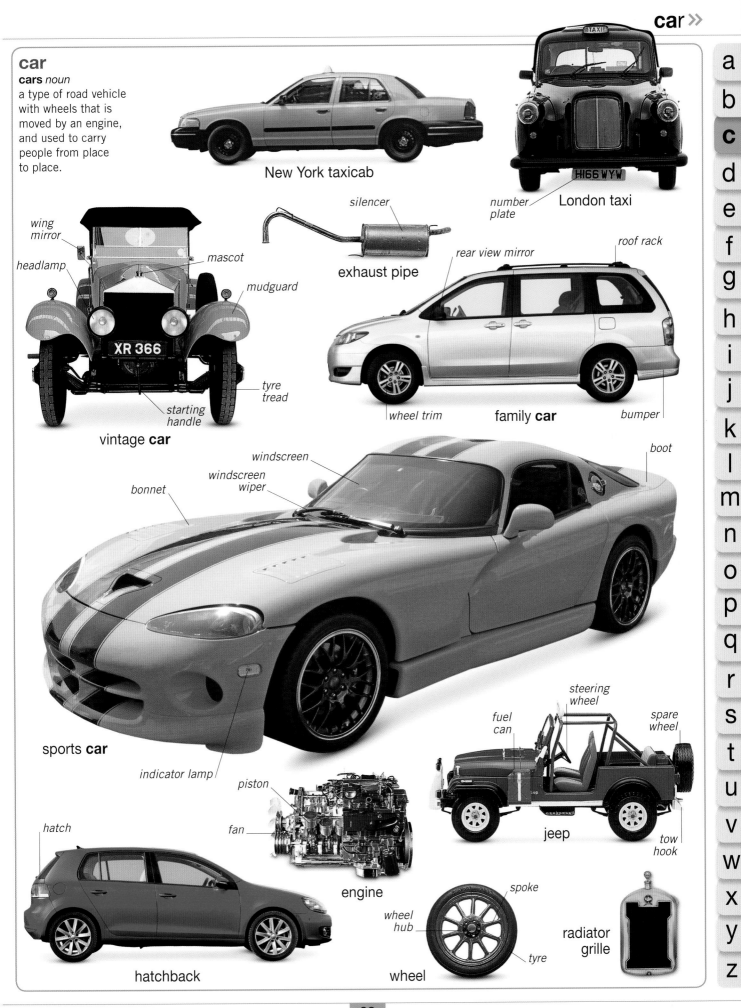

New York taxicab

number plate
London taxi

silencer
exhaust pipe

wing mirror
headlamp
mascot
mudguard
tyre tread
starting handle

XR 366

vintage **car**

rear view mirror
roof rack
wheel trim
family **car**
bumper

windscreen
windscreen wiper
bonnet
boot

sports **car**

indicator lamp

steering wheel
fuel can
spare wheel
jeep
tow hook

piston
fan
engine

hatch
hatchback

spoke
wheel hub
tyre
wheel

radiator grille

A B C D E F G H I J K L M N O P Q R S T U V W X Y Z

caravan
caravans *noun*
1 a home on wheels in which people live or have holidays.
2 a group of people travelling together for safety, usually across deserts.

cardboard
noun
a very strong, stiff type of paper used to make boxes.

care
cares caring cared *verb*
1 to be interested.
I care about what you do.
2 to look after someone.
I care for my sick mother.
3 to feel affection for someone.
He cares for his girlfriend.

career
careers *noun*
the jobs someone has during their working life, usually in the same occupation.
She taught in three schools during her career.

careful
adjective
being aware of dangers or problems.

Be careful when you cross the river.
■ opposite **careless**

cargo
cargoes *noun*
all the different goods that a ship or aircraft carries.
A cargo of bananas.

carnival
carnivals *noun*
a special event with a street procession, music, and dancing.

carrot
carrots *noun*
a hard, sweet-tasting root vegetable.

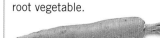

carry
carries carrying carried *verb*
to hold something while you move it somewhere.

carton
cartons *noun*
a small cardboard container for holding liquid or food.

cartoon
cartoons *noun*
1 a funny drawing that makes people laugh.
2 a moving film made by photographing thousands of drawings one by one.

cartridge
cartridges *noun*
a container of ink for use in a pen or computer printer.

carve
carves carving carved *verb*
to cut something into a shape.

carving a spoon out of wood

case
cases *noun*
1 a container.
2 a particular event or example.
There have been several cases of flu at school.

cast
casts casting cast *verb*
1 to choose someone for a part in a play or film.
He was cast as the king.
2 to shape something in a mould.
A statue cast in bronze.

castle
castles *noun*
a large house with high stone walls and strong defences against attacking armies.

cat
cats *noun*
a mammal that is often kept as a pet. Cats eat small animals and are fierce hunters (see **pet** on page 148).

catalogue
catalogues *noun*
a book that shows you the things you can buy from a shop or a company.
■ say **kat**-a-log

catch
catches catching caught *verb*
1 to get hold of something that is thrown to you.

2 to get on a vehicle.
I catch the bus to work.
3 to get an infection.
I caught measles from my sister.

caterpillar
caterpillars *noun*
the larva of a butterfly or moth.

cattle
noun
cows, bulls, or oxen.

cauliflower
cauliflowers *noun*
a vegetable with a short stem and a hard centre, made of small flowers.

caution
noun
attention to possible danger.
*Drive with **caution**.*
■ say **kor**-shun
cautious *adjective*

ceiling
ceilings *noun*
the surface of a room that is above your head.
■ say **see**-ling

celebrate
celebrates celebrating celebrated *verb*
to do something enjoyable for a special reason.
*We had a party to **celebrate** my birthday.*
■ say **sell**-ee-brate
celebration *noun*

cell
cells *noun*
1 a small room in a prison.

2 the smallest living part of an animal or plant.

*human **cell***

cellar
cellars *noun*
an underground room.

cellphone
noun
American usage only: a hand-held mobile telephone that connects to other telephones by radio waves.

*She is speaking on her **cellphone**.*

cement
noun
a clay powder that becomes hard when mixed with water.

centipede
centipedes *noun*
a tiny, blind animal with many pairs of legs, which lives in dark places. Centipedes paralyse their prey with a poisonous bite.
■ say **sen**-tee-peed

centre
centres *noun*
1 the middle.

*The tomato is in the **centre** of the plate.*
2 a building where particular events take place.
*A sports **centre**.*

century
centuries *noun*
a period of a hundred years.
*The building is several **centuries** old.*
■ **sent**-yoo-ree

cereal
cereals *noun*
1 a grain crop grown on farms. Wheat, rye, barley, and oats are cereals.

oats   *wheat*

rye   *barley*

2 a breakfast food made from the grains of a cereal crop.
■ say **seer**-ree-al

certain
adjective
sure, or definite.
*Are you **certain** this is the right train?*
■ opposite **uncertain**

certificate
certificates *noun*
a piece of paper that proves certain facts.
*She received a **certificate** for passing her maths exam.*

chain
chains *noun*
metal loops joined together to make a strong cable.

chair
chairs *noun*
a piece of furniture for sitting on.

chalk
chalks *noun*
a soft, white rock made from the fossils of tiny seashells. Chalk is often made into sticks used for writing or drawing on blackboards.

*coloured **chalk***

challenge
challenges challenging challenged *verb*
to ask someone to try to do something better than you.
*He **challenged** her to a race.*

chameleon
chameleons *noun*
a type of lizard that lives in trees in hot regions and eats insects, rodents, and small birds. Chameleons can change colour to match their surroundings.

■ say ka-**mee**-lee-on

a b c d e f g h i j k l m n o p q r s t u v w x y z

A B C D E F G H I J K L M N O P Q R S T U V W X Y Z

champion
champions *noun*
someone who is the best at something, often a sport.

chance
chances *noun*
an opportunity, or possibility. *He was given the **chance** to study abroad.*

change
changes changing changed *verb*
1 to become different or to make something different.

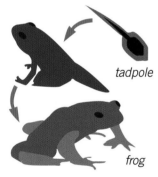

tadpole

frog

*Tadpoles **change** into frogs.*
2 to give up something in return for something else. *He **changed** seats.*
change *noun*

change
noun
small amounts of money.

channel
channels *noun*
1 a passage or track for water to flow along.
2 a television or radio station. *What's on the other **channel**?*

chaos
noun
complete confusion.
■ say **kay**-os

chapter
chapters *noun*
a section of a book.

character
characters *noun*
1 what a person is like. *A miserable **character**.*
2 a person in a play or film. *He played the **character** of the young king.*

charity
charities *noun*
an organization that gives aid to those who need it. *The Red Cross is a **charity**.*

chart
charts *noun*
a map or diagram that provides information.

*a pie **chart** showing popular forms of transport*

chase
chases chasing chased *verb*
to run after something or somebody.

cheap
adjective
not costing much money.
■ opposite **expensive**

an expensive ring

£250

*a **cheap** ring*

50p

cheat
cheats cheating cheated *verb*
to trick someone, or to be dishonest so that you have an advantage over them.

check
checks checking checked *verb*
to look at something to make sure it is all right.
check *noun*

check
checks *noun*
a pattern of regular squares in different colours, often on cloth or paper.

cheek
cheeks *noun*
the side of your face below your eye.

cheek

cheer
cheers cheering cheered *verb*
to shout out loudly and happily.

cheer *noun*

cheese
cheeses *noun*
a food made from the thickened parts of milk.

cheetah
cheetahs *noun*
a spotted mammal that belongs to the cat family. Cheetahs live on the dry plains of Africa and prey on other animals. They are extremely fast runners.

chef
chefs *noun*
a person whose job it is to cook and prepare food.
■ say **shef**

chemical
chemicals *noun*
any substance that can change when joined or mixed with another. Chemicals can be natural or manufactured.
■ say **kem**-ik-al

cheque
cheques *noun*
a piece of paper from a bank that you can use to pay for things.
■ say **check**

cherry
cherries *noun*
a round, soft fruit with a small stone in its centre.

chess
noun
a board game for two people. The winner is the person who takes the other player's king.

chest
chests *noun*
1 the front of your body below your shoulders and above your stomach.

chest

2 a wooden box with a lid, used for keeping things in.

chew
chews chewing chewed *verb*
to use your teeth to break up food.
■ say **choo**

chick
chicks *noun*
a young bird.

child
children *noun*
a young person. A child legally becomes an adult at the age of 18.
■ opposite **adult**

chimney
chimneys *noun*
a pipe above a fire that takes smoke out of a building.

chimpanzee
chimpanzees *noun*
a mammal that lives in groups in forests in central Africa. Chimpanzees are a type of ape. Their main diet is fruit and nuts, though sometimes they eat small animals.

chin
chins *noun*
the part of your face between your mouth and your neck.

chin

china
noun
a type of delicate pottery made from fine, white clay.

chip
chips *noun*
1 a small piece of something that has broken off something larger.

wood **chips**

2 a gap or mark on something, showing the place where a small part has broken off.

chip

3 a fried piece of potato.
4 a small piece of material with many tiny electronic circuits printed on it. Chips are used in electronic devices for storing information.

silicon
chip

chocolate
chocolates *noun*
a sweet food made from crushed and roasted cocoa beans, milk, and sugar.

choir
choirs *noun*
a group of singers.
■ say **kwire**

choke
chokes choking choked *verb*
to stop or almost stop breathing.
The fire-fighters almost **choked** *in the dense smoke.*

choose
chooses choosing chose chosen *verb*
to decide that you want one thing and not another.
I **chose** *the blue trousers instead of the red ones.*
choice *noun*

chop
chops chopping chopped *verb*
to cut up something with a sharp tool.

a b c d e f g h i j k l m n o p q r s t u v w x y z

chopstick
chopsticks *noun*
a thin piece of wood or plastic, used in pairs for eating food.

chorus
choruses *noun*
lines in a song that are repeated at the end of each verse.
■ say **kor**-us

Christian
Christians *noun*
a person who believes in and follows the teachings of Jesus Christ and believes that Jesus is the son of God.

church
churches *noun*
a building where Christians hold religious services.

chute
chutes *noun*
a sloping channel for sliding things down.
Water **chute**.
■ say **shoot**

cigarette
cigarettes *noun*
a rolled-up piece of paper filled with tobacco, which can be lit and smoked. Cigarettes can harm your heart and lungs.

cinema
cinemas *noun*
a building where people pay to watch films.

circle
circles *noun*
a flat, exactly round shape.
circular *adjective*

circuit
circuits *noun*
1 any completed path or track.
2 the completed path of an electric current.

electrical **circuit**
■ say **sir**-kit

circus
circuses *noun*
a show with clowns, jugglers, and acrobats that travels around the world.

citizen
citizens *noun*
a person who lives in, and belongs to, a particular place.
A British **citizen**.

city
cities *noun*
a very large, important town.
London, Glasgow, and Cardiff are British **cities**.

civilization
civilizations *noun*
a large group of people living in a well-organized way.
The Aztec **civilization**.
■ say siv-il-ize-**ay**-shun

claim
claims claiming claimed *verb*
to say that something is yours.
She **claimed** *first prize in the competition.*

clang
clangs clanging clanged *verb*
to make a deep, loud, ringing sound.
Bells **clang**.

clank
clanks clanking clanked *verb*
to make a short, metallic sound.

Chains **clank**.

clap
claps clapping clapped *verb*
to make a short, sharp sound with your hands.

Clap your hands.
clap *noun*

clash
clashes *noun*
a loud, metallic sound.

Cymbals **clash**.

class
classes *noun*
1 a group of pupils who are taught together.
My **class** *is learning French.*
2 a group of people, animals, or things that are similar to each other in some way.
Butterflies belong to the **class** *of insects.*

classify
classifies classifying classified *verb*
to sort things out into groups of different types.
Books can be **classified** *as fiction or non-fiction.*

clatter
clatters clattering clattered *verb*
to make a repeated rattling sound.

The plates **clattered** *to the floor.*

claw
claws *noun*
one of the long, curved, pointed nails that many animals and birds have on their feet.

owl's **claw**

clay
noun
a type of earth that is soft and sticky when wet, and hard when dried or heated. Clay is used to make pots and bricks.

modelling **clay**

clean
cleans cleaning cleaned *verb*
to remove dirt or stains.

clean
adjective
without any dirt or stains.
clean silver
■ comparisons **cleaner cleanest**

clear
clears clearing cleared *verb*
to move things that are in the way.
*The walkers **cleared** a path through the bushes.*

clear
adjective
1 easy to see through.

*The water was so **clear** that I could see the fish.*
2 easy to understand.
*A **clear** explanation.*
■ comparisons **clearer clearest**

clench
clenches clenching clenched *verb*
to curl up your hand or hands tightly.

*a **clenched** fist*

clever
adjective
able to learn and understand things easily.
■ comparisons **cleverer cleverest**

click
clicks clicking clicked *verb*
to make a short, sharp sound with your fingers.
***Clicking** your fingers.*

cliff
cliffs *noun*
the high, steep side of a mountain or rock.

climate
climates *noun*
the type of weather that a place has over a long time.
*The **climate** in southern Africa is hot and dry.*

climb
climbs climbing climbed *verb*
to move upwards using your hands and feet.

climb *noun*

cling
clings clinging clung *verb*
to hold on to something very tightly.

***clinging** upside-down*

clink
clinks clinking clinked *verb*
to make a soft, ringing sound.
*The ice **clinked** in the glass.*

clip
noun
1 a small metal or plastic object to fasten something together.
*A paper **clip**.*
2 a short section of a film.

clock
clocks *noun*
an instrument that shows the time.

clockwise
adverb
moving in the same direction as the hands on a clock.
■ opposite **anti-clockwise**

close
closes closing closed *verb*
to shut something.
■ say **kloze**

close
adjective
near to something.
***Close** to the house.*
■ say **klose**
■ comparisons **closer closest**

clot
clots *noun*
a soft lump in a liquid.
*A blood **clot**.*

cloth
noun
woven material that is used to make clothes and other things.

clothes
noun
the things that we wear.
clothing *noun*

cloud
clouds *noun*
a mass of tiny drops of water, or pieces of ice, floating high in the air. The water falls as rain, and the ice falls as hail or snow.

cloudy *adjective*

clown
clowns *noun*
a circus performer who wears funny clothes and makes people laugh.

club
clubs *noun*
1 a group of people who get together for a purpose, and the place where they meet.
*A drama **club**.*
2 a thick, heavy stick that is used as a weapon.
3 a stick with a shaped head that is used to hit balls in golf (see **sport** on page 197).

clue
clues *noun*
a piece of information that helps to solve a mystery.

a b c d e f g h i j k l m n o p q r s t u v w x y z

A B C D E F G H I J K L M N O P Q R S T U V W X Y Z

clumsy

adjective
moving awkwardly, or without skill.

*He spilled the milk because he was **clumsy**.*
■ comparisons **clumsier clumsiest**

coach

coaches *noun*
1 a long-distance bus.

2 a person who teaches people a special skill.
*An athletics **coach**.*

coach

coaches coaching coached
verb
to teach somebody how to do something.
*She **coaches** the hockey team every Saturday.*

coal

noun
a hard, brittle, brown or black rock that is burned as a fuel. Coal is made from fossilized plants that died millions of years ago.

coast

coasts *noun*
the seashore.
coastal *adjective*

coat

coats *noun*
1 an item of clothing you wear over your clothes to keep warm outside.

2 an animal's fur.
3 a layer of paint.

cobra

cobras *noun*
a large, poisonous snake that lives in hot regions. Cobras can flatten the bones of their neck into a hood shape when threatened. They kill their prey with a bite that paralyses them.

cobweb

cobwebs *noun*
a very fine, sticky net made by spiders to trap flies.

cockatoo

cockatoos *noun*
a parrot with head feathers that it can lift up or flatten. Cockatoos eat fruit, nuts, and plant roots (see **bird** on page 28).

cockerel

cockerels *noun*
a young, male chicken.

cocoa

noun
a powder made from cocoa beans, the dried seeds of the cacao tree. Cocoa is used to make chocolate and as a flavour in food and drink.
■ say **koe**-koe

cocoa beans   *cocoa drink*

coconut

coconuts *noun*
the fruit of the coconut palm tree. The hard outer shell has a layer of sweet, white, edible flesh inside, and contains a thin liquid known as coconut milk.

cod

noun
a large sea fish that lives in shoals close to the ocean floor. Cod use their sharp teeth to eat smaller fish, shellfish, and worms.

code

codes *noun*
1 a set of rules.
*The highway **code**.*
2 a series of signs, symbols, or letters for sending messages secretly or quickly.

*SOS message in Morse **code***

coffee

noun
a drink made from the roasted and crushed seeds of the coffee plant. When roasted, the seeds are called beans.

coffee

*roasted **coffee** beans*

cog

cogs *noun*
1 a wheel with shapes cut out around its edge. Cogs are used together in machines to turn other things round.

2 the tooth-shaped, metal parts around such a wheel.

coil

coils *noun*
something that is twisted around into circles.

coil of metal

coin

coins *noun*
a piece of money made of metal.

cold
adjective
having a low temperature.
*A **cold** day.*
■ opposite **hot**

cold
colds *noun*
an infection that often makes
you sneeze and cough and may
give you a sore throat.

collapse
**collapses collapsing
collapsed** *verb*
1 to fall down suddenly.
*The tent **collapsed**.*
2 to fold up.
*My umbrella **collapses** so
I can put it in my bag.*
collapsible *adjective*

collect
collects collecting collected
verb
to bring together.
*I **collect** autographs.*
collection *noun*

collide
collides colliding collided *verb*
to crash into something.

*The cars **collided**.*
collision *noun*

colour
colours *noun*
what something looks like
when light is shining on it.
Yellow, green, red, and
blue are the names of
some colours.

*fruits of different **colours***
colourful *adjective*

column
columns *noun*
1 a tall, vertical, round post
that is used as a support or
to decorate buildings.

2 a list in which
things are written
underneath
each other.

    33
    27
    46
    58
    19
    ———
    183

*adding up a **column**
of figures*

comb
combs *noun*
a piece of wood, metal, or
plastic with teeth. A comb
is used to arrange hair.

combine
**combines combining
combined** *verb*
to bring things together to
make something else.

*Blue and yellow paint
combine to make green.*
combination *noun*

come
comes coming came *verb*
to move towards, or arrive
at, one place from another.
*Hurry up! The train is **coming**.*

comedy
comedies *noun*
a film, play, or radio or
television show that makes
you laugh.

comet
comets *noun*
a huge ball of dust, ice, and
gases that travels around
the Sun, often followed by
a luminous trail of gases.

comfortable
adjective
pleasant and easy, especially
to sit in or wear.
*A **comfortable** chair.*
■ opposite **uncomfortable**

comic
comics *noun*
a magazine
that contains
stories told
in pictures.

comical
adjective
funny.
*He speaks in a **comical** way.*

command
**commands commanding
commanded** *verb*
to order someone to do
what you want.
*The teacher **commanded**
them to sit down.*
command *noun*

common
adjective
often seen, or normal.
*Seagulls are a **common**
sight along the coast.*

common sense
noun
the ability to act sensibly
in different situations.
***Common sense** stopped us
from driving in the fog.*

communicate
**communicates
communicating
communicated** *verb*
to talk, write, or send a
message to someone else.

***communicating** by telephone*
■ say kom-**yoo**-ni-kate
communication *noun*

community
communities *noun*
a group of people who live
together in the same place.
■ say kom-**yoo**-ni-tee

commuter
commuters *noun*
a person who travels a long
distance to and from work
every day.
commute *verb*

compact disc
compact discs *noun*
a small, flat circle of plastic
that can have sounds, words,
and pictures recorded on it.
Compact disc is shortened
to CD.

a b c d e f g h i j k l m n o p q r s t u v w x y z

47

A
B
C
D
E
F
G
H
I
J
K
L
M
N
O
P
Q
R
S
T
U
V
W
X
Y
Z

company
noun
1 a group of people who work together to make or sell something.
A computer **company**.
2 people or animals with whom you spend time.
My cat is good **company**.

compare
compares comparing compared *verb*
to look at several things to see how they are the same and how they are different.
My teacher **compares** *me with my sister all the time.*
comparison *noun*

compass
compasses *noun*
1 an instrument that shows the direction you are facing. The magnetic compass needle always points north.

magnetic needle

2 a tool with one fixed leg and one movable leg, which is used for drawing circles.

competition
competitions *noun*
an event where one person or a team of people try to do better than their opponents.

She won the tennis **competition**.
compete *verb*

complain
complains complaining complained *verb*
to say that you are not happy about something.
The passengers **complained** *about the late train.*

complete
completes completing completed *verb*
to finish something.

completing *the jigsaw*
complete *adjective*

complicated
adjective
hard to understand, or difficult.

a **complicated** *knot*
■ opposite **simple**

composer
composers *noun*
a person who writes music.
compose *verb*

compromise
compromises compromising compromised *verb*
to end an argument by both sides deciding to give up part of what they want.
They both wanted to ride the bike, but had to **compromise** *by taking turns.*
■ say **kom**-pro-mize
compromise *noun*

compulsory
adjective
that must be done.
Maths is a **compulsory** *subject at school.*

computer
computers *noun*
an electronic machine that arranges and stores information digitally, using a set of instructions called a program. It is also used for communication.

laptop **computer**

concentrate
concentrates concentrating concentrated *verb*
to think carefully about something.

concentrating *on the puzzle*
■ say **kon**-sen-trate
concentration *noun*

concert
concerts *noun*
an event where people sing or play music for an audience to listen to.

conclusion
conclusions *noun*
1 the end of something.
The story's **conclusion** *was a happy one.*
2 a decision that is based on all the things you know.
She came to the **conclusion** *that it was a sensible idea.*
conclude *verb*

concrete
noun
a mixture of sand, cement, stones, and water, which is used for building.

concrete *paving stones*

condition
noun
1 the state that something is in.

Grooming helps to keep a horse in good **condition**.
2 a rule.
He went out on the **condition** *that he would be back before dark.*

confident
adjective
believing you can do something, or being sure something will happen.
I'm **confident** *I'll win.*
confidence *noun*

confiscate
confiscates confiscating confiscated *verb*
to punish by taking something away from someone.
I had my football **confiscated**.

confuse
confuses confusing confused *verb*
1 to make someone puzzled because of some difficulty in understanding.
The instructions confused me.
2 to find it difficult to tell one thing from another.
I always confuse the twins.

congratulate
congratulates congratulating congratulated *verb*
to say to someone that they have done well.

congratulating the winner
congratulations *noun*

conifer
conifers *noun*
a tree that has needles instead of leaves. Conifers stay green all year round, and have cones instead of flowers.

Scotch pine

connect
connects connecting connected *verb*
to link up two things.

connecting the phone to the battery charger
connection *noun*

conscience
consciences *noun*
a feeling inside you that tells you what is right and wrong.
A guilty conscience.
■ say **kon**-shuns

conscious
adjective
awake and aware of what is happening.
The man was still conscious after the accident.
■ say **kon**-shus
■ opposite **unconscious**

conservation
noun
the protection and careful use of something. Conservation groups try to protect animals, plants, and the environment.

consider
considers considering considered *verb*
to think about something carefully.
She considered going out, but decided not to.

considerate
adjective
thoughtful towards other people.

He is very considerate.

consonant
consonants *noun*
any letter of the alphabet that is not a vowel (see **alphabet** on page 16).

constant
adjective
going on without stopping.
A constant problem.
constantly *adverb*

constellation
constellations *noun*
a group of stars.

construct
constructs constructing constructed *verb*
to build.

constructing a wooden chair
construction *noun*

contact
contacts contacting contacted *verb*
to communicate with someone.
You can contact me by phone while I'm away.
contact *noun*

contain
contains containing contained *verb*
to have something inside.

The glass contains juice.
container *noun*

content
contents *noun*
an object inside something, such as a box, bag, or book.
■ say **kon**-tent

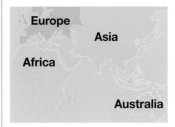

lunch box contents

content
adjective
happy and satisfied.
■ say kon-**tent**
contented *adjective*

contest
contests *noun*
a match or competition between people.
A juggling contest.

continent
continents *noun*
one of the seven large areas of land on Earth that usually includes several countries.

Europe
Asia
Africa
Australia

four of the seven continents of the world

continual
adjective
happening often, or without stopping.
Continual noise.
continually *adverb*

continue
continues continuing continued *verb*
to carry on.
The match continued after the rain had stopped.
continuous *adjective*

a b c d e f g h i j k l m n o p q r s t u v w x y z

contract
contracts contracting contracted *verb*
to shrink or make smaller.
The pupils of your eyes **contract** *when light is shone on them.*

contract
contracts *noun*
a formal agreement.

contradict
contradicts contradicting contradicted *verb*
to say the opposite of what someone else has said.
The politicians **contradicted** *each other.*
contradiction *noun*

contribute
contributes contributing contributed *verb*
to give a part of something.
We all **contributed** *to the meal.*
contribution *noun*

control
controls controlling controlled *verb*
to have the power to make something or someone do what you want.

He **controlled** *the ball with his feet.*

convenient
adjective
useful, or easy for you.
A **convenient** *time.*
■ say kon-**vee**-nee-ent
■ opposite **inconvenient**

conversation
conversations *noun*
talk between two or more people.

a friendly **conversation**

convince
convinces convincing convinced *verb*
to persuade somebody to believe something.
■ say kon-**vins**

cook
cooks cooking cooked *verb*
to prepare and heat food so that it can be eaten.

cookery *noun*

cook
cooks *noun*
someone who prepares food.

cool
adjective
slightly cold.

This box keeps drinks **cool**.
■ opposite **warm**

co-operate
co-operates co-operating co-operated *verb*
to work with someone in a helpful way.
We **co-operated** *on a project.*
co-operation *noun*

copper
noun
a red-brown coloured metal that goes green when it comes into contact with moist air.

copper *ore*   **copper** *pipe*

copy
copies copying copied *verb*
to do the same thing as someone else.
Copy *me! I'll show you how to do it.*
copy *noun*

coral
corals *noun*
a hard substance that is made of the skeletons of small sea animals. Coral is found in warm seas.

core
cores *noun*
the middle part of something.
An apple **core**.

cork
noun
the soft, springy bark of the cork oak tree, which is used to make mats, tiles, and seals for bottles.

cork *oak bark*   *wine* **cork**

corn
noun
a general name for the seeds or the plants of wheat, barley, rye, and oats.

corner
corners *noun*
the place where two lines or surfaces meet at an angle.
A street **corner**.

correct
adjective
right, with no mistakes.
■ opposite **incorrect**
correction *noun*

corridor
corridors *noun*
a long indoor passage, with doors leading off it into rooms.

cosmetics
noun
the things that people use to change the way their skin or hair looks.

lipstick   *eye pencil*

cost
costs costing cost *verb*
to have a price.
A computer **costs** *hundreds of pounds.*
cost *noun*

costume

costumes *noun*
1 an outfit worn in a particular period of time. *Historical* **costume**.
2 an outfit worn for a special reason. *Theatrical* **costume**.

gauntlets

silk stockings

doublet

ruff

chemise

corset

petticoat

16th-century **costume**

19th-century lingerie

drawers

crinoline frame

tunic (chiton)

wig

beauty patch

cravat

hose

sandals

ancient Greek **costume**

waistcoat

cuff

handbag

headdress

trimming

pendant

mules

girdle

brim

cloche hat

breeches

stockings

petticoat

pantaloons

buckle

pumps

braces

19th-century **costume**

18th-century **costume**

14th-century **costume**

a b **c** d e f g h i j k l m n o p q r s t u v w x y z

A B C D E F G H I J K L M N O P Q R S T U V W X Y Z

cotton
noun
1 soft, white hairs that surround the seeds on a cotton plant.
2 thread or cloth woven from cotton plants.

cotton thread

cough
coughs coughing coughed
verb
to force air out of your lungs with a sharp noise.
■ say **kof**

council
councils *noun*
a group of people who are chosen to make decisions for an organization or community.

counter
counters *noun*
a flat surface in a shop or bank where you are served.
*The cheese **counter**.*

country
countries *noun*
1 an area of land with its own borders, people, and laws.

China

*China is one of the biggest **countries** in world.*
2 land outside towns and cities.

courage
noun
being brave when you are in danger or difficulty.
*It takes **courage** to admit that you are wrong.*
■ say **kur**-rij
courageous *adjective*

course
courses *noun*
1 the plan of lessons that students must follow in a school or college subject.
*Our history **course** starts on Monday.*

2 the ground where many outdoor sports, such as golf and horse-racing, take place.

*golf **course***

court
courts *noun*
1 the place where it is decided whether people have broken the law and what punishment they should receive.
2 an area of ground, marked with lines, on which some sports are played.
*A badminton **court**.*

cousin
cousins *noun*
a child of the sister or brother of someone's parent.

cover
covers covering covered *verb*
to put something over or on something else.

*You should **cover** your mouth when you sneeze.*
cover *noun*

cow
cows *noun*
1 a female mammal that eats grass and is reared on farms to produce milk and beef.

2 the female of some large animals, such as elephants and whales.

coward
cowards *noun*
a person who is easily scared.

crab
crabs *noun*
a shellfish with 10 legs and a soft body protected by a hard covering. The front pair of legs ends in claws which the crab uses to catch its prey.

*coral **crab***

crack
cracks cracking cracked *verb*
to become damaged so that it splits, but does not break.
*The mirror **cracked** when he dropped it.*
crack *noun*

cracker
crackers *noun*
1 a thin, dry biscuit often eaten with cheese.

2 a long, round package of coloured paper containing a small present. Crackers are used at parties and make a loud noise when pulled apart.

craft
crafts *noun*
1 an activity that requires skill.

*paper **craft***

2 a boat, aeroplane, or spaceship.

crane
cranes *noun*
1 a machine that lifts and moves heavy objects.

2 a large bird that lives near marshes and lakes, and feeds on plants, small insects, and animals. Cranes have a loud, echoing cry.

*crowned **crane***

crash
crashes crashing crashed *verb*
to fall or collide with a loud noise.
*The tray of china **crashed** to the floor.*
crash *noun*

crate

crates *noun*
an open container for storing and carrying things, usually bottles.

crawl

crawls crawling crawled *verb*
to move along on your hands and knees.

*Most babies **crawl** before they learn to walk.*

crayfish

noun
a spiny shellfish that looks like a small lobster. Crayfish live under stones during the day and hunt for small fish and insects at night.

crazy

adjective
foolish or strange.
■ comparisons **crazier craziest**

creak

creaks creaking creaked *verb*
to make a low, squeaking sound.
*The door **creaked** open.*

cream

noun
1 the oily part of milk that rises to the top. Cream is often used to make sweets and puddings.

*a jug of **cream***

2 a yellow-white colour.

crease

creases *noun*
a line or fold, usually made in cloth or paper.

crease

crease *verb*

create

creates creating created *verb*
to design and make something.
*She **created** a beautiful painting.*
■ say kree-**ate**

creature

creatures *noun*
any living thing.

creek

creeks *noun*
a small, narrow inlet or bay in the coast.

creep

creeps creeping crept *verb*
to walk forwards very slowly and quietly.

*The cat **crept** up on the birds.*

crew

crews *noun*
1 the people who work on a ship or aeroplane.
2 a team of people who work together in a job.
*The film **crew** was ready to begin shooting.*

cricket

crickets *noun*
1 a jumping insect that eats plants. Crickets rub their wings together to make a singing sound. They have long back legs for jumping.

2 a team game played with 11 players in each team. The winning team is the one with the most points, called runs. Runs are scored by the person batting (see **sport** on page 197).

cried

*from the verb **to cry***
*The baby **cried** all night.*

crime

crimes *noun*
an activity that is against the law.
*Murder is a very serious **crime**.*

criminal

criminals *noun*
a person who carries out a crime.

crisp

adjective
dry and easily broken into pieces.

crisp biscuits

■ comparisons **crisper crispest**

criticize

criticizes criticizing criticized *verb*
to say what you think is wrong with something.
*He was upset when I **criticized** his painting.*
■ say krit-i-size
criticism *noun*

crocodile

crocodiles *noun*
a reptile that lives on land and in water. Crocodiles are fierce hunters, and hunt at night for fish, mammals, and frogs (see **skeleton** on page 188).

crop

crops *noun*
a vegetable or plant that is grown on a farm for food.
*The potato **crop**.*

cross

crosses crossing crossed *verb*
1 to go over something, from one side to another.
***Crossing** the street.*
2 to place two things across each other in a cross shape.

*He **crossed** his fingers.*

cross
crosses *noun*
an object or sign made by two lines crossing each other.

cross
adjective
angry.

crossly *adverb*

crossword
crosswords *noun*
a word puzzle with clues. You write down the answers by putting each letter of the answer into a separate square.

B	E	A	N	
U		W		S
S	H	A	R	P
Y		R		O
	W	E	S	T

crouch
crouches crouching crouched *verb*
to bend down low, with your legs curled underneath you.

crowd
crowds *noun*
a large number of people gathered close together.

crown
crowns *noun*
a circle of precious metals and jewels. Kings and queens wear crowns on their heads on special occasions.

cruel
adjective
unkind and hurtful.

crumb
crumbs *noun*
a very small piece of food, such as bread, cake, or biscuits.

crunch
crunches crunching crunched *verb*
to crush or chew something noisily.
*She **crunched** a juicy apple.*

crush
crushes crushing crushed *verb*
to damage something by squeezing it very hard.

crushing a can

crust
crusts *noun*
1 a hard covering.

*pie **crust***

2 the thick, hard outer covering of Earth.

crutch
crutches *noun*
a support for someone who has difficulty walking.

cry
cries crying cried *verb*
to have tears falling from your eyes because you are upset or frightened.

crystal
crystals *noun*
a piece of clear quartz with flat sides that has been formed naturally.

■ say **kris**-tal

cub
cubs *noun*
a young mammal, such as a fox, lion, or bear.

*lion **cub***

cube
cubes *noun*
a solid shape with six square sides.

cucumber
cucumbers *noun*
a green vegetable with a crisp, white flesh that grows on vines. Cucumbers are a popular vegetable to use in salads.

cuddle
cuddles cuddling cuddled *verb*
to hug someone in a loving way.

*She **cuddled** her brother.*

culprit
culprits *noun*
a person who has done something wrong.
*The **culprit** had stolen the money from his pocket.*

cunning
adjective
able to trick people.

cup
cups *noun*
a small container used for drinking liquids out of.

cure
cures curing cured *verb*
to make somebody well again after they have been ill.

curious
adjective
1 eager to find out about things.
*She was **curious** to see what was behind the door.*
2 strange but interesting.
*I saw a very **curious** animal the other day.*
■ say **kew**-ree-us

curl
curls *noun*
a small, curved piece of hair.

*His hair is a mass of **curls**.*
curly *adjective*

currency
currencies *noun*
the money of a country.
*The **currency** of France is the Euro.*

current
currents *noun*
1 a flow of water or air moving in a certain direction.
*The **current** carried the boat out to sea.*
2 the flow of electricity through a wire.
*Switch off the **current** when you change a light bulb.*

curry
curries *noun*
1 a hot, spicy dish made of meat, fish, or vegetables, usually served with rice.

*vegetable **curry***

2 a mixture of hot spices used to flavour food.

***curry** powder*

curtain
curtains *noun*
pieces of material, usually fabric, that is hung from a bar and pulled across a window or space.

curtsy
curtsies *noun*
a formal way for women to greet someone.

■ also spelt **curtsey**

curve
curves *noun*
a line that bends smoothly.

curve *verb*

cushion
cushions *noun*
a type of pillow used for sitting or leaning on.

customer
customers *noun*
a person who buys something from a shop or a company.

cut
cuts cutting cut *verb*
to divide something into parts using a sharp tool.

***cutting**
with scissors*

cut
cuts *noun*
a wound, often made by something sharp.

cutlery
noun
knives, forks, and spoons.

cycle
cycles cycling cycled *verb*
to ride a bicycle.

cyclist

cycle
cycles *noun*
changes that happen regularly in a particular order.
*The life-**cycle** of a butterfly.*

cyclone
cyclones *noun*
a tropical storm with very strong winds.
■ say **sye**-klone

cylinder
cylinders *noun*
a solid or hollow object with circular ends and straight sides (see **shape** on page 182).
■ say **sil**-in-der

cymbal
cymbals *noun*
a round, hollow, brass musical instrument, which makes a loud, clashing sound when hit.

A B C **D** E F G H I J K L M N O P Q R S T U V W X Y Z

Dd

daffodil

daffodils *noun*
a plant that grows from
a bulb and has a large,
trumpet-shaped flower
at the end of each stem.

dagger

daggers *noun*
a knife with a short, sharp,
pointed blade, that is used
as a weapon.

daily

adverb
every day.
*Letters are delivered **daily**.*
daily *adjective*

dairy

dairies *noun*
a place where milk and
cream are stored and butter
and cheese are made.

daisy

daisies *noun*
a common plant with white
or pink flowers. Daisies close
their petals when it is dark.
Some kinds of daisy are wild,
while others are grown as
garden plants.

dam

dams *noun*
a wall built across a river or
stream to hold back the flow
of water.

damage

**damages damaging
damaged** *verb*
to harm something.

*The collision **damaged** the
front of the boat.*
■ say **dam**-ij
damage *noun*

damp

adjective
slightly wet or moist.
*A **damp** towel.*
■ comparisons **damper dampest**
damp *noun*

dance

dances dancing danced *verb*
to move about to music.

dance *noun*

dandelion

dandelions *noun*
a common wild plant with a
thick root and a single yellow
flower on each stem. Fine
hairs attached to the seeds
mean that the seeds can be
easily blown away by the wind.

fine
hairs
on seeds

danger

dangers *noun*
a situation that might
be harmful to you.

Danger ahead!
dangerous *adjective*

dare

dares daring dared *verb*
1 to challenge someone to
do something frightening
to show they are not afraid.
2 to be bold or foolish enough
to do something frightening
or dangerous.

dark

adjective
1 not much light, or no light.

*The street was **dark** away
from the street lights.*
dark *noun*
2 with a lot of black in it.
Dark blue.
■ comparisons **darker darkest**
■ opposite **light**

dash

dashes dashing dashed *verb*
to run very quickly for a
short distance.
*I **dashed** onto the platform,
but the train had just left.*

data

noun
facts and figures
about something.
■ say **day**-ter

database

databases *noun*
a large amount of information
stored in a computer.

date

dates *noun*
1 the day, month, and year.
2 a sweet, sticky fruit with
a stone in the middle.

daughter
daughters *noun*
a person's female child.
■ say **daw**-ter

dawdle
dawdles dawdling dawdled
verb
to move or do things slowly.

*Stop **dawdling**!*

dawn
dawns *noun*
the early part of the day when it starts to become light.

■ opposite **dusk**

day
days *noun*
1 the part of the day when it is light.
■ opposite **night**
2 a period of 24 hours, starting and ending at midnight.

dazed
adjective
not able to think clearly.
*He has a **dazed** look in his eyes.*
■ say **day**-zd

dazzle
dazzles dazzling dazzled *verb*
to shine a bright light into someone's eyes so that they find it difficult to see.

dazzling *adjective*

dead
adjective
no longer living.

***dead** leaves*
■ opposite **alive**

dead
noun
a time when everything is still and quiet.
*The **dead** of night.*

deadly
adjective
able to kill.

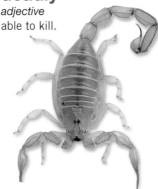

*A scorpion's sting is **deadly**.*

deaf
adjective
not able to hear well or not able to hear at all.
deafness *noun*

dear
adjective
1 expensive.
*The café prices are very **dear**.*
2 loved very much.
*A **dear** friend.*
■ comparisons **dearer dearest**

debt
debts *noun*
money or a favour that you owe to someone.
■ say **det**

decade
decades *noun*
a period of 10 years.
*The **decade** of 1920 to 1929.*

decay
decays decaying decayed *verb*
to rot away.
*Your teeth will **decay** if you don't look after them.*
decay *noun*

deceive
deceives deceiving deceived
verb
to trick a person into thinking something is true when it isn't.
deceit *noun*

decibel
decibels *noun*
a unit of measurement that shows how loud a sound is.
■ say **des**-ee-bel

decide
decides deciding decided *verb*
to make up your mind.

*He couldn't **decide** what to eat.*
decision *noun*

deciduous
adjective
losing leaves every year.

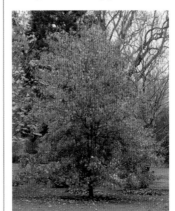

■ opposite **evergreen**
■ say dis-**id**-yoo-us

decimal
adjective
counting numbers and parts of numbers in tens.

3.752

*a **decimal** number*
decimal *noun*

deck
decks *noun*
one of the floors of a ship.

deck

declare
declares declaring declared
verb
to say something to everyone.
*The judges **declared** the winner at the end of the competition.*

decline
declines declining declined
verb
to decrease or get worse.
*His health **declined** steadily.*
decline *noun*

decorate
decorates decorating decorated *verb*
to make something look better by painting it or by adding extra things to it.

***decorating** a Christmas tree*
decoration *noun*

A B C **D** E F G H I J K L M N O P Q R S T U V W X Y Z

decrease
decreases decreasing decreased *verb*
to become smaller.
The number of whales in the world is decreasing.
- opposite **increase**

deep
adjective
going down a long way.

deep in the ocean
- comparisons **deeper deepest**

deer
noun
a mammal with hooves that eats grass and leaves. A male deer is called a stag and has large, branching horns called antlers. A female deer is called a doe.

stag

defeat
defeats defeating defeated *verb*
to win a game or a battle against someone.
She defeated her brother at chess.

defend
defends defending defended *verb*
to protect or guard.
Birds stay with their eggs to defend them from attackers.
defence *noun*

define
defines defining defined *verb*
to describe accurately what something means.
definition *noun*

definite
adjective
certain and clear.
Are you definite about that?
definitely *adverb*

degree
degrees *noun*
1 a unit used to measure temperature and angles. The symbol for a degree is °.
2 a certificate awarded by a college or university.

delay
delays delaying delayed *verb*
to take place later than expected.
The aeroplane's departure was delayed for seven hours.
delay *noun*

delete
deletes deleting deleted *verb*
to remove something.

word deleted

deliberately
adverb
on purpose.
He deliberately pushed me.
deliberate *adjective*

delicate
adjective
easily broken or damaged.

delicate butterfly wings

delicious
adjective
tasting very nice.
The ice-cream was delicious.

delighted
adjective
very pleased.

She was delighted with her birthday present.

deliver
delivers delivering delivered *verb*
to bring something to someone.
He delivered the parcel this morning.
delivery *noun*

demand
demands demanding demanded *verb*
to ask someone for something firmly, not expecting them to refuse.
She demanded to know the truth.
demand *noun*

demolish
demolishes demolishing demolished *verb*
to destroy something.

They started demolishing the house yesterday.

demonstrate
demonstrates demonstrating demonstrated *verb*
1 to show someone how to do something.
He demonstrated the new food mixer.
2 to take part in a public rally or meeting to show that you feel very strongly about something.
The marchers demonstrated against the new road.
demonstration *noun*

denim
noun
a type of strong, cotton cloth that is often dyed blue.

dense
adjective
thick.
A dense fog.

dent
dents *noun*
a hollow left in the surface of something after it has been hit or pressed.
The car had a dent in its bonnet.
dent *verb*

dentist
dentists *noun*
a person who examines and repairs your teeth.

dentist

patien[t]

depart

departs departing departed
verb
to leave.

The ship departed on time.
departure *noun*

depend

depends depending depended *verb*
to need or rely on someone or something.
I'm depending on you to be there on time.

describe

describes describing described *verb*
to say or write what something or someone is like.
***Describe* your house to me.**
description *noun*

desert

deserts deserting deserted
verb
to leave without permission, not planning to return.
He deserted the army.
■ say de-**zert**

desert

deserts *noun*
a large, dry, sandy or stony area of land, with few plants.
■ say **dez**-ert

deserve

deserves deserving deserved *verb*
to have earned some reward because of something you have done.
He deserved a rest after working so hard.

design

designs designing designed
verb
to plan what something is going to look like.

designing a page on my computer
design *noun*

desire

desires *noun*
a strong wish.
desire *verb*

desk

desks *noun*
a table that you use for working on, often with drawers in it.

desperate

adjective
1 ready to do anything without thinking of the risks.
A desperate escape plan.
2 very serious or hopeless.
A desperate situation.

dessert

desserts *noun*
a sweet dish eaten at the end of a meal.

■ say de-**zert**

destination

destinations *noun*
the place someone or something is going to.
She was looking for the shortest route to her destination.

destroy

destroys destroying destroyed *verb*
to completely ruin something.
The fire destroyed the hut.
destruction *noun*

detail

details *noun*
a small part of something.
The news report gave few details of the robbery.
detailed *adjective*

detective

detectives *noun*
a person who investigates crimes.

detergent

detergents *noun*
a soapy powder or liquid that is used for cleaning things such as clothes or dishes.
■ say de-**ter**-jent

bottle of detergent

determined

adjective
not letting anything stop you from doing something.

He was determined to reach the top of the mountain.
determination *noun*

develop

develops developing developed *verb*
to grow and become more complete.
The bud developed into a beautiful flower.
development *noun*

device

devices *noun*
a machine or tool invented for a special purpose.

A corkscrew is a device for pulling corks out of bottles.

dew

noun
small drops of water that form on cool surfaces outside during the night.

a b c **d** e f g h i j k l m n o p q r s t u v w x y z

A B C D E F G H I J K L M N O P Q R S T U V W X Y Z

diagonal
adjective
sloping at an angle from one edge to another.

diagonal stripes

diagram
diagrams *noun*
a drawing or plan that shows or explains something.

*a **diagram** of the inside of a volcano*

dial
dials *noun*
the face of a measuring device that has numbers on it.

dial

diameter
diameters *noun*
the width of a circle, measured by a straight line.

diameter

diary
diaries *noun*
a book in which you write down your thoughts and daily events (see **time** on page 216).

dice
noun
cubes with a different number of dots, from one to six, on each side. Dice are used in indoor games. A single cube is sometimes called a die.

dictionary
dictionaries *noun*
a book that contains an alphabetical list of words with their meanings.

die
dies dying died *verb*
to stop living.
death *noun*

diet
diets *noun*
the food that you usually eat.

*Fruit and vegetables are part of a healthy **diet**.*

different
adjective
not like something else.

*two **different** shells*
■ opposite **same**
difference *noun*

difficult
adjective
hard to do.
*It was **difficult** to cut the string with blunt scissors.*
■ opposite **easy**

dig
digs digging dug *verb*
to make a hole in the earth.

digest
digests digesting digested *verb*
to break food down so that the body can use it.
■ say die-**jest**
digestion *noun*

digit
digits *noun*
1 a number from nought to nine, shown as a figure rather than written in words.
2 a finger or toe.

digital
adjective
1 showing number information in figures.
2 storing information using the digits zero and one.

digital camera

dilute
dilutes diluting diluted *verb*
to make thinner or weaker, often by adding water.
dilution *noun*

diluting cordial

dim
adjective
not bright.
*A **dim** light bulb.*
■ comparisons **dimmer dimmest**

dinghy
dinghies *noun*
a small, open sailing boat (see **boat** on page 31).
■ say **ding**-ee

dingo
dingoes *noun*
a wild dog that lives in Australia. Dingoes hunt alone or in small packs and eat birds, reptiles, and small animals.

dinner
dinners *noun*
the main meal of the day.

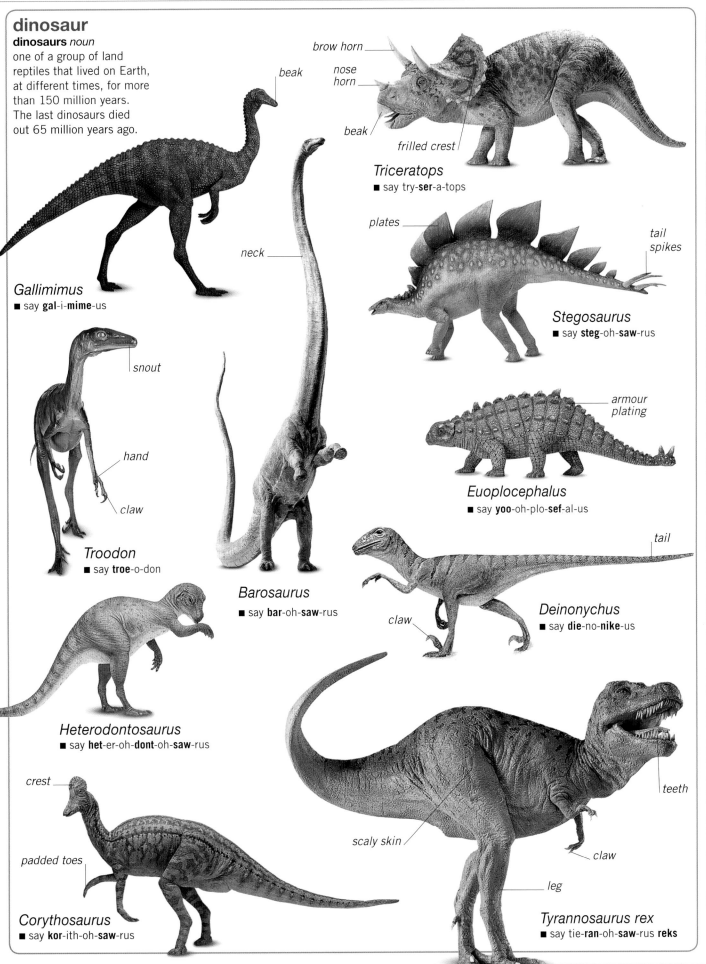

dinosaur

dinosaurs *noun*
one of a group of land reptiles that lived on Earth, at different times, for more than 150 million years. The last dinosaurs died out 65 million years ago.

beak

Gallimimus
■ say **gal**-i-**mime**-us

snout

hand

claw

Troodon
■ say **troe**-o-don

neck

Heterodontosaurus
■ say **het**-er-oh-**dont**-oh-**saw**-rus

crest

padded toes

Corythosaurus
■ say **kor**-ith-oh-**saw**-rus

brow horn

nose horn

beak

frilled crest

Triceratops
■ say try-**ser**-a-tops

plates

tail spikes

Stegosaurus
■ say **steg**-oh-**saw**-rus

armour plating

Euoplocephalus
■ say **yoo**-oh-plo-**sef**-al-us

tail

Barosaurus
■ say **bar**-oh-**saw**-rus

claw

Deinonychus
■ say **die**-no-**nike**-us

scaly skin

teeth

claw

leg

Tyrannosaurus rex
■ say tie-**ran**-oh-**saw**-rus **reks**

dip
dips dipping dipped *verb*
1 to put something into a liquid or a soft substance and then take it out again immediately.

*brush **dipped** in paint*
2 to slope downwards.
*The road **dips** slightly here.*

direct
directs directing directed *verb*
1 to show or tell someone how to get to a particular place.

*He **directed** the tourist to the castle.*
direction *noun*
2 to be in charge of the making of a play or a film.

directing a film

direct
adjective
going the shortest way.
*A **direct** route.*

directory
directories *noun*
a book that contains information about people and organizations, usually listed in alphabetical order.
*A telephone **directory.***

dirty
adjective
not clean.

■ comparisons **dirtier dirtiest**
■ opposite **clean**

disabled
adjective
not having a limb, or being without power or strength, especially of movement, in part of your body because of injury or disease.
disability *noun*

disagree
disagrees disagreeing disagreed *verb*
to think differently from someone about something.
*We always **disagree**.*
■ opposite **agree**
disagreement *noun*

disappear
disappears disappearing disappeared *verb*
to go out of sight.

*The rabbit **disappeared** into its burrow.*
■ opposite **appear**
disappearance *noun*

disappoint
disappoints disappointing disappointed *verb*
to make someone sad by not doing something they expected.
*I **disappointed** my friends by not going to the match with them.*
disappointed *adjective*

disaster
disasters *noun*
a terrible event that may cause damage and suffering.

*Forest fires are natural **disasters**.*
■ say di-**zah**-ster
disastrous *adjective*

disc
discs *noun*
any thin, flat, circular object.
*A compact **disc**.*

discover
discovers discovering discovered *verb*
to find or find out.

*The pirates **discovered** a chest of buried treasure on the island.*

discuss
discusses discussing discussed *verb*
to talk about something with someone else.
*We **discussed** where to go for our holiday.*
discussion *noun*

disease
diseases *noun*
an illness.
*Measles is an infectious **disease**.*

disgraceful
adjective
so bad that the person involved should be ashamed.
*Do this work again – it's **disgraceful**!*

disguise
disguises *noun*
an outfit that you wear to hide who you really are.

■ say dis-**gize**
disguise *verb*

disgusting
adjective
very unpleasant.
*There was a **disgusting** smell coming from the drains.*

dish
dishes *noun*
1 a plate or bowl that is used to hold food.

*a **dish** for serving vegetables*

2 one part of a meal.

*the main **dish***

dishonest
adjective
telling lies or stealing.
■ opposite **honest**

disinfectant
disinfectants *noun*
a chemical that is used
for killing germs.
disinfect *verb*

dislike
dislikes disliking disliked *verb*
to think someone or something
is not very nice.

*She **disliked** the smell.*
■ opposite **like**

disobey
**disobeys disobeying
disobeyed** *verb*
to refuse to do something that
someone tells you to do.
*You mustn't **disobey** orders.*
■ opposite **obey**
disobedient *adjective*

disperse
verb
to scatter widely.
*The dandelion seeds were
dispersed by the wind.*
dispersal *noun*

display
displays displaying displayed
verb
to put something in a place
where people can look at it.

***displaying** paintings*

disposable
adjective
for throwing away after use.

dissolve
**dissolves dissolving
dissolved** *verb*
to mix something with water
or another
liquid so it
becomes
part of
the liquid.

*a tablet
dissolving
in water*

distance
distances *noun*
the space measured between
two places.

distinguish
**distinguishes distinguishing
distinguished** *verb*
to be able to tell the
difference between things.
*Can you **distinguish** between
the twins?*
■ say dis-**ting**-gwish

distract
**distracts distracting
distracted** *verb*
to take someone's attention
away from what they are doing.
*The noise outside **distracted**
her from her work.*

distribute
**distributes distributing
distributed** *verb*
to give something out.

*The teacher **distributed** the
books to the children.*

district
districts *noun*
an area in a town, city,
county, or country, which
is sometimes marked out
for a particular purpose.
*Postal **district**.*

disturb
disturbs disturbing disturbed
verb
to interrupt the peace
and quiet of a place
or person.

*The noise of the drill
disturbed her.*
disturbance *noun*

ditch
ditches *noun*
a long channel that drains
away water.

dive
**dives diving
dived** *verb*
to jump
head first
into water.

diver
divers *noun*
a person who swims beneath
the water, often taking an air
supply to breathe with.

*scuba **diver***

divide
divides dividing divided *verb*
1 to split something up
into parts.

*The cheese is **divided** into
eight portions.*

2 to separate a number into
equal parts.

$8 \div 2 = 4$

*Eight **divided** by two
equals four.*
division *noun*

a b c d e f g h i j k l m n o p q r s t u v w x y z

A B C D E F G H I J K L M N O P Q R S T U V W X Y Z

divorce

divorces divorcing divorced
verb
to end a marriage legally.
divorce *noun*

dock

docks *noun*
1 a place where ships load
and unload cargo.
dock *verb*

2 the place in a courtroom
where the person on trial
stands or sits.

doctor

doctors *noun*
a person who is trained to
treat sick or injured people.

patient   *doctor*

dodge

dodges dodging dodged *verb*
to avoid being hit by
something by moving out
of the way very quickly.
*She **dodged** the ball
coming towards her.*

dog

dogs *noun*
a mammal that is often
kept as a pet. Dogs mainly
eat meat and can be trained
to carry out certain tasks,
such as herding sheep.
Dogs are related to wolves
and foxes (see **pet** on
page 148).

*collie **dog***

doll

dolls *noun*
a toy that is made to look
like a human being.

dolphin

dolphins *noun*
a fish-eating sea mammal.
Dolphins breathe air, so they
must swim to the surface
often. They are friendly
animals and are known for
their intelligence. Dolphins
are a type of small whale.

■ say **doll**-fin

domino

dominoes *noun*
a small, flat piece of wood
or plastic with dots marked
on it. Dominoes are used
in a table game, also
called dominoes.

donation

donations *noun*
a gift, usually of money,
that is made to a charity
or another organization.
*He made a large **donation**.*

donkey

donkeys *noun*
a member of the horse family
that has long ears and a soft,
furry coat. Donkeys eat grass
and in some countries are used
for carrying people and goods.

door

doors *noun*
a piece of wood, glass,
or metal that opens
and shuts
to provide
a way
into a room,
cupboard,
building,
or vehicle.

dot

dots *noun*
a very small, round spot.
*A full stop is a **dot**.*

double

adjective
twice as much.

*a **double** six*
■ say **dub**-ul

doubtful

adjective
not sure, or unlikely.
*He was **doubtful** about
his chances of winning.*
■ say **dowt**-ful
doubt *verb*

dough

noun
a mixture of flour and either
milk or water that is used
to make bread or cakes.
■ say **doh**

doughnut

doughnuts *noun*
a sweet, round cake made
from dough, which is fried
in fat and
covered
in sugar.

■ say **doh**-nut

dove

doves *noun*
a bird that is a member
of the pigeon family.
Doves are
often used
as a symbol
of peace.

down

down
adverb
to a lower place.

*The leaves floated **down**.*
■ opposite **up**

downcast
adjective
sad and upset.
*He looked **downcast**.*

downhill
adjective
sloping down.

***downhill**
skiing*

download
verb
to transfer information content
such as music or film from one
electronic device to another.

downpour
downpours *noun*
a large, heavy
amount of rain.

downstairs
adverb
to a lower floor.

*He ran **downstairs**
to answer the phone.*

downstairs
adjective
on a lower
floor than
the one
you are on.
*She was
in the
kitchen
downstairs.*

doze
dozes dozing dozed *verb*
to sleep lightly for
a short time.
*She **dozed** in the chair.*

dozen
dozens *noun*
12 of something.

*a **dozen** candles*

drag
drags dragging dragged *verb*
to pull
something
along the
ground.

*She **dragged**
her schoolbag.*

dragon
dragons *noun*
a fierce, imaginary animal in
myths and fairy tales, that
breathes fire and has
a large, scaly body
and wings.

dragonfly
dragonflies *noun*
a long, thin insect with two pairs
of wings, often found near ponds
and rivers. Dragonflies feed
on small flying insects, which
they catch with their legs
while flying.

drain
drains *noun*
a pipe or channel that
takes away waste water
and other liquids.

drain
drains draining drained *verb*
to flow away slowly.
*The water **drained** away.*

drama
dramas *noun*
1 a play.
*My favourite **drama** is
Shakespeare's* Hamlet.
2 plays, or the theatre
in general.
3 an exciting or
frightening event.
*There was **drama** today
when the school caught fire.*

draw
draws drawing drew drawn
verb
1 to make a picture or diagram
with a pencil or crayon.

2 to move together by pulling.
*He **drew** the curtains.*

drawer
drawers *noun*
a box-shaped container that
slides in and out of a piece of
furniture. Drawers are used to
store things in.

*a chest of **drawers***

dream
**dreams dreaming dreamed
or dreamt** *verb*
1 to have thoughts and
pictures going through
your mind
while you
are asleep.

*I **dreamt** I saw a
fierce lion.*
2 to hope for something.
*She **dreamed** of travelling
around the world.*
dream *noun*

drench
**drenches drenching
drenched** *verb*
to soak with water.
*The rain **drenched** her.*

dress
**dresses dressing
dressed** *verb*
to put on
clothes.

*He **dressed**
for school.*
■ opposite
undress

a b c d e f g h i j k l m n o p q r s t u v w x y z

A B C D E F G H I J K L M N O P Q R S T U V W X Y Z

dress
dresses *noun*
a piece of clothing that
has a top joined to a skirt.

dried
from the verb **to dry**
He **dried** his clothes outside.

dried
adjective
with water or liquid removed.

*dried
apricots*

drift
drifts drifting drifted *verb*
1 to move slowly
without control.
*The boat **drifted** along.*
2 to be carried along by
water or air.

drift
drifts *noun*
a pile of snow or sand made
by the wind.

drill
drills drilling drilled *verb*
to bore a hole in something
using a drill.

*electric
drill*

drill
drills *noun*
1 a tool used to make holes.
2 a practice.
*Fire **drill**.*

drink
drinks drinking drank drunk
verb
to swallow liquid.

drink *noun*

drip
drips dripping dripped *verb*
to fall slowly, drop by drop.
*Water **dripped** from the tap.*

drip *noun*
dripping *adjective*

drive
drives driving drove driven
verb
to make a car, train, or
other vehicle move.
*They **drove** along the
country roads.*
drive *noun*

drizzle
drizzles drizzling drizzled *verb*
to rain in small, fine drops,
like a mist.
drizzle *noun*

droop
droops drooping drooped *verb*
to hang down in a weak or
tired way.

*The tulip **drooped** over the
edge of the vase.*
■ rhymes with **hoop**

drop
drops *noun*
1 a small amount
of liquid.
2 a long way down.

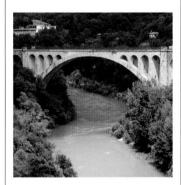

*It was a big **drop** from the
bridge to the river below.*

drop
drops dropping dropped *verb*
to let something fall.

*He **dropped** the ball.*

drought
droughts *noun*
a period of time when there
is not enough rain.

*Many crops died during
the **drought**.*
■ say **drowt**

drown
drowns drowning drowned
verb
to die because you have gone
under water and have not been
able to breathe.

drowsy
adjective
sleepy.

drug
drugs *noun*
1 a chemical substance used
as a medicine to treat people
who are ill or in pain.
2 an illegal chemical substance
which people take to make
them feel different. Taking this
kind of drug is dangerous and
can kill you.

drum
drums *noun*
a hollow musical instrument
that has a covering across
one or both ends. You hit the
drum with sticks, special wire
brushes, or your hands to
make different sounds.

*Japanese **drum***

drum
drums drumming drummed
verb
to tap or hit continuously,
or to play a drum.

dry
adjective
not wet.
*They came in from the rain
and changed into **dry** clothes.*
■ comparisons **drier driest**
■ opposite **wet**
dry *verb*

duck
ducks *noun*
a water bird that has oily,
waterproof feathers, and
webbed feet for swimming.
Ducks eat fish, small plants,
and small animals. Male
ducks are called drakes.

*drake
(male)*

*duck
(female)*

duet
duets *noun*
a piece of music to be played
or sung by two people.

*a violin **duet***
■ say dew-**et**

dug
*from the verb **to dig***
*Our dog **dug** up part of
the lawn this morning.*

dull
adjective
1 not bright.
*It was a **dull** day.*
2 not exciting.
*I thought the film was
very **dull**.*
■ comparisons **duller dullest**

dummy
dummies *noun*
a model of a
person's body,
for making or
displaying
clothes on.

*dressmaker's
dummy*

dump
dumps dumping dumped
verb
to put something down,
or throw it away carelessly.
*They **dumped** the shopping
bags on the floor.*

dune
dunes *noun*
a hill of sand, near the sea
or in a desert, which is made
by the wind.

dungeon
dungeons *noun*
an underground prison cell
in an old building, such as
a castle.
■ say **dun**-jun

duplicate
duplicates *noun*
an exact copy.

*One key is
a **duplicate**
of the other.*
■ say **dew**-pli-kate

during
preposition
1 at some time in.
*I fell asleep **during** the film.*
2 the whole time of.
***During** the summer months
we go swimming in the sea.*

dusk
noun
the time of evening when
it starts to get dark.
■ opposite **dawn**

dust
noun
tiny pieces of dirt that
float in the air and settle
on surfaces.
dusty *adjective*

duty
duties *noun*
things that you ought to
do or feel you should do.
*It is the guard's **duty** to make
sure the doors are locked.*

dvd
noun
a plastic disc that contains
digital recordings of sounds
and images (see **abbreviations**
on page 246).

dye
dyes dyeing dyed *verb*
to change the colour of
something by soaking
it in coloured liquids.
*She **dyed** her white dress
yellow for the party.*
dye *noun*

dynamite
noun
a powerful
substance
that explodes
when it
is burnt.

dynasty
dynasties *noun*
a series of rulers from
the same family.
■ say **din**-as-tee

dyslexia
noun
a learning difficulty that
can affect reading, writing,
or spelling.
■ say dis-**lek**-see-a
dyslexic *adjective*

a b c **d** e f g h i j k l m n o p q r s t u v w x y z

Ee

each
adjective
every single one.
*They **each** received a present.*

eager
adjective
wanting to do or have
something very much.
*The riders were **eager**
to start the race.*
eagerly *adverb*

eagle
eagles *noun*
a large bird of prey that lives
in mountainous areas. Eagles
eat animals and birds, and
have good eyesight for spotting
prey a long way off.

*golden
eagle*

ear
ears *noun*
1 the part
of your body
that you
hear with.

ear / earlobe

early
adverb
1 near the beginning.
*The hero dies **early** in the film.*
2 before the expected time.
*He arrived **early** for the show.*
■ comparisons **earlier earliest**
■ opposite **late**

earn
earns earning earned *verb*
to get something because
you have worked for it or
deserve it.
*They **earned** some pocket
money by cleaning cars.*

earring
earrings *noun*
a piece of jewellery that
can be attached
to, or hung from,
the earlobe
(see **jewellery**
on page 112).

Earth
noun
the planet
that we
live on.

2. the top of a cereal stalk
where the seeds grow.

ear of wheat

earth
noun
1 the surface of the land
or ground.
2 the material that plants
grow in.

earthquake
earthquakes *noun*
a violent shaking of the ground,
because of movement from
within Earth.

east
noun
one of the four main
compass directions. East
is the direction in which
the Sun rises.

north
west east
eastern
adjective
south

easy
adjective
simple, not difficult.
■ comparisons **easier easiest**
■ opposite **difficult**

eat
eats eating ate eaten *verb*
to take in
food through
your mouth.

e-book
noun
a book in a digital format (see
abbreviations on page 246).

e-book reader
noun
a portable device on which to
read e-books (see **abbreviations**
on page 246).

echo
echoes *noun*
a sound that bounces off a
surface and repeats itself.
*My voice **echoed** in the cave.*
■ say **eh**-ko
echo *verb*

eclipse
eclipses *noun*
1 a time when the Moon comes
between Earth and the Sun,
hiding the Sun's light.

*an **eclipse** of the Sun*

2 a time when Earth comes
between the Sun and the
Moon, hiding the Moon's light.
*An **eclipse** of the Moon.*

ecology
noun
the study of how animals,
plants, and humans affect
one another and how they
live in their environment.
■ say ee-**kol**-o-jee

edge
edges *noun*
the border of something.

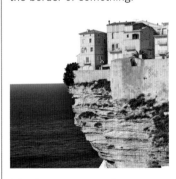

*The houses are at the
cliff's **edge**.*

edible
adjective
safe to eat.
*Are these mushrooms **edible**?*

educate
educates educating educated verb
to teach someone so that they learn and understand things.
education noun

eel
eels noun
a long, thin fish that lives in rivers and the sea. Eels eat tiny sea plants, animals called plankton, and other fish.

ribbon eel

effect
effects noun
the result of an action or event on another person or thing.
Seeing the crash on the news had a bad effect on me.

effort
efforts noun
the energy you need to do something.

It took a lot of effort to lift the bar.

egg
eggs noun
a rounded object that is produced by some female animals. Eggs contain the animal's babies, which hatch when developed.

crow's egg   *hen's egg*

elastic
noun
a stretchy fabric.
The pencils are held together with an elastic band.

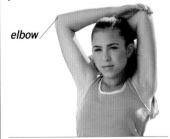
elastic band

elbow
elbows noun
the joint in the middle of your arm.

elbow

elderly
adjective
rather old.

elect
elects electing elected verb
to choose someone to do something by voting for them.

election
elections noun
the time when people vote for someone to be in charge.
Council elections.

electric
adjective
powered by electricity.

electric whisk

electricity
noun
a form of energy that is used for heating and lighting, and for making machines work.
electrical adjective

electronic
adjective
involving computers or other complex electric devices.

elephant
elephants noun
a huge mammal that lives in southern Asia and Africa. Elephants eat tree bark, roots, leaves, grass, and other plants.

Asian elephant

elevator
elevators noun
a large box or cage that carries people and goods between the floors of a building. Elevators are also called lifts.

email
noun
messages sent electronically between computers.

embarrass
embarrasses embarrassing embarrassed verb
to make someone feel ashamed or shy.
It embarrasses me to have to speak in public.
embarrassment noun

emergency
emergencies noun
a sudden, dangerous event.

Helicopters are sometimes used in emergencies.
■ say ee-**mer**-jen-see

emigrate
emigrates emigrating emigrated verb
to leave your own country to go to live in another.
My best friend is emigrating to New Zealand.
emigration noun

emotion
emotions noun
a strong feeling people have.
Love and hate are emotions.

employ
employs employing employed verb
to pay somebody to do a job.
I employ six people in my office.

empty
adjective
having nothing inside.

an empty bottle

A B C D E F G H I J K L M N O P Q R S T U V W X Y Z

emu
emus *noun*
a large bird that lives on the hot, grassy plains of Australia and eats leaves and insects. Emus can't fly, but they can run very fast.

■ say **ee**-mew

encourage
encourages encouraging encouraged *verb*
to help someone feel happy and confident about what they are doing.

*Cheerleaders **encourage** their team.*
■ say en-**kur**-rij

encyclopedia
encyclopedias *noun*
a book, or set of books, that contains facts and information about lots of different things.
■ say en-sye-kloh-**pee**-dee-a

end
ends ending ended *verb*
to finish.
*The film **ends** at 8.30 pm.*

end
ends *noun*
the place where something finishes.

*There is a rubber at the **end** of this pencil.*

endangered
adjective
in danger of becoming extinct.

*Turtles are **endangered** animals.*

enemy
enemies *noun*
1 a person who dislikes you or would like to harm you.
2 the opposing country or army during a time of war.

energy
noun
1 the strength that makes a person or animal lively and active.

*She has lots of **energy**.*
energetic *adjective*

2 the power or ability of something to make something else work.

*wind **energy***

engine
engines *noun*
a machine that uses fuel to make something move.

*jet **engine***

engineer
engineers *noun*
a person who is trained to design, build, or repair things such as machines, buildings, or bridges.

enjoy
enjoys enjoying enjoyed *verb*
to like doing something.

enormous
adjective
very large.

*an **enormous** tree*

enough
adjective
as much as is needed.
*Do you have **enough** money?*
enough *noun*

enter
enters entering entered *verb*
1 to go into a place.
*The cat **entered** the house through the cat flap.*
entrance *noun*
2 to take part in.
*She **entered** the diving competition with her friends.*
3 to write down a name or some other information.
*I **entered** my name at the top of the test paper.*

entertain
entertains entertaining entertained *verb*
to amuse people or provide a pleasant way to pass the time.

*The juggler **entertained** the children all afternoon.*
entertainment *noun*

enthusiastic
adjective
very interested in something.
*He is an **enthusiastic** skier.*
■ say en-**thyoo**-zee-as-tik
enthusiasm *noun*

entire
adjective
whole.
*The **entire** class came to my party.*
entirely *adverb*

envelope
envelopes *noun*
a folded paper container for letters or cards.

environment

environments *noun*
the surroundings in which
a person, plant, or
animal lives.
*A city environment is often
noisy and polluted.*
environmental *adjective*
■ say en-**vire**-o-ment

envy

envies envying envied *verb*
to feel unhappy because you
want something that someone
else has.
I envy her long holidays.
envious *adjective*
envy *noun*

episode

episodes *noun*
one part of a television or
radio series.
*The first episode was so
exciting that he couldn't
wait to see the next one.*

equal

adjective
the same.

equal in length
■ say **ee**-kwul

equator

noun
an imaginary line around
the middle of Earth that
divides the northern half of
the world from the southern
half. The equator is drawn
onto maps and globes.
■ say ee-**kway**-tor

equator

equipment

noun
the things that you need
for a job or
an activity.

*snorkelling
equipment*

error

errors *noun*
a mistake.
*She failed the exam because
her paper was full of errors.*

erupt

erupts erupting erupted *verb*
to explode suddenly.

The volcano erupted.
eruption *noun*

escalator

escalators *noun*
a moving staircase that carries
people between levels or floors.

escape

escapes escaping escaped
verb
to run away from
somewhere or
someone.

*The bird escaped from
its cage.*

establish

**establishes establishing
established** *verb*
to organize or set up.
*They established a camp
at the foot of the mountain.*

estimate

**estimates estimating
estimated** *verb*
to make a thoughtful guess
about something.
*We estimated that the journey
would take 10 hours.*
estimate *noun*

evaporate

**evaporates evaporating
evaporated** *verb*
to dry up gradually, changing
from a liquid to a gas.
The water slowly evaporated.
evaporation *noun*

even

adjective
1 flat or level.

smooth and even grass
■ opposite **uneven**
2 a number that can
be divided by two.
■ opposite **odd**

evening

evenings *noun*
the end of the day when the
Sun sets and it grows dark.

event

events *noun*
something important that
happens or is organized.

*The fireworks display is a big
event each year.*

eventually

adverb
in the end or finally.
*After arguing for hours
we eventually reached
an agreement.*

evergreen

adjective
having green leaves
all year round.

*Lawson
cypress
branch*

■ opposite **deciduous**

every

adjective
all, or each one.
■ *We couldn't use the car
park as every space was full.*
■ *Everybody in the family
loves chocolate.*
■ *We can't take everyone
with us, as there are only
four places on the bus.*
■ *Everything in the house
was stolen.*
■ *There were daffodils
everywhere they looked.*

a
b
c
d
e
f
g
h
i
j
k
l
m
n
o
p
q
r
s
t
u
v
w
x
y
z

A B C D E F G H I J K L M N O P Q R S T U V W X Y Z

evidence
noun
proof that something
has happened.

*The footprint was **evidence**
that the suspect had been
at the scene of the crime.*

evil
adjective
wicked.

evolution
noun
the gradual development
of animals and plants over
a very long time.

Mesohippus

Pliohippus

Equus

***evolution** of the horse*

ewe
ewes *noun*
a female
sheep.
■ say **you**

ewe

lamb

exact
adjective
accurate or precise.

*She pointed to the **exact** place
on the map.*
■ say egg-**zact**
■ opposite **approximate**
exactly *adverb*

exaggerate
**exaggerates exaggerating
exaggerated** *verb*
to say more about something
than is really true.

*She **exaggerated** the size
of her catch.*
■ say egg-**za**-jur-rate
exaggeration *noun*

exam
exams *noun*
an important test to find out
how much you know about
something. Exam is short
for examination.

examine
**examines examining
examined** *verb*
to look at
an object
closely and
carefully.

■ say egg-**za**-min

example
examples *noun*
something that is typical of
other similar things, or how
a rule works.
*Can you think of an
example of a plant that
has blue flowers?*

excellent
adjective
extremely good.

*The **excellent** flower
arrangement won first prize.*

except
preposition
but, or other than.

*All the pins were straight
except one.*
exception *noun*

exciting
adjective
thrilling.

*The roller coaster ride was
very **exciting**.*
excitement *noun*

excuse
excuses *noun*
a reason you give for not
doing what you should
have done.
■ say ex-**kew**-s
excuse *verb*

exercise
exercises *noun*
1 activities
or training
that you do
to become
fit or to
stay fit.

exercise *verb*
2 a piece of work that practises
a skill or a person's knowledge
of something.
*A maths **exercise**.*

exhausted
adjective
extremely tired.

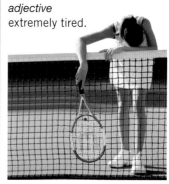

*She was **exhausted** after the
tennis match.*
exhaustion *noun*

exhibition
exhibitions *noun*
an event where things are displayed for people to look at.

a sculpture **exhibition**
■ say ex-i-**bish**-un

exist
exists existing existed *verb*
to be or to live.
Dinosaurs **existed** *long before humans.*
existence *noun*

exit
exits *noun*
a way out.

They left the train by the nearest **exit**.

expand
expands expanding expanded *verb*
to become larger.
Water **expands** *as it freezes.*
■ opposite **contract**
expansion *noun*

expect
expects expecting expected *verb*
to think that something is likely to happen.

He was **expecting** *rain.*

expedition
expeditions *noun*
an adventurous journey that is made for a special reason, such as exploring.

They set off on an **expedition** *across the mountains.*

expensive
adjective
costing a lot of money.
■ opposite **cheap**

an **expensive** *watch*
£300

£2

a cheap watch

experience
experiences *noun*
1 an important event that you remember for a long time.
Travelling around the world was a fantastic **experience**.
experience *verb*
2 knowledge or skill gained from doing something for a long time.
She has years of **experience**.
■ say ex-**peer**-ree-ens
experienced *adjective*

experiment
experiments *noun*
a test that you do in order to find out something.

expert
experts *noun*
a person who knows a lot about a subject.
The space shuttle was designed by **experts**.
expert *adjective*

explain
explains explaining explained *verb*
to help somebody to understand something.
Our teacher **explained** *how rainbows occur.*
explanation *noun*

explode
explodes exploding exploded *verb*
to burst apart suddenly, often into many pieces.
explosion *noun*

explore
explores exploring explored *verb*
to look around somewhere carefully for the first time.
After we arrived on the island, we set off to **explore**.
exploration *noun*

extinct
adjective
no longer existing.

Dinosaurs are **extinct**.

extra
adjective
more than is usual.

an **extra** *scoop of ice-cream*
extra *adverb*

extraordinary
adjective
very unusual.
What an **extraordinary** *car! It must be 10 metres long.*

extreme
adjective
very great, or much more than usual.
He was in **extreme** *danger.*

eye
eyes *noun*
the part of the body that you see with.

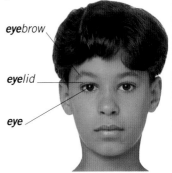

*eye*brow
*eye*lid
eye

A
B
C
D
E
F
G
H
I
J
K
L
M
N
O
P
Q
R
S
T
U
V
W
X
Y
Z

Ff

fable
fables noun
a story, often with animal characters, that tries to teach us in an amusing way.

fabric
fabrics noun
cloth.

façade
façades noun
the front of a building.

■ say fa-**sard**

face
faces noun
the front of your head, where your nose, eyes, and mouth are.

fact
facts noun
a piece of information that is known to be true.

factory
factories noun
a building where people make things using machines.

fade
fades fading faded verb
1 to lose colour or strength.

The colours **fade** to white.
2 to disappear slowly.
The music **faded** away.

fail
fails failing failed verb
to be unsuccessful at doing something.
He **failed** his driving test.
failure noun

faint
adjective
not very strong.
She heard a **faint** noise coming from the cupboard.

faint
faints fainting fainted verb
to become unconscious for a short time.

He **fainted** in the heat.
faint noun

fair
adjective
1 light in colour.

fair hair
■ opposite **dark**
2 done in a way that is right and honest.
Everyone gets a **fair** share.
■ opposite **unfair**
3 dry and sunny.
Fair weather.
■ comparisons **fairer fairest**

fair
fairs noun
an outdoor event with stalls, competitions, games, and other entertainment.

fairy
fairies noun
a small, imaginary creature from stories. Fairies often have magical powers.

toy **fairy**

faith
noun
a strong feeling of trust in someone or something.
I have **faith** in my doctor.

faithful
adjective
trustworthy or reliable.
A **faithful** friend.

fake
adjective
imitation, not real.

fake jewels
fake noun

falcon
falcons noun
a bird with a sharp beak and claws that is related to the eagle. Falcons are good hunters and can fly very fast. They eat birds, reptiles, and small mammals.
■ say **fol**-kon

fall
falls falling fell fallen verb
to drop from a higher
place to a lower place.

*She used a parachute to **fall**
safely to the ground.*
fall noun

fall
falls noun
the American name
for autumn.

false
adjective
not real or true.
*He wore
a **false** beard.*

familiar
adjective
well-known to you.
*I saw a **familiar** face
in the crowd.*
■ opposite **unfamiliar**

family
families noun
1 a group of people who are
closely related to each other.
*I come from a large **family** of
five brothers and sisters.*
2 a group of animals or plants
that are related
to each other.

*These butterflies belong
to the same **family**.*

famine
famines noun
a time when there is not
enough to eat, usually because
of a drought or a war.

famous
adjective
well-known to many people.

*The Taj Mahal is a
famous building.*

fan
fans noun
1 a device that moves air
around to make you feel cooler.

electric
fan

2 a person who is very
interested and enthusiastic
about something.

*They played to their **fans**.*

fanatic
fanatics noun
someone who believes in
something so strongly that
it controls their life.
*A football **fanatic**.*

fang
fangs noun
1 a long, pointed tooth that
meat-eating animals use
for tearing up their food.

fang

2 a snake's long, sharp tooth
that can give a poisonous bite.

fantastic
adjective
1 difficult to believe.
*A **fantastic** tale about giants.*
2 very pleasing or wonderful.
*We had a **fantastic** holiday.*

fantasy
fantasies noun
something that is imaginary
and not real.

far
adverb
1 to or from a long way away.
*Have you come **far**?*
2 how distant something is.

*a quiet road **far** from the city*
■ comparisons **farther farthest** or
further furthest
■ opposite **near**

fare
fares noun
the money that you must
pay to travel on a bus, train,
or aeroplane.
*What is the **fare** to Glasgow?*

farm
farms noun
a place where crops are grown
or animals are reared for food.

farm verb

fascinate
**fascinates fascinating
fascinated** verb
to interest someone so
much that they think of
nothing else.
*Dinosaurs **fascinate** me.*
■ say **fas**-in-ate
fascination noun

fashion
fashions noun
a way of dressing
that people like and
want to copy at a
particular time.

*Long, straight
dresses were
the **fashion**
in the 1920s.*
fashionable
adjective

fast
adjective
at great speed.

*The sports car was very **fast**.*
■ comparisons **faster fastest**
■ opposite **slow**
fast adverb

fast
adverb
firmly held.
*Stuck **fast** in the mud.*

A
B
C
D
E
F
G
H
I
J
K
L
M
N
O
P
Q
R
S
T
U
V
W
X
Y
Z

fast
fasts fasting fasted *verb*
to go without food for
a special reason.
Muslims **fast** *during
the time of Ramadan.*
fast *noun*

fasten
fastens fastening fastened
verb
to join something together
so that it holds.

fastening her collar

fat
fats *noun*
1 the oily substance that
is stored under the skin
and in the cells of animals
and people.
2 an oily, solid substance that
is used in cooking. Lard, oil,
butter, and margarine are
all fats.

butter

fat
adjective
having a lot of fat or flesh.

■ comparisons **fatter fattest**

fatal
adjective
resulting in death.
Fatal injuries.
■ say **fay**-tal
fatally *adverb*

father
fathers *noun*
a male parent.

father and son

fault
faults *noun*
1 something that is wrong.
A **fault** *in the computer.*
2 a mistake that someone
has made.
It was my **fault** *we were late.*
3 a split in Earth's crust.
The San Andreas **Fault** *is
in California.*
■ say **folt**

favour
favours *noun*
a kind and helpful action.
Will you do me a **favour**?

favourite
adjective
liked the
best.

This is her **favourite** *toy.*
favourite *noun*

fawn
fawns *noun*
a young deer.

fax
faxes *noun*
a picture or message that
is recorded electronically on
a fax machine. A fax is sent
by telephone lines to another
fax machine where it is
printed out.
fax *verb*

fear
fears *noun*
the feeling of being afraid.
He had a **fear** *of spiders.*
fear *verb*

feather
feathers *noun*
part of the soft,
light covering that
a bird has on its
body (see **bird** on
page 28).

fee
fees *noun*
money that you pay to
a person or organization
for a service.

feed
feeds feeding fed *verb*
1 to give someone or something food.

2 to eat food.

Caterpillars
feed *on leaves.*

feel
feels feeling felt *verb*
1 to experience an emotion.
2 to experience
something
through
touch.
feeling
noun

She was
feeling *cold.*

fell
from the verb **to fall**
I **fell** *off my bike last week.*

female
adjective
belonging to the sex that can
give birth to babies, or produce
eggs or seeds.
■ opposite **male**
female *noun*

feminine
adjective
of or like women or girls.
■ say **fem**-in-nin
■ opposite **masculine**

fence
fences *noun*
a barrier that separates one
piece of land from another.

fern
ferns *noun*
a type of plant that has feathery leaves and doesn't produce flowers (see **plant** on page 151).

ferocious
adjective
fierce, dangerous, and cruel.
ferociously *adverb*

ferry
ferries *noun*
a boat or ship that regularly sails a short distance between two places, carrying vehicles, passengers, or cargo.

fertile
adjective
where something grows well.
Fertile farmland.

festival
festivals *noun*
a celebration or special event, often with music, dancing, and plays.

a dance **festival**

fetch
fetches fetching fetched *verb*
to go and get something and bring it back.

The dog **fetched** *the stick.*

fever
fevers *noun*
a condition caused by an illness in which your body temperature is very high and your pulse is fast.

few
adjective
not many, or a small number of something.
There are a **few** *pencils in the jar.*
■ opposite **many**

fiancé / fiancée
fiancés / fiancées *noun*
someone who is engaged to be married.
■ say fee-**on**-say
■ a **fiancé** is a man and a **fiancée** is a woman

fibre
fibres *noun*
a fine thread of something.
rope **fibre**

fiction
noun
a story or poem that has been made up and is not about real events.
I read a lot of crime **fiction**.
■ opposite **non-fiction**

field
fields *noun*
an area of land where grass grows, crops are grown, or animals graze.

fierce
adjective
violent or dangerous.

a **fierce** *dog*
■ comparisons **fiercer fiercest**
fiercely *adverb*

fig
figs *noun*
a small, soft fruit with a tough skin and sweet flesh, which is full of tiny seeds. Figs can be eaten fresh or dried.

fight
fights fighting fought *verb*
to struggle against a person or animal.

fighting *with swords*
fight *noun*

figure
figures *noun*
1 a symbol that represents a written number.
2 the shape of the human body.
He saw a shadowy **figure** *walking through the mist.*
■ say **fig**-gur

file
files *noun*
1 a folder for keeping paper and other pieces of information together.

2 a metal tool with rough sides that is used to smooth edges.

3 a line of people, animals, or vehicles.

The ducklings walked in single **file**.

fill
fills filling filled *verb*
to put as much of something into a container as it can hold.

a b c d e f g h i j k l m n o p q r s t u v w x y z

film
films filming filmed *verb*
to use a movie, video, or phone camera to take moving pictures of something.

film
films *noun*
1 a series of moving pictures shown on a screen.

We went to see a film at the cinema.
2 a long, thin piece of special plastic that is used in cameras for taking photographs.
3 a thin layer of something. *A film of oil.*

filter
filters *noun*
a device that only allows some things, such as water or air, to pass through it.

coffee filter

filter *verb*

fin
fins *noun*
1 the part of a fish that sticks out from its body and helps it to swim and maintain its balance (see **fish** on page 79).
2 a device that helps vehicles keep steady while moving fast (see **universe** on page 229).

final
adjective
last in a series.
This is the final call for the flight to Paris.
finally *adverb*

find
finds finding found *verb*
to discover something.
He found the key under the mat.

fine
fines *noun*
money you have to pay as a punishment.
A parking fine.

fine
adjective
1 all right.
I feel fine.
2 dry and sunny.
Fine weather.
3 very thin or delicate.
The pen has a fine tip.
4 having many small parts.
Fine sand.
5 very good.
Fine food.

■ comparisons **finer finest**

finger
fingers *noun*
one of the separate parts at the end of your hand.

fingernail   *finger*

thumb

fingerprint
fingerprints *noun*
the mark that your finger or thumb makes when it touches something.

finish
finishes finishing finished *verb*
to come to the end of something.

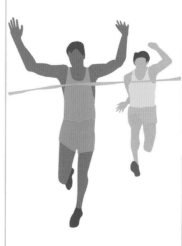

He finished the race ahead of him.

fire

fire
fires *noun*
the heat, light, and flames of something burning.

fire alarm
fire alarms *noun*
a bell that rings to warn people of a fire.

fire engine
fire engines *noun*
the vehicle that fire-fighters travel in to get to a fire.

fire extinguisher
fire extinguishers *noun*
a device filled with water, powder, or chemicals that is used for putting out fires.

fire-fighter
fire-fighters *noun*
someone whose job is to put out fires and rescue people in danger.

firework
fireworks *noun*
a device that burns or explodes when lit, creating a colourful display.

firm
adjective
1 solid.
A firm mattress.
2 fixed so it cannot move.
3 determined and definite.
A firm decision.
firmly *adverb*

A B C D E F G H I J K L M N O P Q R S T U V W X Y Z

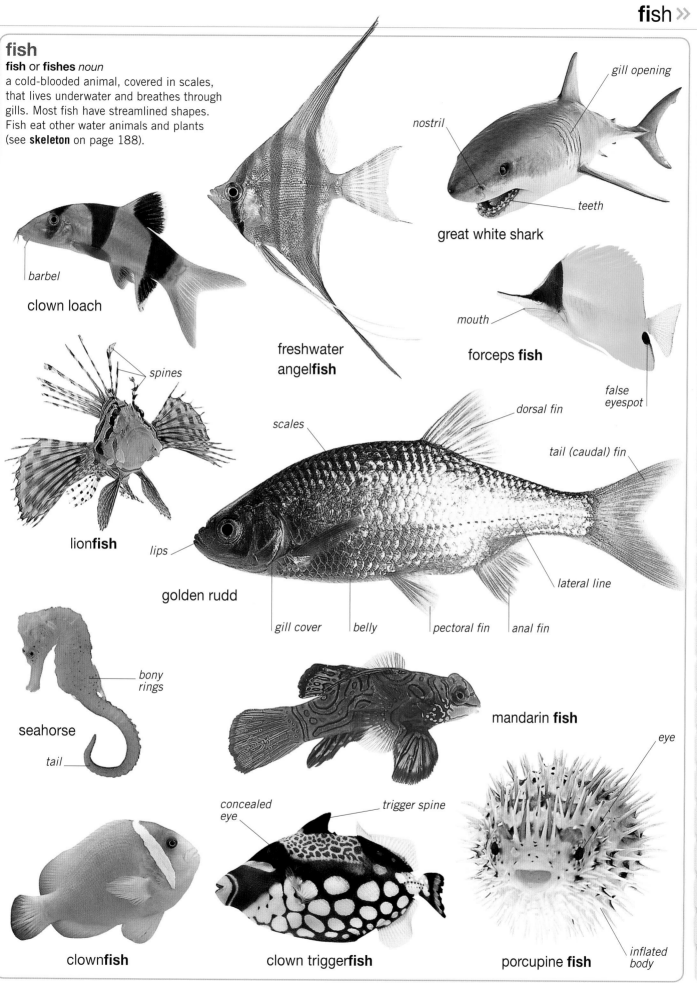

fish

fish or **fishes** *noun*
a cold-blooded animal, covered in scales, that lives underwater and breathes through gills. Most fish have streamlined shapes. Fish eat other water animals and plants (see **skeleton** on page 188).

clown loach

barbel

freshwater angel**fish**

great white shark

nostril

gill opening

teeth

forceps **fish**

mouth

false eyespot

lion**fish**

spines

golden rudd

lips

scales

dorsal fin

tail (caudal) fin

lateral line

gill cover *belly* *pectoral fin* *anal fin*

seahorse

bony rings

tail

mandarin **fish**

clown**fish**

clown trigger**fish**

concealed eye *trigger spine*

porcupine **fish**

eye

inflated body

A B C D E F G H I J K L M N O P Q R S T U V W X Y Z

fish
fishes fishing fished *verb*
to try to catch fish.
fishing *noun*

fist
fists *noun*
the shape your hand makes when you curl up your fingers and thumb tightly.

fit
fits fitting fitted or **fit** *verb*
1 to be the right size or shape.

She checked to see if the shoes **fitted** her.

2 to put something in place.
I **fitted** a lock to the door.

fit
adjective
healthy.
■ comparisons **fitter fittest**

fix
fixes fixing fixed *verb*
1 to mend something.

fixing a car engine

2 to make something secure. They **fixed** the shelf to the wall.

fizzy
adjective
full of bubbles.

a **fizzy** drink
fizz *verb*

flag
flags *noun*
a piece of cloth with a design that represents a country or an organization. Flags are often flown from flag-poles.

flag-pole
United Nations **flag**

flake
flakes *noun*
a small, thin piece of something.

flakes of pastry
flake *verb*

flame
flames *noun*
a bright point of burning gas in a fire.

flammable
adjective
catching fire easily.
■ opposite **non-flammable**

flap
flaps flapping flapped *verb*
1 to hang or swing loosely. The washing **flapped** in the wind.
2 to move up and down. Birds **flap** their wings in order to fly.

flash
flashes *noun*
1 a sudden, bright light. A **flash** of lightning.
flash *verb*
2 a short period of time. It was all over in a **flash**.

flask
flasks *noun*
a container for liquids that usually has a narrow top and a tight-fitting lid.

laboratory **flask**

flat
adjective
1 level or even. A **flat** roof.
2 without air inside it.

a **flat** beach ball

flat
flats *noun*
a home with several rooms that is part of a larger building.

flavour
flavours *noun*
the taste of food or drink.

This dessert has a chocolate **flavour**.

flea
fleas *noun*
a very small, jumping insect without wings that sucks the blood of humans and animals.

flew
from the verb **to fly**
He **flew** to France yesterday.

flexible
adjective
easy to bend.

She has a **flexible** body.

flick
flicks flicking flicked *verb*
to touch or hit something in a quick, light way.

*The horse **flicked** the flies away with its tail.*
flick *noun*

flight
noun
1 the action of flying.

*a parakeet in **flight***
2 a journey through the air.
■ say **flite**

fling
flings flinging flung *verb*
to throw something suddenly and forcefully.
*He **flung** his shoes into the corner.*

float
floats floating floated *verb*
to rest on the surface of water or another liquid without sinking.

floating *adjective*

flock
flocks *noun*
a group of birds, or animals such as sheep or goats.
*A **flock** of geese.*

flood
floods flooding flooded *verb*
to cover an area that is normally dry with a large amount of water.
*The river burst its banks, **flooding** the town.*
flood *noun*

floodlight
floodlights *noun*
a large, bright lamp that is used at night to light up an open area, such as a sports ground.

floodlit *adjective*

floor
floors *noun*
1 a surface that you walk on inside a building.
*A marble **floor**.*
2 a level of a building.
*I live on the sixth **floor** of our block of flats.*

florist
florists *noun*
a person who sells and arranges flowers.

flour
noun
a powder made by crushing grain such as wheat. Flour is used in foods such as bread and cakes.
■ say **flower**

flow
flows flowing flowed *verb*
to move along steadily.
*A steady **flow** of traffic.*

flower
flowers *noun*
the part of a plant that contains the seeds. Flowers often have colourful petals (see **plant** on page 151).

petal

flu
noun
an infectious illness, caused by a virus, which often affects the nose and throat. Flu is short for influenza.

fluff
noun
soft fibres or threads from fabrics such as cotton or wool.
fluffy *adjective*

fluid
fluids *noun*
a substance that flows. Gases and liquids are fluids.

fluorescent
adjective
giving off light.

*a **fluorescent** shirt*
■ say flooer-**es**-ent

flush
flushes flushing flushed *verb*
1 to become red in the face.
*She **flushed** with anger when her friend shouted at her.*
2 to clean with a sudden and quick flow of water.
*He **flushed** the dirty water away.*

flute
flutes *noun*
a wind instrument made of wood or metal. You play it by covering holes with your fingers or special pads and blowing across a hole at one end.

flutter
flutters fluttering fluttered *verb*
to move or flap quickly.

*The flag **fluttered** in the wind.*

a b c d e f g h i j k l m n o p q r s t u v w x y z

A B C D E F G H I J K L M N O P Q R S T U V W X Y Z

fly
flies noun
a flying insect with two wings and six legs. Most flies feed on rotting plants and animals. There are many different kinds of fly.

bluebottle **fly**

fly
flies flying flew verb
to travel through the air.

foal
foals noun
a young horse.

foam
noun
lots of very small air bubbles. Foam can be liquid or solid.

shaving **foam**

focus
focuses focusing focused verb
to adjust something to make a clearer and sharper image.
He **focused** *his camera on the flower.*
focus noun

fog
noun
a thick cloud of tiny water droplets and dust that hangs in the air, close to the ground.
foggy adjective

fold
folds folding folded verb
to bend one part of something over another.

a **fold**

fold noun

follow
follows following followed verb
to go behind or after someone or something.
The dog **followed** *him all the way home.*

food
noun
all the things that humans and animals eat to help them live and grow.

Pasta is an Italian **food**.

foolish
adjective
not sensible.
foolishly adverb

foot
foot
feet noun
the part of your body that you stand on.

football
noun
1 a game for two teams of 11 players. The winning team is the one that scores the most goals by heading or kicking a large ball into a net. Football is also called soccer.
2 a ball used in American football and football games.

an American **football**

footprint
footprints noun
the mark left by a foot or shoe.

footstep
footsteps noun
the sound of somebody walking.
I heard **footsteps** *behind me.*

forbid
forbids forbidding forbade forbidden verb
to tell a person that they must not do something.
I **forbid** *you to drive.*
■ opposite **allow**
forbidden adjective

force
forces forcing forced verb
1 to make a person do something.
I was **forced** *to make a choice.*
2 to push strongly.
They **forced** *the safe open.*

force
forces noun
1 a power.

The **force** *of the wind blew her hat off.*
2 a group of people who together have power.
The armed **forces**.

forearm
forearms noun
the part of your arm between your elbow and your wrist.

forearm

forecast
forecasts forecasting forecast verb
to predict that something will happen in the future.

forecasting the weather
forecast noun

forehead

foreheads noun
the part of your face above your eyes and below your hair.

forehead

foreign

adjective
belonging to another country.
Foreign languages.
■ say **for**-in
foreigner noun

forest

forests noun
a very large area of trees.

forget

forgets forgetting forgot forgotten verb
to not remember something.
I forgot my sister's birthday.
■ opposite **remember**

forgive

forgives forgiving forgave forgiven verb
to stop blaming or being angry with somebody for something they said or did.
I forgave my brother for losing my favourite game.
forgiveness noun

fork

forks noun
1 a tool with two or more narrow spikes that is used for lifting things.

table fork

form

forms noun
1 the shape or the type of something.
Trains are a form of transport.
2 a printed piece of paper with spaces in which you write information.
I filled in a form about my health for my doctor.

formula

formulas or **formulae** noun
1 a type of recipe or code that shows chemists what chemicals are made of.

$$H_2O$$

chemical formula for water
2 instructions or a recipe for making or doing something.

fortnight

noun
a period of time lasting two weeks.
fortnightly adjective
fortnightly adverb

fortune

noun
1 luck.
He had the good fortune to be rescued from the wreck.
■ opposite **misfortune**
2 a lot of money.

2 the place where something divides into two parts.

a fork in the road

forwards

adverb
moving towards the front.
He fell forwards onto his hands.

fossil

fossils noun
the remains or print of a plant or animal that died many years ago. Fossils are found preserved in rocks.
fossilized adjective

foster

fosters fostering fostered verb
to give a home for a period of time to a child who comes from another family.
They have fostered three children in the past two years.

fought

from the verb **to fight**
The team fought back, but in the end they lost the game.
■ say **fort**

found

from the verb **to find**
She found her wallet this morning.

fountain

fountains noun
a statue or structure that sprays water up into the air.

fox

foxes noun
a mammal that belongs to the dog family and lives in the countryside and in towns. Foxes eat small animals, birds, and scraps from dustbins.

fraction

fractions noun
1 a number that is part of a whole number.

$\frac{1}{3}$

One-third is a fraction.
2 a very small part of something.
You can fly there in a fraction of the time it takes to drive.

fracture

fractures fracturing fractured verb
to break.

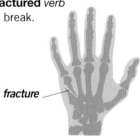

fracture

The X-ray showed where the bone had fractured.
fracture noun

fragile

adjective
delicate and easily broken.

fragile coral
■ say **fra**-jil

A B C D E F G H I J K L M N O P Q R S T U V W X Y Z

frame
frames noun
a structure that surrounds the edge of something, holding it in place.

*a picture **frame***

frantic
adjective
very upset and excited, because of fear, worry, or pain.
*The **frantic** animal tried to escape from its cage.*
frantically *adverb*

freckle
freckles noun
a small, light brown spot on the skin.

freckles

free
adjective
1 costing no money.
*Please accept this **free** gift.*
2 not restricted by rules or limits.
*Have you any **free** time this week?*
free *adverb*
free *verb*

freedom
noun
being free.
*The **freedom** to do as you like.*

freeze
freezes freezing froze frozen
verb
to reach such a low, cold temperature that a liquid becomes a solid.

*We **froze** fruit juice to make an ice lolly.*

freezer
freezers noun
a machine that freezes food so that it can be stored for a long time without going bad.

freight
noun
goods that are carried by road, rail, sea, or air.
■ rhymes with **mate**

freight ship

frequent
adjective
happening often.
*There is a **frequent** train service to the city.*
■ say **free**-kwent
frequently *adverb*

fresh
adjective
new, not stale or preserved.

fresh parsley

dried parsley

friend
friends noun
somebody that you like and who likes you.
friendly *adjective*

frighten
frightens frightening frightened *verb*
to make somebody feel afraid.
*She was always trying to **frighten** her brother.*
frightening *adjective*

fringe
fringes noun
1 a border made up of loose, hanging pieces of material or thread.

fringe

2 the hair that hangs over your forehead.

frog
frogs noun
an amphibian that lives in or near water. Frogs eat spiders, worms, small fish, and insects.

front
fronts noun
the part of something that faces forwards.

***front** of a truck*

frontier
frontiers noun
the border between two regions or countries, especially if one of them is wild and unknown.
■ say **frun**-teer

frost
frosts noun
tiny ice crystals that form on surfaces outside in very cold weather.
frosty *adjective*

frown
frowns frowning frowned *verb*
to pull your eyebrows together and wrinkle your forehead to show that you are not happy about something.

frozen
adjective
preserved by being kept very cold.

frozen peas

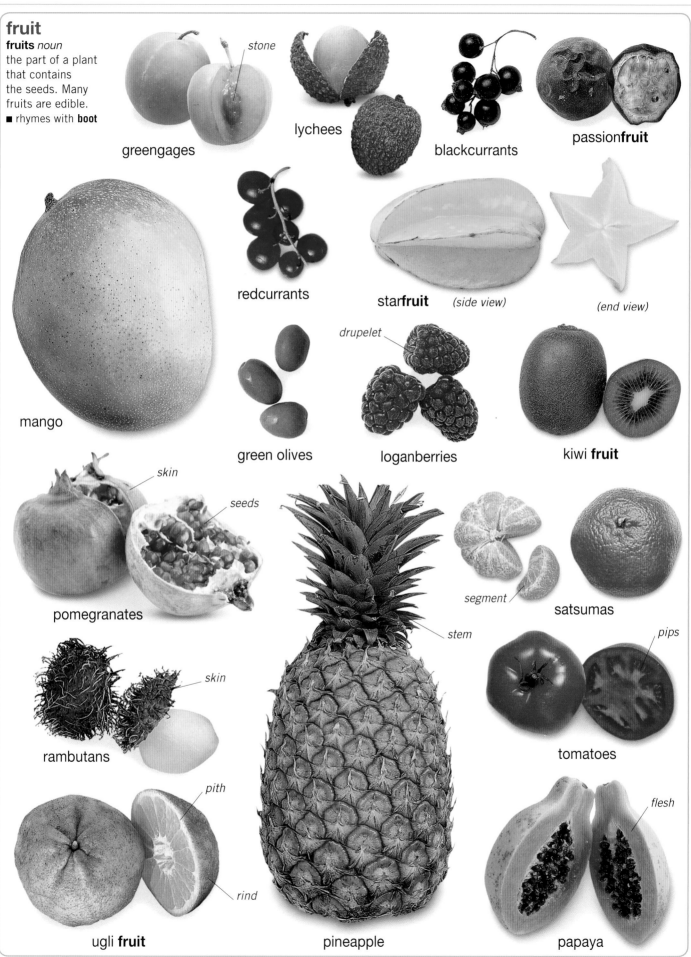

fruit

fruits *noun*
the part of a plant that contains the seeds. Many fruits are edible.
■ rhymes with **boot**

stone

greengages

lychees

blackcurrants

passion**fruit**

mango

redcurrants

star**fruit** *(side view)*

(end view)

drupelet

green olives

loganberries

kiwi **fruit**

skin

seeds

pomegranates

pineapple

segment

satsumas

pips

stem

tomatoes

skin

rambutans

pith

rind

ugli **fruit**

flesh

papaya

frustrate
frustrates frustrating frustrated
verb
to upset someone by keeping them from doing something they want to do.
*It was **frustrating** that the last tickets for the concert had already been sold.*
frustration *noun*

fry
fries frying fried *verb*
to cook something in hot fat.

frying pan

fuel
fuels *noun*
something that is burnt to give heat or power.
*Wood, coal, and petrol are types of **fuel**.*

full
adjective
without space for any more.

*This jar is **full** of sweets.*

fumes
noun
smoke or gas that is often strong-smelling and unpleasant. Some fumes are poisonous.
*Exhaust **fumes**.*

fun
noun
an enjoyable activity.
*The treasure hunt was great **fun**.*

fund
funds *noun*
an amount of money collected for a special reason.
*The church has started a **fund** to repair the roof.*

funeral
funerals *noun*
a formal occasion during which the body of someone who has died is buried or burned.

fungus
fungi or **funguses** *noun*
a plant with no flowers or leaves. Fungus grows in damp places, and has seeds called spores.

fly agaric

funnel
funnels *noun*
1 a tube that is wide at one end and narrow at the other. Funnels are used for pouring liquids through small openings.

2 the chimney on a ship.

funnel

funny
adjective
1 making you laugh or smile.

2 strange or odd.
*What's that **funny** noise?*
■ comparisons **funnier funniest**

fur
noun
the soft, hairy covering that some animals have on their bodies.

furry *adjective*

furious
adjective
very angry.
*She was **furious** to discover that her wallet was missing.*
■ say **fyoor**-ree-us

furnace
furnaces *noun*
an oven that heats metals to a very high temperature, so that they melt.
■ say **fur**-nis

*steel-making **furnace***

furniture
noun
chairs, beds, cupboards, and other movable things that you have in the place where you live or work.

cupboard

armchair

double bed

furrow
furrows *noun*
a groove in the earth made by a plough.

fuse
fuses *noun*
a safety device for electrical machines that stops the current from flowing if it is too strong.

fuss
fusses fussing fussed *verb*
to be more anxious than is necessary about something.
*Don't **fuss**!*
fussy *adjective*

future
noun
the time that is to come.
*In the **future**, people might travel to Mars.*
■ opposite **past**

Gg

gadget
gadgets *noun*
a small, useful tool.
■ say **ga**-jit

galaxy
galaxies *noun*
a large group of stars.
The Milky Way is a galaxy.

gale
gales *noun*
a strong wind.

gallop
gallops galloping galloped
verb
to move in the way that
a horse does when it runs
as fast as it can.

gamble
gambles gambling gambled
verb
to bet money on the result of
a race, game, or competition.

game
games *noun*
an activity that
you play for fun,
or a sport. Many
games have
rules and a
scoring system.
*They played
a board game.*

gang
gangs *noun*
a group of people who do
things together.
A gang of road workers.

gaol
gaols *noun*
another spelling
of the word "jail".
■ say **jayl**

gap
gaps *noun*
a space between two things.

a gap between the teeth

gape
gapes gaping gaped *verb*
to stare at something with your
mouth open.
*They gaped at the acrobat
on the tightrope.*

garage
garages *noun*
1 a place where cars and other
vehicles are stored.
2 a place where cars and other
vehicles are mended.

■ say **ga**-rarj or **ga**-rij

garbage
noun
things that have been
thrown away.
■ say **gar**-bij

garden
gardens *noun*
a piece of ground where fruit,
flowers, vegetables, and other
plants are grown.

*The garden looked beautiful
in the summer.*

garlic
noun
a plant with an
onion-shaped bulb,
made up of sections
called cloves. Garlic
is used in cooking
to add flavour
to food.

*garlic
cloves*

string of garlic

gas
gases *noun*
a substance
that is not
a liquid
or a solid.

*This camping stove is powered
by a gas called butane.*

gash
gashes *noun*
a long, deep cut.

gasp
gasps gasping gasped *verb*
to struggle to breathe, taking
in air in short, quick breaths.
*He rose to the surface of
the water, gasping for air.*
gasp *noun*

gate
gates *noun*
a type of outside door that
is fitted into walls or fences.

gather
gathers gathering gathered
verb
to collect together.

gathering berries

a b c d e f g h i j k l m n o p q r s t u v w x y z

gave
from the verb **to give**
She **gave** *me a kite for my birthday last week.*

gaze
gazes gazing gazed *verb*
to stare at something for a long time.
He **gazed** *out of the window.*

gem
gems *noun*
a jewel or precious stone.

emerald

aquamarine   fire opal

heliodor   yellow sapphire

general
adjective
1 usual, or to do with most people.
The **general** *opinion is that exercise is good for you.*
2 having to do with the main parts, but not the details.
The newspaper reported the **general** *points of the President's speech.*
generally *adverb*

generation
generations *noun*
all the people who are in approximately the same age group. There is usually a period of about 30 years between one generation and the next.

three different generations   child   parent   grandparent

generous
adjective
kind and ready to give.
It was **generous** *of him to lend us the car.*
generously *adverb*

genius
geniuses *noun*
a person who is extremely intelligent.
Many people think that Albert Einstein was a **genius**.
■ say **jee**-nee-us

gentle
adjective
kind and careful.

Be **gentle** *with the kitten.*
■ comparisons **gentler gentlest**
gently *adverb*

genuine
adjective
real, or not imitation.
A **genuine** *leather bag.*
■ say **jen**-yoo-in

geography
noun
the study of Earth's surface and its inhabitants.
■ say jee-**og**-raf-ee

geometry
noun
the study of shapes, surfaces, and angles.
■ say jee-**om**-met-ree

germ
germs *noun*
a tiny plant or animal that can cause illness.

germinate
germinates germinating germinated *verb*
to start to grow.

a seed **germinating**

gesture
gestures *noun*
a sign that you make with your hands or body.

ghost
ghosts *noun*
the spirit of a dead person. Some people believe they can see ghosts.

■ say **goest**
ghostly *adjective*

giant
giants *noun*
a huge, imaginary person from fairy tales or legends.

giant
adjective
very large.

giant *tortoise*

gift
gifts *noun*
a present.

gigantic
adjective
huge or enormous.
A **gigantic** *house with 20 bedrooms.*
■ say jie-**gan**-tik

giggle
giggles giggling giggled *verb*
to laugh in a nervous or silly way.

gill

gills *noun*
the organ that a fish uses to breathe (see **fish** on page 79).

gimmick

gimmicks *noun*
a way of making people aware of something or somebody.
*Gifts are often given away as a **gimmick** to draw attention to a new product.*

ginger

noun
a spicy root that is used to add flavour to food.

ground **ginger**

root **ginger**

giraffe

giraffes *noun*
a very tall mammal that lives on dry plains in Africa. Giraffes eat leaves on trees, which they can reach with their long necks.

girl

girls *noun*
a young female person.

give

gives giving gave given *verb*
to let somebody have something.

*He **gave** his friend a book.*

glacier

glaciers *noun*
a huge river of ice that moves very slowly.

glad

adjective
pleased and happy.
*I am **glad** to be back home.*

gladiator

gladiators *noun*
a man who was trained to fight for entertainment in ancient Rome.

glance

glances glancing glanced *verb*
to take a quick look at something.
*She **glanced** at the clock to see if it was time to go out.*

gland

glands *noun*
one of the parts of your body that makes the chemicals your body needs.
Glands near your eyes make tears.

glare

glares glaring glared *verb*
1 to look at someone in an angry way.
2 to shine very brightly.
*The sun **glared** down.*
glare *noun*

glass

noun
1 a transparent, fragile substance that is used to make things such as windows and bottles.

*stained **glass***

2 a container that is used to drink from.

*a **glass***

glasses

noun
a pair of lenses in frames. People wear glasses to help them see better.

gleam

gleams gleaming gleamed *verb*
to shine or glow.

glider

gliders *noun*
a very light aircraft with no motor that flies using air currents.

glimpse

glimpses glimpsing glimpsed *verb*
to see something or someone for just a few moments.
*He **glimpsed** his friend in the crowd.*

glitter

glitters glittering glittered *verb*
to shine with a bright, sparkling light.

a b c d e f g h i j k l m n o p q r s t u v w x y z

globe
globes *noun*
the world, or a model
of the world.

gloomy
adjective
dull and dark.
*A **gloomy** winter day.*

glossy
adjective
shiny.
***Glossy** paper.*
■ comparisons **glossier glossiest**

glove
gloves *noun*
a piece of clothing that you
wear on your hands.

glow
glows glowing glowed *verb*
to give off a steady light.

*The stick **glowed** in the dark.*

glue
glues *noun*
a substance that is used
to stick things together.

glue *verb*

gnat
gnats *noun*
a small, biting insect with
wings and long, fine legs.
*A mosquito is a type of **gnat**.*
■ say **nat**

gnaw
gnaws gnawing gnawed *verb*
to chew something.

*The mouse **gnawed** the wood.*
■ say **naw**

goal
goals *noun*
1 the target that you have to aim the ball at in some games.
*An ice hockey **goal**.*
2 a point scored for sending a ball into a net.

*He scored a **goal** in the last minute of the game.*
3 an aim or an ambition.
*My **goal** in life is to become a doctor.*

goat
goats *noun*
a mammal, with horns,
from the same animal
group as sheep. Goats eat
grass and other plants and
are often kept on farms
for their milk. A baby
goat is called a kid.

gobble
gobbles gobbling gobbled
verb
to eat something quickly and in
a greedy way.

God
noun
the being that Christians, Jews,
and Muslims worship and
believe made the world.

god
gods *noun*
a being that people worship
and believe has
power over
their lives.

*Ganesha, a
Hindu **god***

goggles
noun
special glasses worn to protect
the eyes.

*swimming **goggles***

gold
noun
a soft, bright,
yellow metal
that is very
valuable.

***gold** ore*

***gold** ring*

goldfish
noun
an orange fish that is often
kept in aquariums and ponds
as a pet.

golf
noun
a game played on a grass
course, with a ball, and sticks
called clubs. Players hit the
ball into holes around the
course. The player who
completes the
course in the
fewest shots
is the winner.

gong
gongs *noun*
a metal disc that you hit to make a loud noise.

good
adjective
1 pleasant or of high quality.
*That was a **good** film!*
2 useful.
*This knife is **good** for cutting.*
3 kind or well-behaved.
*A **good** child.*
4 skilful.
*She's very **good** at maths.*
■ comparisons **better best**

goodbye
interjection
a word that you say when someone leaves.

goods
noun
things that can be bought and sold.

goose
geese *noun*
a large bird that lives on or near water. Geese eat grasses and grain. A male goose is called a gander. Some types of geese are kept by farmers for their eggs, meat, and feathers.

gorge
gorges *noun*
a deep, narrow valley.

gorgeous
adjective
very nice to look at or taste.
*The long, sandy beach looked **gorgeous** in the photograph.*
■ say **gor**-jus

gorilla
gorillas *noun*
a large mammal covered in dark hair that lives in rainforests in Africa. Gorillas eat fruit, nuts, and leaves. They are the largest and strongest apes in the world.

*baby **gorilla***

gossip
gossips gossiping gossiped *verb*
to talk about someone or something without always knowing whether what you say is true or not.
*People often **gossip** about film stars.*

government
governments *noun*
a group of people who run a country.
■ say **guv**-er-ment
govern *verb*

grab
grabs grabbing grabbed *verb*
to take hold of something in a quick, rough way.

*They **grabbed** each other practising judo.*

graceful
adjective
moving in a beautiful way.

*Ballet dancers are very **graceful**.*
gracefully *adverb*

gradually
adverb
happening slowly, little by little.
*The path **gradually** became steeper.*
gradual *adjective*

graffiti
noun
writing and drawing on walls in public places.

■ say gra-**fee**-tee

grain
grains *noun*
1 a seed of a cereal crop such as wheat or barley, or a quantity of these seeds.

*barley **grains***

2 a small, hard piece of something.
*Sand is made up of many tiny **grains**.*
3 the pattern in wood.

*different wood **grains***

grammar
noun
the rules for writing and speaking a language.

grand
adjective
large and impressive.
*The **grand** house had a huge iron gate.*
■ comparisons **grander grandest**

» grandchild

A B C D E F **G** H I J K L M N O P Q R S T U V W X Y Z

grand

grandchild
grandchildren *noun*
a son or daughter's child.
A grandchild can be a granddaughter or a grandson.

grandfather
grandfathers *noun*
the father of a parent.
A grandfather can also be called granddad or grandpa.

grandmother
grandmothers *noun*
the mother of a parent.
A grandmother can also be called grandma or granny.

grape
grapes *noun*
a small, round fruit with a smooth green or black skin and soft, juicy flesh. Grapes can be used to make wine.

bunch of grapes

grapefruit
grapefruit or **grapefruits** *noun*
a large, round, juicy fruit with a thick skin and a sour taste.

graph
graphs *noun*
a diagram that shows how amounts and numbers of things compare with each other.

■ say **grarf**

grasp
grasps grasping grasped *verb*
1 to take hold of something firmly.

baby grasping hand
2 to understand something.
They couldn't grasp how the computer worked.

grass
grasses *noun*
a plant with long, thin, green leaves. Grass is an important food for many animals.

grasshopper
grasshoppers *noun*
a jumping insect that feeds on plants. Grasshoppers have two sets of wings and strong back legs.

grateful
adjective
feeling thankful to someone because they have done something for you.

She was grateful to her friend for his help on her project.
gratefully *adverb*

grave
graves *noun*
a hole in the ground in which a dead body is buried.

grave
adjective
very serious and important.

gravel
noun
a mixture of tiny pieces of stone, used for covering paths and roads.

gravity
noun
1 the natural force that pulls everything down towards Earth.

Apples fall downwards rather than upwards because of gravity.
2 seriousness.
The gravity of a crime.
■ say **grav-it-ee**

gravy
noun
the juice that comes out of meat when it is cooked. Gravy is served as a sauce.
■ say **gray-vee**

graze
grazes grazing grazed *verb*
1 to move around eating grass and plants, in the way that cattle and other animals do.

grazing cow
2 to scrape your skin.
When I grazed my knee it was very painful.

grease
noun
a soft, thick oil or fat.
greasy *adjective*

great
adjective
1 very big.
a great volcano

2 important or powerful.
A great leader.
3 very good.
That was a great goal.
■ say **grayt**
■ comparisons **greater greatest**

greedy
adjective
wanting much more of something than you need.
A greedy person.
■ comparisons **greedier greediest**

92

green
noun
a colour.

greenhouse
greenhouses *noun*
a building made mainly of glass, used for growing plants.

greet
greets greeting greeted *verb*
to welcome someone.

greeting
greetings *noun*
an action, or words, used when meeting someone.

grey
noun
a colour that is a mixture of black and white.

grief
noun
great unhappiness.

grill
grills *noun*
a set of metal bars for cooking food on.
grill *verb*

barbecue grill

grin
grins grinning grinned *verb*
to have a big smile.
grin *noun*

grind
grinds grinding ground *verb*
to crush something into a powder by rubbing it.

grinding spices

grip
grips gripping gripped *verb*
to hold on to something very firmly.
She gripped her briefcase.

groan
groans groaning groaned *verb*
to make a long, deep sound because you are unhappy or in pain.

groceries
noun
food, cleaning materials, and other things that you buy regularly to use at home.

■ say **grow**-sir-eez

groom
grooms grooming groomed *verb*
to make an animal clean by brushing it.

groove
grooves *noun*
a long, fine line that is cut into a flat surface.

grotesque
adjective
ugly and strange.
■ say grow-**tesk**

ground
noun
1 the surface of Earth.

She could see the ground from the top of the tower.
2 a place where some sports are played.
A cricket ground.

group
groups *noun*
people, animals, or things that are connected in some way.

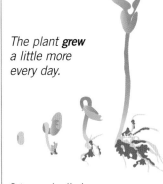
a group of schoolchildren

grow
grows growing grew grown *verb*
1 to become bigger.

The plant grew a little more every day.

2 to gradually become something.
Growing older.

growl
growls growling growled *verb*
to make a long, low, angry sound deep down in the throat.
The dog growled every time I came near.

» growth

A B C D E F G H I J K L M N O P Q R S T U V W X Y Z

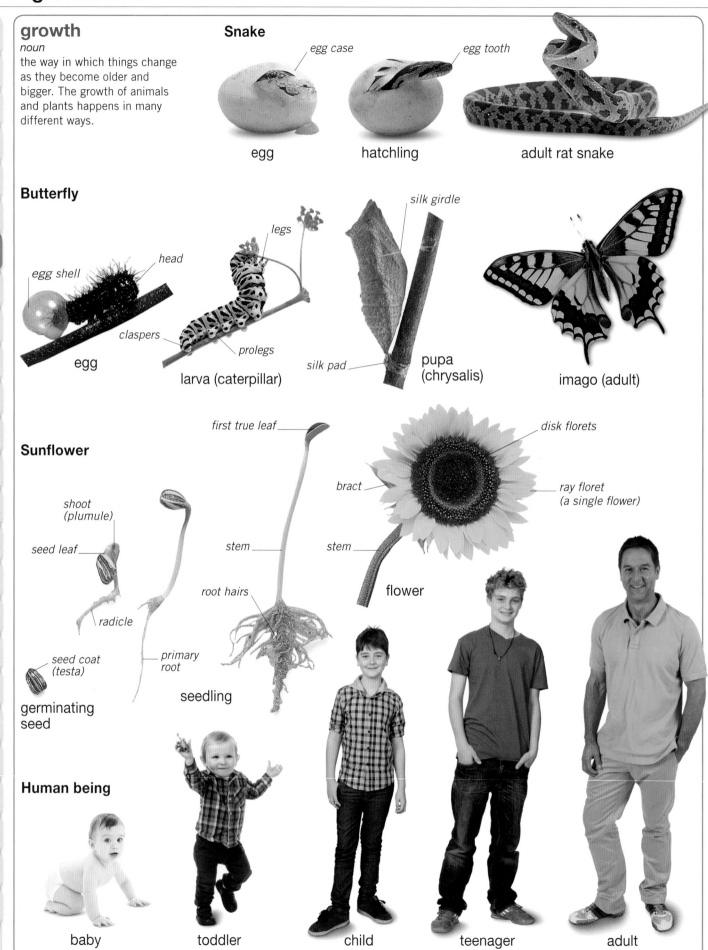

growth
noun
the way in which things change as they become older and bigger. The growth of animals and plants happens in many different ways.

Snake
egg case
egg tooth
egg
hatchling
adult rat snake

Butterfly
egg shell
head
legs
silk girdle
egg
claspers
prolegs
silk pad
larva (caterpillar)
pupa (chrysalis)
imago (adult)

Sunflower
first true leaf
disk florets
shoot (plumule)
seed leaf
stem
stem
bract
ray floret (a single flower)
radicle
root hairs
flower
seed coat (testa)
primary root
seedling
germinating seed

Human being
baby
toddler
child
teenager
adult

grub
grubs noun
the larva of a newly hatched insect before it becomes an adult. A grub looks like a thick, soft worm.

grumble
grumbles grumbling grumbled verb
to complain crossly, usually in a quiet voice.

grunt
grunts grunting grunted verb
to make a short sound like the noise a pig makes.

guarantee
guarantees noun
1 a promise from a company that if one of their products goes wrong they will mend or replace it.
A one-year guarantee.
2 a promise that something will happen.
■ say ga-ran-**tee**

guard
guards guarding guarded verb
to watch over something to keep it safe.
The building was guarded at night.
■ say **gard**

guard
guards noun
1 someone who watches over and protects something or someone.

security guard

2 something that prevents damage or injury.

face guard

guess
guesses guessing guessed verb
to suggest an answer to a question, without being sure it is the right one.

She had to guess what was inside the box.
guess noun

guest
guests noun
someone who visits or stays at a house or a hotel.
■ rhymes with **best**

guide
guides noun
1 someone whose job is to show people around places.
The guide took us around the museum.
2 a book with maps and information about a place.
guide verb

guilty
adjective
having done something wrong.

guilt noun

guitar
guitars noun
a musical instrument with six or twelve strings. You pull the strings with your fingers to make different sounds.

electric guitar

gulp
gulps gulping gulped verb
to swallow something fast or in large amounts.
He gulped the drink quickly.

gum
gums noun
1 the firm part inside your mouth around your teeth.
2 a sticky substance that is usually made from plants.
3 Chewing-gum.

gun
guns noun
a weapon that fires bullets.

18th-century gun

gurgle
gurgles gurgling gurgled verb
to make small bubbling sounds in the throat.
The baby gurgled when his mother tickled him.

gust
gusts noun
a sudden, strong rush of wind.
A gust of wind blew off his hat.

gym
gyms noun
a large room or building where people can play sports or exercise, often using special equipment. Gym is short for gymnasium.
■ say **jim**

gymnast
gymnasts noun
a person who is skilled in gymnastics.
■ say **jim**-nast

gymnastics
noun
a sport in which people perform exercises that develop physical strength and ability.
■ say jim-**nass**-ticks

a
b
c
d
e
f
g
h
i
j
k
l
m
n
o
p
q
r
s
t
u
v
w
x
y
z

Hh

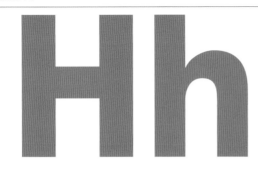

habit
habits *noun*
1 something that you usually do without thinking.

*Biting your nails is a bad **habit**.*

2 a type of clothing worn by monks and nuns.

*monk's **habit***

habitat
habitats *noun*
the natural place where an animal, bird, or plant lives and grows.

hail
noun
frozen rain that falls in small, hard balls.

hair

hair
noun
1 thin strands that grow on the skin of animals and people.
2 a mass of thin strands that covers your head.

long hair

hairy *adjective*

hairbrush
hairbrushes *noun*
a brush for hair.

haircut
haircuts *noun*
a style in which hair is cut.
*Have you seen his new **haircut**?*

hairdresser
hairdressers *noun*
someone whose job it is to cut hair.

halal
adjective
food that is prepared so that it satisfies the rules of the Islamic religion.

half
halves *noun*
one of two equal parts of something.

halve *verb*

hall
halls *noun*
1 a corridor or small room at the entrance of a house.
2 a large, open room in a building, used for meetings or other group activities.

halt
halts halting halted *verb*
to stop walking or moving forwards.
■ say **holt**

ham
noun
meat from the leg of a pig that has been preserved with salt or smoke.

hamburger
hamburgers *noun*
a flat piece of chopped beef, grilled and served in a roll.

hammer
hammers *noun*
a tool with a metal end that is used to knock nails into wood and to hit things.
hammer *verb*

hammock
hammocks *noun*
a bed made of cloth or net, hung by rope and fastened at two ends.

hand
hands *noun*
the part of your body at the end of your arm that has four fingers and one thumb.

hand
hands handing handed *verb*
to give something to someone with your hand.
***Hand** the hammer to me.*

handkerchief
handkerchiefs *noun*
a small piece of cloth or paper, used for blowing your nose.

handle
handles *noun*
a part of something that is designed to be grasped or held by the hand.

*door **handle***

handle
handles handling handled *verb*
to touch or hold something.
*Please **handle** that vase carefully!*

handlebar
handlebars *noun*
a bar at the front of a bicycle that you turn to steer (see **transport** on page 221).

handsome
adjective
attractive and pleasant to look at.
A handsome man.

handstand
handstands *noun*
an upside-down position, standing on your hands, with your legs in the air.

handwriting
noun
writing done by hand, not typed or printed.

Jane – see you later at the park.

hang
hangs hanging hung *verb*
to support something from above.

hanging up her clothes

hangar
hangars *noun*
a very large building where aircraft are stored.

hang-glider
hang-gliders *noun*
a huge kite that a person can hang from. The hang-glider rides on currents of air, in the same way as a glider.

happen
happens happening happened *verb*
to take place.
What happened to your car?

happy
adjective
pleased and content.
He felt happy on his birthday.
■ comparisons **happier happiest**
happiness noun

harbour
harbours *noun*
a sheltered place where ships can anchor and unload safely.

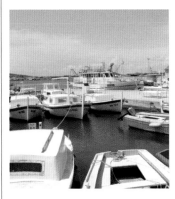

hard
adjective
1 solid and firm to touch.
Hard ground.
2 difficult to understand or do.
These sums are hard.
■ comparisons **harder hardest**
hard *adverb*

hare
hares *noun*
a furry, plant-eating mammal that belongs to the same animal group as rabbits. Hares can run fast and have very good hearing. Males are called jacks and females are called jills.

harm
harms harming harmed *verb*
to damage or injure something or somebody.

harmful
adjective
able to damage or injure someone or something.
■ opposite **harmless**

harmony
harmonies *noun*
a collection of musical notes played or sung together to make a pleasant sound.
They sang in perfect harmony.

harp
harps *noun*
a musical instrument that has a large frame with strings stretched across it. Harps are played by pulling the strings with your fingers.

frame
harp

harvest
harvests harvesting harvested *verb*
to gather a crop, such as fruit or wheat, when it is ready to be used or eaten.

combine harvester

harvesting wheat
harvest *noun*

hat
hats *noun*
something that is worn on the head.

hatch
hatches hatching hatched *verb*
to be born by coming out of an egg.

hate
hates hating hated *verb*
to dislike something or someone very much.
hatred *noun*

haul
hauls hauling hauled *verb*
to pull with force.

hauling a boat

a b c d e f g h i j k l m n o p q r s t u v w x y z

A B C D E F G H I J K L M N O P Q R S T U V W X Y Z

haunted

adjective

having ghosts or other spirits in it.
*A **haunted** house.*

hawk

hawks *noun*

one of a group of birds that hunt animals for food. Falcons, buzzards, and vultures are all hawks.

long-legged buzzard

hay

noun

grass that has been cut and dried to be fed to animals. Hay is often stored in large heaps called haystacks.

Hay is often hung in a net for horses to eat.

hazard

hazards *noun*

a risk or dangerous obstacle.

*Icy pavements are a **hazard** to pedestrians in winter.*
hazardous *adjective*

head

head

heads *noun*

1 the part of your body that contains your brain, and is where your ears, eyes, nose, and mouth are.

2 a leader of a group.
*She is the **head** of a large company.*

headache

headaches *noun*

a pain in your head.

headlamp

headlamps *noun*

a light at the front of a vehicle, used when driving at night.

headlamp

headline

headlines *noun*

the title of a report in a newspaper.
*Have you seen the **headlines** today?*

headphones

noun

a device worn over the ears that is used for listening to the radio or to recorded music.

healthy

adjective

well and strong.

■ say **hell**-thee
■ comparisons **healthier healthiest**
health *noun*

heap

heaps *noun*

a collection of things lying on top of each other.

*She left her clothes in a **heap** on the chair.*

hear

hears hearing heard *verb*

1 to notice a sound.
*Did you **hear** that bird?*
2 to listen to.
*I'd like to **hear** you play the piano.*

heart

hearts *noun*

1 the organ in your chest that pumps blood around your body.

heart

2 a shape.

■ say **hart**

heat

heats heating heated *verb*

to make or become warmer.
*We **heated** some water.*
heat *noun*

heave

heaves heaving heaved *verb*

to lift, pull, or throw something with a lot of effort.

*He **heaved** the sack onto the back of the truck.*

heavy

adjective

weighing a large amount.

*a **heavy** stone*   *a light feather*

■ say **hev**-ee
■ comparisons **heavier heaviest**
■ opposite **light**

hedge

hedges *noun*

a line of bushes grown so that they make a boundary between two places.

hedgehog

hedgehogs *noun*

a small, nocturnal mammal covered in spines. Hedgehogs hunt for insects and small animals. They roll into a ball when they feel threatened.

heel
heels *noun*
1 the back part of your foot.

heel

2 the higher back part of a shoe.

heel

height
heights *noun*
the measurement of how tall or high someone or something is.

*She measured his **height**.*
■ say **hite**

held
from the verb **to hold**
*I **held** a snake when we went to the zoo yesterday.*

helicopter
helicopters *noun*
a type of aircraft that uses rotating blades to make it fly and hover.

helmet
helmets *noun*
a strong hat, worn to protect the head.

cycling **helmet**

help
helps helping helped *verb*
to make something easier or better for someone.
help *noun*

helpless
adjective
unable to take care of yourself.
*A baby is completely **helpless**.*

hemisphere
hemispheres *noun*
one half of the world.

northern **hemisphere**

southern **hemisphere**

herb
herbs *noun*
a plant that is used fresh or dried to flavour food or to make medicines.

oregano   rosemary

*two different types of **herbs***
herbal *adjective*

herd
herds *noun*
a group of large, grazing animals.

*a **herd** of elephants*

here
adverb
in this place.
*Is there a doctor **here**?*

hero / heroine
heroes / heroines *noun*
1 a very brave person.
2 the main character in a story, film, or play.
■ **hero** is male and **heroine** is female

hesitate
hesitates hesitating hesitated *verb*
to pause because you are not sure what to do.

*He **hesitated** before jumping into the icy pool.*
hesitation *noun*

hexagon
hexagons *noun*
a shape with six sides (see **shape** on page 182).

hibernate
hibernates hibernating hibernated *verb*
to go to sleep for the winter.

*a dormouse **hibernating***
■ say **hie-ber-nate**
hibernation *noun*

hiccup
hiccups *noun*
a sudden movement in your chest that causes a quick breath and a short gulp.
■ also spelt **hiccough**
hiccup *verb*

hide
hides hiding hid hidden *verb*
to put yourself or something out of sight.

hieroglyphics
noun
a type of writing that uses pictures to represent sounds, words, and letters.

ancient Egyptian **hieroglyphics**

■ say **hie-roh-gli-fiks**

a b c d e f g **h** i j k l m n o p q r s t u v w x y z

high
adjective
tall or a long way up.

high *above the ground*
- say **hye**
- comparisons **higher highest**

highway
highways *noun*
a main road.

hi-jack
hi-jacks *noun*
a crime in which a vehicle or an aircraft is seized by force, and people are held prisoner.
hi-jack *verb*

hill
hills *noun*
an area of high ground.
hilly *adjective*

Hindu
Hindus *noun*
a follower of Hinduism (cultural and religious beliefs and practices that originated in India centuries ago).

hinge
hinges *noun*
a metal device that holds doors and gates in place, allowing them to open and close.

hint
hints hinting hinted *verb*
to suggest something in a vague way.
He hinted that he knew about my secret.

hip
hips *noun*
a joint at the top of each of your legs, between your waist and your thigh.

hip

hippopotamus
hippopotamuses or **hippopotami** *noun*
a large mammal that lives in Africa. Hippopotamuses spend most of the time in lakes or rivers, and eat water plants.

hire
hires hiring hired *verb*
to pay money so you can borrow something or use someone's services.
They hired a car for two weeks.

hiss
hisses hissing hissed *verb*
to make a noise like air escaping from a tyre.

Snakes hiss.
hiss *noun*

history
noun
the study of things that have happened to people in the past.
We are studying the history of the USA.
historical *adjective*

hit
hits hitting hit *verb*
to come into contact with someone or something in a forceful way.

The tennis player hit the ball over the net.

hit
hits *noun*
a success.
The song was a big hit.

hoax
hoaxes *noun*
an unpleasant trick or a joke where a person tries to make someone believe something that isn't really true.
A hoax phone call.
- say **hoe**-ks

hobble
hobbles hobbling hobbled *verb*
to walk with difficulty and pain.

hobby
hobbies *noun*
an activity that you do for enjoyment in your spare time.

His hobby is playing the guitar.

hold
holds holding held *verb*
1 to keep something in a certain position.

holding a cup and saucer
2 to contain.

This container holds kitchen utensils.

hold
holds *noun*
a place inside a ship or an aircraft where cargo is stored.
The cars were driven into the ferry's hold.

hole
holes *noun*
a hollow place or gap in something.

holiday
holidays *noun*
a period of time off from school or work.

hollow
adjective
with a space inside.

*The mouse ran through the **hollow** pipe.*

home
homes *noun*
the place where a person or an animal lives or comes from.

honest
adjective
truthful or able to be trusted.
■ say **on**-nist
■ opposite **dishonest**
honesty *noun*

honey
noun
a sweet, sticky food, made by bees from the nectar of flowers.
■ say **hun**-ee

*jar of **honey***

honeycomb

hood
hoods *noun*
the part of a coat, jacket, or sweatshirt that covers your head.

hood

hoof
hoofs or **hooves** *noun*
the hard, nail-like part of the foot of a horse, deer, or similar animal.

*horse's **hoof***

hook
hooks *noun*
a curved metal object used for hanging things on or for catching things.

*clothes **hook***

hoop
hoops *noun*
a round strip of plastic, wood, or metal.

hoot
hoots hooting hooted *verb*
1 to make a sound like the noise an owl makes.
2 to blow a horn or whistle.
hoot *noun*

hop
hops hopping hopped *verb*
to jump on one leg.

hop *noun*

hope
hopes hoping hoped *verb*
to want something to happen, and think that it might.
*I **hope** I'll be in the team.*
hopeful *adjective*

horizon
horizons *noun*
the line in the distance where the land or the sea seems to meet the sky.

■ say hor-**ize**-on

horizontal
adjective
parallel to the ground.
*A table top is **horizontal**.*
■ opposite **vertical**
horizontally *adverb*

horn
horns *noun*
1 a tough, pointed, bony part on the head of some animals.

*goat's **horn***

2 a brass wind instrument that you play by holding down its valves with your fingers and blowing through the narrow end of the tube.

*French **horn***

3 a device that is used to make a warning signal.

*old-fashioned car **horn***

horoscope
horoscopes *noun*
a prediction of what might happen to you in the future, made from the position of the stars and your date of birth.

horrible
adjective
very unpleasant or frightening.
horribly *adverb*

horror
noun
a feeling of shock and fear.
*They watched in **horror** as the house burned down.*

a b c d e f g h i j k l m n o p q r s t u v w x y z

A
B
C
D
E
F
G
H
I
J
K
L
M
N
O
P
Q
R
S
T
U
V
W
X
Y
Z

horse

horses *noun*
a large plant-eating mammal that is often used for riding and pulling equipment. There are many different breeds of horse, and their coats can be a variety of colours.

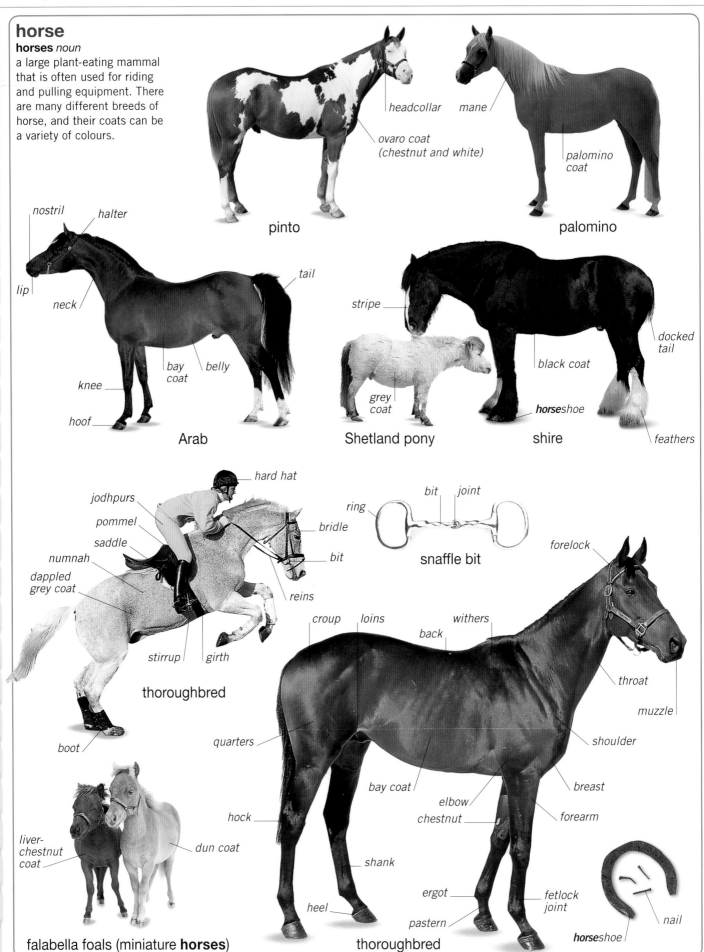

headcollar

mane

ovaro coat (chestnut and white)

pinto

palomino coat

palomino

nostril

halter

lip

neck

tail

bay coat

belly

knee

hoof

Arab

stripe

grey coat

black coat

*horse*shoe

docked tail

Shetland pony

shire

feathers

hard hat

jodhpurs

pommel

saddle

numnah

dappled grey coat

bridle

bit

reins

stirrup

girth

boot

thoroughbred

ring

bit

joint

snaffle bit

forelock

croup

loins

back

withers

throat

muzzle

quarters

shoulder

breast

bay coat

elbow

chestnut

forearm

hock

liver-chestnut coat

dun coat

shank

heel

ergot

pastern

fetlock joint

nail

*horse*shoe

falabella foals (miniature **horses**)

thoroughbred

102

hose
hoses *noun*
a long, narrow tube, through which liquids can be sent.

garden hose

hospital
hospitals *noun*
a place where sick or injured people are treated.

hostage
hostages *noun*
a person who is taken prisoner by someone who demands something in return for the prisoner's safety.

hot
adjective
1 very warm.

*The bars of the heater are very **hot**.*
2 very spicy.

*Chilli peppers taste very **hot**.*
■ comparisons **hotter hottest**

hotel
hotels *noun*
a building with bedrooms that people pay to stay in. Most hotels have a restaurant and a bar.

hotel building

hour
hours *noun*
a period of time lasting 60 minutes. There are 24 hours in a day.
■ say **ow**-er
hourly *adjective*

house
houses *noun*
a building that people live in.

houseboat
houseboats *noun*
a small boat that people live on.

household
households *noun*
all the people that live together in one home.

hover
hovers hovering hovered *verb*
to stay in one place in the air.

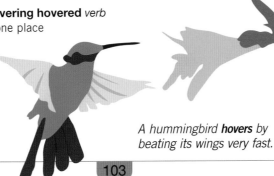

*A hummingbird **hovers** by beating its wings very fast.*

hovercraft
hovercraft *noun*
a vehicle that rides on a cushion of air. A hovercraft can travel across land and sea.

how
adverb
in what way.
How does this work?

howl
howls howling howled *verb*
to make a long, whining sound like a wolf.

huddle
huddles huddling huddled *verb*
to push or squeeze together.
*They **huddled** under the shelter.*

hug
hugs hugging hugged *verb*
to hold someone close in a loving way.

huge
adjective
very large or enormous.
*He was so hungry that he ate a **huge** plateful of food.*

hum
hums humming hummed *verb*
to make a musical sound with your lips closed.
humming *noun*

human being
human beings *noun*
a man, woman, or child.

■ say **hew**-mun
human *adjective*

humane
adjective
kind and merciful.
■ say hew-**mane**
humanely *adverb*

humid
adjective
warm and damp.
*The weather was **humid**.*

humiliate
humiliates humiliating humiliated *verb*
to make someone feel ridiculous or ashamed.
■ say hew-**mil**-lee-ate

humour
noun
the ability to see or show that something is funny.
*A good sense of **humour**.*
■ say **hew**-mer
humorous *adjective*

hump
humps *noun*
a large, round lump.

*This camel has two **humps**.*

hung
*from the verb **to hang***
*I **hung** my coat up when I arrived this morning.*

hungry
adjective
wanting or needing something to eat.

***hungry** chicks*
■ comparisons **hungrier hungriest**
hunger *noun*

hunt
hunts hunting hunted *verb*
1 to chase an animal, often to kill it for food.

*Lions **hunt** in packs.*
2 to search for something in many places.

*I **hunted** all over the house for my key.*
hunt *noun*

hurl
hurls hurling hurled *verb*
to throw something as hard as you can.

*He **hurled** the javelin.*

hurricane
hurricanes *noun*
a violent storm with very strong winds.

hurry
hurries hurrying hurried *verb*
to act quickly, because there is not a lot of time.

*He had to **hurry** to deliver the parcel on time.*

hurt
hurts hurting hurt *verb*
1 to cause pain or injury.
*I **hurt** my leg when I fell.*
2 to be painful.
*My broken arm **hurts**.*

husband
husbands *noun*
a married man.
■ opposite **wife**

hush
noun
silence.
*There was a **hush** as the teacher came into the room.*

hut
huts *noun*
a small shelter.

*Tourists stayed in **huts** on the beach.*

hutch
hutches *noun*
a large box made of wood and wire for a small pet to live in.

*rabbit **hutch***

hydrogen
noun
a gas that is lighter than air, burns easily, and has no taste, colour, or smell.
■ say **hye**-dro-jen

hyena
hyenas *noun*
a fierce mammal from Africa and Asia that looks like a large dog. Hyenas hunt for food and have a strange bark which sounds like a laugh.

■ say hye-**ee**-na

hygiene
noun
cleanliness and health.

*Good **hygiene** is important in the kitchen.*
■ say **hye**-jeen

hysterical
adjective
crying or laughing wildly.
■ say his-**ter**-rik-al

Ii

ice

ice
noun
frozen water.

iceberg
icebergs *noun*
a huge piece
of ice floating
in cold seas.

ice-cream
ice-creams *noun*
a sweet, frozen
food made mainly
from cream or milk.

ice-cube
ice-cubes *noun*
a small block of ice
used in drinks.

ice-rink
ice-rinks *noun*
a surface of ice, either inside
or outside a building, that
people skate on.

ice-skate
ice-skates *noun*
a boot with a
metal blade on
the sole,
used for
skating
on ice.

icicle
icicles *noun*
a hanging
piece of
ice, formed
by dripping
water that
has frozen.

idea
ideas *noun*
a thought or suggestion
about something.
*Do you have any better **ideas**?*

ideal
adjective
perfect in every way.
*That's an **ideal** solution.*
ideal *noun*

identical
adjective
exactly the same.

identical candles

identify
**identifies identifying
identified** *verb*
to recognize
something
or someone
by name.

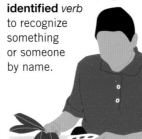

*Can you **identify** which tree
these leaves come from?*
identification *noun*

identity
identities *noun*
who someone is or what
something is.

*The card around his neck
shows his **identity**.*

idle
adjective
lazy, or doing nothing.

igloo
igloos *noun*
a round building made of
snow and ice.

ignorant
adjective
not knowing about something.
ignorance *noun*

ignore
ignores ignoring ignored *verb*
to take no notice of someone
or something.

iguana
iguanas *noun*
a large lizard found mainly
in Central and South America.
The common iguana lives
near rivers and streams.
It eats plants, insects, and
small animals.

*common **iguana***

ill
adjective
feeling sick or unwell.
illness
noun

illegal
adjective
not allowed by law.
*It is **illegal** to park there.*
■ opposite **legal**
illegally *adverb*

illustrate
**illustrates illustrating
illustrated** *verb*
to supply with pictures.

illustrating a book
illustration *noun*

image
images *noun*
a picture of something
or someone, or a
picture in your mind.

A B C D E F G H I J K L M N O P Q R S T U V W X Y Z

imaginary
adjective
not real.
- say i-**mag**-in-ery

imagine
**imagines imagining
imagined** *verb*
to create a picture of
something in your mind.
- say i-**ma**-jin
imagination *noun*

imitate
**imitates imitating
imitated** *verb*
to copy the way that
someone talks or
does something.

imitation
imitations *noun*
a copy.

*These **imitations** of fruit
don't look real.*
imitation *adjective*

immediately
adverb
without delay.
*Go home **immediately**!*
immediate *adjective*

immigrate
**immigrates immigrating
immigrated** *verb*
to go to a country
in order to live
there permanently.
immigration *noun*

impact
impacts *noun*
1 the action of one object
hitting another with force.

*The **impact** of the crash
wrecked both cars.*
2 something that has enough
power to create strong feelings
in someone.
*Travelling abroad had
a great **impact** on me.*

impatient
adjective
1 not willing
to wait.

*He became **impatient** when
the train was late.*
2 easily annoyed.
*She was often **impatient** with
her little brother.*
impatience *noun*

important
adjective
1 meaning a lot.
*Winning this competition
is very **important** to me.*
2 having great power
or influence.
*An **important** visitor.*
importance *noun*

impossible
adjective
not able to be done.
*It is **impossible** for people
to fly like birds.*
- opposite **possible**

impress
**impresses impressing
impressed** *verb*
to make someone have a good
opinion of something.

*She **impressed** the audience
with her speech.*

improve
**improves improving
improved** *verb*
to make or become better.

*We **improved** the flower pot
by decorating it.*
improvement *noun*

include
includes including included
verb
to put something in as part
of a whole.
*The travel brochure **includes**
pictures of the hotels.*
inclusion *noun*

inconvenient
adjective
not easy or not suitable.
*Steep stairs are **inconvenient**
for a lot of people.*
- say in-kon-**vee**-nee-ent
- opposite **convenient**
inconvenience *noun*

increase
**increases increasing
increased** *verb*
to become bigger in
size or number.
- opposite **decrease**
increase *noun*

incredible
adjective
difficult to believe.
*He tells some
incredible stories.*

independent
adjective
not controlled by anyone
or anything.
- opposite **dependent**
independently *adverb*

index
indexes or **indices** *noun*
an alphabetical list of subjects
and page numbers, usually
found at the back of a book.

indignant
adjective
upset and annoyed because
something is unfair.
*They were **indignant** about
the way they were treated.*
indignantly *adverb*

individual
adjective
separate or for just one person.

individual teaching
individual *noun*

indoors
adverb
inside a building.
*Let's go **indoors** now.*
■ opposite **outdoors**

industry
industries *noun*
a trade or business, and all the people and processes involved in it.

*the food **industry***
industrial *adjective*

infant
infants *noun*
a very young child.

infancy *noun*

infection
infections *noun*
a disease caused by germs, which can be passed from one person to another.
infect *verb*
infectious *adjective*

infinite
adjective
with no end.
infinity *noun*

inflate
inflates inflating inflated *verb*
to make something bigger by filling it with air or gas.

inflatable *adjective*

influence
influences influencing influenced *verb*
to have an effect on someone so that they change their ideas or behaviour.
■ say **in**-floo-ens
influence *noun*

information
noun
useful facts about something.

*The board gave **information** about the park.*

infuriate
infuriates infuriating infuriated *verb*
to make someone very angry.
■ say in-**fyoo**-ree-ate

ingredient
ingredients *noun*
one of the parts of a mixture.

***ingredients** for a salad*

■ say in-**gree**-dee-ent

inhabitant
inhabitants *noun*
a person who lives in a place.
*The desert has very few **inhabitants**.*
inhabit *verb*

initial
initials *noun*
the first letter of a word or name.

*Robert Anderson's **initials***
■ say i-**nish**-al

inject
injects injecting injected *verb*
to put a substance into your body using a hollow needle and a syringe.
injection *noun*

injure
injures injuring injured *verb*
to hurt yourself or somebody else.

*He **injured** his leg when he fell down the stairs.*
injured *adjective*
injury *noun*

ink
inks *noun*
a black or coloured liquid used for writing or drawing.

inland
adjective
away from the sea, towards the middle of the country.

inlet
inlets *noun*
a small opening or bay along the coast.

*an **inlet***

innocent
adjective
not guilty.
*He was arrested for stealing, but was found to be **innocent**.*
innocence *noun*
innocently *adverb*

inquire
inquires inquiring inquired *verb*
to ask for information.

*She **inquired** about the way to the mall.*
■ also spelt **enquire**
inquiry *noun*

a b c d e f g h i j k l m n o p q r s t u v w x y z

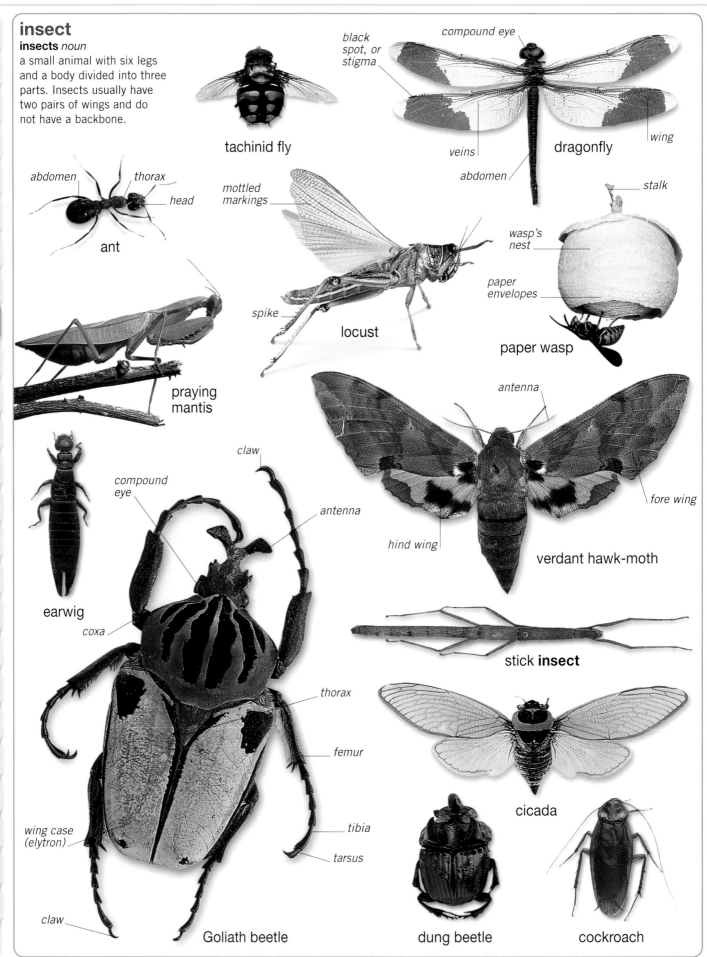

insect

insects *noun*
a small animal with six legs and a body divided into three parts. Insects usually have two pairs of wings and do not have a backbone.

tachinid fly

compound eye

black spot, or stigma

veins

abdomen

wing

dragonfly

abdomen *thorax*

head

ant

mottled markings

spike

locust

stalk

wasp's nest

paper envelopes

paper wasp

praying mantis

compound eye

claw

antenna

earwig

coxa

antenna

hind wing

fore wing

verdant hawk-moth

stick **insect**

thorax

femur

cicada

tibia

tarsus

wing case (elytron)

claw

Goliath beetle

dung beetle

cockroach

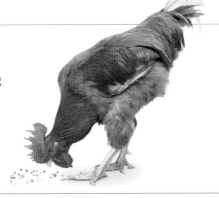

insert
inserts inserting inserted *verb*
to put one thing inside another.

inside
preposition
in the interior of.

inside the box

inside
adverb
in or into something.
Come inside!
inside *noun*

insist
insists insisting insisted
verb
to say something very firmly.
*She insisted that she had
seen a ghost.*
insistence *noun*
insistent *adjective*

inspect
inspects inspecting inspected
verb
to check something carefully.

*Cars are inspected for faults
before leaving the factory.*
inspection *noun*

instant
adjective
immediate.
She was an instant success.

instead
adverb
in place of.
*I chose the red pen instead
of the blue one.*

instinct
instincts *noun*
a strong natural feeling
that makes animals or
people do things that
they haven't learnt.
*Birds have a
pecking instinct.*

instruction
instructions *noun*
information about something.
*Read the instructions before
you use the machine.*
instruct *verb*

instrument
instruments *noun*
a device or tool that
has a special use.

a navigational instrument

insult
insults insulting insulted *verb*
to upset someone by saying
unpleasant things to them
or about them.
insult *noun*

intelligent
adjective
quick to learn, think,
and understand.

*She was intelligent, so she
solved the puzzle quickly.*
intelligence *noun*

interest
interests interesting interested
verb
to hold the attention of.
*Anything to do with space
interests me.*
interesting *adjective*

interfere
**interferes interfering
interfered** *verb*
to involve yourself in something
that isn't anything to do
with you.

*She kept interfering as
he tried to prepare lunch.*

interior
interiors *noun*
the part that is inside something.

interior of a doll's house
interior *adjective*

interjection
interjections *noun*
a word, such as "goodbye"
or "please", that can be
used on its own.

internal
adjective
on the inside.

*the internal workings
of a pocket watch*
■ opposite **external**
internally *adverb*

international
adjective
involving several countries.
An international event.

internet
noun
a worldwide computer network
for sharing information and
sending messages.

interrupt
**interrupts interrupting
interrupted** *verb*
1 to stop someone from
talking by breaking into
the conversation.
*Please don't interrupt while
I'm speaking!*
2 to stop something
happening temporarily.
*The tennis match was
interrupted by rain.*

intersection
intersections *noun*
a place where lines or
roads cross each other.

a busy road intersection

a b c d e f g h i j k l m n o p q r s t u v w x y z

interval
intervals noun
a period of time between events.
There was a short **interval** *between the two acts.*

interview
interviews noun
a meeting where someone is questioned.

a job **interview**
interview verb

intestine
intestines noun
an organ that leads from the stomach. Food is digested in the intestine as well as in the stomach.
■ say in-**tes**-tin

introduce
introduces introducing introduced verb
to present a person or idea to someone for the first time.
Introduce *me to your friend.*
introduction noun

invade
invades invading invaded verb
to enter a place as an enemy.
invasion noun

invent
invents inventing invented verb
to design an original device or process.
This device was **invented** *to record sound and play it back.*
invention noun

investigate
investigates investigating investigated verb
to look at a situation carefully to find out what is happening or what has happened.
The police are **investigating** *yesterday's robbery.*
investigation noun

invisible
adjective
unable to be seen.
■ opposite **visible**

invitation
invitations noun
a written or spoken request asking someone to come and be with you.
A party **invitation**.
invite verb

involve
involves involving involved verb
to include or affect something.
Two cars were **involved** *in the accident.*

involved
adjective
complicated.
An **involved** *plan.*

iris
irises noun
1 a tall, flowering plant that grows from a bulb or a root-like stem.

2 the round, coloured part of the eye.
■ say **eye**-ris

iris

iron
noun
1 a strong, heavy metal found in rocks, which is used to make things such as tools and gates.

wrought **iron** *gate*

2 a piece of electrical equipment that heats up and is used to remove creases in clothing.

irrigate
irrigates irrigating irrigated verb
to supply land with water.
irrigation noun

irritate
irritates irritating irritated verb
to annoy someone.
irritation noun

Islam
noun
the Muslim religion. Muslims believe there is one God, Allah, and that Mohammed is His prophet.
Islamic adjective

island
islands noun
a piece of land completely surrounded by water.

■ say **eye**-land

itch
itches itching itched verb
to have a feeling in your skin that makes you want to scratch.

He scratched his head because it was **itching**.
itch noun

ivy
ivies noun
an evergreen climbing plant.

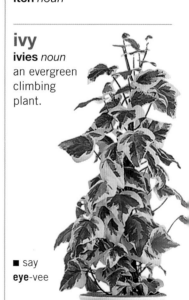

■ say **eye**-vee

Jj

jab
jabs jabbing jabbed *verb*
to push a finger or a pointed tool into something in a quick, sharp way.
*He **jabbed** his finger into his friend's ribs.*
jab *noun*

jacket
jackets *noun*
a short coat.

jagged
adjective
having rough, sharp edges.
***Jagged** rocks.*

jaguar
jaguars *noun*
a meat-eating mammal that belongs to the cat family. Jaguars live in the forests and marshes of North and South America.

jail
jails *noun*
a place where criminals are kept locked up.

jam
jams *noun*
1 a sweet food made from boiled fruit and sugar.

*strawberry **jam***

2 a group of people or things that are squashed together.

*traffic **jam***

jar
jars jarring jarred *verb*
to make an unpleasant sound or a jolt.
jarring *adjective*

jar
jars *noun*
a glass container with a wide top, used for storing foods.

javelin
javelins *noun*
a long, pointed stick that is thrown like a spear in athletic competitions.

jaw
jaws *noun*
the U-shaped bone that supports your mouth, allowing it to open and close.

*The crocodile opened its wide **jaws**.*

jazz
noun
a type of popular music with strong rhythms, first played in the USA.

jealous
adjective
annoyed and unhappy because others have something you would like.
*He was **jealous** of his friend's computer.*
■ say **jel**-lus
jealousy *noun*

jeans
noun
trousers made of denim.

jeep
jeeps *noun*
a small, open vehicle for driving over rough ground (see **car** on page 39).

jelly
jellies *noun*
a soft, firm, clear food made from fruit juice and sugar.

jellyfish
jellyfish or **jellyfishes** *noun*
a sea animal that has a transparent, soft body. Jellyfish feed on fish and tiny sea animals, which they catch by stinging them with their long tentacles.

*mangrove **jellyfish***

jet
jets *noun*
1 a sudden spray or stream of liquid or gas.
*The water was thrown up in a huge **jet**.*
2 a fast aircraft that is powered by an engine that sucks in air, heats it, and then pushes it out again.

*supersonic **jet***

Jew
Jews *noun*
a person whose ancestors were Hebrew or whose religion is Judaism.
Jewish *adjective*

jewel
jewels *noun*
1 a precious stone that has been cut and polished. Diamonds, rubies, and emeralds are all jewels.
2 an ornament made of gems and precious metals that people wear.

a b c d e f g h i j k l m n o p q r s t u v w x y z

A B C D E F G H I J K L M N O P Q R S T U V W X Y Z

jewellery

noun

ornaments that people wear. Jewellery is usually made from metals and decorated with jewels.

silver

hook

filigree bead

gold chain

Viking armband

earrings

lapis lazuli

gold amulet

cornelian

turquoise

amethyst

Egyptian necklace

diamond

amethyst

pendant

peridot

red garnet

drop earrings

heliodor

solitaire ring

scarf pin

spacer

pearl

choker

emerald

setting

opal

malachite

cufflinks

green garnet

citrine

fire opal

ruby

sapphires

amethyst

eternity ring

pearl

pearl

diamond

collar

gold

tourmaline

cameo brooch

diamanté

clasp

jigsaw puzzle
jigsaw puzzles *noun*
a puzzle with oddly shaped pieces that fit together to make a picture.

job
jobs *noun*
1 a task or some work that you have to do.
Jobs to do around the house.
2 work that someone is paid to do.
I have an outdoor job.

jockey
jockeys *noun*
a person who rides a horse in races.

jog
jogs jogging jogged *verb*
to run steadily and slowly.

join
joins joining joined *verb*
1 to put two things together.

joining hands

2 to become a member of something, such as a club.

joint
joints *noun*
the place where two pieces of something join together. The bones in your body meet at joints to help you move around.

ankle joint

joke
jokes *noun*
something that someone says or does to make people laugh.
joke *verb*

jolt
jolts jolting jolted *verb*
to shake or move in a bumpy way.

jolting along a bumpy track
jolt *noun*

journalist
journalists *noun*
a person who gathers and writes news.
■ say **jer**-nal-list

journey
journeys *noun*
a distance travelled.
■ say **jer**-nee

Judaism
noun
the religion of Jewish people. Jews believe in one God, and in the teachings of the Old Testament and the Talmud, the Jewish holy books.
■ say **joo**-day-izm

judge
judges judging judged *verb*
to decide whether something is right or wrong, good or bad.
judgement *noun*

judge
judges *noun*
1 a person in charge of a court, who decides the punishment of those people that the jury finds guilty.
2 a person who decides the winner of a competition or contest.

judo
noun
a sport from Japan, in which two people fight using special movements to try to throw each other to the ground.

jug
jugs *noun*
an open container that is used to hold liquids, and that has a handle and a spout.

juggle
juggles juggling juggled *verb*
to keep several objects in the air at the same time by throwing and catching.

juice
juices *noun*
a liquid from fruit or meat.
juicy *adjective*

jump
jumps jumping jumped *verb*
to throw yourself into the air.

junction
junctions *noun*
a place where several things join, such as roads or railways.

jungle
jungles *noun*
a dense, tropical forest.

junior
adjective
younger or less experienced.

jury
juries *noun*
a group of 12 people, chosen from the public, who sit in court and decide whether the person on trial is guilty or not guilty.

justice
noun
a fair and honest judgement.
■ say **jus**-tis

a b c d e f g h i j k l m n o p q r s t u v w x y z

kaleidoscope
kaleidoscopes *noun*
a tube with mirrors and small pieces of colourful plastic inside that you can look through. When the tube is turned, the pieces move, making a pattern of colours.
■ say kal-**eye**-do-skope

kangaroo
kangaroos *noun*
a marsupial from Australia that eats leaves and plants. Kangaroos can hop fast on their strong back legs. The females carry their young in a stomach pouch.

karate
noun
a sport from Southeast Asia, in which people fight with their hands and feet, using special movements.
■ say ka-**rah**-tee

kayak
kayaks *noun*
a covered canoe for one person, originally made from sealskins.
■ say **kie**-ak

kebab
kebabs *noun*
pieces of meat and vegetables, usually cooked over a grill on a sharp spike of wood or metal called a skewer.

keep
keeps keeping kept *verb*
1 to have something and not give it away.
She **keeps** a goldfish as a pet.
2 to remain.
Keep still!
3 to continue.
He **kept** walking.

kennel
kennels *noun*
a shelter outdoors for a dog.

key
keys *noun*
1 a piece of metal that has been cut so that it will lock and unlock a door or padlock.

keyhole

2 a small lever that you press with your finger.
Computer **keys**.

keyboard
keyboards *noun*
a row of keys that you use to play a musical instrument, or to use a computer or a typewriter.

computer **keyboard**

kick
kicks kicking kicked *verb*
to hit something or someone with your foot.

kick *noun*

kidnap
kidnaps kidnapping kidnapped *verb*
to take someone away against their will and keep them prisoner.
kidnapping *noun*

kidney
kidneys *noun*
one of two organs in your body that filters your blood and helps to keep it clean.

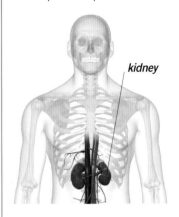

kidney

kill
kills killing killed *verb*
to make someone or something die.
She **killed** the wasp with a rolled-up newspaper.

kind
kinds *noun*
a type or sort of something.

nailbrush   *pastry brush*   *floor brush*

different **kinds** *of brushes*

kind
adjective
helpful and generous to other people.
■ comparisons **kinder kindest**
■ opposite **unkind**

king
kings *noun*
a male ruler of a country.

kingfisher
kingfishers *noun*
a bird with a long, straight bill and a small body. Kingfishers eat insects or fish and live in river banks or holes in trees.

kiss
kisses kissing kissed *verb*
to touch someone with your
lips in an affectionate way.
kiss *noun*

kitchen
kitchens *noun*
a room in which food
is prepared and cooked.

kite
kites *noun*
a light, material-covered frame
that is flown in the air. Kites
are attached to a string held
by a person on the ground.

kitten
kittens *noun*
a young cat.

kiwi
kiwis *noun*
a nocturnal bird from
New Zealand. Kiwis have
hair-like feathers but they
cannot fly. They have long,
curved bills, which they use
to hunt for insects and worms
(see **bird** on page 28).
■ say **kee**-wee

knee
knees *noun*
the joint
between the
upper and
lower bones
of your leg.

knee

■ say **nee**

kneel
kneels kneeling kneeled or
knelt *verb*
to go down on your knees.
■ say **neel**

knew
from the verb **to know**
I **knew** *the answers to
the test this morning.*
■ say **new**

knife
knives *noun*
a sharp blade
with a handle,
that is used
for cutting.
■ say **nife**

knight
knights *noun*
a soldier from
medieval times
who rode a horse.
A knight fought on
behalf of a lord, or
for the king
or queen.
■ say **nite**

lance

shield

knit
knits knitting knitted *verb*
to make clothes and
blankets from wool,
using large plastic
or metal needles.
■ say **nit**
knitting *noun*

knob
knobs *noun*
a round handle made of metal,
china, plastic, or wood that is
fitted to a piece of furniture.
■ say **nob**

knock
knocks knocking knocked
verb
to strike something sharply
and quickly.
She **knocked** *at the door.*
■ say **nok**

knot
knots *noun*
a twisted or tied
piece of string,
rope, or
other cord.
■ say **not**
knot *verb*

know
knows knowing knew known
verb
1 to understand something
or be sure about something.
Do you **know** *her name?*
2 to have met
somebody before.
I have **known** *him for years.*
■ say **no**

knowledge
noun
the things that someone
knows, or all the things
that are known.
■ say **nol**-lidj
knowledgeable *adjective*

knuckle
knuckles *noun*
one of the bony joints at
the base of your fingers.

knuckle

■ say **nuk**-ul

koala
koalas *noun*
a marsupial from Australia.
Koalas eat the leaves and bark
of the eucalyptus trees, in
which they live.

kosher
adjective
food that is prepared so
that it satisfies the rules
of the Jewish religion.
Kosher *meat.*
■ say **koh**-shur

a b c d e f g h i j k l m n o p q r s t u v w x y z

label
labels *noun*
a small notice attached to something that gives you information about it.

label for bottle of orange juice

laboratory
laboratories *noun*
a place where scientists work.

lace
noun
1 a material with a pattern of small holes.

lace border

2 a cord that is used to fasten things.

lace
laces lacing laced *verb*
to thread a lace through holes.

shoelace

lack
noun
a state of not having enough or any of something.
*The plants died from **lack** of water.*
lack *verb*

ladder
ladders *noun*
a wooden or metal frame with rungs or steps, which you use for climbing up or down.

rung

ladle
ladles *noun*
a large, deep, round spoon used to serve soup and other liquids.

ladybird
ladybirds *noun*
a small, flying insect with spotted wing covers. Ladybirds eat other small insects.

lagoon
lagoons *noun*
a shallow lake, cut off from the sea or a larger lake by coral, rocks, or sand banks.

laid
*from the verb **to lay***
1 *He **laid** his paintings on the table, so we could see them.*
2 *Our hen **laid** two eggs this morning.*

lake
lakes *noun*
a large area of water surrounded by land.

lamb
lambs *noun*
1 a young sheep.

2 meat from a young sheep.

lamp
lamps *noun*
a light that works by using electricity, oil, or gas.

land
lands landing landed *verb*
to arrive on the ground after flying.

*The plane **landed** on the runway.*

land
lands *noun*
1 the parts of the world that are not covered by sea.
2 a country, or an area of ground.
*The farmer owns all the **land** around the village.*

language
languages *noun*
the words or movements that people use to communicate with each other.

*They spoke using sign **language**.*
■ say **lang**-gwij

lantern
lanterns *noun*
a light that is inside a transparent case to protect it from winds.

lap
laps *noun*
1 the top of your legs when you are sitting down.

*The baby sat on his mother's **lap**.*
2 one circuit of a race track.
*The runners were on the last **lap** of the race.*

lap
laps lapping lapped *verb*
1 to splash gently against something.
*The waves **lapped** against the beach.*
2 to drink using the tongue, in the way an animal does.

*The kittens **lapped** up the milk.*

large
adjective
great in size.

a small tomato   *a large tomato*

- comparisons **larger largest**
- opposite **small**

larva
larvae *noun*
an insect after it has hatched out of its egg, but before it has become an adult (see **growth** on page 94).

laser
lasers *noun*
a machine that produces a beam of powerful light. Lasers are used to cut metal, to perform surgery, or for light shows.

last
adjective
1 the only one left.
*The **last** roll on the plate.*
- opposite **first**
2 the most recent.
*We stayed in **last** night.*

last
lasts lasting lasted *verb*
to take a certain amount of time.
*My riding lesson **lasts** an hour.*

late
adjective
after the correct time.
*They were **late** for dinner.*
- comparisons **later latest**
- opposite **early**

laugh
laughs laughing laughed *verb*
to make a noise with your voice because you think that something is funny.
- say **larf**
laughter *noun*

launch
launches launching launched *verb*
1 to put a boat or ship into the water.

2 to start something off.

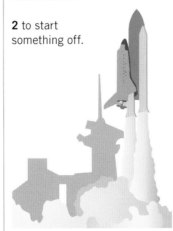

*They **launched** the space shuttle successfully.*

law
laws *noun*
a set of rules that people live by, usually made by the government of a country.
*It is against the **law** to drop litter.*

lawn
lawns *noun*
an area of grass that is regularly cut in a park or a garden.

lay
lays laying laid *verb*
1 to arrange or put something down on a surface carefully.

***Lay** the cards on the table.*
2 to produce an egg.

lay
from the verb **to lie**
*He **lay** down on the bed.*

layer
layers *noun*
a single thickness of something.

*There is a **layer** of nuts on top of the cake.*

lazy
adjective
not wanting to work or do anything energetic.
- comparisons **lazier laziest**

lead
leads leading led *verb*
1 to go first to show someone the way.
*Our tour guide **led** us to the coach.*
- opposite **follow**
2 to be in charge of something.
*She **led** the expedition to the South Pole.*

lead
leads *noun*
1 a thin strap or chain attached to a dog's collar and used to control it.
2 the first place in a race.
*She was in the **lead** all the way around the race track.*
3 a clue.
*The police followed up every **lead**.*
- rhymes with **feed**

lead
noun
a soft, heavy metal used in building and for making weights.

diving belt   *lead weight*
- rhymes with **bed**

leaf
leaves *noun*
one of the thin, flat, green parts of a plant that grows out from the stem or shoots.

leak
leaks *noun*
a hole or crack in a container through which liquid or gas can escape.

*There is a **leak** in this pipe.*
leak *verb*

a b c d e f g h i j k l m n o p q r s t u v w x y z

lean

**leans leaning leaned
or leant** *verb*
to rest on something
or tilt to
one side.

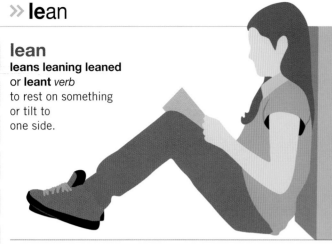

leap

**leaps leaping leaped or
leapt** *verb*
to jump a long distance,
or to jump high into the air.

leap year

leap years *noun*
a year that has 366 days,
instead of 365. A leap year
happens once in every four
years. The extra date in
a leap year is 29th February.

learn

**learns learning learned or
learnt** *verb*
to find out about something,
and to understand it.
*We **learnt** about magnetism
at school today.*
learning *noun*

leather

noun
a material made from the skin
of an animal, usually a cow.

*leather
bag*

leave

leaves leaving left *verb*
1 to go away.
*We'll **leave** after lunch.*
2 to let something stay as it is.
***Leave** those cakes alone!*

lecture

lectures *noun*
a talk given by one person
to an audience.

leek

leeks *noun*
a long vegetable with layers
of tight leaves. Leeks are
part of the onion family.

left

adjective
the side that is opposite
to the right.

*He drew around his **left** hand.*
left *noun*

leg

legs *noun*
1 the part of your body
between your hip and your foot.

2 a support for furniture.

leg

table leg

legal

adjective
allowed by law, or to do
with the law.
■ say **lee**-gal
■ opposite **illegal**

legend

legends *noun*
a well-known old story, which
may or may not be true.
■ say **lej**-und

leisure

noun
a time when you don't have
to work.
■ say **lezh**-ur

lemon

lemons *noun*
a sour, juicy fruit with a
tough, yellow skin.

lend

lends lending lent *verb*
to give something to someone
for a short time.
*He **lent** me his umbrella
because it was raining.*
■ opposite **borrow**

length

lengths *noun*
1 the measurement of
something from one end
to the other.
*Thirty centimetres in **length**.*
2 a piece cut from
a longer piece.

*a length
of ribbon*

lens

lenses *noun*
a curved piece of plastic
or glass that is used to help
you to see things in a clearer
way. Lenses are an important
part of telescopes, cameras,
and spectacles.

*contact
lens*

lens case

■ say **lenz**

leopard

leopards *noun*
a large mammal that lives
in Africa and Asia and belongs
to the cat family. Leopards
hunt at night, and are good
at climbing trees.

■ say **lep**-ard

leotard

leotards *noun*
a tight piece
of clothing worn
for dancing and
other kinds
of exercise.

■ say **lee**-o-tard

A B C D E F G H I J K L M N O P Q R S T U V W X Y Z

less
adjective
not as much.
Three is less than four.
■ opposite **more**

lesson
lessons *noun*
a period of time for teaching
and learning.

a violin lesson

let
lets letting let *verb*
to allow someone to
do something.
*The farmer let the children
stroke the donkey.*

letter
letters *noun*
1 a written symbol that
is part of the alphabet
(see **alphabet** on page 16).
2 a written message that
you send to someone by post.

lettuce
lettuces *noun*
a green vegetable with large
leaves around a short, central
stem. Lettuce
is often
used in
salads.

■ say **let**-iss

level
adjective
smooth and flat.
A sports field should be level.

lever
levers *noun*
1 a bar that is used to lift heavy
weights or to force things open.
2 a long bar or handle for
operating a machine.

espresso coffee machine

liberty
liberties *noun*
freedom.
*The prisoner's relatives
campaigned for his liberty.*

library
libraries *noun*
a place where books and other
sources of information are
collected and may be borrowed.

*He replaced the book on the
shelf in the library.*

licence
licences *noun*
an official certificate that
shows you have permission
to do something.
A driving licence.
■ say **lie**-sens
license *verb*

lick
licks licking licked *verb*
to touch
something
with your
tongue to
eat it or
make
it wet.

licking an ice-lolly

lid
lids *noun*
the top of a container.

lid

lie
lies lying lied *verb*
to say something that you know
is untrue.
lie *noun*

lie
lies lying lay lain *verb*
to be in a horizontal position.

lying down

life
lives *noun*
1 all things that are living.
Life on Earth.
2 the time that you are alive.
*My grandma had a long,
happy life.*

lifeboat
lifeboats *noun*
a boat for rescuing people who
are in trouble at sea.

lifeguard
lifeguards *noun*
a person whose job
it is to rescue people
who are in trouble
in the sea or in a
swimming pool.

lift
**lifts lifting
lifted** *verb*
to pick
something up.

lift
lifts *noun*
1 a machine that carries
people up to or down from
high places, either in
a building or outside.

a ski lift
2 a ride in a vehicle that you
don't have to pay for.
Can I give you a lift into town?

light
lights lighting lit *verb*
to make something catch fire,
or to turn on a light.
Lighting a candle.

light
lights *noun*
something that shines to help
you see in the dark.
*I had to turn on the light
so I could see the way.*

a b c d e f g h i j k l m n o p q r s t u v w x y z

light
adjective
1 weighing little.

a light balloon   a heavy bucket

- comparisons **lighter lightest**
- opposite **heavy**

2 not dark in colour.
Her dress was light blue.

lighthouse
lighthouses *noun*
a tall tower with a bright, flashing light that guides or warns ships around dangerous areas of coast.

lightning
noun
a flash of light in the sky during a thunderstorm.

like
likes liking liked *verb*
to think that someone or something is pleasant.
- opposite **dislike**
likeable *adjective*

like
adjective
similar to.
He looks like his brother.

lily
lilies *noun*
a tall plant that grows from a bulb, with large, trumpet-shaped blooms.

lime
limes *noun*
a juicy fruit with a sour flavour, similar to that of a lemon.

limit
limits *noun*
the point where something ends.
The limits of the town.

limp
limps limping limped *verb*
to walk with difficulty because your leg or your foot is injured or stiff.
The dog limped because it had a thorn in its paw.
limp *noun*

limp
adjective

not stiff.
a limp flag

line
lines *noun*
1 a piece of rope or thread.
A fishing line.
2 a long, thin mark.

a wavy line

3 a straight row of something.

a line of cars

liner
liners *noun*
a large passenger ship.

link
links *noun*
1 one of the individual sections that make up a chain.

link

2 a connection between two things.
The motorway will provide a link between the two cities.

lion
lions *noun*
a large mammal that is found in Africa and India. Lions belong to the cat family. They live together in groups called prides. The females, called lionesses, hunt at night for large animals such as antelope and zebra.

lioness

lip
lips *noun*
1 one of the two soft, pink edges of your mouth.

2 the top edge of a container.

lip

lips

liquid
liquids *noun*
a substance that flows and is not a gas.

list
lists *noun*
the names of several people or things written in columns.
A shopping list.

listen
listens listening listened *verb*
to hear and pay attention to something, such as music.

A B C D E F G H I J K L M N O P Q R S T U V W X Y Z

lit
from the verb **to light**
They **lit** a fire last night.

literature
noun
novels, plays, poems, and other written material.

litter
noun
1 rubbish left lying around.
2 baby animals born to the same mother at one time.

*a **litter** of puppies*

little
adjective
1 small in size.

*a **little** ball*   *a **big** ball*

■ comparisons **littler littlest**
■ opposite **big**
2 not much.
*I only have a **little** time.*
■ comparisons **less least**

live
lives living lived *verb*
1 to be alive.
*He **lived** to an old age.*
2 to stay in a place.

*There were a large number of bats **living** inside the cave.*
■ rhymes with **give**
living *adjective*

live
adjective
1 having life.
*A **live** snake.*
2 shown while the event is taking place.
*A **live** television show.*
■ rhymes with **dive**

liver
livers *noun*
an organ in the body that cleans the blood and helps to digest food.

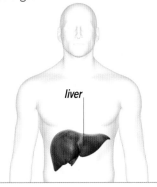

liver

living
noun
the way a person lives or earns money.
*He earns his **living** as a chef.*

lizard
lizards *noun*
a reptile with scales. Most types of lizard have four legs and a long tail. Many lizards live in warm regions and eat insects.

*A gecko is a type of **lizard**.*

load
loads loading loaded *verb*
to put things into a vehicle.
***Loading** the ship with cargo.*

loaf
loaves *noun*
a lump of bread baked as one piece that can be cut into slices.

***loaf** of bread*

lobster
lobsters *noun*
a large shellfish that lives in the sea and has five pairs of legs. One pair of legs are claws, which lobsters use for cutting up dead fish and crushing shellfish to eat.

*European **lobster***

local
adjective
having to do with the area near to a place.
*The **local** paper showed a picture of the flood.*
locally *adverb*

locate
locates locating located *verb*
1 to be in a particular place.
*The company is **located** in the north.*
2 to find where something is.
*He finally **located** the garage down a side street.*

load
loads *noun*
an amount of something that is carried.

*a **load** of gravel*

location
locations *noun*
the place or position of something.

lock
locks *noun*
1 a device that keeps something shut.

combination lock

lock *verb*
2 a device on a canal that raises or lowers the water level, so that boats can move up and down.

locker
lockers *noun*
a small, narrow cupboard with a lock, which is used for storing clothes or books.

log
logs *noun*
a thick piece of tree trunk or branch.

lonely
adjective
feeling sad and alone.
*He was **lonely** with no one to play with.*
■ comparisons **lonelier loneliest**
loneliness *noun*

a b c d e f g h i j k l m n o p q r s t u v w x y z

A B C D E F G H I J K L M N O P Q R S T U V W X Y Z

long
adjective
1 having
great length.

a **long**
string
of beads

a **short**
string
of beads

■ comparisons **longer longest**
■ opposite **short**
2 being a certain length.
*The fish was one metre **long**.*

look
looks looking looked verb
1 to use your eyes
to see something.

***looking** up*
2 to appear a certain way.
*He **looked** tired after
a sleepless night.*

loose
adjective
not firmly
fastened
or held.

***loose**
scarf*

■ say **loos**
■ comparisons **looser loosest**
loosely adverb
loosen verb

lose
loses losing lost verb
1 to no longer
have something.

*She has
lost her
phone.*
■ opposite
find
2 to be defeated in a game
or battle.
*He **lost** the match.*
■ say **looz**
■ opposite **win**

loud
adjective
noisy.
***Loud** music.*
■ comparisons **louder loudest**

loudspeaker
loudspeakers noun
a device that turns electrical
signals into sound.

love
loves loving loved verb
to like someone or something
very much.
love noun

low
adjective
near the ground.

*a **low** table*
■ comparisons **lower lowest**

lower
**lowers lowering
lowered** verb
to let something down to the
ground carefully.

*The crane truck **lowered** the
freight onto the ground.*

luck
noun
something that happens
to you by chance, without
being planned.
*I had the good **luck** to win
a free holiday.*
lucky adjective

luggage
noun
cases and bags containing
your clothes and other
things that you carry when
you travel.

■ say **lug**-ij

lukewarm
adjective
not very warm.
*The hot water system wasn't
working properly, so he had
to have a **lukewarm** shower.*

lull
lulls lulling lulled verb
to calm someone.
*He **lulled** the baby to sleep.*

lullaby
lullabies noun
a song that is sung to help
children to fall asleep.

luminous
adjective
glowing in
the dark.

*The candle
looks **luminous**
in the dark.*
■ say **loo**-min-us

lump
lumps noun
a rough piece of something.
*A **lump** of coal.*

lunch
lunches noun
a meal eaten in the middle
of the day.

lung
lungs noun
one of a pair of organs
inside your body that
you use for breathing.

lung

luxury
luxuries noun
something that is expensive.
*The new car was a **luxury**.*
■ say **luk**-sher-ee
luxurious adjective

lyrics
noun
the words to a song.
■ say **lir**-iks

Mm

machine
machines *noun*
a piece of equipment that is made up of several parts. The parts move together to do a particular job.

*A food mixer is a useful **machine**.*

machinery
noun
machines in general.

mad
adjective
1 crazy or foolish.
*She is **mad** to swim in the sea during winter.*
2 very angry.
■ comparisons **madder maddest**

magazine
magazines *noun*
a collection of news, stories, pictures, and advertisements with a paper cover.

magic
noun
tricks that a person performs that seem to make impossible and surprising things happen.
magical *adjective*

magician
magicians *noun*
someone who performs magic tricks.

magnet
magnets *noun*
a piece of iron that attracts metals with iron or steel in them.

magnetic
adjective
magnetism *noun*

magnificent
adjective
grand and wonderful.
*A **magnificent** fountain.*

magnify
magnifies magnifying magnified *verb*
to make something look bigger than it really is.

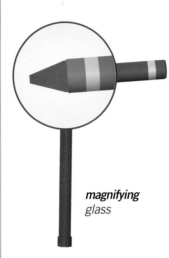

magnifying glass

mail
noun
letters, cards, and parcels that are collected and delivered.

mail *verb*

main
adjective
most important.
*The **main** road.*
mainly *adverb*

major
adjective
big or important.
*Scientists have made a **major** discovery.*
■ opposite **minor**
majority *noun*

make
makes making made *verb*
1 to create, produce, build, or do something.

*She **made** a paper windmill.*
2 to cause something to happen.

*The stone **made** ripples in the pond.*
3 to force someone to do something.
*Our teacher **made** us tidy the classroom.*

make-up
noun
a substance that people put on their faces to change the way that they look.

male
adjective
belonging to the sex that can be a father, but cannot give birth to babies, or produce eggs or seeds.
■ opposite **female**
male *noun*

A
B
C
D
E
F
G
H
I
J
K
L
M
N
O
P
Q
R
S
T
U
V
W
X
Y
Z

mammal

mammals *noun*
one of a group of animals that usually have hair or fur and a backbone, and are warm-blooded. Most female mammals give birth to live babies and feed them on milk.

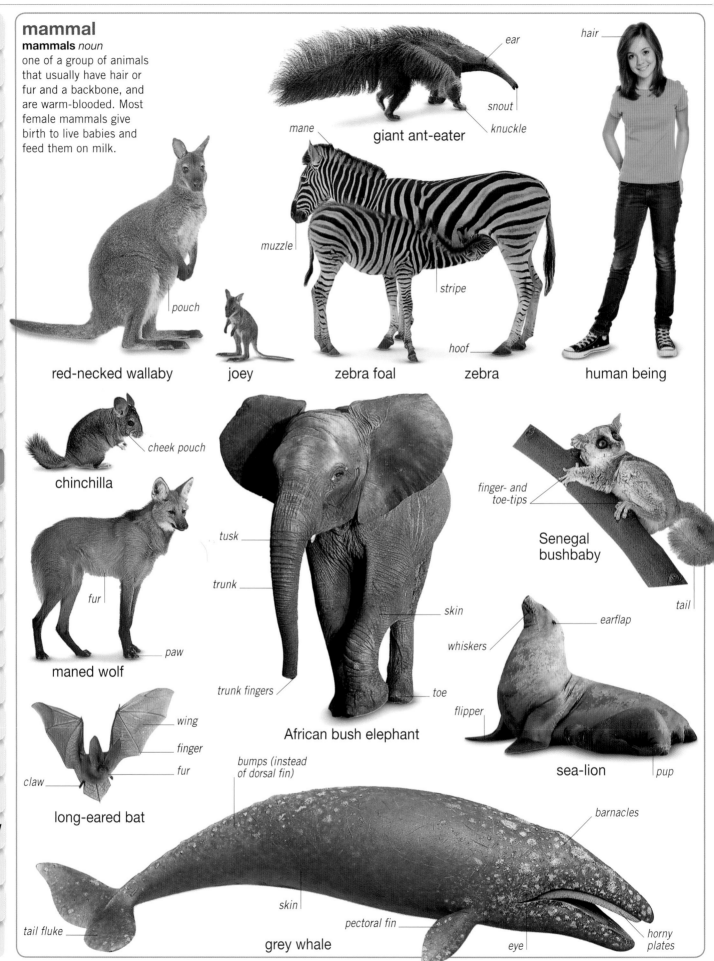

ear
hair
snout
knuckle
mane
giant ant-eater
muzzle
stripe
hoof
red-necked wallaby
joey
zebra foal
zebra
human being
pouch
cheek pouch
chinchilla
finger- and toe-tips
Senegal bushbaby
tail
tusk
trunk
skin
earflap
whiskers
fur
maned wolf
paw
trunk fingers
toe
flipper
sea-lion
pup
African bush elephant
wing
finger
fur
bumps (instead of dorsal fin)
claw
long-eared bat
barnacles
skin
pectoral fin
tail fluke
grey whale
eye
horny plates

man
men *noun*
an adult
male person.

man
noun
people in general.
Apes are related to **man**.

manage
**manages managing
managed** *verb*
1 to be in charge of a business
or part of a business.
She **manages** *a shop, and has
two assistants to help her.*
2 to be able to do something
that is difficult.
She **managed** *to swim right
across the bay.*

manner
noun
a way that a person acts,
or a way something is done.
*She always greets us in
a friendly* **manner**.

manners
noun
the way a person behaves.

He has good **manners**.

manufacture
**manufactures manufacturing
manufactured** *verb*
to make something in large
quantities with a machine.
Manufacturing cars.
■ say man-yoo-**fak**-chur

many
adjective
a large number.
There were so **many** *people
that I couldn't find her.*
■ comparisons **more most**
■ opposite **few**

map
maps *noun*
a drawing of all, or part
of, Earth's surface. Maps
often show where towns,
rivers, and other geographical
features are.

road **map**

marathon
marathons *noun*
a very long running race.
A marathon is 42.195 km
(26.2 miles) long.

marble
noun
1 a hard rock that is used in
buildings to make floors or
for decoration.

marble slab

2 a small, glass ball that
is used to play a children's
game, called marbles.

march
**marches marching
marched** *verb*
to walk with quick,
regular steps.

march
noun

margarine
noun
a food made of vegetable
oil that is used for spreading
on bread, or in baking.
■ say mar-jer-**een**

margin
margins *noun*
a space that forms a border at
the edge of a piece of paper.

margin

marine
adjective
living in the sea, or having
something to do with the sea.

marine life
■ say ma-**reen**

mark
marks *noun*
1 a line or a stain
on something.
A chalk **mark**.
2 a score that shows how well
you have done at something.
I got high **marks** *in French.*

market
markets *noun*
a place with stalls for
buying and selling goods,
often outside.

open **market**

marmalade
marmalades *noun*
a type of jam made from fruit
such as oranges or limes.

orange **marmalade**

marry
**marries marrying
married** *verb*
to become someone's husband
or wife at a wedding.
marriage *noun*

marsh
marshes *noun*
a low area of land that
is always very wet.

a b c d e f g h i j k l m n o p q r s t u v w x y z

A B C D E F G H I J K L M N O P Q R S T U V W X Y Z

marsupial
marsupials *noun*
one of a group of mammals that carry their babies in pouches. Kangaroos and koalas are marsupials (see **mammal** on page 124).
■ say mar-**soo**-pee-al

masculine
adjective
of, or like, men or boys.
■ say **mas**-kul-lin
■ opposite **feminine**

mask
masks *noun*
something that hides or protects the face.

party mask
mask *verb*

mass
masses *noun*
a very large number of people or things.

*A **mass** of bees gathered together.*

mast
masts *noun*
an upright pole that holds the sails on a boat or ship (see **boat** on page 31).

mat
mats *noun*
a covering for a floor, or to put under dishes on a table.

match
matches matching matched *verb*
to be similar to, or to go well with, something else.

*His trousers **matched** his hat and scarf.*
matching *adjective*

match
matches *noun*
1 a sports competition between two people or teams.
*A football **match**.*
2 a small stick of wood or card that you strike against a rough surface to make a flame.

mate
mates mating mated *verb*
to join together as males and females to produce babies.
*Many animals **mate** in the spring, and have their babies in the summer.*
mate *noun*

material
materials *noun*
1 cloth.

*woven **material***

2 things that are used to make or do something.

*building **materials***

mathematics
noun
the study of numbers, quantities, shapes, and sizes. Mathematics is often shortened to maths.

*symbols that are used in **mathematics***
mathematical *adjective*

matter
noun
1 any substance that takes up space and has weight, such as solids, liquids, and gases.
*Everything is made up of **matter**.*
2 a subject that needs to be discussed or decided.
*It was an urgent **matter**.*

mattress
mattresses *noun*
a soft, thick pad that you lie on in a bed.

mature
adjective
fully grown or developed.
mature *verb*
maturity *noun*

maximum
noun
the greatest possible amount.

*This box holds a **maximum** of 12 pencils.*
■ opposite **minimum**

may
might *verb*
1 to ask or have permission to do something.
May I go now?
2 to suggest that something is possible.
*It **may** rain later.*
■ always used with another verb

mayonnaise
noun
a creamy sauce made from eggs, vegetable oil, and vinegar, and eaten with salads.

■ say may-on-**ayz**

maze
mazes *noun*
a system of paths in which it is difficult to find your way around.

meadow
meadows *noun*
a field of grass, often with wild flowers growing in it.
■ say **med**-oh

meal
meals *noun*
food eaten at a particular time of the day.

*The family enjoyed a delicious **meal**.*

mean
adjective
1 unkind or unpleasant.
*That was a **mean** trick!*
2 not generous with money or other things.
*He was too **mean** to buy us an ice-cream.*
■ comparisons **meaner meanest**

meaning
meanings *noun*
the explanation behind what something says or what it is about.
*She didn't understand the **meaning** of the joke.*
mean *verb*

meanwhile
adverb
at the same time.
*Put the pasta on to boil, and **meanwhile** make the sauce.*

measure
measures measuring measured *verb*
to find out how big or how heavy something is.

■ say **mezh**-ur
measurement *noun*

meat
noun
the parts of an animal that can be eaten.

*grilled **meat** kebabs*

mechanic
mechanics *noun*
a person who makes and repairs engines and machines.

mechanical
adjective
worked by a machine.

*a **mechanical** toy*

medal
medals *noun*
a piece of metal that looks like a large coin hanging on a ribbon. Medals are awarded to people for something special that they have done.

*war **medal***

medical
adjective
having to do with medicine or doctors.
***Medical** school.*

medicine
medicines *noun*
a substance given to a sick person to help make them better.

■ say **med**-i-sin

medieval
adjective
coming from the historical period between the 12th and 15th centuries.

medieval costume

■ say med-ee-**ee**-val

medium
adjective
an average size, not particularly large or small.

small **medium** *large*

meet
meets meeting met *verb*
to come face-to-face with another person.
*I **meet** my friend at the bus-stop every day.*
meeting *noun*

melody
melodies *noun*
a tune.
*Do you recognize this **melody**?*
melodic *adjective*

melon
melons *noun*
a round yellow or green fruit with a tough skin, soft flesh, and many seeds.

melt
melts melting melted *verb*
to turn from a solid to a liquid when heated.

*The chocolate **melted** in the sun.*

a b c d e f g h i j k l m n o p q r s t u v w x y z

member

members *noun*
a person who belongs
to a club or an organization.

memorial

memorials *noun*
a structure that is built to
remind us of
people who
have died.

a war **memorial**

memorize

**memorizes memorizing
memorized** *verb*
to learn something so that you
can remember it in detail.
*Memorize the directions before
you set off.*

memory

memories *noun*
1 the ability to
remember things.
*I've got a terrible memory
for people's names.*
2 what you remember of
something that has happened
in the past.
*The photos brought back
happy memories.*

mend

mends mending mended
verb
to repair something that
is broken.

mental

adjective
having to do with the mind.
Mental arithmetic.

menu

menus *noun*
a list of dishes in a restaurant.
■ say **men**-yoo

mercury

noun
a heavy, silver-coloured
metal that is usually in
a liquid form. Mercury
is often used
in thermometers.

mercury

mercy

noun
the ability to forgive
someone or to treat
them sympathetically.
*The prisoners were shown
mercy and released.*
merciful *adjective*

merit

merits meriting merited *verb*
to deserve something.
*She merited a special award
for bravery.*
merit *noun*

mermaid

mermaids *noun*
a sea creature from legends
that has the upper body of a
woman and the tail of a fish.

merry

adjective
happy and cheerful.
■ comparisons **merrier merriest**

mess

messes *noun*
things that are dirty or in the
wrong place and look untidy.
*There was a lot of mess after
they had finished cooking.*
messy *adjective*

message

messages *noun*
a piece of information or an
instruction that you send to
someone or leave for them.

met

from the verb **to meet**
*I met my friend in
town yesterday.*

metal

metals *noun*
a substance that is found in
rocks and can be hammered
or stretched into a shape. Iron,
gold, and copper are all metals.
Electricity and heat can be
passed through metals.

*tin
can*

gold watch

metallic *adjective*

meteorite

meteorites *noun*
a piece of rock that falls to
Earth from space without
burning up. Pieces of rock that
burn up as they enter Earth's
atmosphere are called meteors.

meteorite
■ say **meet**-ee-or-ite

method

methods *noun*
a way of doing something.
Organic farming methods.

microphone

microphones *noun*
a device that is
used to send sound
over a distance
or to make
it louder.

microscope

microscopes *noun*
an instrument that
magnifies very tiny
things so that they
can be seen
in detail.

microwave oven

microwave ovens *noun*
an oven that cooks food very
quickly by passing electrical
energy through it.

midday
noun
12 o'clock in the middle of the day.
■ opposite **midnight**

middle
middles *noun*
the centre, or the part between the outer edges of something.

*He sat in the **middle** of the bench, between his two friends.*

midnight
noun
12 o'clock at night.
■ opposite **midday**

might
*from the verb **may***
*It **might** snow later.*
■ say **mite**

migrate
migrates migrating migrated *verb*
1 to go from one place to another to live there.
***Migrating** from the country to the city.*
2 to go from one place to another every year at the same time.

*Birds **migrate** huge distances.*
■ say my-**grate**
migration *noun*

military
adjective
to do with an army, navy, or air force.

military hat

milk
noun
the liquid that female mammals produce to feed their babies. People also drink goat's and cow's milk.

mill
mills *noun*
1 a building where materials are manufactured.

*paper **mill***

2 a device that grinds or crushes.

*pepper **mill***

millionaire
millionaires *noun*
a very rich person with money and property worth more than a million pounds or dollars.

mime
mimes *noun*
a type of acting that uses movements instead of words.

mime *verb*

mimic
mimics mimicking mimicked *verb*
to imitate what someone says or does.

*Parrots can **mimic** lots of noises.*

mind
minds minding minded *verb*
1 to object to something.
*Do you **mind** if I sit here?*
2 to take care of someone for a time.
*I had to **mind** the baby while my sister went out.*

mind
minds *noun*
1 the thoughts, feelings, and memory of a person.
*I've changed my **mind**.*
2 intelligence.
*She has a quick **mind**.*

mine
mines *noun*
1 a deep hole in the ground from which minerals are dug out of rock.
miner *noun*
2 a type of bomb that can float in the sea or be buried in the ground.

*trucks at an open-cut gold **mine***

mineral
minerals *noun*
a natural substance, such as coal or gold, that is found in rocks and in the ground.

lapis lazuli

miniature
adjective
very small, or made to a small scale.

miniature china
■ say **min**-it-cher
miniature *noun*

minimum
noun
the smallest possible amount or number.
*He was below the **minimum** height for the fairground ride.*
■ opposite **maximum**

minister
ministers *noun*
1 a person who holds religious services in a church.
2 someone in charge of a government department.
*The health **minister**.*

a b c d e f g h i j k l m n o p q r s t u v w x y z

minor
adjective
small or unimportant.
*A **minor** fault delayed the plane's departure.*
■ opposite **major**
minority *noun*

minus
preposition
subtract or less.
*8 **minus** 5 equals 3.*
■ opposite **plus**

minus
minuses *noun*
a symbol in mathematics that means subtract.
minus *adjective*

minute
minutes *noun*
a measurement of time that lasts 60 seconds. There are 60 minutes in an hour.
■ say **min**-it

minute
adjective
extremely small.

*a **minute** bead*
■ say my-**newt**

miracle
miracles *noun*
a sudden, wonderful event that sometimes makes a bad situation better.
*Her recovery after the accident was a **miracle**.*
■ say **mir**-i-kul
miraculous *adjective*

mirage
mirages *noun*
something that looks real from far away, but is not there when you get closer to it.
*The lake that they saw in the desert was only a **mirage**.*
■ say mi-**razh**

mirror
mirrors *noun*
a shiny surface, usually made of glass. Mirrors reflect the images of things placed in front of them.

mischievous
adjective
playful in a way that can be annoying.

*The **mischievous** cat knocked over the plant.*
■ say **mis**-chi-vus
mischievously *adverb*

miserable
adjective
very sad or unhappy.

miss
misses missing missed *verb*
1 to fail to meet, reach, or hit something that you are aiming at.
*He threw the ball at the target, but **missed** it.*
2 to be sad because someone is not there.
*I will **miss** you.*
3 to fail to keep, have, or attend something.
*She has **missed** school for three weeks now.*

mist
mists *noun*
a cloud of tiny water drops in the air.
misty *adjective*

mistake
mistakes *noun*
something that someone does wrong.

$$8 - 5 = 1$$

mistaken *adjective*

mix
mixes mixing mixed *verb*
to combine two or more things together.

mixture *noun*

moan
moans moaning moaned *verb*
to complain or to make a long, low, groaning noise because of pain or sadness.

moat
moats *noun*
a deep ditch filled with water that surrounds a castle.

mobile
adjective
able to move or be carried about.
*A **mobile** phone.*

mobile
mobiles *noun*
a decoration made of small objects hanging on strings.

model
models *noun*
1 a small copy of something larger.

*a **model** of an aeroplane*
model *adjective*
2 a person who demonstrates clothes or other things that are for sale.

*a fashion **model***
3 a person who poses for photographs or for an artist.

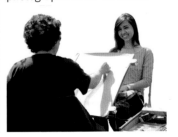

modern
adjective
of the present time.
*A **modern** house.*

modest
adjective
not boasting about your talents
and actions.
*He was too **modest** to say he
had won the first prize.*

moist
adjective
slightly wet.
moisture *noun*

mole
moles *noun*
1 a small, furry mammal that
lives in underground tunnels.
Moles eat worms and insects
and they are almost blind.

2 a small, dark patch
on your skin.

moment
moments *noun*
a short time.
*I'll be back in a **moment**.*

money
noun
the coins
and notes
used to
buy things.

mongrel
mongrels *noun*
a dog that
is a mixture
of more than
one breed.

monk
monks *noun*
a man who lives
in a religious
community.

*Buddhist
monk*

■ say **munk**

monkey
monkeys *noun*
a furry mammal that usually
lives in hot regions. Most
monkeys live in trees and eat
fruit, although some eat small
insects and mammals. There
are many different species
of monkey.

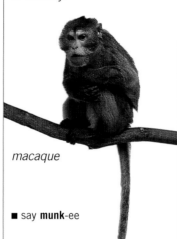

macaque

■ say **munk**-ee

monster
monsters *noun*
a fierce, frightening creature
from myths and fairy tales.

month
months *noun*
a period of between
28 and 31 days. A year
is divided into 12 months.

mood
moods *noun*
a way you feel
at a particular time.
*The sunny day put us all
in a good **mood**.*

moon
moons *noun*
a ball-shaped natural satellite
made of rock that revolves
around a planet (see **universe**
on page 229).

mop
mops *noun*
a tool for cleaning
floors, used with
water and
a bucket.

more
adjective
greater in number
or quantity.
■ opposite **less**

morning
mornings *noun*
the early part of the day,
ending at noon.
*School starts at 8.30 in
the **morning**.*

mosaic
mosaics *noun*
a picture or pattern
made of small squares
of coloured stone.

■ say mo-**zay**-ik

mosque
mosques *noun*
a building where Muslims
go to pray.
■ say **mosk**

mosquito
mosquitoes or **mosquitos**
noun
a small, flying insect found
in hot, wet regions. Female
mosquitoes bite and feed
on the blood of people and
animals, and can infect them
with serious illnesses, such
as malaria.

■ say moss-**kee**-toe

most
adjective
greatest in number
or quantity.
■ opposite **least**

motel
motels *noun*
a hotel specially built
for motorists.

moth
moths *noun*
a flying insect with wings
covered in fine scales. Moths
belong to the same animal
group as butterflies, but they
usually fly at night.

*pine emperor **moth***

mother
mothers *noun*
a female parent.

motion
motions *noun*
movement.
*The rocking **motion** of the boat
made me feel sick.*

a b c d e f g h i j k l m n o p q r s t u v w x y z

A B C D E F G H I J K L M N O P Q R S T U V W X Y Z

motor
motors *noun*
a machine that supplies power to objects to move them or make them work.

motorbike
motorbikes *noun*
a two-wheeled vehicle that is powered by a motor.

motorist
motorists *noun*
a person who drives a car regularly.

motorway
motorways *noun*
a road that is specially designed for cars to travel along quickly.

mountain
mountains *noun*
an area of land that rises up to a great height.
mountainous *adjective*

mourn
mourns mourning mourned
verb
to be sad because someone has died.
■ say **morn**

mouse
mice *noun*
1 a small, furry mammal from the rodent family. Mice have large front teeth which they use to gnaw food. Mice mainly eat plants, but sometimes they eat insects and other small animals too.

mouth
mouths *noun*
1 the opening in your face that you use for eating and talking.

mouth

2 the end of a river where it meets the sea.

move
moves moving moved *verb*
to go from one place to another, or to make something change position.
movement *noun*

moving
adjective
1 making you feel very sad.
*The film was very **moving**.*
2 able to move.
*Keep your fingers away from all **moving** parts.*

mow
mows mowing mowed *verb*
to cut grass.

mowing the lawn
■ rhymes with **go**

2 a control switch for a computer that can be used to move things around on a computer screen.

mud
noun
soft, wet earth.
muddy *adjective*

muddle
muddles *noun*
a confusing or untidy situation.
muddle *verb*

mug
mugs *noun*
a large cup without a saucer.

multiply
multiplies multiplying multiplied *verb*
to increase a number or an amount of something by adding it to itself several times.

9x5=45

*Nine **multiplied** by five equals forty-five.*
multiplication *noun*

munch
munches munching munched *verb*
to make a crunching noise while eating something.
munching some crisps

murder
murders murdering murdered *verb*
to kill someone deliberately.

murmur
murmurs *noun*
a quiet, whispering sound.
murmur *verb*

muscle
muscles *noun*
the fleshy parts of your body that help it to move.

*biceps **muscle***

■ say **mus**-ul
muscular *adjective*

museum
museums *noun*
a place where objects from other times and places, or of special interest, are displayed.
■ say mew-**zee**-um

mushroom
mushrooms *noun*
a common fungus that grows in warm, damp areas. Some mushrooms can be eaten, but others are poisonous.

field mushrooms

music
noun
the sound that people make when they sing, or play musical instruments.

musical instrument

musical instruments *noun*
an instrument for making music, usually played by hitting, blowing, or pulling or hitting strings.

treble clef | sharp sign | crotchet | minim | flat sign | crotchet | semibreve
key signature | time signature | quavers | semiquavers | bar line | repeat sign

Musical symbols

Wind instruments

didgeridoo
(Australian Aboriginal pipe)

reed

bassoon   keys   bell

ocarina

Pan-pipes

reed

Brass instruments

piston valve

flared bell

mouthpiece

carrying cord

coils of tubing

tuba

mouthpiece

nfir
(Moroccan trumpet)

String instruments

sound hole

fret   string   peg box

balalaika

fingerboard   tuning peg

tuning peg

bridge

sound box

soundboard

sitar   fiddle   bow

Percussion instruments

animal skin

castanets

steel bead

cabaca (rattle)   djeme (African drum)

mu-yus (Chinese temple blocks)

beaters

133

A
B
C
D
E
F
G
H
I
J
K
L
M
N
O
P
Q
R
S
T
U
V
W
X
Y
Z

musician
musicians *noun*
a person who sings, plays a musical instrument, or writes music.

- say myoo-**zish**-un

Nn

Muslim
Muslims *noun*
a person who believes in and follows the Islamic religion.
- also spelt **Moslem**

mussel
mussels *noun*
a type of shellfish, which is edible. Some mussels live in the sea, while others live in lakes and streams.

must
verb
to have to do something.
*I **must** post her birthday present today.*
- opposite **must not** or **mustn't**
- always used with another verb

mustard
noun
a spicy powder or sauce, made from mustard seeds and used to add flavour to food.

mutiny
mutinies *noun*
a rebellion by the crew of a ship or by soldiers in an army against the people in charge.
- say **myoo**-tin-ee
mutiny *verb*

mutter
mutters muttering muttered
verb
to talk in a low voice.
*I can't hear when you **mutter**.*

mutual
adjective
shared by two or more.

*We had a **mutual** friend.*
- say **myoo**-tyoo-al

muzzle
muzzles *noun*
1 the mouth and nose of an animal.
2 a cage or straps put over an animal's mouth to stop it biting.

muzzle

mystery
mysteries *noun*
an unusual and puzzling event.
*His disappearance is still a **mystery**.*
mysterious *adjective*

myth
myths *noun*
an ancient story that tries to explain how the world became the way it is.
mythical *adjective*

nail
nails *noun*
1 a long, thin, pointed metal spike that is hammered into pieces of wood to fasten them together.
nail *verb*

2 a hard substance that grows at the ends of your fingers and toes.

*finger**nail***

naked
adjective
not wearing any clothes.
- say **nay**-kid

name
names *noun*
a word that a person or thing is known by.
*My dog's **name** is Rover.*

nap
naps *noun*
a short sleep.

*He had a quick **nap** before supper.*

narrator
narrators *noun*
someone who tells a story, either by writing it or by reading it aloud.

narrate *verb*

narrow
adjective
with sides or edges that are very close together.

*The path was very **narrow**.*
- comparisons **narrower narrowest**
- opposite **wide**

nasty
adjective
unpleasant or cruel.
- comparisons **nastier nastiest**

nation
nations *noun*
a group of people who usually share the same history, language, and way of life, and live in the same country.
national *adjective*

natural
adjective
produced by nature.

natural sponge

nature
noun
all the things in the world that are not made by humans, such as the weather, animals, plants, and the sea.
■ say **nay**-cher

naughty
adjective
disobedient or badly behaved.

The **naughty** dog made a big mess.
■ say **nor**-tee
■ comparisons **naughtier naughtiest**

nautical
adjective
relating to ships, sailors, or sailing.

anemometer

map dividers

nautical instruments   sextant

navigate
navigates navigating navigated *verb*
to steer a boat, ship, or aircraft in a particular direction using special instruments and maps.

navigation *noun*

navy
noun
1 a country's warships and sailors.
2 a dark blue colour.

near
preposition
close to or not far from.

*three boats **near** each other*
■ opposite **far**
near *adjective*
near *adverb*

nearby
adverb
not far away.
*Do you live **nearby**?*

nearly
adverb
not quite, but almost.
*It's **nearly** bedtime.*

necessary
adjective
needed.
***Necessary** equipment for survival at sea.*
■ say **nes**-es-er-ee
■ opposite **unnecessary**
necessarily *adverb*

hand-held flare

parachute flare

neck
necks *noun*
the part of the body that supports your head and joins it to the rest of your body.

neck

necklace
necklaces *noun*
a chain or beads worn around the neck as a piece of jewellery.

nectar
noun
a sweet liquid that bees and some birds collect from flowers. Bees use nectar to make honey.

need
needs needing needed *verb*
to want something because you have to have it.
*Do you **need** anything from the shops?*

life jacket

needle
needles *noun*
1 a small, thin piece of pointed steel.

*sewing **needle***
2 a plastic or metal stick used for knitting.

3 a thin, pointed leaf of some plants, such as pine trees.
4 a part that points on a dial.
*A compass **needle**.*

negative
adjective
1 saying or meaning no.
*A **negative** answer.*
2 smaller than zero.
*A **negative** number.*
■ opposite **positive**

neglect
neglects neglecting neglected *verb*
to pay too little or no attention to someone or something.

He **neglected** the house plant.
neglect *noun*

negotiate
negotiates negotiating negotiated *verb*
to discuss something in order to reach an agreement.
■ say neg-**oh**-she-ate
negotiation *noun*

neighbour
neighbours *noun*
someone who lives near you.
■ say **nay**-ber

neighbourhood
neighbourhoods *noun*
the people and the area where you live.
■ say **nay**-ber-hood

a b c d e f g h i j k l m n o p q r s t u v w x y z

nephew

nephews noun
the son of a person's brother, sister, brother-in-law, or sister-in-law.
■ say **nef**-few

nerve

nerves noun
1 a thin fibre that connects your brain to all parts of your body. Nerves carry messages to and from your brain so that you can feel and move.
2 courage.
*To lose your **nerve**.*

nerve

nervous

adjective
slightly worried or frightened about what is happening or going to happen.

*She was **nervous** about the test.*
nervously adverb

nest

nests noun
the home that a bird or animal builds out of leaves, grass, and other materials.

nest verb

squirrel's **nest**

net

nets noun
a material made of knotted threads, string, or rope. Nets are often used to catch fish.

nettle

nettles noun
a plant with stinging hairs on its stems and leaves. These hairs can cause a rash on your skin if you touch the plant.

network

networks noun
1 a system of connected lines, roads, people, computers, or organizations.

*plan of a rail **network***

2 a group of connected radio or television stations that can broadcast the same programmes.

neutral

adjective
1 not being on anyone's side.
*A **neutral** country.*
2 not very definite.
*Grey is a **neutral** colour.*
■ say **new**-trul

never

adverb
not ever.
*I've **never** been here before.*

new

adjective
1 recently made, or unused.

*She tried on a **new** T-shirt today.*
2 unfamiliar or recently changed.
*A **new** job.*
■ comparisons **newer newest**
■ opposite **old**

news

noun
information about recent events around the country or around the world.
*Have you heard the **news**?*

newspaper

newspapers noun
large sheets of paper, printed with pictures and news reports.

*daily **newspapers***

next

adjective
1 coming immediately after.
*The **next** day.*
2 nearest.
*It's in the **next** room.*
next adverb

nib

nibs noun
the point at the end of an ink pen where the ink comes out.

nib

nibble

nibbles nibbling nibbled verb
to eat by taking quick, small bites out of something.

nibbling some nuts
nibble noun

nice

adjective
1 pleasant or delightful.
*A **nice** day.*
2 kind.
*He is a **nice** person.*
■ comparisons **nicer nicest**

nickel

noun
a strong, silvery-white metal. Nickel is often used as a covering for metal objects because it doesn't rust easily.

nickel ore

nickname
nicknames *noun*
a shortened form of a name or an extra name that people may use instead of a person's proper name.
*She was so clever that she earned the **nickname** Brains.*

niece
nieces *noun*
the daughter of a person's brother, sister, brother-in-law, or sister-in-law.
■ say **neess**

night
nights *noun*
the time between sunset and sunrise, when the sky is dark.

■ opposite **day**

nightmare
nightmares *noun*
an unpleasant and frightening dream.

*The **nightmare** woke up the boy.*

nimble
adjective
able to move quickly and easily.
***Nimble** fingers.*

nitrogen
noun
a gas with no taste or smell. All living things contain nitrogen, and air is mainly made of nitrogen.
■ say **nite**-tro-jen

nobody
noun
no person.
***Nobody** came to the party.*

nocturnal
adjective
active at night.

*Bats are **nocturnal** animals.*

nod
nods nodding nodded *verb*
to move your head up and down.
nod *noun*

noise
noises *noun*
any kind of sound, especially a sound that is too loud or unpleasant.

*He was making a lot of **noise**.*

noisy
adjective
making loud sounds.
noisily *adverb*

non-fiction
noun
information that is written about real events, things, and people.
■ opposite **fiction**

nonsense
noun
words that are silly or do not make sense.

noodle
noodles *noun*
a type of pasta that is made in long, flat, narrow strips.

noon
noun
12 o'clock midday.

noose
nooses *noun*
a circle of rope with a sliding knot. The loop tightens when the rope is pulled.

normal
adjective
usual or ordinary.
*Come at the **normal** time.*
normally *adverb*

north
noun
one of the four main compass directions. North is to your right when you are facing the setting Sun.

north
west   east
south

northern *adjective*

nose
noses *noun*
the part of your face that you smell and breathe with through two openings called nostrils.

nose
nostril

note
notes *noun*
1 a short, written message to remind you of something, or a short letter.
2 a piece of paper money.

3 a single sound in a piece of music.

nothing
noun
1 not anything.
*There's **nothing** to worry about.*
2 zero.

notice
notices noticing noticed *verb*
to see or be aware of something and pay attention to it.

*He **noticed** that he had a mark on his sleeve.*
noticeable *adjective*

a b c d e f g h i j k l m n o p q r s t u v w x y z

A B C D E F G H I J K L M N O P Q R S T U V W X Y Z

notice
notices *noun*
1 a written or printed sign that provides information.

notices on a board
2 attention.
Take no notice of them.

noun
nouns *noun*
a word that is used as a name. A noun can name a person, a place, a thing, or an idea.

novel
novels *noun*
a fictional written story in book form.

nowhere
adverb
not in any place.

His dog was nowhere to be seen.

nozzle
nozzles *noun*
a spout fitted to the open end of a pipe or hose, through which water or other liquids are sprayed.

nozzle

nuclear energy
noun
energy that is released by splitting the centre, or nucleus, of particular atoms.
■ say **new-klee-er**

nude
adjective
with no clothes on.

nudge
nudges nudging nudged *verb*
to push or poke someone gently to draw their attention to something.

nudge *noun*

nugget
nuggets *noun*
a lump of something, usually used for minerals.

a gold nugget

nuisance
nuisances *noun*
an annoying person or thing.

The dog was being a nuisance.
■ say **new-sans**

numb
adjective
unable to feel anything.
His fingers were numb with cold.
■ say **num**

number
numbers *noun*
a figure used in counting that shows the quantity or total of something.

848 is a three-figure number.

numeral
numerals *noun*
a symbol that stands for a number.

VI is the Roman numeral for 6.

numerous
adjective
very many.
Too numerous to count.

nun
nuns *noun*
a woman who lives in a religious community.

nurse
nurses *noun*
a person who is trained to care for and treat sick people, usually in a hospital.

nurse *patient*

nursery
nurseries *noun*
1 a room or building where young children are looked after.

nut
nuts *noun*
1 a tree fruit that consists of a seed, or kernel, surrounded by a hard shell.

almond *kernel*
brazil nut *kernel*

2 a small piece of metal with a hole in it that is screwed onto a bolt.

bolt *nut*

nutmeg
nutmegs *noun*
the hard seed of the tropical, evergreen nutmeg tree. Nutmegs can be used as a spice in cooking.

nutrient
nutrients *noun*
a part of a food that gives living things what they need to be healthy or to grow.

2 a place where trees and plants are grown and sold.

Oo

oak

oaks *noun*
a large deciduous tree that has fruit called acorns. Oak wood is often used for making furniture (see **tree** on page 223).

oak leaf

oar

oars *noun*
a long pole with a wide, flat end used for rowing a boat.
■ say **or**

oasis

oases *noun*
a place in the desert where there is water and where plants and trees can grow.

■ say oh-**ay**-sis

oats

noun
a type of cereal grown on farms. Oats are used to make food and to feed cattle, horses, and other animals.

obey

obeys obeying obeyed *verb*
to do something that someone tells or orders you to do.

She taught the dog to **obey** *her commands.*
■ opposite **disobey**
obedient *adjective*

object

objects *noun*
anything you can see or touch that isn't alive.
■ say **ob**-jekt

object

objects objecting objected *verb*
to dislike or disagree with something.
He **objected** *to people dropping litter in the street.*
■ say ob-**jekt**

oblong

adjective
longer than it is wide, with sides nearly parallel.

an **oblong** *box*
oblong *noun*

observatory

observatories *noun*
a building from which people observe stars, the planets, and the weather, using powerful telescopes.

observe

observes observing observed *verb*
to watch something.
observation *noun*

obstacle

obstacles *noun*
a thing that blocks your way. *He had to jump over 10* **obstacles** *to win the race.*

obstinate

adjective
difficult to persuade.

She was very **obstinate** *and refused to tidy up her room.*
obstinately *adverb*

obstruct

obstructs obstructing obstructed *verb*
to block or to prevent something or someone from passing.

She **obstructed** *his path.*
obstruction *noun*

obvious

adjective
easy to see or understand.
■ say **ob**-vee-us
obviously *adverb*

occasion

occasions *noun*
1 a special event. *The park opening was a grand* **occasion**.
2 a time when something happens. *I have flown in an aeroplane on two* **occasions**.

occupation

occupations *noun*
the work that someone does to earn a living.

occupy

occupies occupying occupied *verb*
1 to keep someone busy. *Sport* **occupies** *my time for most of the weekend.*
2 to take up a space or live in a place. *The company* **occupied** *the top two floors of the building.*
3 to control a place by force. *The army* **occupied** *the city.*

occur

occurs occurring occurred *verb*
1 to happen or exist. *When did the problem* **occur**?
2 to come into your mind. *That never* **occurred** *to me.*

a b c d e f g h i j k l m n o p q r s t u v w x y z

A B C D E F G H I J K L M N O P Q R S T U V W X Y Z

ocean
oceans *noun*
a very large area of sea, usually separating continents.

octagon
octagons *noun*
a flat shape with eight straight sides (see **shape** on page 182).

octopus
octopuses or **octopi** *noun*
a sea animal that does not have a backbone. Octopuses have eight arms, which they use for catching crabs, shellfish, and fish. They have good eyesight and are thought to have the ability to learn things.

odd
adjective
1 strange or unusual.
*That's a very **odd** thing to do!*
■ comparisons **odder oddest**
2 not belonging to a pair or a set of things.

*wearing **odd** socks*
3 any number that cannot be divided exactly by two.
■ opposite **even**

odour
odours *noun*
a strong smell.

*The sour milk gave off a bad **odour**.*
■ say **oh**-der

offend
offends offending offended *verb*
1 to upset or annoy someone.
offensive *adjective*
2 to break a law.

offer
offers offering offered *verb*
to ask someone if they would like something, or if you can do something for them.

*He **offered** her some grapes.*
offer *noun*

office
offices *noun*
a place where people organize and run a business.

official
adjective
properly approved by someone in charge.
■ say o-**fish**-al
officially *adverb*

often
adverb
many times.
*I **often** go to school by bus.*

oil
oil
noun
1 a thick liquid that occurs naturally underground. Oil is used to make products such as fuel and plastics.
2 a greasy substance that is found in the seeds and fruits of some plants. This type of oil is often used for cooking.

oily *adjective*   sunflower **oil**

oil rig
oil rigs *noun*
a structure and machinery used for drilling into the ground in search of oil and gas. Some oil rigs are used at sea, while others are used on land.

oil slick
oil slicks *noun*
a patch of oil, usually spilt accidentally, that floats on the surface of the sea.

oil-tanker
oil-tankers *noun*
a ship that transports huge amounts of oil.

ointment
ointments *noun*
a substance that you put on your skin or on a wound to make it better.

old
adjective
1 having been in use for a long time.

*an **old** teddy bear*
■ opposite **new**
2 having existed for a long time.
■ opposite **young**
■ comparisons **older oldest**

olive
olives *noun*
a small, oval fruit that grows in countries near the Mediterranean Sea. Olives are eaten in salads and crushed to make olive oil.

Olympic Games
noun
a sporting competition for athletes from countries all over the world, held every four years.

omit
omits omitting omitted *verb*
to leave something out, or not to do something.
*His name was **omitted** from the list.*

onion
onions *noun*
a small, round root vegetable with a strong taste. Onions have a thin, papery skin with many layers inside.

only
adjective
without any others.
*He's the **only** person
wearing green.*

only
adverb
1 just.

*There were **only** a few beads
left in the box.*
2 no more than.
***Only** five of us went
to the park.*

open
adjective
1 not closed or shut, so
that people or things can
go in and out.

***open** car doors*
■ opposite **shut**
2 with plenty of space,
or not closed in.
***Open** fields.*

opera
operas *noun*
a musical play where
the words are sung instead
of spoken.

***opera** singer*

operate
**operates operating
operated** *verb*
1 to work a piece
of machinery.

*You must take care when
operating machinery.*
2 to carry out surgery
in a hospital.

operating *adjective*
operation *noun*

opinion
opinions *noun*
a person's belief or judgement
about something.
*Who is the best football
player, in your **opinion**?*

opponent
opponents *noun*
someone who is on the
opposite side in a fight
or competition.

*karate **opponents***

opportunity
opportunities *noun*
a chance, or a suitable time
to do something.
*He had the **opportunity** to go
to Europe for a year.*

oppose
**opposes opposing
opposed** *verb*
to argue or fight against
someone or something.
*They **opposed** the decision
to close the park.*
opposition *noun*

opposite
adjective
1 on the other side.

*They rode their horses in
opposite directions.*
2 completely different.
*Tall is the **opposite** of short.*
opposite *noun*

optician
opticians *noun*
a person whose job is to test
people's sight and to sell
spectacles and contact lenses.
■ say op-**tish**-un

optimistic
adjective
expecting or hoping that things
will go well.
***Optimistic** about the future.*
■ opposite **pessimistic**
optimism *noun*

option
options *noun*
a choice.
*You have several **options**: you
can travel by car, train,
or plane.*
optional *adjective*

orange
oranges *noun*
1 a colour made
by mixing red and
yellow together.

2 a juicy fruit with
a tough skin.

orang-utan
orang-utans *noun*
a large ape that lives in
tropical forests in Southeast
Asia. Orang-utans eat mainly
fruit, but also eat leaves, bark,
and birds' eggs. They live in
nests called platforms, which
they build in trees.

■ say or-**rang**-a-tan

orbit
orbits orbiting orbited *verb*
to move around a planet,
a moon, or the Sun in space.
*The Earth **orbits** the Sun.*
orbit *noun*

orchard
orchards *noun*
an area of land where fruit
trees are grown.

*pear **orchard***

a b c d e f g h i j k l m n o p q r s t u v w x y z

orchestra

orchestra
orchestras *noun*
a large group of musicians who play together.
■ say **or**-kes-tra

orchid
orchids *noun*
a type of plant with flowers that are an unusual shape.
■ say **or**-kid

order
orders *noun*
1 an instruction telling someone to do something.

He gave them orders to stop.
2 a request for something in a shop or restaurant.

3 a way that things are placed or arranged.
Alphabetical order.
4 a peaceful, lawful state.
Law and order.
order *verb*

ordinary
adjective
not different or unusual in any way.

The plain cake on the left looked ordinary next to the other one.

organ
organs *noun*
1 a musical instrument with a keyboard and large air pipes. The pipes make a noise when air is forced into them.
2 a part inside your body that does a particular job. Your heart is an organ.

organic
adjective
food grown without using chemicals.

organism
organisms *noun*
any living animal or plant.

organization
organizations *noun*
a group of people with common aims or business.

organize
organizes organizing
organized *verb*
to arrange or plan something.

organizing work into folders
organization *noun*

origin
origins *noun*
the beginning of something, or where something or someone comes from.
The pot was of Roman origin.
■ say **o**-rij-in

original
adjective
earliest or first.
An original design.
■ say or-**rij**-in-nal

ornament
ornaments *noun*
an object that is used as a decoration.

orphan
orphans *noun*
someone whose parents have died.
■ say **or**-fan

ostrich
ostriches *noun*
a tall bird from Africa that can run very fast, but cannot fly. Ostriches live in dry, open countryside and eat plants, fruit, insects, and small animals.

other
adjective
the remaining one, usually of two.

She tried the other hat on.

ought
verb
to do something because it is necessary or should be done.
You ought to be in bed.
■ say ort
■ always used with another verb

out

out
adverb
1 away from a place or not in a place.

The bird pulled the worm out with its beak.
2 into view.
The Sun came out from behind the cloud.
■ opposite **in**
3 no longer lit.
Blow the candle out.

outcome
outcomes *noun*
the result of something.
What was the outcome of the match?

outdoors
adverb
not inside a building.
Shall we eat outdoors today?
■ opposite **indoors**

outfit
outfits *noun*
a set of clothes worn for a particular occasion.

outgrow
outgrows outgrowing
outgrew outgrown *verb*
to grow too big for something.
He had outgrown his clothes.

outline
outlines *noun*
a line that shows the shape of something.

outline of a leaf

outside
outsides *noun*
a part of something that faces out.
They painted the outside of the house green.
outside *adverb*

oval
ovals *noun*
a flat, round shape
like a zero.
oval *adjective*

oven
ovens *noun*
a space for cooking food,
heating, or drying things,
usually inside a stove.

over

over
preposition
above or across.
*She threw the ball **over**
the wall.*

overboard
adverb
over the side of a ship or boat.

*The fisherman cast his
net **overboard**.*

overgrown
adjective
covered in plants that have
been left to grow wild.
*An **overgrown** garden.*

overhear
**overhears overhearing
overheard** *verb*
to hear people talking about
things accidently.

overlap
**overlaps overlapping
overlapped** *verb*
to cover the edge
of something.
*Fish scales **overlap** each other.*

overtake
**overtakes overtaking
overtaken overtook** *verb*
to catch up with and pass by.
*The car **overtook** the lorry.*

owe
owes owing owed *verb*
to have to pay back money
or something else you
have borrowed.
*You **owe** me £5.*

owl

owls *noun*
a nocturnal
bird that
hunts for
mice, and other
small animals.
Owls have good
hearing and can see well in the
dark. They can turn their heads
around to see behind them.

own
owns owning owned *verb*
to have something that
belongs to you.

ox
oxen *noun*
a bull used for carrying or
pulling things.
*A zebu is a type of **ox**.*

oxygen
noun
a gas found in air and water.
You cannot see, smell, or
taste oxygen. All living things
need oxygen in order to live.
■ say **ox**-i-jen

oyster
oysters *noun*
a shellfish that lives in
shallow water. Oysters feed
on tiny bits of food that they
filter through the edge of
their shells.

ozone layer
noun
a layer of ozone gas in Earth's
atmosphere that protects
Earth from the more harmful
rays of the Sun.

pack
**packs packing
packed** *verb*
to put things
into a suitcase,
box, or other
container.

■ opposite **unpack**
2 to fit in as much as possible.
*The hall was **packed**
with people.*

pack
packs *noun*
1 a bundle that you carry.
2 a group of similar animals
or objects.
***Pack** of cards.*

package
packages *noun*
a wrapped parcel or bundle.

pad
pads *noun*
1 a pile of sheets of paper
joined at one end.
2 a thick piece of soft material.
3 the soft, fleshy parts on
an animal's paw.
4 a place where helicopters
land and take off.

paddle
paddles *noun*
a pole with a flat blade at
one or both ends. You hold
the paddle and use it to move
a boat or canoe through water
(see **boat** on page 31).

paddle
**paddles paddling
paddled** *verb*
1 to move a boat through water
using a paddle.

2 to walk around in
shallow water.

paddock
paddocks *noun*
a fenced area of grass, often
where animals are kept.

padlock
padlocks *noun*
a type of portable
lock often used
on gates.

page
pages *noun*
one side of a single piece of
paper forming part of a book,
newspaper, or magazine.

a b c d e f g h i j k l m n o p q r s t u v w x y z

paid
from the verb **to pay**
I **paid** *for the cinema tickets.*

pail
pails *noun*
a bucket, usually made of wood or metal.

pain
pains *noun*
suffering caused by an injury, disease, or sadness.
painful *adjective*

paint
paints *noun*
a coloured liquid used for decorating or for making pictures.

*paint*brush

paint
paints painting painted *verb*
to cover a surface with colour, either for decoration or to create a picture.

painting
paintings *noun*
a painted picture.

pair
pairs *noun*
a set of two things that match each other, or belong together.
A **pair** *of socks.*

palace
palaces *noun*
a large, grand home belonging to an important person.

pale
adjective
of faint colour, almost white.
He painted the hall **pale** *blue.*
■ comparisons **paler palest**

palm
palms *noun*
1 the flat, middle part on the inside of your hand.

2 a tree without branches that grows in hot regions. Palms have long leaves that grow from the top of the trunk (see **tree** on page 223).

pan
pans *noun*
a metal container with a handle, used for cooking.

pancake
pancakes *noun*
a flat, fried cake made of eggs, flour, and milk.

panda
pandas *noun*
a large, bear-like mammal that lives in the mountain forests of China. Pandas mainly eat bamboo shoots, but sometimes eat other plants and small animals.

panic
panics panicking panicked *verb*
to lose control suddenly because you are frightened or do not know what to do.
The man on the bike **panicked** *when he saw the dog.*
panic *noun*

pant
pants panting panted *verb*
to breathe quickly through your mouth because you are hot or out of breath.

panther
panthers *noun*
a black leopard.

pantomime
pantomimes *noun*
a traditional children's play with music, songs, and dancing.

paper
papers *noun*
a material made from wood, and mainly used for writing, printing, and drawing on.

parachute
parachutes *noun*
an apparatus made of material, which helps people and objects fall to the ground safely from an aircraft.

■ say **pa**-ra-shoot

parade
parades *noun*
a procession of people, animals, or vehicles, either for display or inspection.

paragraph
paragraphs *noun*
a section in a piece of writing. Paragraphs start on a new line.

parallel
adjective
being side by side and at the same distance from each other.

parallel lines

paralyse
paralyses paralysing paralysed *verb*
to be unable to move a part of the body because of an injury or disease.
paralysis *noun*

parcel
parcels *noun*
an object wrapped up with paper.

parent
parents *noun*
a father or mother.

park
parks *noun*
an area of grass and trees, which the public may use.

park
parks parking parked *verb*
to drive a vehicle into a position where it can be left.

parliament
parliaments *noun*
a group of people who have been elected to govern and make the laws of their nation.
■ say **par**-li-ment

parrot
parrots *noun*
a large bird that lives in tropical forests and eats fruit and seeds. Parrots are often kept as pets. In the wild, parrots live in large flocks.

part
parts *noun*
1 a piece of something.

*The **parts** of an electric guitar.*
2 a role in a play.

*She played the **part** of the queen in the play.*

particular
adjective
1 a specific one.
*Which **particular** one do you mean?*
2 special, or careful.
*Take **particular** care of that!*

partner
partners *noun*
one of a pair of people who do something together, such as dancing or playing a game.
*A business **partner**.*

party
parties *noun*
1 a group of people invited to celebrate a special occasion.
2 an organized group of people who have the same political beliefs.

pass
passes passing passed *verb*
1 to go by someone or something.
2 to give something to someone with your hand.

*She **passed** the ball to her teammate.*
3 to be successful in an examination or test.

passenger
passengers *noun*
someone travelling in or on a vehicle that is controlled by another person.

*motorcycle **passenger***

passport
passports *noun*
an official certificate that you need for travelling to other countries.

past
noun
the time before now.
past *adjective*

past
adverb
by or beyond.
*He walked **past** the shop.*

pasta
noun
an Italian food, usually made from wheat flour and water.

*different shapes of **pasta***

paste
pastes *noun*
1 a soft, moist, or sticky substance.
2 a type of glue made of flour and water.

pasteurize
pasteurizes pasteurizing pasteurized *verb*
to heat and then cool something to kill the bacteria in it. Milk is usually pasteurized.
■ say **past**-yoor-ize

pastry
pastries *noun*
a dough made of flour, water, and fat that is baked to make small cakes called pastries, or cases for pies and tarts.

cheese pastries

pasture
pastures *noun*
a field of grass where animals graze.

patch
patches *noun*
1 a small piece of material that is placed over a hole to repair it.

patch
2 a small area of something.
*A **patch** of grass.*

path
paths *noun*
a narrow track for walking along, or a route.

patient
adjective
able to wait calmly.
■ say **pay**-shunt
patience *noun*

patient
patients *noun*
a person being treated by a doctor, nurse, or dentist.

patrol
patrols patrolling patrolled *verb*
to guard a place by moving around it and checking it regularly.
patrol *noun*

A B C D E F G H I J K L M N O P Q R S T U V W X Y Z

pattern
patterns *noun*

1 a decorative shape or design.

2 a guide for making things, such as toys or clothes.

patterned *adjective*

teddy bear **pattern**

pause
pauses pausing paused *verb*
to stop what you are doing for a short time.
- say **porz**
pause *noun*

pavement
pavements *noun*
a hard path for pedestrians, usually at the side of a road.

paw
paws *noun*
a soft, padded animal foot with claws or nails.

cat's **paw**

pay
pays paying paid *verb*
to give money in return for something.
payment *noun*

pea
peas *noun*
a small, round, sweet-tasting vegetable that grows in a pod.

pea pod

peace
noun
a period of quietness and calm.
peaceful *adjective*

peach
peaches *noun*
a round fruit with a velvety skin and a large stone inside.

peacock
peacocks *noun*
a large bird that is also called a peafowl. Peacocks live in forests in Africa and India and eat insects, grains, plants, and small animals. The males are known for their beautiful tail-feathers (see **bird** on page 28).

peak
peaks *noun*
the pointed top of a mountain.

peanut
peanuts *noun*
a small, edible nut that grows in pods under the ground.

pear
pears *noun*
a pale green or brown fruit with a thin skin, pale, juicy flesh, and pips.

- rhymes with **hair**

pearl
pearls *noun*
a smooth, shiny, rounded object that grows inside an oyster. Pearls are often used for making jewellery.

pearl

- say **purl**

pebble
pebbles *noun*
a small, smooth, rounded stone.

peck
pecks pecking pecked *verb*
to bite or strike with a beak.

The bird **pecked** *at the food.*

peculiar
adjective
strange, odd, or queer.

pedal
pedals *noun*
a lever that you work with your foot to move or control something (see **transport** on page 221).

pedestrian
pedestrians *noun*
a person travelling on foot.

peel
peels peeling peeled *verb*
to remove or strip something off.

peeling a banana

peep
peeps peeping peeped *verb*
to look quickly and secretly at something or someone.

peer
peers peering peered *verb*
to look closely at something or someone.

peg
pegs *noun*
a wooden or plastic object used to hang clothes on a washing-line.

pelican
pelicans *noun*
a large bird that lives in or near water in warm regions. It has a pouch beneath its bill, which it uses to catch and hold fish.

pen
pens *noun*
1 a tool filled with ink, used for writing.

2 a small area with a fence, for keeping animals in. *A pig pen.*

penalty
penalties *noun*
a fine or a punishment for breaking a law or rule, or for breaking a rule during a sports game.
The penalty for cheating in an exam is severe.

pencil
pencils *noun*
a tool with grey or coloured graphite inside, used for writing and drawing.

penguin
penguins *noun*
a large, fish-eating seabird found in the cold seas of the southern hemisphere. Penguins cannot fly, but are good underwater swimmers (see **bird** on page 28).

penknife
penknives *noun*
a small knife that folds into a case.

pentagon
pentagons *noun*
a flat shape with five sides of equal length (see **shape** on page 182).

people
noun
1 human beings in general.
2 members of a particular race or nation.

pepper
peppers *noun*
1 the dried berries of the pepper plant, used to flavour foods.

ground pepper

peppercorns

2 a bright green, yellow, orange, or red vegetable (see **vegetable** on page 233).

per cent
noun
a fraction of a whole written as part of 100. 50 per cent means 50 parts of 100. Per cent is also written as percentage. The sign for per cent is %.

27%

27% (per cent) of 100 is 27.

perch
perches perching perched
verb
to sit on a branch or other place like a bird.

perching on a branch
perch *noun*

perfect
adjective
having nothing wrong, or just right.
perfectly *adverb*

perform
performs performing performed *verb*
to put on a show for other people.

The band performed at the concert.
performance *noun*

perfume
perfumes *noun*
1 a sweet-smelling liquid that you put on your skin.

2 any sweet or pleasant smell.

perhaps
adverb
maybe or possibly.

perimeter
perimeters *noun*
the outer edge or boundary of something.
■ say per-**rim**-it-ter

period
periods *noun*
a length or portion of time.
A fortnight is a period of two weeks.

permanent
adjective
lasting a long time or for ever.
A permanent job.
■ opposite **temporary**

permission
noun
the act of allowing someone to do something.

She put her hand up to ask for permission to leave the room.
permit *verb*

perpendicular
adjective
crossing at or forming a right angle.
■ say pur-pen-**dik**-yoo-lar

person
persons or **people** *noun*
a human being.

personal
adjective
belonging to, or meant for one person.

personal belongings

personality
personalities *noun*
1 your character or the sort of person you are.
My sister has a friendly personality.
2 someone famous.
A sports personality.

persuade
persuades persuading persuaded *verb*
to make someone believe or do something by giving good reasons.
She persuaded me to go skiing with her.
persuasion *noun*
■ say pur-**swade**

pest
pests *noun*
an insect or animal that is harmful or a nuisance.

Colorado beetle

pet

pets *noun*
a tame animal that is kept because it is loved rather than because it is useful. Pets are often kept in the home.

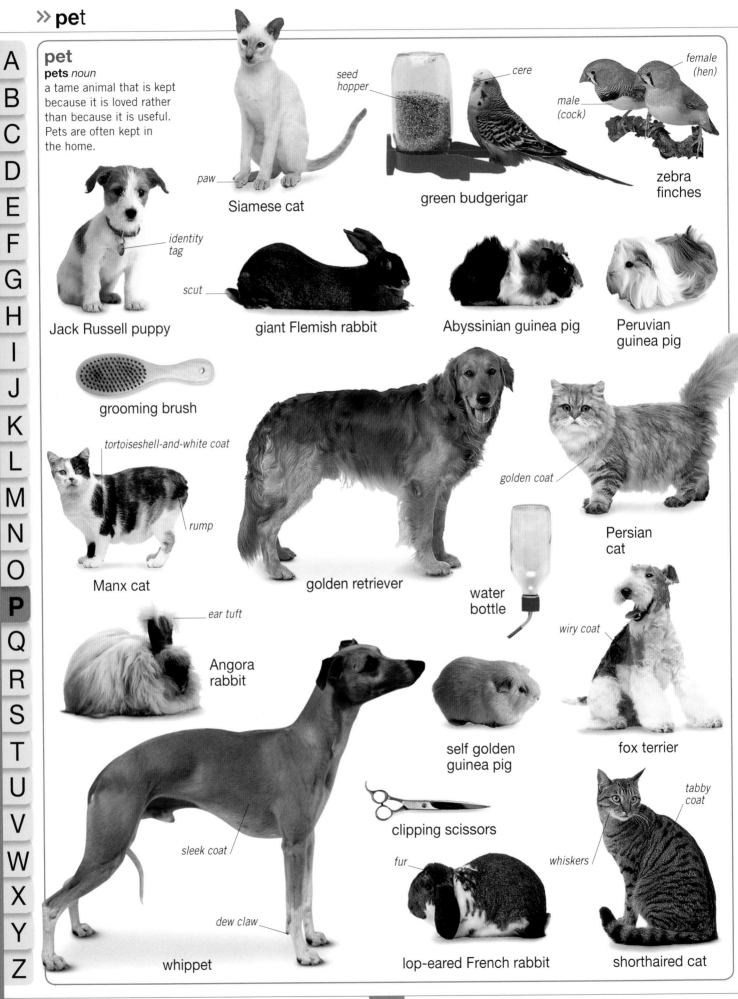

paw

Siamese cat

seed hopper

cere

green budgerigar

male (cock)

female (hen)

zebra finches

identity tag

Jack Russell puppy

scut

giant Flemish rabbit

Abyssinian guinea pig

Peruvian guinea pig

grooming brush

tortoiseshell-and-white coat

rump

Manx cat

golden retriever

golden coat

Persian cat

water bottle

wiry coat

ear tuft

Angora rabbit

self golden guinea pig

fox terrier

clipping scissors

sleek coat

dew claw

whippet

fur

lop-eared French rabbit

whiskers

tabby coat

shorthaired cat

petal

petals *noun*
the coloured outer parts of a flower that are not green (see **plant** on page 151).

petrol

noun
a liquid fuel made from oil, used for powering vehicles.

photocopy

photocopies *noun*
an exact copy of words or pictures, made by a machine.

photocopy *verb*

photograph

photographs *noun*
a picture made using a camera. Photograph can be shortened to photo.

taking a **photograph**

photographer

photographers *noun*
a person who takes photographs.

physical

adjective
to do with the body. ***Physical*** *exercise.*
■ say **fiz**-i-kal

pianist

pianists *noun*
a person who plays the piano.
■ say **pee**-an-ist

piano

pianos *noun*
a large, stringed, musical instrument with black and white keys. Different musical notes are produced by pressing the keys.

grand ***piano***

pick

picks picking picked *verb*
1 to choose something.

She asked him to **pick** *a card.*
2 to remove a flower, fruit, or leaf from a plant.

picking *flowers*

picnic

picnics *noun*
a meal that is eaten in the open air, away from home.

picnic *verb*

picture

pictures *noun*
an image of something, such as a painting or a photograph.

pie

pies *noun*
a pastry case filled with vegetables, meat, fish, or fruit and baked in an oven.

apple ***pie***

piece

pieces *noun*
a bit or a part of something.

a ***piece*** *of cheese*

pier

piers *noun*
a long platform built out into the sea for people to walk along or to tie boats to.

pig

pigs *noun*
an animal with a blunt snout and a curly tail, which is kept on farms to provide meat, such as pork, ham, and bacon.

pigeon

pigeons *noun*
a bird that is common in the town and countryside. Pigeons mainly eat fruit, such as berries, and seeds. Some pigeons can be trained to deliver messages.

■ say **pij**-in

pigment

pigments *noun*
1 a coloured powder that is mixed with other substances to make paint.

windsor red   cadmium yellow

2 the substance that gives colouring to the skin of animals and vegetables.

pile

piles *noun*
a group of things resting or lying one on top of the other.

pill

pills *noun*
a small piece of medicine that is swallowed whole.

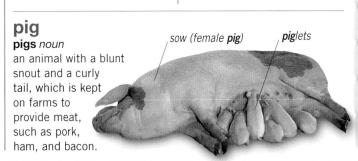

sow (female ***pig****)*   *piglets*

a b c d e f g h i j k l m n o p q r s t u v w x y z

A B C D E F G H I J K L M N O P Q R S T U V W X Y Z

pillow
pillows *noun*
a soft pad for resting your head on in bed.

pilot
pilots *noun*
a person who controls and flies an aircraft.

pin
pins *noun*
a small piece of metal with a sharp point at one end, used to fasten pieces of cloth together.

pin cushion

pinch
pinches pinching pinched *verb*
to squeeze someone's skin between your finger and thumb.

pine
pines *noun*
an evergreen tree that has needle-shaped leaves and produces cones.

pineapple
pineapples *noun*
a tropical fruit with a tough, scaly skin and a sprout of spiky, green leaves at the top (see **fruit** on page 85).

pink
noun
a colour made by mixing red and white together.

pipe
pipes *noun*
a tube through which liquids and gases can flow.

*pipe*line

pirate
pirates *noun*
someone who attacks and robs ships or boats at sea.

pit
pits *noun*
1 a deep hole in the ground.
2 a coal mine.

pitch
pitches *noun*
1 an area where some games or sports are played.
We went to the cricket **pitch** *to watch the game.*
2 how high or low a musical note, a musical instrument, or a human voice is.

pitiful
adjective
making you feel sad or full of pity.
A **pitiful** *sight.*

pity
noun
a feeling of sadness for someone because they are unhappy or in pain.
pity *verb*

pizza
pizzas *noun*
a round, flat piece of dough with tomato, cheese, and other foods on top, which is baked in an oven.

■ say **peet**-sa

place
places *noun*
1 a particular area.
2 a position in a competition or race.

They won the first, second, and third **places** *in the race.*

place
places placing placed *verb*
to put something in a position.
He **placed** *the vase in the centre of the table.*

plain
adjective
1 ordinary, or not fancy.
Her dress was very **plain**.
2 understandable or clear.
His meaning was **plain**.

plain
plains *noun*
a large area of flat land.

plan
plans *noun*
a map or drawing of an area, such as a room, building, or town.

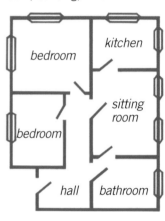

a **plan** *of a flat*

plan
plans planning planned *verb*
to decide how you are going to do something.
plan *noun*

planet
planets *noun*
one of the huge spheres of rock and gas that revolve around the Sun. The eight planets in our Solar System are Mercury, Venus, Earth, Mars, Jupiter, Saturn, Uranus, and Neptune (see **universe** on page 229).

plant
plants planting planted *verb*
to put a seed, bulb, or plant into the soil so that it will grow.

The girl **planted** *a tree.*

plant

plants *noun*
a living thing that cannot move around like animals do, and that makes its own food. Some plants grow in the ground, while others grow in water. Plants usually have a stem, leaves, flowers, and roots.

poppy seedheads

capsule

frond

pinna

fern

spine (leaf)

stigma

stamen

style

petal

flower head

spike

bract

thistle

sepal

flower bud

pedicel (flower stalk)

stem

leaf

magnified pollen grains

bulb

root

tulip

frond

hibiscus

rock

green seaweed

bract

calla lily

pitcher

flower

stalk

stalk

capsule

stalk

moss

stalk

lily pad

cactus

waterlily

pitcher **plant**

plaster
plasters *noun*
1 a powder mixed with water that is spread on walls and ceilings to make them smooth.
2 a small piece of sticky material that is put over a wound to keep it clean.

plastic
plastics *noun*
a light, manufactured material made from chemicals. Many types of plastic can be heated up and moulded into different shapes and products.

plastic duck

plate
plates *noun*
a flat dish that is used for serving food on.

dinner
plate

plateau
plateaus or **plateaux** *noun*
a high, wide, flat area of ground.
■ say **plat**-oh

platform
platforms *noun*
1 the flat, raised area at a station where passengers get on and off trains.

2 a flat, raised area in a hall where speakers or performers stand so they can be seen.

platypus
platypuses or **platypi** *noun*
an Australian mammal with a bill like a duck's, webbed feet, and a long, flat tail. Platypuses live in water and, unusually for a mammal, lay eggs. They eat plants, worms, insects, and water animals.
■ say **plat**-ee-pus

play
plays playing played
verb
1 to take part in a game, usually with other people.

playing football
2 to make music on a musical instrument.

playing the violin
3 to act a part.
She played the fairy.
play *noun*

pleasant
adjective
enjoyable or well-liked.
A pleasant evening.
■ opposite **unpleasant**

please
interjection
a word used when you ask for something politely.

pleasure
pleasures *noun*
enjoyment or satisfaction.
■ say **plezh**-er

pleat
pleats *noun*
a fold that is pressed or sewn into cloth.

pleat
pleat *verb*

plenty
noun
a large amount of something.
Do you want some sweets? I've got plenty.
plentiful *adjective*

plot
plots plotting plotted *verb*
to make a secret plan.
The thieves plotted to rob the bank.
plot *noun*

plot
plots *noun*
1 the story of a book, play, or film.
The book has a complicated plot.
2 a small piece of ground.

plough
ploughs *noun*
a farm tool that has large blades for cutting and turning the soil. Ploughs are used to prepare the soil for planting crops and are pulled by a tractor or an animal.

plough

■ rhymes with **now**
plough *verb*

plug
plugs *noun*
1 a circular piece of plastic or other material used to keep water in a bath or sink.
2 an electrical device that connects the wire from a piece of electrical equipment to a source of electricity.

plum
plums *noun*
a fruit that grows on trees, and has a smooth, thin skin and soft, juicy flesh.

plumber
plumbers *noun*
a person who fits water and heating pipes into buildings and repairs them when they go wrong.

plunge
plunges plunging
plunged verb
to fall or dive very quickly.

*He **plunged** into the river.*
plunge noun

plural
plurals noun
a word used to describe two or more things or people.
*The **plural** of baby is babies.*

plus
preposition
added to.
*4 **plus** 2 equals 6.*
■ opposite **minus**

plus
pluses noun
a symbol in mathematics that means add.

pocket
pockets noun
a small pouch or fold sewn into clothing or a bag where you can put your belongings.

pocket

pod
pods noun
a long seed-case that holds the seeds of some plants.

*bean **pod***

poem
poems noun
a piece of writing, set out in lines which sometimes rhyme. Poems describe things in a thoughtful and imaginative way.

poet
poets noun
a person who writes poetry.

poetry
noun
a general name for poems.

point
points noun
1 the sharp end of an object.

*Each star has six **points**.*
2 a score in a game or competition.
*How many **points** did you get?*
3 the main aim or purpose.
*What's the **point** of this story?*
4 the level, time, or place at which something happens.
*The freezing **point** of water is 0°C.*
5 a dot or speck.

point
points pointing pointed verb
to show where something is with your finger.

poison
poisons noun
a substance that can kill or harm animals or plants.

poison arrow frog

*A deadly **poison** can be made from this frog's skin.*
poisonous adjective

poke
pokes poking poked verb
to push something with a stick, your finger, or another pointed object.

*He **poked** the fire with a stick.*

polar bear
polar bears noun
a large mammal that lives in Arctic regions. Polar bears eat animals such as seals and fish. Their white fur camouflages them against the snow and ice where they live.

pole
poles noun
1 a long, rounded rod made from wood, metal, or plastic.

*a row of flag **poles***

police
noun
an organization that is responsible for keeping law and order and making sure that a country's laws are not broken.

polish
polishes polishing
polished verb
to rub something so that it shines.

polishing shoes

polish
polishes noun
a substance that is rubbed into something to make it shine.

*furniture **polish***

polite
adjective
well-mannered and pleasant to other people.
■ opposite **rude**
politely adverb

2 the most northern and southern end of an imaginary line, or axis, that passes through Earth's centre.

*North **Pole***

*South **Pole***

3 either end of a magnet.

a b c d e f g h i j k l m n o p q r s t u v w x y z

A B C D E F G H I J K L M N O P Q R S T U V W X Y Z

politics
noun
the work of government.
political adjective

pollen
noun
a fine, yellow powder found in the middle of flowers. Pollen is made by the male parts of a flower.

pollinate
pollinates pollinating pollinated verb
to transfer pollen from the male to the female parts of a plant so that a seed can grow.

*The bee **pollinated** the flower.*

pollute
pollutes polluting polluted verb
to make a thing or a place dirty, unclean, or harmful.
*Chemicals from the factory **polluted** the river.*
pollution noun

pond
ponds noun
an area of fresh water that is smaller than a lake.

*duck **pond***

pony
ponies noun
a small horse (see **horse** on page 102).

pool
pools noun
a small area of water, especially one that is made for people to swim in.

*swimming **pool***

poor
adjective
1 not having enough money to live on.
*The family was very **poor**.*
■ opposite **rich**
2 of low or bad quality.
*The house was in a **poor** condition.*
3 unfortunate.
*The **poor** child was soaking wet.*
poor noun

popcorn
noun
a snack made by heating grains from the maize plant until they burst open and puff up.

poppy
poppies noun
a wild flower with delicate petals. When the flowers die, they leave behind a round seed-head (see **plant** on page 151).

popular
adjective
liked by many people.

population
populations noun
all the people living in a district or country.

porch
porches noun
a shelter built around the entrance to a building.

porcupine
porcupines noun
a large rodent that is covered in lots of sharp spines called quills. A porcupine can raise the quills to protect itself from its enemies. Porcupines eat bark, buds, twigs, and leaves.

pork
noun
meat from a pig.

porpoise
porpoises noun
a sea mammal that belongs to the whale family. Porpoises eat shrimp, fish, squid, and other sea animals.

■ say **por**-pus

port
ports noun
a place on a coast or river, where ships load and unload.

portable
adjective
easily carried or moved about.

portable electronic reader

portion
portions noun
a part or share of something.

*a **portion** of fish pie*

portrait
portraits noun
a picture or photograph of a person, especially their face.

pose
poses posing posed verb
to arrange yourself or a thing in a particular position, especially for a painting or a photograph.
pose noun

position
positions noun
1 the way in which a person or thing is placed or arranged.
*A sitting **position**.*
2 a place or location.
*He found the **position** of his house on the map.*

positive
adjective
definite or certain.
■ opposite **negative**

possess
**possesses possessing
possessed** *verb*
to own or have something.
possession *noun*

possible
adjective
able to be done or happen.
*Is it **possible** to walk there?*
■ opposite **impossible**
possibly *adverb*

post
noun
1 the delivery of letters
and other mail, or
the letters themselves.
2 an upright pole of wood,
stone, or metal set in
the ground.

gate-**post**

3 a job or duty and the place
where it is done.

poster
posters *noun*
a large notice or picture that
is displayed on a wall as an
advert or for decoration.

post office
post offices *noun*
a place where you go to buy
stamps, and to send letters
and parcels.

postpone
**postpones postponing
postponed** *verb*
to put something off
until later.
*The game was **postponed**
because of the rain.*

posy
posies *noun*
a small
bunch of
flowers.

pot
pots *noun*
a container with high sides.

coffee
pot

potato
potatoes *noun*
a common root vegetable
that can be boiled, roasted,
fried, or baked.

pottery
noun
a general name
for containers and
ornaments made
from clay, then
baked in a kiln.
kitchen **pottery**

pouch
pouches *noun*
1 a small, open bag or sack
that is used for carrying things
like money.
2 a part of the body that is
shaped like a bag or pocket
(see **mammal** on page 124).

pounce
**pounces pouncing
pounced** *verb*
to spring forwards suddenly
and grab hold of something.

*The cat **pounced**
on the leaf.*

pour
pours pouring poured *verb*
to tip a container up so that
its contents flow out.

poverty
noun
the situation of not having
enough money to live on.
*The family lived in **poverty**.*

powder
noun
a mass of
very fine,
dry grains
of a
substance.

washing
powder

power
powers *noun*
1 the ability to do something.
2 the ability to control what
someone else does.
3 energy or force.

*Batteries provide
the **power** for this torch.*
■ rhymes with **our**

practical
adjective
1 sensible and useful.
*Gloves are very **practical**
in cold weather.*
■ opposite **impractical**
2 having practice at
doing something.
*You need **practical** experience
for this job.*

practise
**practises practising
practised** *verb*
to do something over and
over again in order to be
good at it.

practising the piano
practice *noun*

a
b
c
d
e
f
g
h
i
j
k
l
m
n
o
p
q
r
s
t
u
v
w
x
y
z

A B C D E F G H I J K L M N O P Q R S T U V W X Y Z

praise
praises praising praised *verb*
to tell someone that what they have done is very good.
praise *noun*

pray
prays praying prayed *verb*
to talk to a god, prophet, or saint.
prayer *noun*

precaution
precautions *noun*
care or action taken in advance to prevent something from happening.
*Locks are a **precaution** against theft.*
■ say pri-**kor**-shun

precious
adjective
very valuable or special to someone.

*The ring was very **precious**.*
■ say **presh**-us

precise
adjective
exact or accurate.

*Stopwatches measure the **precise** time.*
■ say pri-**sise**

predict
predicts predicting predicted *verb*
to say what is going to happen in the future.
prediction *noun*

preen
preens preening preened *verb*
to clean and arrange feathers with the beak. Birds preen themselves.

prefer
prefers preferring preferred *verb*
to like something or someone better than another.
*She pointed to the pair of skates she **preferred**.*
preferable *adjective*

pregnant
adjective
expecting a baby.
pregnancy *noun*

prehistoric
adjective
belonging to the time before any records were written.

prehistoric fossil

prejudice
prejudices *noun*
a strong feeling about something, which has been formed unfairly or before all the facts are known.
■ say **pre**-joo-dis

prepare
prepares preparing prepared *verb*
to make something or yourself ready.

preparing sandwiches for lunch

preposition
prepositions *noun*
a word that shows how one person or thing relates to another.
*The bird was **on** the chair **in** the garden.*

prescription
prescriptions *noun*
an order for medicine written by a doctor.

present
noun
1 the time now.
*The story takes place in the **present**.*
present *adjective*
2 a gift to someone.

■ say **prez**-ent

present
presents presenting presented *verb*
to award or give something to someone.
*The judge **presented** the rider with a cup.*
■ say pri-**zent**

preserve
preserves preserving preserved *verb*
1 to keep something the way it is.
2 to keep food so that it lasts.

*tomatoes **preserved** in a jar*

press
presses pressing pressed *verb*
to squeeze or push something down, often in order to flatten it.

*He **pressed** the mouse button.*

pretend
pretends pretending pretended *verb*
1 to try to make people believe something that isn't true.
2 to believe something for fun.

*She **pretended** to be a witch.*
pretence *noun*

pretty
adjective
nice to look at.
■ comparisons **prettier prettiest**

prevent
**prevents preventing
prevented** verb
to stop something
from happening.
*The barrier **prevented** anyone
from falling down the hole.*
prevention noun

previous
adjective
happening or existing before.
*The **previous** day.*
■ say **pree**-vee-us

prey
noun
creatures that are hunted and
eaten by other animals.

*The owl swooped
down on its **prey**.*
■ say **pray**
prey verb

price
prices noun
the amount of money needed
to buy something.

prickly
adjective
having many
little sharp
points
or needles.

*a **prickly** cactus*

■ comparisons **pricklier
pricky**
prick verb

priest
priests noun
a person who is trained
to lead religious services.

prince / princess
princes / princesses noun
a son or daughter of a king
or queen. The wife of a prince
is also a princess.
■ **prince** is male and **princess**
is female

principle
principles noun
a general rule, belief, or truth.
*Scientific **principles**.*

print
prints printing printed verb
1 to write the letters of words
separately, rather than joining
them up.
2 to put words, pictures,
or patterns onto paper,
using paint or ink,
and printing blocks.

***printing** a picture*
printed adjective

printer
noun
a machine that prints on
paper, usually linked to
a computer.

prison
prisons noun
a secure place in which
criminals are kept
as punishment.

private
adjective
belonging only to one person
or a few people, or not open
to the public.
*My diary is **private**.*
■ say **pry**-vit
privately adverb

prize
prizes noun
a reward for winning something.

*The **prize** was a silver cup.*

probable
adjective
likely to happen.
probably adverb

problem
problems noun
something that is difficult to
do or hard to understand.

process
processes noun
the method of making or
doing something.
■ say **proh**-sess

procession
processions noun
a line of people or vehicles
following each other.

*a **procession** of musicians*

prod
prods prodding prodded verb
to poke or push something,
often with something sharp.

produce
**produces producing
produced** verb
1 to make something happen.

*The magician **produced**
a rabbit out of his hat.*
2 to make, grow, manufacture,
or create something.
*The orange trees **produced**
a large crop of fruit this year.*
■ say pro-**juce**
product noun
production noun

produce
noun
things that
are grown
or made.

*farm
produce*
■ say **prod**-yoos

profession
professions noun
1 a job or occupation where
special knowledge of
a subject is needed.
2 all the people who do such
a job.
*The medical **profession**.*

professional
adjective
1 having to do with
a profession.
*He took **professional** advice.*
2 earning a living from
an occupation that is not
usually thought of as a job.
*A **professional** footballer.*

A B C D E F G H I J K L M N O P Q R S T U V W X Y Z

profile
profiles *noun*
the side view of a face or object.

profit
profits *noun*
the extra money made when something is sold for more than it cost to make or buy.
■ opposite **loss**
profitable *adjective*

program
programs *noun*
a set of instructions that tells a computer how to do something.

programme
programmes *noun*
1 a television or radio show.
2 a list of planned events.
3 a small book of information about a play or concert.

progress
noun
the process of moving forwards or improving.

*He made slow **progress** through the swamp.*
progress *verb*

prohibit
prohibits prohibiting prohibited *verb*
to ban, or to forbid someone to do something.

Littering is prohibited.

project
projects *noun*
a piece of work involving research and study of a particular subject.

*He is doing a science **project**.*
■ say pro-**jekt**

project
projects projecting projected *verb*
to stick out or throw outwards.
*The rock **projected** over the valley.*
■ say pro-**jekt**

promise
promises promising promised *verb*
to say, and mean that you will, or will not, do something.
promise *noun*

promotion
promotions *noun*
1 a campaign to improve the sale of a product or event by advertising it.

*He took part in the **promotion** of the new chicken restaurant.*
2 a change to a more important job or position.
promote *verb*

prompt
prompts prompting prompted *verb*
to encourage someone to do or say something.

prompt
adjective
on time, or without delay.

pronoun
pronouns *noun*
a word such as "he" or "she" that is used in a sentence to replace a noun.
*Jane was ill today, so **she** didn't go to school.*

pronunciation
pronunciations *noun*
the way a word is said.
■ say pro-nun-see-**ay**-shun
pronounce *verb*

proof
noun
a thing or happening that shows something is true.

*The passport was **proof** of his identity.*

propeller
propellers *noun*
a device with revolving blades. Propellers spin round to move a boat through the water, or to power an aeroplane through the air (see **boat** on page 31 and **transport** on page 221).

proper
adjective
suitable and correct.

*This is the **proper** way to hit a golf ball so that it rolls along the ground.*
properly *adverb*

property
noun
1 the things that belong to a person.
2 a general name for the buildings and land owned by someone.

prosecute
prosecutes prosecuting prosecuted *verb*
to accuse someone of a crime in a law court.
■ say **pros**-i-kyoot
prosecution *noun*

protect
protects protecting protected *verb*
to keep someone or something from being harmed.

*The gloves **protect** the scientist from harmful chemicals.*
protection *noun*

protest
protests protesting
protested *verb*
to say very clearly that you disagree with something.

*They **protested** against the building of a new road.*
■ say pro-**test**
protest *noun*

proud
adjective
feeling very pleased or satisfied.

*She was **proud** to be graduating.*
■ say **prowd**
proudly *adverb*

prove
proves proving proved *verb*
to show that something is true.
■ say **proov**

proverb
proverbs *noun*
a short common saying that comments on life.
*"Many hands make light work" is a **proverb**.*

provide
provides providing provided *verb*
to supply something that is useful or needed.

*The runners were **provided** with drinks along the route.*

prowl
prowls prowling
prowled *verb*
to move around quietly while searching for something.

*The lion **prowled** through the grass.*

public
adjective
open to everybody.

publish
publishes publishing
published *verb*
to produce and print a book, newspaper, or magazine.

puddle
puddles *noun*
a shallow pool of rain-water or other liquid on the ground.

puff
puffs *noun*
a small, sudden gust of smoke, air, or breath.

*a **puff** of smoke*

pull
pulls pulling pulled *verb*
to move something with force towards you or in the same direction as you are going.

pulling on a rope

pulley
pulleys *noun*
a device made of a wheel with a rope or a chain round it that is used for lifting heavy objects.

pulp
noun
the soft, inside part of a plant, particularly fruits (see **fruit** on page 85).

pulse
pulses *noun*
the regular sound of your blood as the heart pumps it through your body.

*feeling her **pulse***

pump
pumps pumping
pumped *verb*
to fill or inflate something by forcing air or liquids into it.

pumping up a balloon

pump
pumps *noun*
a device that pushes liquids or gases into or out of something.

*bicycle **pump***

punch
punches *noun*
1 a hard blow made with your fist.

punch *verb*
2 a machine that stamps holes, letters, or patterns in something.

*hole **punch***

3 a sweet drink made by mixing fruit juices and other liquids together. Punch is usually served from a large bowl.

puncture
punctures *noun*
a hole, often made by a sharp point, that lets the air out of something.
*My tyre has a **puncture**.*
puncture *verb*

A B C D E F G H I J K L M N O P Q R S T U V W X Y Z

punish

punishes punishing punished *verb*
to make someone suffer in some way for things they have done wrong.
punishment *noun*

pupa

pupae *noun*
the stage of an insect's development when it changes from a larva to a winged insect inside a rounded case (see **growth** on page 94).
■ say **pew**-pa

ladybird
pupa

pupil

pupils *noun*
1 a student at school.

2 the small, dark part at the centre of your eye, which expands or contracts to let in the right amount of light.

pupil

puppet

puppets *noun*
a doll or animal figure that is moved by pulling on its strings or by making hand movements inside it.

finger **puppet**

string **puppet**

puppy

puppies *noun*
a young dog (see **pet** on page 148).

purchase

purchases purchasing purchased *verb*
to buy something.

■ say **pur**-chis

pure

adjective
clean, or not mixed with anything.
***Pure** gold.*
■ comparisons **purer purest**

purple

noun
a colour made by mixing red and blue together.

purpose

purposes *noun*
a reason for doing something, or an aim.

purr

purrs purring purred *verb*
to make a low, rumbling noise like a cat makes.

purse

purses *noun*
a small bag for carrying money.

push

pushes pushing pushed *verb*
to move something away from you by pressing hard against it.

*He had to **push** the car to a garage when it broke down.*

put

puts putting put *verb*
to place or position something somewhere.

*She **put** her books into her school bag.*

puzzle

puzzles *noun*
1 a problem or question that it is difficult to find the answer to.
2 a game in which you have to find the answers to a problem.

puzzle

puzzles puzzling puzzled *verb*
to try to work out something you do not understand.

pyjamas

noun
a matching jacket and trousers that are worn in bed.

pyramid

pyramids *noun*
1 a solid shape with a square base and four triangular faces which meet in a point (see **shape** on page 182).
2 an ancient tomb or temple, shaped like a pyramid.

*the **pyramids** of Egypt*
■ say **pir**-a-mid

python

pythons *noun*
a large snake that is found in hot regions. Pythons kill by wrapping themselves around their prey and squeezing. They eat small mammals.

■ say **pie**-thun

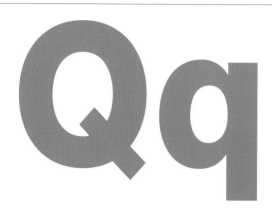

Qq

quake
quakes quaking quaked *verb*
to shake or tremble.
*He **quaked** with fear when he saw the crocodile.*
- say **kwake**

qualify
qualifies qualifying qualified *verb*
to prove that you are fit or suitable for something.
*I hope I **qualify** for the team!*
- say **kwol**-i-fie
qualification *noun*

quality
qualities *noun*
1 a judgement of how good or bad something is.
*High **quality**.*
2 something that is special about someone or something.
*She has many good **qualities**.*
- say **kwol**-i-tee

quantity
quantities *noun*
an amount or number.

*a large **quantity** of pencils*
- say **kwon**-ti-tee

quarrel
quarrels quarrelling quarrelled *verb*
to have an argument or disagreement with someone.
- say **kwor**-rul
quarrel *noun*

quarry
quarries *noun*
a place where stone, sand, or gravel is cut out of the ground.

*a stone **quarry***
- say **kwor**-ee

quarter
quarters *noun*
one of four equal pieces of a whole.

four orange quarters
- say **kwor**-ter

quartz
noun
a hard mineral, often found in crystal form.

- say **kworts**

quay
quays *noun*
an area by a harbour where ships are loaded and unloaded.
- say **kee**

queen
queens *noun*
a female ruler of a country or the wife of a king.

query
queries *noun*
a question or inquiry, because you have a doubt or problem about something.

*The teacher helped to answer the student's **query**.*
- say **kweer**-ree
query *verb*

question
questions questioning questioned *verb*
to ask someone for information or an answer.
- opposite **answer**
question *noun*

queue
queues *noun*
a line of people or vehicles that are waiting for something.
- say **kew**
queue *verb*

quick
adjective
fast or sudden.
*A **quick** movement.*
- comparisons **quicker quickest**
- opposite **slow**
quickly *adverb*

quiet
adjective
silent and peaceful.
- comparisons **quieter quietest**

quill
quills *noun*
a large feather, especially one that has been made into an ink pen.
- say **kwil**

quill pen

quilt
quilts *noun*
a thick, soft cover for a bed.

patchwork quilt

quite
adverb
1 fairly.
*I am **quite** good at running.*
2 completely.
*You are **quite** right.*

quiz
quizzes *noun*
a game in which you are asked questions to find out how much you know.

quote
quotes quoting quoted *verb*
to repeat something that someone else has said or written.
quotation *noun*

a b c d e f g h i j k l m n o p q r s t u v w x y z

Rr

A B C D E F G H I J K L M N O P Q R S T U V W X Y Z

rabbi
rabbis *noun*
a teacher of the Jewish religion and law.
■ say **rab**-eye

rabbit
rabbits *noun*
a small mammal with long front teeth that lives underground in burrows. Rabbits are normally active in the evening or at night. They eat grass, roots, and leaves.

race
races *noun*
1 a competition of speed.

a horse race
race *verb*
2 a group of people who share the same ancestors and may share some physical characteristics.
racial *adjective*

racket
rackets *noun*
1 a bat with strings used for playing sports such as tennis and badminton (see **sport** on page 197).

badminton racket

2 a loud, annoying noise.
He was making a racket with his drums.

radar
noun
a device that tells you the position and speed of ships, cars, and aircraft by sending out radio waves.

an airport radar screen
■ say **ray**-dar

radiator
radiators *noun*
1 a thin, metal tank with hot water flowing through it, which heats a room.
2 a metal tank that allows air to cool the hot water in the engine of a vehicle.
■ say **ray**-dee-ay-tor

radio
radios *noun*
a device that sends or receives electrical signals and changes them into sound.

radioactivity
noun
the energy released by the centre of atoms breaking up in some substances. High amounts of radioactivity can be harmful to living things.
They tested for radioactivity outside the nuclear power station.
■ say **ray**-dee-oh-ak-**tiv**-i-tee
radioactive *adjective*

radius
radii or **radiuses** *noun*
a straight line drawn from the centre of a circle to its outer edge.

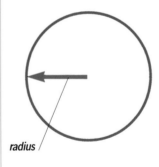

radius

raft
rafts *noun*
1 a floating platform made of logs that have been tied tightly together.

2 a hollow mat made of rubber or plastic and filled with air, which can be used as a boat.

life raft

rag
rags *noun*
a small, torn piece of cloth.

rage
rages *noun*
anger or uncontrolled temper.
In her rage, she slammed the door shut.

raid
raids *noun*
a sudden surprise attack by a group of people.
The police made a raid on the house, arresting two women.
raid *verb*

rail
rails *noun*
1 a long bar for holding on to, or for hanging clothes on.
Use the rail to help you climb the stairs.
2 a long line of metal track that trains run along.

3 the railway.
We travelled by rail around Europe.

railway
railways *noun*
1 a network of tracks that trains run on.
2 a transport system that uses rail tracks, together with trains, stations, and land.

rain

rain
rains *noun*
water that falls from the clouds in drops.

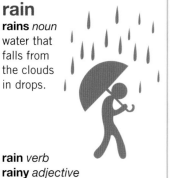

rain *verb*
rainy *adjective*

rainbow
rainbows *noun*
an arch of colours that appears in the sky when the sun shines during rain.

raindrop
raindrops *noun*
a single drop of rain.

rainfall
noun
the amount of rain that falls over a particular area.
*The chart shows the annual **rainfall** in South America.*

rainforest
rainforests *noun*
a dense, hot, wet jungle that grows in tropical areas.

rake
rakes raking raked *verb*
to gather up leaves into a pile or to smooth over soil.

rake

rally
rallies *noun*
1 a large, public meeting held to discuss something that is important or worrying to people.

*The party held a political **rally** in the park.*
2 a long-distance car race that tests drivers' skills.

ram
rams *noun*
1 a male sheep.

2 a device for pushing against something with force.

*They used the log as a **ram** to break down the door.*
ram *verb*

ran
*from the verb **to run***
1 *Last week, he **ran** a 400 metre race.*
2 *She **ran** a bookshop.*

ranch
ranches *noun*
a huge farm where cattle or other animals are reared, usually found in America.

rang
*from the verb **to ring***
1 *He **rang** the doorbell.*
2 *She **rang** me twice today.*

ranger
rangers *noun*
a person who looks after a forest or a wildlife park.

rapid
adjective
quick or swift.

rare
adjective
unusual or not common.

*a **rare** blue morpho butterfly*

■ comparisons **rarer rarest**
■ opposite **common**

rascal
rascals *noun*
a mischievous person.

rash
rashes *noun*
a patch of red, itchy spots on your skin.

raspberry
raspberries *noun*
a juicy, red fruit that grows on a bush with thorns.

■ say **rarz**-bur-ree

rat
rats *noun*
a common rodent that looks like a large mouse. Some kinds of rats eat plants, while others eat small animals. They can gnaw through stone, wood, and even metal with their strong front teeth.

rate
rates *noun*
1 a speed.
*Ostriches can run at a **rate** of 50 kilometres per hour.*
2 a level of payment.
*The holiday company charges high **rates** for its apartments.*

a b c d e f g h i j k l m n o p q r s t u v w x y z

rather
adverb
1 fairly or quite.
*It was **rather** hot the other day.*
2 preferably.

*He'd **rather** wear the yellow shirt than the stripy one.*

ration
rations *noun*
a fixed amount of something that someone is allowed.
*Food **rations**.*
■ say **rash**-un
ration *verb*

raw
adjective
1 in its natural condition, not processed or cooked.

raw carrot
2 not experienced.
*A **raw** recruit.*
3 painful to touch.
*A **raw** wound.*

ray
rays *noun*
a long, narrow beam of light, heat, or other powerful force.

rays of light

razor
razors *noun*
a device with a blade that people use to shave.

reach
reaches reaching reached *verb*
1 to stretch out your hand and arm to touch something.

2 to arrive at a place.
*After a long trek they **reached** the other side of the island.*

react
reacts reacting reacted *verb*
to say or do something in response to an event.
*He **reacted** badly to the news.*
■ say ree-**akt**
reaction *noun*

read
reads reading read *verb*
to look at and understand written words.

■ rhymes with **seed**

ready
adjective
prepared, or able to start.
■ say **red**-ee

real
adjective
actually existing, or genuine.

realize
realizes realizing realized *verb*
to become aware, or to understand completely.

*She **realized** that she was running late.*

really
adverb
very, or actually.
*The trip was **really** good fun.*

rear
rears rearing reared *verb*
1 to feed and care for young animals as they grow up.
*Our cat has **reared** 10 kittens.*
2 to rise up on the back legs.

*a **rearing** horse*

rear
noun
the back of something, or the part that is opposite or behind the front.

*the **rear** of a car*
rear *adjective*

reason
reasons *noun*
an explanation of why or how something has happened.

rebel
rebels *noun*
someone who fights against those in charge.
■ say **reb**-ul
rebellion *noun*

receipt
receipts *noun*
a written or printed piece of paper that shows you have received and paid for something.
■ say re-**seet**

receive
receives receiving received *verb*
to take something given or sent to you.

*He **received** an award.*

recent
adjective
not long ago.
*A **recent** storm.*
■ say **ree**-sunt
recently *adverb*

recipe
recipes noun
instructions that tell you how to make and cook food, or how to make a drink.

recipe book
■ say **res**-i-pee

recite
recites reciting recited verb
to say aloud something that you have learned by heart.

reckon
reckons reckoning reckoned verb
1 to suppose or think something.
*What do you **reckon** that is?*
2 to work out the amount of something.
■ say **rek**-un

recognize
recognizes recognizing recognized verb
to see someone or something and know who they are or what it is.
recognition noun

record
records recording recorded verb
1 to store sounds or pictures, on tape, film, record, compact disc (CD), digital versatile/video disc (DVD), or other digital device.
2 to write down information on paper.

*The doctor **recorded** the patient's results.*
■ say ri-**cord**

record
records noun
1 a round plastic disc with tiny grooves in the surface, on which sounds are recorded.
2 information that is written or printed.

*She kept a **record** of the day's events in her diary.*
3 the fastest or best performance in an activity or sport.
*They tried to beat the **record** for the number of people who can stand on a chair.*
■ say **rek**-ord

recorder
recorders noun
a small wooden or plastic wind instrument that you blow into. The air is forced out through holes, which you cover with your fingers to make different sounds.

recover
recovers recovering recovered verb
1 to get better after being ill.
2 to get something back.

*He was **recovering** from a broken arm.*

recreation
noun
the things we like to do in our spare time, such as playing sports and having hobbies.

recruit
recruits noun
a new member of an organization or group.
■ say ri-**krute**

rectangle
rectangles noun
a flat four-sided shape with four right angles in its corners (see **shape** on page 182).

recycle
recycles recycling recycled verb
to use things again, often by turning rubbish into new products. Glass, plastics, paper, and metal can all be recycled.

*materials for **recycling***

red
noun
a colour.

reduce
reduces reducing reduced verb
to make something smaller in size or amount.
*The shop **reduced** the price of hats by half.*
■ say ri-**dews**
reduction noun

reed
reeds noun
a tall plant with a long, stiff, straight stem that grows in wet areas. Reeds are used to make house roofs and paper.
*common **reed***

reef
reefs noun
a raised, narrow ridge of rock, sand, or coral, just above or below the surface of the sea.

*coral **reef***

referee
referees noun
someone who watches over a game or contest to see that people keep to the rules.

reference
adjective
providing information.
*The **reference** book was full of interesting facts.*
reference noun

refinery
refineries noun
a large factory where natural substances are processed into other products. Oil is made into petrol at a refinery.

*oil **refinery***

A B C D E F G H I J K L M N O P Q R S T U V W X Y Z

reflect
reflects reflecting reflected *verb*
1 to throw back light, heat, or sound that has come from somewhere else.
*Shiny surfaces **reflect** light.*
2 to give back, or show, an image of something or someone.

*His face was **reflected** in the mirror.*
reflection *noun*

refrigerator
refrigerators *noun*
a machine that keeps food and drink cool and fresh. Refrigerator can be shortened to fridge.

refugee
refugees *noun*
someone who leaves their home and belongings and escapes to another place, usually because he or she is in danger.
■ say ref-yoo-**jee**

refuse
refuses refusing refused *verb*
to say that you will not do something.

*He **refused** to give her the ball.*

region
regions *noun*
an area or district of a country.

*a mountain **region***
■ say **ree**-jun

regret
regrets regretting regretted *verb*
to be sorry or sad about something that has happened.
*He **regretted** being angry with his sister.*

regular
adjective
1 normal, or happening at certain times.
*A **regular** bus service.*
2 even in shape or sound.

*These wooden cubes are **regular** shapes.*
■ opposite **irregular**
regularly *adverb*

rehearse
rehearses rehearsing rehearsed *verb*
to practise doing something before giving a performance in public.

*She **rehearsed** for the play.*
■ say re-**herss**
rehearsal *noun*

reign
reigns reigning reigned *verb*
to rule a country or region as a queen or king.
■ say **rain**
reign *noun*

rein
reins *noun*
a long, thin, leather strap that a rider uses to control a horse (see **horse** on page 102).
■ say **rain**

reindeer
reindeer or **reindeers** *noun*
a deer with large antlers that lives in cold, Arctic regions. Reindeer herds migrate great distances every summer and winter in search of plants to eat. Some reindeer are tamed and used to pull sledges.

relative
relatives *noun*
a member of someone's family.

relax
relaxes relaxing relaxed *verb*
to rest and feel comfortable.

*She **relaxed** with her favourite book.*

relay
relays *noun*
a team race in which runners carrying a baton take it in turns to run part of the distance.

release
releases releasing released *verb*
to let someone or something go free.

*She **released** the balloons.*

reliable
adjective
able to be trusted.

relief
noun
1 the removal of worry, pain, or unhappiness.
*It was a **relief** when the exam was over.*
2 help given to people who need it.
■ say ri-**leef**

religion
religions *noun*
a belief in God or gods, and the way people express this belief in their life and worship.
religious *adjective*

reluctant
adjective
unsure or unhappy about doing something.

*The dog was **reluctant** to come out from under the chair.*

rely
relies relying relied *verb*
to depend on someone for something with complete trust.
*Young birds **rely** on their parents for food.*
■ say ri-**lie**

remain
remains remaining remained *verb*
1 to stay behind.

*She **remained** at the bus stop.*
2 to be left behind.
3 to stay unchanged.
*She **remained** calm while everyone else panicked.*
remains *noun*

remember
remembers remembering remembered *verb*
to think about a place, person, object, or past event again.
*She suddenly **remembered** she had left her bag on the bus.*

remind
reminds reminding reminded *verb*
to make someone remember something.

*A calendar **reminds** you of future events.*

remote
adjective
far away, distant.
*A **remote** farmhouse.*

remove
removes removing removed *verb*
to take something off or away.

*She **removed** her shoe to get a stone out.*

renew
renews renewing renewed *verb*
to begin, make, or get again.
*He **renewed** his bus pass.*

rent
rents *noun*
a regular payment that you make to the owner of something so that you can use it.
rent *verb*

repair
repairs repairing repaired *verb*
to mend something that is broken.

repairing a bicycle
repair *noun*

repeat
repeats repeating repeated *verb*
to say or do something again.
repetition *noun*

replace
replaces replacing replaced *verb*
1 to put something back where it came from.

*She **replaced** the book on the shelf.*
2 to exchange or renew.
*He **replaced** his bicycle with a bigger, more expensive one.*
replacement *noun*

replay
replays replaying replayed *verb*
1 to play a sports match again.
2 to play a recording of something again.

replica
replicas *noun*
an exact copy of something.
*She made a **replica** of the ship out of matchsticks.*

reply
replies replying replied *verb*
to answer.
*He **replied** to the invitation immediately.*
reply *noun*

report
reports *noun*
a spoken or written account of a situation or event.

reporter
reporters *noun*
a person who gathers information on events and writes or speaks about them for a television programme, newspaper, or radio station.

represent
represents representing represented *verb*
to mean or show something.

*Sailors use this flag to **represent** the word "yes" when they signal to other ships.*

a b c d e f g h i j k l m n o p q r s t u v w x y z

reptile

reptiles *noun*
one of a group of cold-blooded animals that have a backbone, lungs for breathing, dry, scaly skin, and clawed fingers or toes. Reptiles lay their eggs on dry land.

crest

nostril

external ear

crested water dragon

scales

head

banded skin

tail

milk snake

camouflaged skin

padded toe

swivelling eye

horn

camouflaged skin

beak

fold of skin

Jackson's chameleon

tortoise hatching

tokay lizard

carapace

forked tongue

shell

starred tortoise

plastron

tail with rattle

rattlesnake

eye

red-eared terrapin

leg

covered eardrum

leopard gecko

webbed foot

tail crest

hindlimb

scute

snout

belly

digit (finger)

claw

caiman

forefoot

nostril

tail

flying gecko

request
requests requesting requested *verb*
to ask for something formally.
*The prisoner **requested** a visit to his mother.*
■ say ri-**kwest**
request *noun*

rescue
rescues rescuing rescued *verb*
to save someone who is injured or in danger.
■ say **res**-kew

research
researches researching researched *verb*
to study a subject in order to learn new facts or develop new ideas.

*The scientists were doing **research**.*
research *noun*

reserve
reserves reserving reserved *verb*
to arrange to have something kept for a later time.
*They **reserved** a table at the restaurant for 8 o'clock.*
reservation *noun*

reservoir
reservoirs *noun*
a large storage area where water is collected and stored for future use.

■ say **rez**-ur-vwah

resign
resigns resigning resigned *verb*
to give up your job.
■ say ri-**zine**

resist
resists resisting resisted *verb*
to try to stop something from happening.
*He **resisted** temptation.*

resort
resorts *noun*
a place where many people go for a holiday.

*a ski **resort***

resource
resources *noun*
a supply of something useful or valuable, such as oil or gas.
*The country is rich in natural **resources**.*
■ say ri-**zorse**

respect
noun
1 admiration for someone.
*I have great **respect** for her.*
2 politeness.
respect *verb*
respectful *adjective*

response
responses *noun*
a reply, in actions or words, to something.
respond *verb*
responsive *adjective*

responsible
adjective
1 sensible and dependable.
2 in charge of something.

*The girl was **responsible** for feeding her dog.*

rest
noun
1 the time when you are relaxing.
rest *verb*
2 something that is left over.
*Most people left yesterday, but the **rest** went this morning.*
3 when something is still.
*The ball came to **rest** at the teacher's feet.*

restaurant
restaurants *noun*
a place where people go to buy and eat a meal.

■ say **rest**-er-ront

restless
adjective
unable to stay still or relax.

*The baby had a **restless** night.*

restore
restores restoring restored *verb*
to mend something old or worn, so that it looks new or can be used again.

result
results *noun*
the effect of certain actions or events.
*What was the **result** of the experiment?*
result *verb*

retire
retires retiring retired *verb*
to give up working, usually because of old age or illness.

return
returns returning returned *verb*
1 to come back from somewhere.

*The boomerang **returned** easily to his hand.*
2 to give something back to a person.
*She **returned** the book he had lent her.*
return *noun*

A B C D E F G H I J K L M N O P Q R S T U V W X Y Z

revenge

noun
harm or injury that a person does to another, in return for something unpleasant previously done to them.

reverse

reverses reversing reversed *verb*
to go backwards, usually in a vehicle.

*She **reversed** her car into the parking space.*

reverse

adjective
at the opposite side, inside, or back of an object.

*The **reverse** side of the coat is lined with white material.*
reverse *noun*

revise

revises revising revised *verb*
to look back over work, either to check for mistakes, or to prepare for a test.
revision *noun*

revolution

revolutions *noun*
1 one complete turn.
2 a time when people fight to change the government of their country.
*The French **Revolution**.*

reward

rewards *noun*
a prize given because of a good thing someone has done.

LOST

£50 reward

*They offered a **reward** to anyone who found their cat.*

rhinoceros

rhinoceroses *noun*
a heavy mammal that lives in hot regions. Rhinoceroses have one or two horns and thick skin with hardly any hair.

■ say ry-**noss**-er-rus

rhubarb

noun
a large-leaved plant. Its long stems can be cooked and eaten as a dessert.

■ say roo-**barb**

rhyme

rhymes *noun*
words which have the same or similar sound and are often found in a poem.
■ say **rime**

rhythm

rhythms *noun*
a regular pattern of sound, such as beats in music.
■ say **rith**-um

rib

ribs *noun*
one of the bones that curves round from your spine to the front of your chest. Ribs protect your internal organs (see **skeleton** on page 188).

ribbon

ribbons *noun*
a thin strip of decorative material often used for tying hair or wrapping up presents.

rice

noun
a grass-like plant that grows in warm, wet regions. The small white or brown grains can be cooked and eaten.

*cooked **rice***

rich

adjective
1 having a lot of money.
2 having a lot of something.
*Milk is **rich** in calcium.*
■ comparisons **richer richest**
■ opposite **poor**

riddle

riddles *noun*
a word puzzle in which you have to guess the answer from clues, often in a rhyme.

ride

rides riding rode ridden *verb*
1 to travel on the back of a horse.

2 to travel on anything that moves.

***riding** on a Ferris wheel*
ride *noun*

ridiculous

adjective
crazy, funny, or not making sense.

*She looked **ridiculous**.*
■ say ri-**dik**-yoo-lus

right

adjective
1 the opposite direction to left.
*My **right** hand.*
2 correct or lawful.
*The **right** answer.*
right *noun*

right-angle

right-angles *noun*
an angle that measures
90 degrees, formed by two
lines that are perpendicular
to one another (see **shape**
on page 182).
*The four inside corners of
a square are **right-angles**.*

rim

rims *noun*
the edge or border
of something.

*He looked over the **rim** of
the volcano into the crater.*

ring

**rings ringing
rang rung** *verb*
1 to strike metal
or play a bell
so that it
makes a
pleasant
sound.

2 to make a
telephone call.
*I have tried to
ring her three
times today.*

ring

rings *noun*
a piece of jewellery that
is worn on your finger
(see **jewellery** on
page 112).

rinse

rinses rinsing rinsed *verb*
to wash something
in water with
no soap in it.

riot

riots *noun*
uncontrolled fighting
among a crowd of people
who are angry or protesting
about something.
■ say **ry**-ut

rip

rips ripping ripped *verb*
to tear something, usually cloth
or paper.

*He **ripped** the
piece of paper in half.*

ripe

adjective
ready to pick or eat, usually
used about fruit.
■ comparisons **riper ripest**
■ opposite **unripe**

ripple

ripples *noun*
a small wave on the
surface of water.

ripple

*When the duck dived,
it made **ripples** on the
water's surface.*

rise

rises rising rose risen *verb*
to go upwards or
become higher.
*Heat **rises**.*
rising *adjective*

risk

risks risking risked *verb*
to take the chance of harming
or losing something.
*He **risked** his life to save her.*
risk *noun*
risky *adjective*

river

rivers *noun*
a large stream of water
that flows into another river,
a lake, or the ocean.

road

roads *noun*
a path for vehicles to
travel on, usually with a
hard, smooth surface.

roar

roars roaring roared *verb*
to make a loud,
deep, rumbling
noise like
the noise a
lion makes.

roast

roasts roasting roasted *verb*
to cook food in a hot oven
or over a fire.

rob

robs robbing robbed *verb*
to steal from someone, often
by using violence.
*They **robbed** the bank.*
robbery *noun*

robber

robbers *noun*
a person who robs you of
something, usually money
or goods.

robot

robots *noun*
a machine that can imitate
some human actions. Robots
are often used
in factories,
but can also
be used
in homes.

*This amazing
robot can
walk like a
human being.*

rock

rocks *noun*
a hard, stony substance that
covers most of Earth's surface,
or a large lump of
this substance.

*granite **rock***
rocky *adjective*

rock

rocks rocking rocked *verb*
to move gently
backwards and
forwards, or from
side to side.

*rocking
chair*

rocket

rockets *noun*
1 an engine that powers a spacecraft. Hot gases are released from the rear of the engine, causing the craft to move forwards.

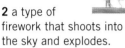

2 a type of firework that shoots into the sky and explodes.

rode

from the verb **to ride**
She **rode** her horse last week.

rodent

rodents *noun*
a small, usually nocturnal mammal with long front teeth for gnawing food. Some rodents eat insects and plants, while others only eat plants. Rats, mice, and squirrels are rodents.
■ say **roh**-dent

roll

rolls rolling rolled *verb*
1 to move by turning over and over.

The girl **rolled** down the hill.
2 to move along on wheels.
3 to tilt from side to side, like a ship on a rough sea.

4 to flatten something by moving a tool over it.

roll

rolls *noun*
1 paper, cloth, film, or other material that has been wound onto a tube.

rolls *of wrapping paper*

2 a rounded piece of bread, cake, or pastry.

bread **rolls**

roof

roofs *noun*
1 the outside covering on top of a vehicle or a building.
2 the highest surface inside your mouth or a cave.

room

rooms *noun*
1 one of the separate areas inside a building.

bathroom
2 space.
Is there any **room** in the car for me?

roost

roosts roosting roosted *verb*
to settle down for the night, used about birds.

root

roots *noun*
the part of a plant that usually grows underground. A plant's roots supply it with water and minerals from the soil (see **plant** on page 151).

rope

ropes *noun*
a strong, thick piece of twisted string or wire.

coil of **rope**

rose

roses *noun*
a plant with thorns along its stem and flowers with many petals.

rose

from the verb **to rise**
The Sun **rose** in the sky.

rot

rots rotting rotted *verb*
to go bad, or to weaken and break down.
rotten *adjective*

rotate

rotates rotating rotated *verb*
to turn around a central point like a wheel does.

axis

The Earth **rotates** on its axis.
rotation *noun*

rough

adjective
1 uneven, or not smooth.
A **rough** sea.
2 approximate, or not exact.
A **rough** guess.
■ comparisons **rougher roughest**

round

adjective
shaped like a circle, with no corners.

route

routes *noun*
the way you go to get from one place to another.

We drew our **route** on the map in red.
■ say **root**

row

rows *noun*
an argument or quarrel.
■ rhymes with **now**

row

rows *noun*
a line of several things next to each other.

■ rhymes with **toe**

row

rows rowing rowed *verb*
to make a boat move forwards by pulling it through the water with oars.

royal
adjective
to do with a king, queen, or members of his or her family.

rub
rubs rubbing rubbed *verb*
to press something backwards and forwards over the surface of something else.

*She **rubbed** her wet hair with a towel.*

rubbish
noun
the things that people throw away because they no longer have use for them.

rude
adjective
speaking or behaving in a way that does not show respect.
■ opposite **polite**

rug
rugs *noun*
1 a small carpet made of thick material.

2 a soft blanket.

rugby
noun
a sport in which two teams, of 15 players each, throw and kick an oval ball, trying to score points by running over a line with it or kicking it between the goal posts.

*a **rugby** union game*

ruin
ruins *noun*
the broken remains of a building.

ruined *adjective*

ruin
ruins ruining ruined *verb*
to spoil or damage something.

*She **ruined** her top by spilling ink on it.*

rule
rules *noun*
an instruction of what must or must not be done, for example in a game.

rule
rules ruling ruled *verb*
to govern a country or a group of people.

ruler
rulers *noun*
1 a straight piece of wood, metal, or plastic that is used for measuring and drawing straight lines.
2 a person, such as a king or queen, who rules a country.

rumble
rumbles rumbling rumbled *verb*
to make a long, low sound, like the noise thunder makes.
rumble *noun*

rumour
rumours *noun*
a tale passed from one person to another, about something that may not be true.

run
runs running ran *verb*
1 to move quickly on your legs.

2 to organize something.
*He **runs** a swimming club.*

runway
runways *noun*
a long, flat strip of ground with a hard surface from which aircraft take off and land.

runway

rural
adjective
to do with the countryside or farms.
*A **rural** village.*
■ say **roo**-ral

rush
rushes rushing rushed *verb*
to hurry, or to do something quickly.

rust
noun
the red-brown coating that forms on some metals when they get wet.

*The sickle was covered with **rust**.*

rustle
rustles rustling rustled *verb*
to make a soft, whispering sound.
*The leaves on the tree **rustled** in the wind.*

rye
noun
a grass with light-brown grains, grown to make bread, and as cattle food.

a b c d e f g h i j k l m n o p q r s t u v w x y z

Ss

A B C D E F G H I J K L M N O P Q R S T U V W X Y Z

sack
sacks *noun*
a large, strong bag made of cloth, plastic, or paper, which is used for carrying or storing things.

sacred
adjective
holy, or connected with the worship of God or gods.
*The Qur'an is the **sacred** book of Muslims.*
■ say **say**-krid

sad
adjective
not feeling happy.
■ comparisons **sadder saddest**
■ opposite **happy**

saddle
saddles *noun*
a seat for a rider on a horse or a bicycle (see **horse** on page 102 and **transport** on page 221).

*horse **saddle***

safari
safaris *noun*
an expedition to hunt or observe wild animals, usually in Africa.

■ say sa-**far**-ree

safe
adjective
1 protected from harm or danger.
***Safe** on dry land.*
2 not dangerous.
*A **safe** driver.*
■ comparisons **safer safest**
safety *noun*

safe
safes *noun*
a lockable metal box that is used for storing money and valuable things.

sag
sags sagging sagged *verb*
to bend or sink, especially in the middle.
*The sofa **sagged** in the middle.*

said
from the verb **to say**
1 *She **said** "Good morning".*
2 *The clock **said** half past four.*

sail
sails sailing
sailed *verb*
to travel across water in a ship or boat.

sail
sails *noun*
a piece of material attached to the mast of a boat or ship that catches the wind and helps to move the vessel along (see **boat** on page 31).

salad
salads *noun*
a mixture of vegetables, fruit, or other foods, usually served cold.

*mixed
salad*

salary
salaries *noun*
an amount of money regularly paid to someone for work they have done.
*A monthly **salary**.*

sale
sales *noun*
1 the act of offering something to be sold.

*The house is for **sale**.*
2 an event where things are sold at reduced prices.
*Half-price **sale**!*

saliva
noun
the fluid that is produced in your mouth to help you to chew and digest food.

salmon
noun
a large, edible fish. Salmon hatch in rivers, but then swim to the sea to live. They swim back up rivers to lay their eggs.

■ say **sam**-un

salt
noun
a substance made of small, white crystals that we put on food in order to add flavour.

salt mill
salty *adjective*

salute
salutes saluting saluted *verb*
to give a sign of respect by raising the right hand to the forehead or by firing guns into the air.
salute *noun*

same
adjective
1 matching exactly.
*She was wearing the **same** dress as me.*
2 mentioned or seen before.
*He looks like the **same** person who was there yesterday.*
■ opposite **different**

sample
samples *noun*
a small part of something that shows what the rest is like.

The outdoor market was giving away free samples of cheese.
sample *verb*

sand
noun
very small grains of broken rock, found on beaches or in deserts.

sandal
sandals *noun*
a shoe with a top made of straps, usually worn in warm weather.

sandwich
sandwiches *noun*
slices of bread with another food in between.

sang
from the verb **to sing**
The blackbird sang loudly outside my window.

sank
from the verb **to sink**
1 *The ship sank at sea.*
2 *The balloon sank slowly.*

sari
saris *noun*
a long, light cloth wrapped around the body and shoulder that is worn mainly by women of India, Bangladesh, Nepal, and Sri Lanka.

sarong
sarongs *noun*
a traditional Asian skirt worn by men and women and made from a piece of cloth wrapped around the waist or chest.

sash
sashes *noun*
a band of fabric worn around the waist or over the shoulder.

sash

sat
from the verb **to sit**
1 *I sat down on the floor.*
2 *She sat an English exam.*

satellite
satellites *noun*
1 an object in orbit around a larger object in space. Planet satellites are called moons.
2 an artificial device in space that receives and transmits information around the world.
an Earth observation satellite
■ say **sat**-a-lite

satisfy
satisfies satisfying satisfied *verb*
to please someone, or give someone what they want or need.
His answer didn't satisfy the teacher.
satisfaction *noun*

sauce
sauces *noun*
a liquid or soft food that is eaten with a meal.

raspberry sauce

■ say **sors**

saucepan
saucepans *noun*
a metal container with a handle, used for cooking.

■ say **sors**-pan

saucer
saucers *noun*
a small, shallow plate that is placed beneath a cup.

■ say **sor**-ser

sausage
sausages *noun*
a food made from a mixture of chopped meat, fat, and cereal inside a tube of thin skin.
■ say **sos**-ij

save
saves saving saved *verb*
1 to rescue.
The fire-fighter saved him from the burning house.
2 to not waste.
Save power – turn off the light!
3 to keep something to use later.
He saved all his pocket money.

saw
saws *noun*
a tool for cutting wood, which has a handle and a blade with sharp teeth.

saw
saws sawing sawed *verb*
to use a saw.

sawing a plank of wood

saw
from the verb **to see**
I saw my face in the mirror.

say
says saying said *verb*
1 to speak words out loud.
"Hurry up!" I said.
2 to give a message or some information.
The sign says "No Entry".

a b c d e f g h i j k l m n o p q r s t u v w x y z

scald
scalds scalding scalded *verb*
to burn with hot liquid
or steam.
- say **skold**

scale
scales *noun*
1 a series of regular
marks along a line used
for measuring.
*Thermometers have a scale
for measuring temperature.*
2 a set sequence of musical
notes going from the highest
to the lowest, or from the
lowest to the highest.

3 a small, hard plate on
the skin of a fish, insect,
or reptile (see **fish** on
page 79, **insect** on page
108, **reptile** on page 168).
4 the size of a map or a model
compared with the actual size
of the object.

*This model of a building has
been made to scale.*

scales
noun
a machine that is used
to weigh things.

*kitchen
scales*

scar
scars *noun*
a mark left on the skin
after a wound has healed.
scar *verb*

scarce
adjective
not great in amount,
or not often found.
Snow is scarce in May.
- say **skairs**

scare
scares scaring scared *verb*
1 to become frightened.
2 to make someone
else frightened.

*The large spider
scared the girl.*

scarecrow
scarecrows *noun*
a figure made from sticks and
old clothes, which is used to
scare birds away from crops.

scarf
scarves *noun*
a piece of cloth that you wear
around your shoulders, neck,
or head for decoration or to
keep warm.

scatter
scatters scattering scattered
verb
to spread in many
different directions.
The wind scattered the seeds.

scavenger
scavengers *noun*
an animal or person who
searches through rubbish.

scavenge *verb*

scene
scenes *noun*
1 the place where
something happened.
The scene of the crime.
2 a part of a play or film, set in
a particular time or place.
3 a view.

a winter scene
- say **seen**

scenery
noun
1 the way a place looks.

*The scenery in the mountains
was amazing.*
2 an artificial background used
in a play or a film.
- say **seen**-er-ree

scent
scents *noun*
1 a trail of smell left by
an animal or a person.
The dog followed the scent.
2 perfume.
- say **sent**

scheme
schemes *noun*
1 a secret plan.
2 a way of arranging things.
A colour scheme.
- say **skeem**

school
schools *noun*
a place where children
go to learn.
- say **skool**

science
sciences *noun*
the study of things
in the world, which involves
observing, measuring, and
experimenting to test ideas.
- say **sye**-ens
scientific *adjective*

scientist
scientists *noun*
someone who does
scientific work.
- say **sye**-en-tist

scissors
noun
a tool with handles
and two blades joined
together. Scissors are
used for cutting
things, such as
paper and hair.

- say **siz**-ers

scold
scolds scolding scolded *verb*
to speak to someone angrily
because they have done
something wrong.
*My father scolded me
for being late.*

scoop
scoops scooping scooped *verb*
to lift something up using your hand or a tool shaped like a deep spoon.

*The ice-cream was **scooped** into the bowl.*

score
scores scoring scored *verb*
to win points in a game.

scorn
scorns scorning scorned *verb*
to show by words or your expression that you do not think much of something or someone.
*The journalist **scorned** the plans for the power station.*
scornful *adjective*

scorpion
scorpions *noun*
a small, nocturnal animal that is part of the same animal group as spiders. Scorpions usually live in hot regions. They eat insects and spiders, which they kill with the poisonous stingers on their tails.

imperial **scorpion**

scowl
scowls scowling scowled *verb*
to frown in an angry or bad-tempered way.
*She **scowled** when she was given extra homework.*
scowl *noun*

scramble
scrambles scrambling scrambled *verb*
1 to crawl or climb fast, using your hands.

*She **scrambled** up the cliff face.*
2 to mix together.
Scrambling an egg.

scrap
noun
1 a small piece of something.

scraps of paper

2 anything that is worn out or no longer of any use.

*The cars were sold as **scrap**.*
scrap *verb*

scrape
scrapes scraping scraped *verb*
to drag an object across something, often removing part of the surface.

scraping wallpaper off the walls

scratch
scratches scratching scratched *verb*
1 to make a mark on the surface of something with a sharp object.

*The cat **scratched** the tree trunk with its claws.*
2 to rub skin with fingernails or claws to stop it itching.
scratch *noun*

scream
screams screaming screamed *verb*
to cry out in a loud, high voice, possibly because you are frightened or in pain.
scream *noun*

screen
screens *noun*
1 a flat surface onto which moving images are projected.
*Some cinemas have six **screens**.*
2 a barrier that is used to hide, separate, or protect something.
*She dressed behind a **screen**.*
3 the part of a computer or television on which the picture or text appears.

screen

screw
screws *noun*
a metal pin used for fastening things together.

screwdriver
screwdrivers *noun*
a tool for turning screws.

script
scripts *noun*
1 a written version of a play, film, radio, or television show.
2 handwriting.

scrub
scrubs scrubbing scrubbed *verb*
to clean by rubbing hard.

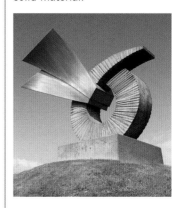

*He **scrubbed** the car.*

sculpture
sculptures *noun*
a piece of art made from wood, stone, metal, or another solid material.

sea
seas *noun*
the salt water that covers two-thirds of Earth's surface.

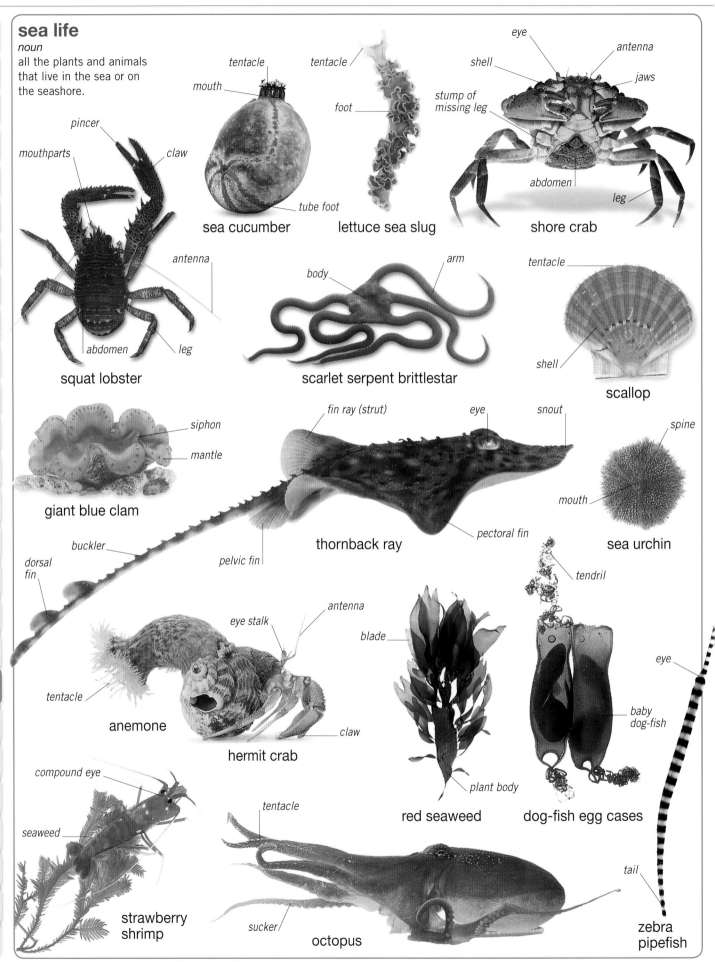

sea life

noun

all the plants and animals that live in the sea or on the seashore.

pincer

mouthparts

claw

squat lobster

antenna

abdomen

leg

tentacle

mouth

tube foot

sea cucumber

tentacle

foot

lettuce sea slug

eye

antenna

shell

jaws

stump of missing leg

abdomen

leg

shore crab

body

arm

scarlet serpent brittlestar

tentacle

shell

scallop

siphon

mantle

giant blue clam

fin ray (strut)

eye

snout

spine

mouth

sea urchin

buckler

dorsal fin

pelvic fin

thornback ray

pectoral fin

tentacle

anemone

eye stalk

antenna

claw

hermit crab

blade

plant body

red seaweed

tendril

baby dog-fish

dog-fish egg cases

eye

tail

zebra pipefish

compound eye

seaweed

strawberry shrimp

tentacle

sucker

octopus

seal

seals *noun*

1 a sea mammal usually found in cold seas. Seals eat fish and are excellent swimmers. Some seals are clumsy on land, where they move by rolling or sliding along.

2 a piece of paper or wax that is used to mark something or to close it so that you can tell whether it has been opened.

wax **seal**

seal

seals sealing sealed *verb*
to close something securely or tightly.
Seal the envelope.

search

searches searching searched *verb*
to look hard for something.

They **searched** *for the golf ball in the long grass.*
search *noun*

season

seasons *noun*
1 one of the four divisions of the year marked by particular kinds of weather.
Our **seasons** *are spring, summer, autumn, and winter.*
2 a particular part of the year.
The football **season** *starts next week.*

seat

seats *noun*
anything that is used for sitting on.

child's car safety **seat**   **seat**-belt

second

seconds *noun*
a very short period of time. There are 60 seconds in one minute.

secret

secrets *noun*
something that is not known by everyone.
Can you keep a **secret**?
secret *adjective*

secretary

secretaries *noun*
a person whose job is to assist other people by making business appointments, writing letters, and keeping records.

section

sections *noun*
a separate part or portion of something.
The library has a children's **section**.

secure

adjective
1 well fastened.

2 safe and confident.
My baby brother needs his teddy to make him feel **secure**.

a **secure** *window*
secure *verb*

see

sees seeing saw seen *verb*
to notice something with your eyes.

You can **see** *a long way with binoculars.*

seed

seeds *noun*
a small, hard part of some flowering plants, from which new plants may grow (see **growth** on page 94).

sunflower **seeds**

seek

seeks seeking sought *verb*
to search for something, or try to achieve something.
Seeking *help.*

seem

seems seeming seemed *verb*
to appear to be.
She **seems** *worried about something.*

seesaw

seesaws *noun*
a balancing toy. Children play on a seesaw by sitting at either end of a board and rocking up and down.

seize

seizes seizing seized *verb*
to take hold of something suddenly.
The thief **seized** *her bag.*
■ say **seez**

seldom

adverb
not often, or rarely.
I **seldom** *get home before six.*

select

selects selecting selected *verb*
to choose something you want from a number of things.

He **selected** *the trousers.*
selection *noun*

selfish

adjective
only caring about yourself.
He was very **selfish** *and never shared his toys.*

sell

sells selling sold *verb*
to give something to someone in return for money.
They **sell** *all sorts of vegetables in the market.*

a b c d e f g h i j k l m n o p q r s t u v w x y z

A B C D E F G H I J K L M N O P Q R S T U V W X Y Z

semaphore
noun
a way of sending messages by signalling with two flags. The flags are held in different positions to represent each letter of the alphabet.
■ say **sem**-a-for

send
sends sending sent *verb*
to make someone or something go to another place.
Send me a postcard!

senior
adjective
older, more experienced, or more important.
The headteacher is senior to the other teachers.
■ say **seen**-ee-or

sense
senses *noun*
1 one of the five ways in which we can receive information about the world. The five senses are sight, hearing, touch, smell, and taste.

You need your sense of hearing to use a telephone.
2 a feeling.
A sense of disappointment.
3 reasonable decisions or good judgement.
She has a lot of sense.
4 a meaning that can be understood.
It makes sense.

sensible
adjective
thinking clearly or in a practical way.

She was sensible about dressing for the cold weather.
sensibly *adverb*

sensitive
adjective
1 quick to feel, understand, or react to something.

Sensitive hairs on this plant make the leaves close when they are touched.
2 easily upset or hurt.
His skin was very sensitive where he had been burnt.

sentence
sentences *noun*
1 a group of words that make sense together. Sentences start with a capital letter and end with a full stop. They usually include a verb.
2 a punishment decided by a judge in a law court.
He received a four-year prison sentence.

separate
separates separating separated *verb*
to set apart from each other.

He separated the yellow marbles from the green ones.
separate *adjective*
separately *adverb*

sequel
sequels *noun*
something that follows an earlier event, or continues a story from a previous book or film.
A film sequel.
■ say **see**-kwul

sequence
sequences *noun*
a number of things that follow in a particular order.
■ say **see**-kwens

sequin
sequins *noun*
a small, shiny, metal or plastic disc that is sewn onto material as a decoration.
■ say **see**-kwin

serial
serials *noun*
a story that is broadcast or published in a series of parts.

series
noun
1 a group of similar things that follow one another in order.
a series of books on nature

2 a television or radio show that is broadcast in regular episodes, or a set of novels about the same characters.

serious
adjective
1 requiring careful thought.
A serious question.
2 worrying or dangerous.
3 not smiling or laughing.

He had a serious expression.

servant
servants *noun*
a person whose job it is to work for someone in that person's home.

serve
serves serving served *verb*
1 to help someone, usually by giving them something they want or need.
2 to start play in games like tennis by hitting the ball to your opponent.

service
services *noun*
1 the act of serving.
Good restaurant service.
2 employment in the armed forces or in a public organization.
Military service.
3 the supply of something that helps or serves people.
A telephone service.
4 religious worship.
A church service.
5 the act of checking and repairing machinery so that it continues to work well.
A car service.

set
sets *noun*
a group of things that belong together.

a toy construction set

set
sets setting set *verb*
1 to put in position or arrange something.
She set the vase on the table.
2 to give someone a task to do.
The teacher set the class some homework.
3 to go below the horizon.
The Sun sets in the west.
4 to go hard.
The cement took a long time to set.

settle
settles settling settled *verb*
1 to calm down, or stop moving.

The dog settled down to sleep.

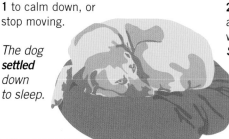

2 to decide or agree about something without any doubts.
Settle an argument.

several
adjective
a number, usually three or more, but not many more.
Several people waved as they walked past.

severe
adjective
1 extremely bad.
A severe accident.
2 strict or hard.
The rock face was a severe test for the climbers.
severely *adverb*

sew
sews sewing sewn *verb*
to join something together using a needle and thread.

sewing on a shirt button
■ say **so**

sewer
sewers *noun*
a large, underground pipe or channel that takes dirty water and waste matter away.
■ say **soo**-er

sex
sexes *noun*
one of two groups, male or female, that people, animals, and plants are divided into.

shade
shades *noun*
1 a cool place where the Sun's direct light doesn't reach.

He lay down in the shade to read.
shady *adjective*
2 a slight difference in colour.

different shades of pencil

shadow
shadows *noun*
a dark shape made by something that is blocking the light.

shadow

shaft
shafts *noun*
1 a long, vertical passageway.
A lift shaft.
2 a long, straight part of something.
A shaft of light.

shaggy
adjective
having long, rough, untidy hair.

■ comparisons **shaggier shaggiest**

shake
shakes shaking shook shaken *verb*
1 to move something rapidly up and down, or from side to side.

shaking hands
2 to tremble with fear, shock, or cold.

shall
verb
a word used to show that something will happen in the future.
I shall go shopping later.
■ always used with another verb

shallow
adjective
not deep.

They played in shallow water.

shame
shames *noun*
1 a sad thing that happens.
It's a shame you can't come.
2 an uncomfortable, guilty feeling about something you have done.
ashamed *adjective*

shampoo
shampoos *noun*
a soapy liquid that is used for washing hair.

shampoo *verb*

shape

shapes *noun*
the outline or form of an object.
Everything has a shape. Some shapes
are two-dimensional, because they have
width and length, but no height. Some
shapes are three-dimensional, because
they have width, length, and height.

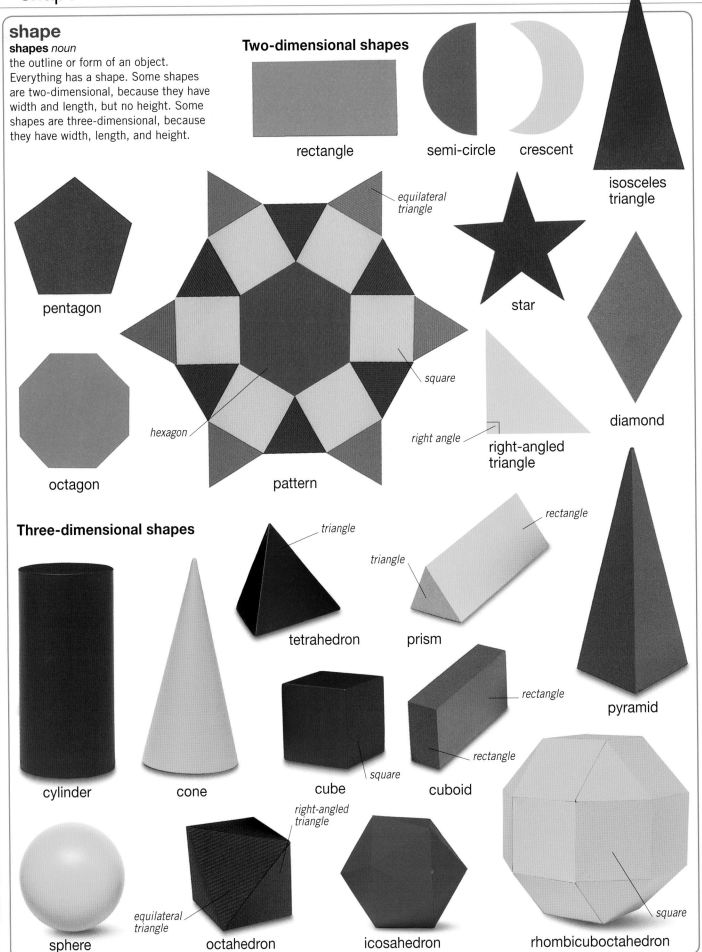

Two-dimensional shapes

rectangle

semi-circle

crescent

isosceles
triangle

pentagon

*equilateral
triangle*

star

square

diamond

octagon

hexagon

pattern

right angle

right-angled
triangle

Three-dimensional shapes

triangle

rectangle

triangle

cylinder

cone

tetrahedron

prism

rectangle

pyramid

cube

square

cuboid

rectangle

rectangle

*right-angled
triangle*

sphere

*equilateral
triangle*

octahedron

icosahedron

rhombicuboctahedron

square

share
shares sharing shared verb
1 to have or use together.
2 to divide something into parts to give to others.

*They **shared** the melon.*

shark
sharks noun
a large fish with rows of sharp teeth, which lives in both cold and warm seas. Sharks eat fish or small water animals and are able to detect smells and sounds at great distances.

*leopard **shark***

sharp
adjective
with a thin edge or a fine point that may be used for cutting things.
*Careful – that knife is **sharp!***
■ comparisons **sharper sharpest**

shatter
shatters shattering shattered verb
1 to break into many pieces.

*The glass **shattered**.*
2 to ruin someone's plans, or to make someone upset.
*The loss of their jobs **shattered** their dreams of buying a home.*

shave
shaves shaving shaved verb
to remove hair from the skin with a razor.

shawl
shawls noun
a large piece of cloth worn over the shoulders.

shear
shears shearing sheared shorn verb
to cut off wool or fur.
*We **shear** sheep for their wool.*

shed
sheds noun
a small building for storing things such as garden tools.

shed
sheds shedding shed verb
to drop, lose, or separate from something.

*Snakes **shed** their skins.*

sheep
sheep noun
a farm animal reared for its wool and meat.

sheer
adjective
1 very steep.
*It was a **sheer** drop.*
2 complete or absolute.
***Sheer** exhaustion.*

sheet
sheets noun
a large, thin, flat piece of cloth, paper, plastic, or metal.
*A **sheet** of steel.*

shelf
shelves noun
a horizontal piece of wood or metal for storing things on.

shell
shells noun
the hard, outer covering that protects some living things. Eggs, nuts, and animals such as snails, crabs, and tortoises have shells (see **reptile** on page 168).

*egg **shell***   *nut **shell***

*crab's **shell***

shellfish
noun
any small, edible water animal that has a shell.

shelter
shelters noun
a thing that protects someone or something from the weather or from danger.

*They took **shelter** from the sun.*
shelter verb
sheltered adjective

sheriff
sheriffs noun
1 in Scotland, a senior judge of a particular area.
2 in America, a person who is elected to keep the law and order in a particular area.

shield
shields noun
a strong piece of metal or leather that soldiers used to carry in battle to protect their bodies from their opponents' weapons.

*an ancient Indian **shield***

shield
shields shielding shielded verb
to protect.

*She **shielded** her eyes from the sun.*

A
B
C
D
E
F
G
H
I
J
K
L
M
N
O
P
Q
R
S
T
U
V
W
X
Y
Z

shin
shins *noun*
the front part of your leg below the knee.

shin

shine
shines shining shone *verb*
to give out or reflect light.

*The car headlights **shone** on the road ahead.*
shiny *adjective*

ship
ships *noun*
a large vessel for transporting people and cargo by sea. A ship is powered by a motor or sails, and is bigger than a boat.

shipwreck
shipwrecks *noun*
1 the destruction of a ship at sea.
*The whole of the ship's cargo was lost in the **shipwreck**.*
2 the remains of a ship that was destroyed at sea.

■ say **ship**-rek

shirt
shirts *noun*
a piece of clothing for covering the top half of your body. Shirts have sleeves and usually have a collar and buttons down the front.

shiver
shivers shivering shivered *verb*
to tremble with cold or fear.

*He **shivered** in the cold wind.*

shock
shocks *noun*
1 an unpleasant experience.
shock *verb*
shocking *adjective*
2 pain and injury caused by a flow of electricity through a person's body.
3 a state of weakness caused by injury or pain, or by an unpleasant experience.
*He was in **shock** after the accident.*

shoe
shoes *noun*
a protective covering worn on your feet, often made of leather.

shook
*from the verb **to shake***
*The dog **shook** himself dry.*

shoot
shoots shooting shot *verb*
1 to fire a bullet from a gun or another weapon.

*He used his bow to **shoot** the arrow.*
2 to wound or kill with a bullet or other weapon.
*The hunters **shot** the birds.*
3 to take pictures with a camera.
*She **shoots** lots of animal photographs.*

shop
shops *noun*
a place where people can go to buy things they need or want.
shop *verb*

shore
shores *noun*
the edge of an ocean, sea, or lake.

*sea**shore***

short
adjective
1 not long in measurement.

short hair

2 not lasting a long time.
*The film was very **short**.*
■ comparisons **shorter shortest**
■ opposite **long**
3 not having enough of something.
*We are **short** of milk.*

shortage
shortages *noun*
a situation where there is not enough of something.
*There is a **shortage** of bread in the supermarket.*

shorten
shortens shortening shortened *verb*
to make something shorter.

*She **shortened** the little girl's skirt for her.*

shorts
noun
a pair of short trousers that usually finish above the knees (see **sport** on page 197).

shot
shots *noun*
the act of shooting.
*She fired a **shot** at the target.*

should
verb
a word used to show that something must be done, ought to be done, or is expected to happen.
*I **should** do my homework.*
■ opposite **should not / shouldn't**
■ always used with another verb

shoulder
shoulders *noun*
the place below your neck where your arms join your body.

shoulder

shout
shouts shouting shouted *verb*
to call out loudly.
shout *noun*

shovel
shovels *noun*
a broad tool like a spade that you use to scoop up material such as earth, sand, or rubbish.

show
shows showing showed *verb*
to allow something to be seen, or to make something clear to other people.

*He **showed** the class his favourite picture in the book.*

show
shows *noun*
a public performance or exhibition.

shower
showers *noun*
1 a device that sends out a fine spray of water, used for washing your body.

2 a short, sudden fall of rain.
3 a sudden fall of something in large quantities.
*A **shower** of sparks.*
■ rhymes with **our**
shower *verb*

shred
shreds *noun*
a small, narrow strip that has been cut or torn off something.

***shreds** of paper*

shriek
shrieks shrieking shrieked *verb*
to cry out in a high-pitched voice because you are excited or afraid.
*He **shrieked** when he saw the mouse.*
■ say **shreek**
shriek *noun*

shrill
adjective
making a sharp, high sound.
*A **shrill** whistle.*
■ comparisons **shriller shrillest**

shrink
shrinks shrinking shrank shrunk *verb*
to become smaller.

*His jumper had **shrunk** in the wash.*

shrivel
shrivels shrivelling shrivelled *verb*
to become small and wrinkled, or dry out.
*Water your plants or they will **shrivel** and die.*

shrub
shrubs *noun*
a large plant that is smaller than a tree, often with many stems and little or no trunk.

shrug
shrugs shrugging shrugged *verb*
to raise your shoulders to show that you do not care or do not know.

shudder
shudders shuddering shuddered *verb*
to shake or tremble violently for a short time.
*The thought of spiders makes me **shudder**.*

shuffle
shuffles shuffling shuffled *verb*
1 to mix things up to change their order.

*He **shuffled** the cards.*
2 to move by dragging your feet along the ground.

shut
shuts shutting shut *verb*
to close something.
*He **shut** the book carefully.*
■ opposite **open**
shut *adjective*

shutter
shutters *noun*
1 a hard cover for a window.

*The house has **shutters** at every window.*
2 the part of a camera inside the lens that opens and closes to allow light to fall onto the film.

shy
adjective
timid and lacking confidence with people.
■ comparisons **shyer shyest**
shyly *adverb*

sick
adjective
ill, or not healthy.
■ comparisons **sicker sickest**

A B C D E F G H I J K L M N O P Q R S T U V W X Y Z

side
sides *noun*
1 the edge of something. *Triangles have three **sides**.*
2 the outside surfaces of something, but not the front or back.

*a car viewed from the **side***
3 a team or group of people that is against another group. *Which **side** are you on?*

sideways
adverb
towards the side or from the side. *Crabs walk **sideways**.*

siege
sieges *noun*
the action of surrounding a place to try to force the people inside to surrender.
■ say **seej**

sieve
sieves *noun*
a container made of plastic or metal, that has mesh or small holes for sorting solids from liquids, or fine grains from larger pieces.

■ say **siv**
sieve *verb*

sift
sifts sifting sifted *verb*
to sort through something carefully in order to separate larger pieces from smaller pieces.

sifting for gold

sigh
sighs sighing sighed *verb*
to let out a long, deep breath slowly.
■ say **sye**

sight
noun
1 the ability to see. *She lost her **sight** in an accident.*
2 something that can be seen. *The ship was a fine **sight** as it sailed up the river.*
■ say **site**

sign
signs signing signed *verb*
1 to write your signature.

*The boy **signed** his friend's cast.*
2 to use sign language to communicate with people who have hearing difficulties.
■ say **sine**

sign
signs *noun*
1 a symbol that represents something. *The **sign** for pound is £.*
2 a movement that expresses a meaning. *He nodded his head as a **sign** that he wanted to leave.*
3 a public notice that gives information.

*a no swimming **sign***
4 anything that indicates something is going to happen. *Is there any **sign** of snow?*

signal
signals *noun*
1 an action or object that is used to send a message without words.

*He put his right arm out as a **signal** that he wanted to turn right.*
2 the electrical current by which sounds and pictures are transmitted to radios, televisions, and telephones.

signature
signatures *noun*
your special way of writing your own name.

■ say **sig**-na-chur

significant
adjective
very important, or having a special meaning. *A **significant** event.*

Sikh
Sikhs *noun*
a person who follows Sikhism, an Indian religion. Sikhs believe in a single God.
■ say **seek**

silent
adjective
not making any sound.
silence *noun*
silently *adverb*

silhouette
silhouettes *noun*
a dark outline of something seen against a pale background.
■ say sil-oo-**et**

silk
silks *noun*
a thin, soft fabric made from threads spun by a silkworm.

silly
adjective
not sensible. *What a **silly** idea!*
■ comparisons **sillier silliest**

silver
noun
1 a precious metal found in the ground, which is used in making coins and jewellery.

silver

silver ring
2 the colour of the metal silver.
silver *adjective*

similar
adjective
almost, but not exactly, the same.

*These mugs are **similar**.*

simmer
simmers simmering simmered *verb*
to cook something so that it bubbles very gently.
Leave the soup to simmer for 20 minutes.

simple
adjective
1 easy to understand or solve.
A simple solution.
■ opposite **complicated**
2 plain.

simple earrings   ornate earrings
■ comparisons **simpler simplest**

simplify
simplifies simplifying simplified *verb*
to make something easier.

sincere
adjective
honest, or not pretending.
She was sincere when she said she was sorry.
■ say sin-**seer**
sincerely *adverb*

sing
sings singing sang sung *verb*
1 to make a musical sound with your voice.

She likes to sing.
2 to perform by singing.
She is singing in an opera.

single
adjective
something that is only for one person, or only one of something.

single bed

sink
sinks sinking sank sunk *verb*
1 to go down below the surface of water.
The boat was sinking fast.
2 to go down slowly.
The Sun sank below the horizon.

sink
sinks *noun*
a basin with a water supply, taps, and a drain.

kitchen sink

sip
sips sipping sipped *verb*
to drink in small amounts.

He sipped his coffee slowly.
sip *noun*

siren
sirens *noun*
a device that makes a loud noise, and is used as a warning signal.
A fire-engine's siren.
■ say **sye**-ren

sister
sisters *noun*
a female person who has the same mother and father as someone else.

sit
sits sitting sat *verb*
1 to rest your body by supporting your weight on your bottom, rather than on your feet.

2 to rest or be positioned.
The bird sat on its perch.
3 to take an exam.

site
sites *noun*
an area of ground used for a particular purpose.

a building site

situation
situations *noun*
what is happening in a particular place at a particular time.

He found himself in a desperate situation.
■ say sit-yoo-**ay**-shun

size
sizes *noun*
a measurement of how large or small something is.

These screwdrivers are different sizes.

sizzle
sizzles sizzling sizzled *verb*
to make a hissing sound during cooking.
The sausages sizzled under the grill.

skate
skates skating skated *verb*
to slide along on a hard surface wearing special shoes with blades or wheels.

skating noun   roller skate

skateboard
skateboards *noun*
a small board on wheels that people stand on to ride along.

a b c d e f g h i j k l m n o p q r s t u v w x y z

A B C D E F G H I J K L M N O P Q R S T U V W X Y Z

skeleton

skeletons *noun*
a group of connected bones that support a person's or animal's body. There are 206 bones in a human skeleton.

seal **skeleton**

horny shield layer
ribs
bony layer

tortoise **skeleton**

bird **skeleton**

frog **skeleton**

horn

goat skull

tusk

elephant skull

bony plates   *radial*

fish **skeleton**

monkey **skeleton**

spine
rib
skull

snake **skeleton**

skull (cranium)
collar bone (clavicle)
jawbone (mandible)
shoulder blade (scapula)
breast bone (sternum)
upper arm bone (humerus)
rib cage
spine
main forearm bone (ulna)
small forearm bone (radius)
hip bone (pelvis)
coccyx
hand bones (carpals)
metacarpal
phalanx
thigh bone (femur)
kneecap (patella)
main shin bone (tibia)
small shin bone (fibula)
foot bones (tarsals)
metatarsal
phalanx

human **skeleton**

crocodile **skeleton**

sketch

sketches *noun*
1 a quick drawing.

*a **sketch** of a ship*
2 a short play.

ski

skis skiing skied *verb*
to move over snow or ice
on two long pieces of wood,
metal, or plastic
attached to
special boots.

■ say **skee**
ski *noun*

skid

skids skidding skidded *verb*
to slide out of control.

*The car **skidded** on the
icy road.*

skill

skills *noun*
an ability to do something.
*Juggling is a difficult **skill**
to learn.*
skilful *adjective*

skin

skins *noun*
1 the thin, protective layer
that animals and people have
on the outside of their bodies
(see **mammal** on page 124).
2 a thin layer that covers
the flesh of vegetables and
fruit (see **fruit** on page 85).

skip

skips skipping skipped *verb*
1 to move along, hopping
lightly from one foot
to another.
*She **skipped** down the road.*
2 to jump over a turning rope.

*skipping
rope*

3 to miss something
out deliberately.
*We'll **skip** the next question.*

skirt

skirts *noun*
a piece of clothing worn
by a girl or woman, that
hangs down from the waist.

skull

skulls *noun*
the bone frame
of the head that
protects the brain
and supports the
face (see **skeleton**
on page 188).

*ram's **skull***

sky

skies *noun*
the air around the Earth as
we see it. The sky usually
looks blue.
*Not a cloud in the **sky**.*

skyscraper

skyscrapers *noun*
a very tall building with
many storeys.

slam

slams slamming slammed *verb*
to shut something with
a bang.
***Slam** the door.*

slang

noun
everyday words and phrases
that are not normally used
in writing or formal speaking.

slant

slants slanting slanted *verb*
to slope sideways.

*One shelf was **slanted**.*

slap

slaps slapping slapped *verb*
to hit quickly with the palm
of your hand.
slap *noun*

slave

slaves *noun*
someone who is forced to
work without being paid
and is not free to leave.

sledge

sledges *noun*
a low platform with curved
strips of metal or wood
underneath. Sledges are
used to carry people and
things over snow and ice.

sleek

adjective
smooth and shiny.
*Seals have **sleek** fur.*

sleep

sleeps sleeping slept *verb*
to rest your body and mind
with your eyes closed.

sleep *noun*

sleeve

sleeves *noun*
the part of a piece of clothing
that covers the arm.

sleeve

a b c d e f g h i j k l m n o p q r s t u v w x y z

A B C D E F G H I J K L M N O P Q R S T U V W X Y Z

sleigh
sleighs noun
a large sledge, usually pulled by an animal and used for travelling over snow or ice.

■ say **slay**

slender
adjective
long and thin.
*A **slender** branch.*

slice
slices noun
a thin, flat piece cut from something.

*a **slice** of bread*
slice verb

slide
slides sliding slid verb
to move smoothly over a surface.
*She **slid** across the ice on her skates.*

slide
slides noun
1 a piece of children's play equipment for sliding down.

2 a transparent photo in a cardboard or plastic frame.

slight
adjective
very small in amount.
*There's a **slight** chance he'll come.*
■ say **slite**
■ comparisons **slighter slightest**
slightly adverb

slim
adjective
fairly thin.
■ comparisons **slimmer slimmest**

slime
noun
an unpleasantly wet and slippery substance.
*Snails leave a trail of **slime** as they move along.*
slimy adjective

sling
slings noun
a piece of material used to support an injured arm.

sling

slip
slips slipping slipped verb
1 to move, or to move something easily or quietly.
*She **slipped** the note under the door.*
2 to slide or fall over by accident.
*He **slipped** in the mud.*

slipper
slippers noun
a soft, comfortable, loose shoe worn indoors.

slippery
adjective
smooth and difficult to grip.
*She couldn't keep hold of the **slippery** fish.*

slit
slits noun
a long, narrow, straight cut.
slit verb

slither
slithers slithering slithered verb
to slide along.
*Snakes **slither** over sand.*

slope
slopes noun
ground that slants.

*The skier went down the steep **slope**.*
slope verb

slot
slots noun
a small, narrow opening for putting something in.

*She put a coin in the **slot**.*
slot verb

slouch
slouches slouching slouched verb
to sit, stand, or walk so that your shoulders are bent over and your back is not straight.
■ rhymes with **ouch**

slow
adjective
1 taking a long time, or not hurrying.

*Tortoises move very **slowly**.*
2 behind the time.
*This watch is 5 minutes **slow**.*
■ comparisons **slower slowest**
■ opposite **fast**
slowly adverb

sly
adjective
doing things in a sneaky or secretive way.
*She had a **sly** plan to trick her brother.*
■ comparisons **slyer slyest**
slyly adverb

smack
smacks smacking smacked verb
to slap with the hand, usually as a punishment.

small
adjective
little in size, or not great or big.

***small** tin of paint*   *big tin of paint*

■ comparisons **smaller smallest**
■ opposite **big**

smart
adjective
1 quick and intelligent.
*A **smart** remark.*
2 well-dressed.
*She looked
very **smart**
in her
new clothes.*

■ comparisons **smarter smartest**

smartphone
smartphones *noun*
a mobile phone that can
carry out many functions
similar to a computer.

smash
**smashes smashing
smashed** *verb*
to break something into pieces.

*The plate **smashed**
on the ground.*

smear
smears smearing smeared
verb
to spread something
sticky or messy.

*He **smeared** glue onto the
back of the picture.*
■ say **smeer**
smear *noun*

smell
smells smelling smelled or
smelt *verb*
1 to use your nose to
notice odours.

smelling a rose
2 to have an odour.
*The barn **smelled** of hay.*

smell
smells *noun*
1 the sense you use to notice
odours through your nose.
***Smell** is one of the
five senses.*
2 the odour of something,
usually unpleasant.
*What a **smell**!*

smile
smiles smiling smiled *verb*
to show you are happy by
widening your mouth and
turning up the corners of
your lips.

smile *noun*

smoke
noun
the cloud of gas and small
ash particles that rises
from a fire.
smoke *verb*

smooth
adjective
having an even surface,
without sharp edges or lumps.
*As **smooth** as silk.*
■ opposite **rough**

smoulder
**smoulders smouldering
smouldered** *verb*
to burn very slowly, without
any flames.
■ say **smole**-der
smouldering *adjective*

smudge
smudges *noun*
a dirty mark made by rubbing
or smearing something onto
a surface.

*She had a **smudge** of chalk
on her cheek.*
smudge *verb*

smuggle
**smuggles smuggling
smuggled** *verb*
to take something into a
place secretly and illegally.

snack
snacks *noun*
a small amount of food eaten
between meals or instead of
a meal.

snail
snails *noun*
a slow-moving animal
with a spiral shell. Snails
live on land or
in water and
eat mainly plants.
When in danger,
snails pull their
soft bodies back
into their shells.

snake
snakes *noun*
a long, thin reptile with no
legs. Snakes eat insects, eggs,
fish, or animals. Some snakes
are poisonous, while
others kill by
squeezing their
prey tightly.

*vine **snake***

snap
snaps snapping snapped *verb*
1 to make a sudden
cracking noise.
***Snap** your fingers.*
2 to break
suddenly.

*She **snapped**
the stick in half.*
3 to talk in a
quick, angry way.
*"Why haven't you done your
homework?" he **snapped**.*

snarl
snarls snarling snarled *verb*
to growl fiercely, showing
the teeth.
*The guard dog **snarled**
at the burglar.*

a
b
c
d
e
f
g
h
i
j
k
l
m
n
o
p
q
r
s
t
u
v
w
x
y
z

A B C D E F G H I J K L M N O P Q R S T U V W X Y Z

snatch

snatches snatching snatched *verb*
to take hold of something suddenly.
I snatched my coat and ran out of the house.

sneak

sneaks sneaking sneaked *verb*
to move or act in a quiet or secret way.

She sneaked in through the door.
sneaky *adjective*

sneer

sneers sneering sneered *verb*
to show scorn about something or someone.
"My bike is better than yours," *she sneered.*
sneer *noun*

sneeze

sneezes sneezing sneezed *verb*
to force air out of your nose in a sudden, uncontrolled way.

sneeze *noun*

sniff

sniffs sniffing sniffed *verb*
1 to breathe in noisily through your nose.
Stop sniffing and blow your nose!
2 to breathe in through your nose, trying to smell something.
Dogs find out about things by sniffing them.

snip

snips snipping snipped *verb*
to cut something with scissors in one quick movement.

snipping the top off the packet

snore

snores snoring snored *verb*
to breathe noisily as you sleep.

snorkel

snorkels *noun*
a short tube that a swimmer holds in his or her mouth in order to breathe underwater.

snorkel

snorkels snorkelling snorkelled *verb*
to swim using a snorkel.

snout

snouts *noun*
an animal's long nose and jaws (see **dinosaur** on page 61, **mammal** on page 124, and **reptile** on page 168).

snow

snow

noun
soft, white flakes of ice that fall from the clouds in cold weather.
snow *verb*
snowy *adjective*

snowball

snowballs *noun*
a ball shape made by pressing snow together.

snowdrift

snowdrifts *noun*
snow that has been blown into a pile by the wind.

snowflake

snowflakes *noun*
a group of ice crystals that falls as a tiny piece of snow.

snowman

snowmen *noun*
a figure that you build with snow.

snowplough

snowploughs *noun*
a machine used to clear snow off the roads or off railway tracks.

snowstorm

snowstorms *noun*
a storm during which a lot of snow falls.

snug

adjective
comfortable and warm.

The cat looked very snug curled up inside the basket.

snuggle

snuggles snuggling snuggled *verb*
to lie close together in order to keep warm.

soak

soaks soaking soaked *verb*
to make or become thoroughly wet.

She got soaked in the pouring rain.

soap

soaps *noun*
a substance used for washing.

soar

soars soaring soared *verb*
to fly high in the air.
The eagle soared above them.

sob
sobs sobbing sobbed *verb*
to cry noisily, catching
your breath.

The little boy was sobbing in his cot.

soccer
noun
another name for football.
Soccer is played by two teams
of 11 players. The winning
team is the one that scores
the most goals by kicking or
heading a large ball into a net.

social
adjective
to do with people living
together in communities.
Social history.
■ say **so**-shul

society
societies *noun*
1 all the people who live in
a group or in a country, and
their way of life.
Laws protect society.
2 a club or an organization.
An animal welfare society.
■ say sow-**sye**-eh-tee

sock
socks *noun*
a piece of clothing
that covers your
foot and the
lower part of
your leg.

socket
sockets *noun*
a hole that something, such
as a plug or bulb, fits into.
An electric socket.

soft
adjective
1 easy to put out of shape by
touching, or not firm or hard.
A soft pillow.
■ opposite **hard**
2 gentle or smooth
to the touch.

a **soft** ball of wool
■ opposite **rough**
3 not harsh or loud.
A soft sound.
■ comparisons **softer softest**

software
noun
programs that are put into
a computer to make it work.

soil
soils *noun*
the top layer of earth in
which plants can grow.

*You can grow some vegetables
in pots of soil.*

solar
adjective
having to
do with the
power of the
Sun or any
other light.

solar panel

a solar-powered calculator

sold
from the verb **to sell**
*She sold her bike when she
grew too big for it.*

soldier
soldiers *noun*
a person who
is part of
an army.

*ancient
Greek
soldier*

■ say **sole**-jer

sole
soles *noun*
1 the bottom part
of your foot.

sole

2 the bottom of a shoe.

3 an edible type of flat fish.

sole
adjective
one or only.
*He was the sole survivor
of the crash.*

solemn
adjective
serious.
A solemn promise.
■ say **sol**-em

solid
solids *noun*
a substance that keeps its
shape, and is not a liquid
or a gas.
Ice, rock, and jelly are solids.

solid
adjective
1 made of the same
thing all the
way through.

*This cat is carved from
a solid block of wood.*
2 firm or strongly made.
*They built a solid wall
around the castle.*

solo
adjective
on your own.
*She made a solo flight
around the world.*
■ say **so**-low

solo
solos *noun*
a piece of music that is played
or sung by one person.

She played a violin solo.

solution
solutions *noun*
1 the answer to a problem.
The solution to the crossword.
2 a liquid that has something
dissolved in it.
A solution of salt and water.
■ say so-**loo**-shun

a b c d e f g h i j k l m n o p q r s t u v w x y z

A B C D E F G H I J K L M N O P Q R S T U V W X Y Z

solve

solves solving solved *verb*
to find the answer to
a problem or mystery.

*To **solve** the puzzle you must
end up with one marble in
the middle.*

some

adjective
1 several or a few, but not
a definite number or amount.
*Could you buy **some**
apples, please?*
2 part of, but not all.
*I ate **some** cake.*
◆ **Some**body has taken
my ruler.
◆ I must get there **some**how.
◆ Will **some**one lay the
table please?
◆ Let's get **some**thing to eat.
◆ **Some**times I go to the
swimming pool after school.
◆ You must have put
it **some**where.

somersault

**somersaults somersaulting
somersaulted** *verb*
to roll or leap forwards
or backwards so that your
whole body turns over.

■ say **summer**-salt
somersault *noun*

son

sons *noun*
a person's male child.

■ say **sun**

sonar

noun
a device that finds and
records the depth of water.
Sonar works by sending out
sound waves and measuring
how long it takes for the echo
to return. Submarines use
sonar to navigate at sea.
■ say **so**-nar

song

songs *noun*
a piece of music with words
that you sing.

soon

adverb
after a short time.
*It will **soon** be lunchtime.*

sore

adjective
aching or
hurting.

*His head was **sore** where
he had bumped it.*
■ comparisons **sorer sorest**

sorry

adjective
feeling sad or unhappy
about what has happened.
*I am **sorry** that I trod on
your toe.*
■ comparisons **sorrier sorriest**
■ opposite **pleased**

sort

sorts *noun*
a group of similar things,
or a type of something.
*What **sort** of holiday will
you have this year?*

sort

sorts sorting sorted *verb*
to arrange
things into
different types
or groups.

*He **sorted** the socks and put
them in pairs.*

sought

*from the verb **to seek**
The two countries
sought peace.*
■ say **sort**

soul

souls *noun*
the spiritual part of a person.
Some people believe that
the soul continues after
a person's body is dead.

sound

sounds *noun*
something that can be heard.

soup

soups *noun*
a liquid food made from fish,
meat, or vegetables, cooked
in water or milk.

*vegetable **soup***
■ say **soop**

sour

adjective
with a sharp taste, like vinegar
or a lemon.
■ rhymes with **power**

source

sources *noun*
the place where something
comes from or is found.
*The **source** of a river.*

south

noun
one of the four main directions
on a compass. South is to your
right when you are facing the
rising Sun.

north

west *east*

south

southern *adjective*

souvenir

souvenirs *noun*
something that you keep
to remind you of a person,
place, or event.
*Holiday **souvenirs**.*
■ say soo-ven-**neer**

sow

sows sowing sowed sown
verb
to put seeds in the soil
so that they will grow
into plants.

*She **sowed** some seeds
in the window box.*
■ say **so**

soya
noun
a bean used for food
or crushed for its oil.

space
noun
1 the place where all the
stars and planets are found.
2 an empty area or gap.

spacecraft
spacecrafts *noun*
a vehicle for travelling
in space.

*Vostok 1 was the first
manned **spacecraft**.*

spade
spades *noun*
a tool that is
used for digging.

spaghetti
noun
a type
of long,
thin pasta.

■ say spa-**ge**-tee

spanner
spanners *noun*
a tool with a specially shaped
end that is used to fasten and
unfasten nuts and bolts.

spare
adjective
more than is needed.

spare wheel

spark
sparks *noun*
a small, burning piece
of material that is thrown
up from a fire.

sparkle
sparkles sparkling sparkled
verb
to reflect tiny flashes of
bright light.

*Diamonds
sparkle.*
sparkling *adjective*

speak
**speaks speaking spoke
spoken** *verb*
to say words, or to talk.

spear
spears *noun*
a long weapon
with a sharp point
that is thrown
by hand.

special
adjective
different from the rest, usually
because it is better.
■ say **spesh**-ul
■ opposite **ordinary**

species
species *noun*
a group of animals or plants
that usually look similar or
behave in a similar way.
*There are about 320 **species**
of salamander in the world.*
■ say **spee**-sheez

specific
adjective
definite or precise.
*Can you be more **specific**?*
■ say spes-**if**-ik

speck
specks *noun*
a very small piece or spot.
*A **speck** of dust.*

speckled
adjective
covered with
tiny marks
or spots.

*a **speckled** egg*

spectator
spectators *noun*
a person who watches an
event but does not take part.

*The **spectators** cheered their
favourite team.*

speech
speeches *noun*
1 the ability to speak
and the way people speak.
***Speech** is a power only
humans have.*
2 a talk given to an audience.

speed
speeds *noun*
a measurement of how fast
something is moving.

spell
spells spelling spelled or
spelt *verb*
to say or write the letters
of a word in the correct order.
*How do you **spell** "special"?*

spell
spells *noun*
words that are supposed
to have a magic power.
*The magician cast a **spell**
on the frog.*

spend
spends spending spent *verb*
1 to use money to buy things.
*I **spent** a lot at the sales.*
2 to pass time.
*We **spent** two weeks camping
in the forest.*

sphere
spheres *noun*
a solid, round shape, like a ball
(see **shape** on page 182).
■ say **sfeer**

spice
spices *noun*
a substance made from dried
parts of a plant and used to
add flavour to food.

cayenne pepper   paprika

cinnamon stick

spicy
adjective
strongly flavoured with spice.

a
b
c
d
e
f
g
h
i
j
k
l
m
n
o
p
q
r
s
t
u
v
w
x
y
z

A B C D E F G H I J K L M N O P Q R **S** T U V W X Y Z

spider
spiders *noun*
a small animal with eight legs. Spiders spin nets of thin, sticky threads called webs, which they use to trap insects for food. They kill their prey with poison.

spike
spikes *noun*
a sharp point, often made of metal or wood, or a pointed part of an animal or plant.

spill
spills spilling spilled or **spilt** *verb*
to let something drop or overflow from a container.

*She **spilt** her drink.*

spin
spins spinning spun *verb*
1 to turn around quickly, or to make something turn quickly.

2 to produce threads. Spiders and silkworms spin threads by producing them from their bodies. People spin raw cotton and wool to make threads.

spine
spines *noun*
1 the column of bones that makes up the backbone of a skeleton (see **skeleton** on page 188).

spine

2 one of the stiff, sharp points on an animal, like a porcupine, or on a plant, like a cactus (see **fish** on page 79, **plant** on page 151, and **sea life** on page 178).
3 the part of a book where the pages are joined and that holds the book together.

spiral
spirals *noun*
an object shaped in a curve that turns around a central point.

spire
spires *noun*
a tall, pointed structure at the top of a tower.

*church **spire***

spirit
spirits *noun*
1 a person's mind and feelings.
*In good **spirits**.*
spiritual *adjective*
2 a being, such as a ghost, that does not have a body.

spit
spits spitting spat *verb*
to force saliva or something else out of your mouth.
*She **spat** out the rotten apple.*

spite
noun
deliberate nastiness.
*He ignored him out of **spite**.*
spiteful *adjective*

splash
splashes splashing splashed *verb*
to scatter water or another liquid.

*The children **splashed** about in the pool.*
splash *noun*

splinter
splinters *noun*
a thin, sharp piece that has broken off something hard, such as wood or glass.

split
splits splitting split *verb*
1 to divide into parts.

*She **split** the logs with an axe.*
2 to tear or crack, perhaps by mistake.
*The bag **split** open.*

splutter
splutters spluttering spluttered *verb*
to make a series of short hissing or spitting noises.
*The sauce **spluttered** in the pan.*

spoil
spoils spoiling spoiled or **spoilt** *verb*
1 to destroy or damage something.
*Don't draw on that – you'll **spoil** it.*
2 to give a child so much that he or she becomes demanding and unpleasant.

spoke
*from the verb **to speak***
*They **spoke** in a whisper in case anyone was listening.*

sponge
sponges *noun*
a soft, flexible material used for washing and cleaning. Some sponges are made of plastic, but real sponges are made from the skeletons of sea creatures.
■ say **spunj**

*bath **sponge***

sponsor
sponsors sponsoring sponsored *verb*
to give money to support a charity or event. Sometimes money is given in return for a person completing an activity.
*The sports shop **sponsored** the cross-country race.*
sponsor *noun*

spoon
spoons *noun*
a small utensil with a curved bowl at one end. Spoons are used for eating or stirring.

*plastic **spoon***

*metal **spoon***

sport

sports *noun*
an activity or game that needs physical effort or skill. People play sport for exercise or pleasure.

windsurfing

ball

tee

mast

sail

batten

boom

buoyancy aid

wetsuit

board

sailboard

golf

shaft

head

wood   iron   putter

golf clubs

American football

face guard

armpad   football helmet

shoulder and chest pads

athletics

spike

track shoes

basketball

basketball ring

basketball

net

singlet

shorts

trainers

squash

strings

frame

throat

shaft

grip

ball

racket

badminton

head

shaft

feathers

shuttlecocks

handle

racket

table tennis

blade

bat   ball

field hockey

goalkeeper's shoe cover

field hockey shoe

head

field hockey stick   ball

ice hockey

skates

blade

puck   *blade*

ice hockey stick

cricket

ball

grip

blade

bail

shaft

stump

wicket   bat

baseball

webbed pocket

barrel

ball

fielding glove   bat

a b c d e f g h i j k l m n o p q r s t u v w x y z

197

spot
spots *noun*
1 a small, round area that is a different colour from the area around it.
*This cup and saucer are covered in white **spots**.*
2 a place.
*It was a perfect picnic **spot**.*

spot
spots spotting spotted *verb*
to notice or see.
*Can you **spot** my car?*

spotlight
spotlights *noun*
a strong light pointed at a small area, usually on a stage.

spout
spouts *noun*
the part of a container that a liquid is poured from.

*teapot **spout***

spray
sprays spraying sprayed *verb*
to scatter a fine shower of liquid onto something.

*He **sprayed** the plant with water.*
spray *noun*

spread
spreads spreading spread *verb*
to open something out or make it cover a bigger area.

*They **spread** the blanket out on the ground.*
■ say **spred**

spring
springs *noun*
1 the season between winter and summer when the weather becomes warmer and many plants start to grow.
2 a coil of thin metal that jumps back into shape after it has been pressed together or pulled apart.

3 a place where water flows out of the ground.

spring
springs springing sprang sprung *verb*
1 to jump upwards in a lively way.

*She **sprang** over the gymnastic apparatus.*
spring *noun*
2 to appear or grow quickly.
*New houses **sprang** up all over the hillside.*

sprint
sprints sprinting sprinted *verb*
to run very fast.

sprint *noun*

sprout
sprouts sprouting sprouted *verb*
to begin to grow.

*Green shoots **sprouted** from the bean.*
sprout *noun*

spy
spies *noun*
a person who gathers information in secret.
spy *verb*

square
squares *noun*
a shape with four equal sides and four right angles (see **shape** on page 182).
square *adjective*

squash
squashes squashing squashed *verb*
1 to crush something so that it becomes flat.
2 to squeeze together.

*The people were **squashed** into the train.*
■ say **skwosh**

squeak
squeaks squeaking squeaked *verb*
to make a short, shrill sound, like the sound a mouse makes.
squeak *noun*

squeal
squeals squealing squealed *verb*
to make a long, shrill sound like the sound a piglet makes.
squeal *noun*

squeeze
squeezes squeezing squeezed *verb*
to press hard, often in order to push something out.

*She **squeezed** the paint out of the tube.*

squirm
squirms squirming squirmed *verb*
to twist the body from side to side, or to wriggle.
*The rabbit **squirmed** under the fence.*
■ say **skwurm**

squirrel
squirrels *noun*
a small, furry rodent. Some types of squirrel live in trees, while others live on the ground. Squirrels eat nuts, berries, fruits, and insects.

squirt
squirts squirting squirted *verb*
to shoot out a thin jet of liquid.

*He **squirted** the washing-up liquid into the bowl.*
■ rhymes with **dirt**

stab
stabs stabbing stabbed *verb*
to pierce or wound with a knife or other pointed object.
*She **stabbed** the potato with a fork to see if it was cooked.*

stable
stables *noun*
a building where horses or other animals are kept.

*a **stable** for horses*

stack
stacks *noun*
a pile of things, one on top of another.

*a **stack** of plates*
stack *verb*

stadium
stadiums or **stadia** *noun*
a sports ground surrounded by seats for spectators.

staff
noun
a group of people who work together in a business, school, or other organization.

*The nursing **staff** at the hospital wear a uniform.*

stag
stags *noun*
a male deer, especially a red deer that is over four years old.

stage
stages *noun*
1 a platform used for plays and other performances.
2 a point reached in the progress of something.
*They made the long journey in several **stages**.*

stagger
staggers staggering staggered *verb*
to walk in an unsteady way.
*They **staggered** home after the long walk.*

stain
stains *noun*
a dirty mark that is difficult to remove.

coffee **stain**

stain *verb*

stair
stairs *noun*
one of a series of steps, set one after the other.

*a flight of **stairs***

stalactite
stalactites *noun*
a spike of rock that is formed from dripping water and hangs down from the roof of a cave.

■ say
stal-ak-tite

stalagmite
stalagmites *noun*
a spike of rock that is formed by dripping water and builds up on the floor of a cave.

■ say
stal-ag-mite

stale
adjective
no longer fresh.
***Stale** bread is hard and dry.*

stalk
stalks *noun*
1 the stem of a plant or a leaf (see **plant** on page 151).
2 a long, thin part of an animal (see **sea life** on page 178).

leaf **stalk**

stall
stalls *noun*
1 an area divided off in a stable or barn for one animal.

2 a table used to display and sell goods, usually at a market.

■ rhymes with **call**

stall
stalls stalling stalled *verb*
to come to a stop suddenly, without meaning to.
*The old car **stalled** at the traffic lights.*

stammer
stammers stammering stammered *verb*
to stutter or speak with difficulty, often stopping in the middle of words and repeating sounds.
stammer *noun*

a b c d e f g h i j k l m n o p q r s t u v w x y z

199

stamp
stamps *noun*
a sticker you put on an envelope or parcel to show that you have paid for it to be delivered.

stamp
stamps stamping stamped *verb*
to bring your foot down very hard.

stamp *noun*

stand
stands standing stood *verb*
to be in an upright position.

*She **stood** on a box to look over the fence.*

standard
standards *noun*
a level of quality that is considered acceptable, or how good something is.
*The **standard** of spelling in this class is very high.*

standard
adjective
ordinary or usual.
*Headlights are **standard** equipment on all cars.*

stank
*from the verb **to stink***
*The boat **stank** of fish.*

staple
staples *noun*
a small, thin strip of metal used to join sheets of paper together.
■ say **stay**-pul

star
stars *noun*
1 an object in the sky that appears as a ball of light. The Sun is the nearest star to Earth.

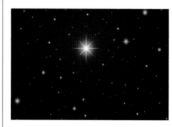

2 a shape with five or more points (see **shape** on page 182).
3 a famous actor, actress, or other performer.

stare
stares staring stared *verb*
to look for a long time at something with your eyes wide open.

*The cat **stared** at the mouse.*

starfish
starfish *noun*
a star-shaped sea animal, usually with five arms. Starfish eat plants and sea animals, such as crabs and other shellfish. They sense things through tentacles on their arms (see **sea life** on page 178).

start
starts starting started *verb*
to begin.

*The runners lined up, ready to **start** the race.*
start *noun*

startle
startles startling startled *verb*
to give someone a surprise or a shock.
*His son **startled** him.*

starve
starves starving starved *verb*
to suffer or die from lack of food.
starvation *noun*

state
states *noun*
1 the condition of something, or what it is like.
*In an untidy **state**.*
2 a group of people under one government. A state can be a whole country or part of a country.
*The United **States** of America.*

state
states stating stated *verb*
to say something clearly.
statement *noun*

station
stations *noun*
1 a place where buses and trains stop so that people can get on and off.

*bus **station***
2 a building used by a public service, such as the police.
*A police **station**.*
■ say **stay**-shun

statue
statues *noun*
a figure of a person or animal made from stone, wood, or another hard material.

Statue of Liberty
■ say **stat**-tyoo

stay
stays staying stayed *verb*
1 to remain in one place.
*Dad **stayed** at home while we went to the show.*
2 to live somewhere for a short time.
*I went to **stay** with my cousin during the holidays.*
3 to continue to be in one state.
*It **stayed** sunny all week.*

steady
adjective
1 firm.
*He held his partner **steady**.*
2 continuous or unchanging.
*A **steady** fall of snow.*

■ say **sted**-ee
■ comparisons
steadier steadiest
steadily *adverb*

steak
steaks *noun*
a thick slice of fish or meat, usually beef.
■ say **stake**

steal
steals stealing stole stolen
verb
to take something that does not belong to you, without the owner's permission.

*The thief **stole** the laptop computer.*

steam
noun
the gas that water turns into when it boils. Steam can be used as a source of power.

steel
noun
a hard, strong metal made from iron mixed with a small amount of carbon. Steel can also be combined with other metals. Stainless steel is a mixture of steel, chromium, and nickel.

grater   *hand whisk*

*Many kitchen utensils are made of **steel**.*

steep
adjective
slanting up or down sharply.
*A **steep** hill.*
■ comparisons **steeper steepest**

steer
steers steering steered *verb*
to control the direction something is going in.
*She **steered** her car into the driveway.*

stem
stems *noun*
the main stalk of a plant that grows up out of the soil (see **growth** on page 94 and **plant** on page 151).

step
steps *noun*
1 the movement made by lifting your foot and putting it down when you walk along or dance.
step *verb*
2 a level surface for putting your foot on to help you climb up or down, usually as part of a staircase or ladder.

3 a stage in a series of things to do.
*The first **step** in learning to swim is to enjoy being in the water.*

stepladder
stepladders *noun*
a portable ladder with flat steps that can stand up without leaning on anything.

stereo
stereos *noun*
equipment for playing recorded sound. The sound comes from two different directions, so that it sounds natural.
■ say **ster**-ree-oh
stereo *adjective*

stern
adjective
firm or strict.
*A **stern** warning.*

stern
noun
the back part of a ship or boat (see **boat** on page 31).

*The dinghy was kept at the **stern** of the yacht.*

stethoscope
stethoscopes *noun*
an instrument used by doctors for listening to the heart and lungs.

stick
sticks *noun*
1 a thin piece of wood.
2 something long and thin.
*A **stick** of celery.*

stick
sticks sticking stuck *verb*
1 to glue or fasten one thing to another.
*She **stuck** the model aeroplane together with glue.*
sticky *adjective*
2 to press a sharp point into something.
*He **stuck** a pin into the balloon.*

stiff
adjective
not easy to bend or move.

*This folder is made of **stiff** plastic card.*
■ comparisons **stiffer stiffest**

still
adverb
1 up until now.
*He is **still** there.*
2 even so, or nevertheless.
*I don't like rice pudding, but I **still** have to eat it.*
3 an even larger amount.
***Still** more snow fell.*

still
adjective
not moving or without sound.

stilt
stilts *noun*
one of a pair or set of long poles used to support a person or thing high off the ground.

*pair of **stilts***

3 to project out.

*The bread **stuck** out of the basket.*

a b c d e f g h i j k l m n o p q r **s** t u v w x y z

A B C D E F G H I J K L M N O P Q R S T U V W X Y Z

sting
stings stinging stung *verb*
to prick the skin, or to cause a sharp pain. Some insects sting when they are frightened or angry, injecting a poison into the skin.

stink
stinks stinking stank stunk *verb*
to have a strong, bad smell. *This bin **stinks**!*
stink *noun*

stir
stirs stirring stirred *verb*
to mix something by moving it around with a spoon or similar tool.

stitch
stitches *noun*
a loop of thread or wool made with a needle in sewing or knitting.

cross stitch

stitch *verb*

stock
stocks stocking stocked *verb*
to keep a supply of something. *Do you **stock** writing paper in this shop?*
stock *noun*

stolen
*from the verb **to steal**
A painting was **stolen** from the gallery.*

stomach
stomachs *noun*
1 the part of your body where food goes after you have eaten it, to be partly digested.

stomach

2 the outside part of your body at the front between your ribs and your hips.
■ say **stum**-uk

stone
stones *noun*
1 the hard material that rocks are made of.

*staircase made of **stone***

2 a small, loose piece of rock.

*The field was full of **stones**.*

stood
*from the verb **to stand**
They **stood** at the bus-stop for an hour.*

stool
stools *noun*
a seat without a back or arms.

*kitchen **stool***

stop
stops stopping stopped *verb*
1 to come, or bring, to an end. *The rain **stopped**.*
2 to prevent something from happening.

*The man **stopped** the boy from running into the road.*

stop-watch
stop-watches *noun*
a watch that can be started and stopped to measure how much time something takes (see **time** on page 216).

store
stores storing stored *verb*
to put something away for when you need it.

*They **stored** the sports equipment in the cupboard.*

storey
storeys *noun*
all the rooms on one floor of a building.

stork
storks *noun*
a large bird with a long beak and long legs that lives near shallow water. Storks eat fish, insects, rodents, and snakes. They live in large nests built in trees and on cliffs.

*marabou **stork***

storm
storms *noun*
a period of bad weather, with strong winds and thunder and lightning, or snow.

story
stories *noun*
a tale, or a description of an event, either real or imaginary. *Tell me a **story**.*

stove
stoves *noun*
a piece of equipment used for cooking or heating.

straight
adjective
not bent or curved.

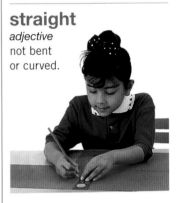

*She drew a **straight** line.*
■ say **strate**
■ comparisons **straighter straightest**

strain
strains straining strained *verb*
1 to try so hard that it hurts or tires you.
*Be careful not to **strain** yourself when you exercise.*
strain *noun*
2 to pass something through a sieve in order to filter out larger pieces.

strand
strands *noun*
1 any thread that is twisted together with others to make a stronger line.
2 anything that looks like a rope or string.
*A **strand** of hair.*

stranded
adjective
unable to leave somewhere.

strange
adjective
unusual or unfamiliar.
■ comparisons **stranger strangest**

stranger
strangers *noun*
a person you have not seen before or who is new to a place.

strap
straps *noun*
a strip of leather or other material, used for fastening or holding things.

shoulder strap

straw
straws *noun*
1 stalks of dried wheat or other cereal plants. Straw is used for farm animals and pets to lie on.

2 a hollow tube used for drinking liquids through.

strawberry
strawberries *noun*
a small, red fruit that is soft and sweet and grows on a plant.

stray
strays straying strayed *verb*
to wander away from someone or somewhere.

*One duckling **strayed** from its mother.*

streak
streaks *noun*
a long, thin mark or smear.
*After the football game his clothes were covered with **streaks** of mud.*

stream
streams *noun*
1 a small river.

2 a steady flow of something.
*A **stream** of cars rushed along the street.*

streamlined
adjective
having a smooth shape that allows quick and easy movement through air or water.

*This cycling helmet has a **streamlined** shape.*
streamline *verb*

street
streets *noun*
a road in a city or town.
*What is the name of the **street** you live in?*

strength
strengths *noun*
the quality of being strong or powerful.

*The weight-lifter had incredible **strength** in his arms.*

strengthen
strengthens strengthening strengthened *verb*
to make something strong or stronger.
*You can **strengthen** your muscles by exercising.*

stress
stresses *noun*
1 a strain on a person or thing.
*He is under a lot of **stress**.*
2 an extra force laid on part of a word when speaking. In the word "stretcher", the stress is on the first syllable.

stretch
stretches stretching stretched *verb*
1 to pull something so that it becomes longer or bigger.
2 to straighten or reach out as much as you can with part of your body.

*She **stretched** out her arms.*

3 to reach one place from another.

*The road **stretches** all the way to the mountains.*

stretcher
stretchers *noun*
a light bed with handles that is used to carry someone who is hurt.

strict
adjective
keeping closely to the rules.
*The teacher was very **strict**.*
■ comparisons **stricter strictest**

a b c d e f g h i j k l m n o p q r s t u v w x y z

A
B
C
D
E
F
G
H
I
J
K
L
M
N
O
P
Q
R
S
T
U
V
W
X
Y
Z

stride
strides striding strode *verb*
to walk with long steps.

stride *noun*

strike
strikes *noun*
the action of stopping work
in order to get better pay
and working conditions, or
to protest about something.
*On **strike**.*

strike
strikes striking struck *verb*
1 to hit something hard.

*The tree was **struck**
by lightning.*
2 to stop work in order to
protest about something.

string
strings *noun*
a long, narrow cord used
for fastening or as part of
a musical instrument (see
musical instrument
on page 133).

strip
strips *noun*
a long, narrow piece
of something.
*A **strip** of paper.*

stripe
stripes *noun*
a long, narrow
band of colour.

*This swimsuit has blue **stripes**.*
striped *adjective*
stripy *adjective*

stroke
strokes stroking stroked *verb*
to rub gently with the hand.

*He **stroked** the rabbit.*

stroll
strolls strolling strolled *verb*
to walk slowly in a relaxed way.
*They **strolled** through
the woods.*
stroll *noun*

strong
adjective
1 tough.
*A **strong** rope.*
2 powerful.
*Elephants are very **strong**.*
■ comparisons **stronger strongest**
■ opposite **weak**

structure
structures *noun*
1 something that
has been built.

*The Eiffel
Tower is a tall,
steel **structure**.*

2 the way that something is
put together or organized.
*A company's **structure**.*

struggle
**struggles struggling
struggled** *verb*
to try hard, or to fight hard.
*He **struggled** with the maths
problem for a long time.*

stubborn
adjective
determined to
have your
own way.

*a **stubborn** dog*
■ say **stub**-ern

stuck
from the verb **to stick**
1 *I **stuck** the label on the jar.*
2 *The thorn **stuck** in her leg.*

student
students *noun*
a person who is studying at
school, college, or university.
■ say **stew**-dent

studio
studios *noun*
1 a room where an artist or
photographer works.
2 a room or building where
television programmes or
films are made.
■ say **stew**-dee-oh

study
studies studying studied *verb*
1 to look at
something carefully.

*She **studied** the flower through
a magnifying glass.*
2 to learn about a subject from
books and lessons.
*She **studied** for her exams.*

stuffy
adjective
without fresh air.
*The room was **stuffy** so she
opened the window to let
some fresh air in.*

stumble
**stumbles stumbling
stumbled** *verb*
to trip up and almost fall.

stump
stumps *noun*
a short part of something left
behind after the rest has been
cut or worn away.

*tree **stump***

*television **studio***

stunt

stunts noun

a dangerous action that is done as part of a film or performance.

*He performed a dangerous **stunt**.*

stupid

adjective

foolish, or not intelligent.

- say **stew**-pid
- comparisons **stupider stupidest**
- opposite **clever**

sturdy

adjective

strong and well made.
*A **sturdy** table.*

- comparisons **sturdier sturdiest**

stutter

stutters stuttering stuttered *verb*

to stammer or speak with difficulty, often stopping in the middle of words or repeating sounds.

stutter noun

style

styles noun

1 the way that something is done or made.
*Which **style** of tennis racket do you prefer, wooden or metal?*
2 a fashion or design.

*A 1950s **style** car.*

- say **stile**

subject

subjects noun

something you are talking, writing, or learning about.

submarine

submarines noun

a vessel that can travel underwater.

- say sub-ma-**reen**

substance

substances noun

a material or object that can be seen or felt.
*There was a sticky **substance** on the table.*

substitute

substitutes noun

someone or something that is used in place of another person or thing.

butter

margarine

*Margarine is used as a **substitute** for butter.*

- say **sub**-sti-tyoot

subtract

subtracts subtracting subtracted *verb*

to take one number away from another number.

$$8-5=3$$

*Five **subtracted** from eight equals three.*
subtraction noun

subway

subways noun

an underground tunnel for pedestrians beneath a road.

succeed

succeeds succeeding succeeded *verb*

to manage to do what you were trying to do.

*They **succeeded** in moving the heavy piano upstairs.*

- say suk-**seed**

success

successes noun

a thing that works out well.
*His magic act was a complete **success**.*

- say suk-**sess**

successful adjective

such

adjective

1 of a particular kind.
*Pins, needles, and **such** things.*
2 so much.

*There was **such** a lot of work to do, she didn't know where to begin.*

suck

sucks sucking sucked *verb*

to pull liquid into your mouth, or to hold something in your mouth and lick it.

*He **sucked** his drink through a straw.*

suddenly

adverb

quickly and without warning.

Suddenly he had an idea.
sudden adjective

suffer

suffers suffering suffered *verb*

to feel pain, or to be ill.
*She is **suffering** from measles.*

suffocate

suffocates suffocating suffocated *verb*

to die because you are unable to breathe.

- say **suf**-a-kate

sugar

noun

a sweet substance made from plants and used in food and drinks.

brown sugar

- say **shoog**-er

suggest

suggests suggesting suggested *verb*

to mention a new idea or plan to someone.
*I **suggested** going to the park to ride our bikes.*

- say su-**jest**
suggestion noun

a b c d e f g h i j k l m n o p q r s t u v w x y z

suicide
noun
killing yourself deliberately.
■ say **soo**-i-side

suit
suits *noun*
a jacket and skirt or trousers, designed to be worn together.

■ rhymes with **boot**

suit
suits suiting suited *verb*
to look good on someone.
Does this suit me?

suitable
adjective
right for a particular purpose or occasion.

These boots are suitable for walking over rough ground.
■ say **soo**-ta-bul

suitcase
suitcases *noun*
a large bag with a handle that is used for carrying clothing and other things when you travel.

sulk
sulks sulking sulked *verb*
to be silent because you are in a bad temper.
sulky *adjective*

sum
sums *noun*
1 a total made by adding two or more numbers together.

$$3+49=52$$

The sum of 3 and 49 is 52.
2 an exercise in arithmetic.
Have you done your sums?

summary
summaries *noun*
a short form of a story or a piece of information that just gives the main points.
They gave a summary of the news at the end of the programme.

summer
summers *noun*
the warmest season of the year. Summer comes between spring and autumn.

summit
summits *noun*
the highest point of something.

The two climbers finally reached the summit of the mountain.

sun

Sun
noun
the star that is the centre of our Solar System (see **universe** on page 229).

sun
noun
the light and heat that we get from the Sun.
The cat was sitting in the sun.

sunflower
sunflowers *noun*
a tall plant with large, yellow flowers. The seeds can be eaten or used to make cooking oil.

sunglasses
noun
glasses with dark lenses that you wear to protect your eyes from sunlight.

sunlight
noun
the light from the Sun.

sunrise
sunrises *noun*
the time when the Sun is coming up over the horizon in the morning.

sunset
sunsets *noun*
the time when the Sun is going down below the horizon in the evening.

sunshine
noun
bright sunlight.

superb
adjective
extremely good.
A superb performance.
■ say soo-**purb**

superior
adjective
higher in rank or position.
Soldiers must salute their superior officers.
■ say soo-**peer**-ee-er
■ opposite **inferior**

supermarket
supermarkets *noun*
a large shop that sells food and other items. People select the goods they want and pay for them at the exit.

supersonic
adjective
faster than the speed of sound.

Concorde was a supersonic aircraft.
■ say soo-per-**son**-ic

superstition
superstitions *noun*
a false belief based on fear or lack of knowledge about something.
A common superstition is that it is unlucky to walk under ladders.
■ say soo-per-**stish**-un
superstitious *adjective*

supper
suppers *noun*
a small meal eaten in the evening.

supply

supplies *noun*
a quantity of something that may be needed.

cleaning supplies
supply *verb*

support

supports supporting supported *verb*
to hold something or someone up to stop it, or them, from falling.

She supported her friend who had hurt his leg.
support *noun*

suppose

supposes supposing supposed *verb*
to think that something is true or likely.
I suppose you are right.

sure

adjective
certain, or with no doubt.
I am sure you will enjoy your stay here.
■ say **shoor**

surf

surfs surfing surfed *verb*
1 to balance on a special board while riding on waves as they begin to break near the seashore.
2 to explore the internet.

surfer

surfboard

surface

surfaces *noun*
the outside or top of something.

These buttons have shiny surfaces.
■ say **sur**-fis

surgeon

surgeons *noun*
a doctor who treats patients by doing operations.

■ say **ser**-jun

surgery

surgeries *noun*
1 a medical operation that involves cutting open part of a patient's body.
2 a place where you go to see a doctor or dentist for treatment.
■ say **ser**-jer-ee

surname

surnames *noun*
the last part of someone's name that shows which family they belong to.

surprise

surprises *noun*
something that happens when you do not expect it.
She got a surprise when she received the parcel!
surprise *verb*
surprising *adjective*

surrender

surrenders surrendering surrendered *verb*
to give yourself up.

The kidnapper finally surrendered to the police.

surround

surrounds surrounding surrounded *verb*
to be or to go on all sides of something.

The bench surrounded the tree trunk.

survive

survives surviving survived *verb*
to continue to live after an event in which you might have died.
They all survived the crash.

survivor

survivors *noun*
a person who is still alive after experiencing an event that might have killed them.
He was one of three survivors of the shipwreck.
■ say sur-**vye**-ver

suspect

suspects suspecting suspected *verb*
1 to think that someone is guilty of something.
I suspect her of being a thief.
suspect *noun*
2 to suppose that something is likely.
I suspect it will rain.

suspend

suspends suspending suspended *verb*
to attach something by its top so that it hangs down.

The baskets are suspended from a hook.

suspense

noun
the feeling of being anxious or excited about what might happen next.
This film is full of suspense.

suspicious

adjective
1 suspecting something bad.
I became suspicious when my friends didn't answer the telephone for a week.
2 behaving in a way that makes people suspect you.

A suspicious character was by the car.
■ say sus-**pish**-us

a b c d e f g h i j k l m n o p q r s t u v w x y z

A B C D E F G H I J K L M N O P Q R S T U V W X Y Z

swallow

swallows swallowing swallowed verb
to make your food go down your throat and into your stomach.

*The snake **swallowed** the egg whole.*

swallow

swallows noun
a small bird with long wings and a forked tail. Swallows eat mainly insects and are found in most parts of the world.

swam

from the verb **to swim**
*I **swam** across the pool.*

swamp

swamps noun
an area of wet or marshy land.

*a mangrove **swamp***

swan

swans noun
a large bird that lives in and around water. Swans feed on water plants, which they grasp with their sharp-edged bills. Swans are related to geese.

■ say **swon**

swap

swaps swapping swapped verb
to give one thing in return for something else.
*He **swapped** his toy for her tennis racket.*

swarm

swarms noun
a large number of insects moving together.
*A **swarm** of bees.*
■ say **sworm**

sway

sways swaying swayed verb
to swing or lean from side to side.

*The trees **swayed** in the wind.*

swear

swears swearing swore sworn verb
1 to make a solemn promise.
*She **swears** that she didn't do it.*
2 to speak rude or unpleasant words.

sweat

noun
the salty liquid that comes out of your skin when you are hot.
*She was covered in **sweat** after the race.*
sweat verb

sweatshirt

sweatshirts noun
a thick, cotton jumper with long sleeves.

sweep

sweeps sweeping swept verb
1 to clean up dust, dirt, or other mess using a brush.

2 to push away.
*The flood **swept** the car off the road.*

sweet

adjective
1 containing sugar or tasting like sugar.
*Grapes are very **sweet**.*
2 very pleasant or kind.
*It was **sweet** of you to bring me flowers.*
■ comparisons **sweeter sweetest**

sweet

sweets noun
a small piece of snack food, made mostly of sugar.

swell

swells swelling swelled swollen verb
to become larger.

*The male frigate bird's throat **swells** up to attract females.*

swelling

swellings noun
a swollen place on the body.
*She had a **swelling** where she had bumped her head.*

swerve

swerves swerving swerved verb
to turn quickly to one side when you are moving.

*The cyclist **swerved** to avoid the car door.*

swift

adjective
moving quickly.
■ comparisons **swifter swiftest**

swim

swims swimming swam swum verb
to move through water using arms, legs, or fins.

swim noun

swimming pool

swimming pools noun
a large, artificial area of water for swimming in.

swing
swings swinging
swung *verb*
to move backwards and
forwards, usually while
hanging from a support.

swing

swing *noun*

swirl
swirls swirling swirled *verb*
to move with a twisting or
circular motion.

*The gymnast
swirled the ribbon.*

switch
switches *noun*
a lever or button used to turn
equipment or a machine on
and off.
switch *verb*

swivel
swivels swivelling swivelled
verb
to turn around on
a central point.

swivelling around on a chair

swoop
swoops swooping swooped
verb
to move downwards through
the air in a curving movement.

*The stunt plane swooped down
out of the sky.*

sword
swords *noun*
a weapon with
a long blade
and a handle.

18th-century sword
■ say **sord**

swore
*from the verb to swear
She swore she was telling
the truth.*

syllable
syllables *noun*
a word or part of a word made
up of a single sound. The word
"once" has one syllable and
the word "single" has two.
■ say **sil**-a-bul

symbol
symbols *noun*
a sign or object that reminds
you of something else, or
represents something else.

A dove is a symbol of peace.
■ say **sim**-bul

symmetrical
adjective
having two halves that match
each other.

*This cut-out shape is
symmetrical through
its middle.*
■ say sim-**meh**-trik-kal
symmetry *noun*

sympathy
noun
a caring feeling shown by
someone for someone else.
*When you're hurt, it's nice
to get sympathy.*
■ say **sim**-pa-thee
sympathetic *adjective*

symptom
symptoms *noun*
a sign that shows you have a
particular illness or disease.
*One of the symptoms of
measles is red spots.*
■ say **simp**-tom

synagogue
synagogues *noun*
a building where Jews
go to worship.
■ say **sin**-a-gog

synthetic
adjective
made with artificial materials
rather than natural ones.

*This frog is made from
synthetic fur.*
■ say sin-**thet**-ik

syringe
syringes *noun*
a tube with a nozzle or hollow
needle attached that is used
for sucking up and squirting
out liquid. Doctors
use syringes to
give injections.

■ say ser-**ringe**

syrup
syrups *noun*
a sweet, sticky
liquid food, often
made from sugar.

maple syrup

■ say **si**-rup

system
systems *noun*
a group of things that work
together in an organized way.
■ say **sis**-tum

a b c d e f g h i j k l m n o p q r s t u v w x y z

Tt

table
tables *noun*
1 a piece of furniture with a flat surface and legs underneath to support it.

2 a list of facts or figures written in columns.
A multiplication table.

tablet
tablets *noun*
1 a small, hard piece of medicine.
2 a compact computer with a flat screen.

tackle
tackles tackling tackled *verb*
1 to try to solve something.
They had to tackle some difficult maths problems.
2 to seize and try to throw someone to the ground, usually in a sport such as rugby or American football.

tactful
adjective
trying to avoid hurting someone's feelings.
She was very tactful when talking about his new haircut.
■ opposite **tactless**
tactfully *adverb*

tactics
noun
methods used to make something happen.
The team used clever tactics to win the match.
tactical *adjective*

tadpole
tadpoles *noun*
a young frog or toad. Tadpoles live in water. As they grow, their tails get smaller and they grow legs.

tail
tails *noun*
the part that sticks out beyond the back end of an animal's body.

lizard's tail

tailor
tailors *noun*
a person who makes or mends clothes. Tailors usually make clothes to fit a particular person.

take
takes taking took taken *verb*
1 to get hold of or carry.
She took her coat off the peg.
2 to bring or lead.
My parents took me to the cinema.
3 to make use of something.
Take the first turning on the left.
4 to require or need.
It takes three hours to cook.
5 to travel by or on something.
Let's take the bus.
6 to remove or steal.

The thief took a wallet from the man's coat pocket.

tale
tales *noun*
a story about things that may not be true.
A fairy tale.

talent
talents *noun*
a special natural skill or ability.

She showed a talent for dancing at an early age.

talk
talks talking talked *verb*
to say words, or to speak.
He talked to his sister on the telephone for an hour.
■ say **tork**
talk *noun*

talkative
adjective
talking a lot.
Our parrot is very talkative.

tall
adjective
1 very high.

The tall office block was surrounded by shorter ones.
■ opposite **short**
2 having a particular height.
He is 1.5 metres tall.
■ comparisons **taller tallest**

tambourine
tambourines *noun*
a musical instrument that is held in the hand and shaken or tapped to provide a rhythm.

■ say tam-bor-**een**

tame
adjective
used to living or working with human beings.
The bird they rescued from the cat became very tame.
■ comparisons **tamer tamest**
■ opposite **wild**

tan
tans *noun*
a brown skin colour caused by the Sun's rays.
tan *verb*

tangle
tangles tangling tangled *verb*
to twist into an untidy mass of knots.

The kittens tangled the wool.
tangle *noun*

teapot »

tank
tanks *noun*
1 a large container for liquid or gas.
2 a heavy vehicle with guns that moves along on metal belts instead of wheels.

tanker
tankers *noun*
a vehicle or large ship that carries oil or other liquids.

tantrum
tantrums *noun*
a noisy display of bad temper.

*She often has **tantrums** when she is tired.*

tap
taps tapping tapped *verb*
to hit gently with your fingers.

*She **tapped** on his shoulder.*
tap *noun*

tap
taps *noun*
a device that you turn to control the flow of liquid or gas from a pipe.

tape
tapes *noun*
1 a long, narrow strip of material such as paper, plastic, or metal.

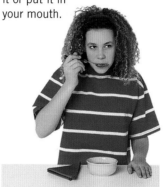

*three types of sticky **tape***

2 a strip of plastic coated with magnetic powder that is used for recording sounds, video pictures, and computer information.

tape measure
tape measures *noun*
a tape marked in centimetres or inches that is used for measuring length.

tar
noun
a thick, dark, sticky liquid that is made from coal or wood. Tar is used in making road surfaces.

target
targets *noun*
an object that you try to hit when shooting or throwing something.

*archery **target***

tartan
adjective
decorated with a special pattern of lines and squares. Tartan patterns originally came from Scotland.

***tartan** scarf*

task
tasks *noun*
a piece of work or a duty.
*My **task** was cleaning the car.*

taste
noun
1 one of the body's five senses which we use to find out the flavour of something.
2 the flavour of something when you have licked it or put it in your mouth.

*She tried the soup to see if she liked the **taste**.*
taste *verb*
tasty *adjective*

tattoo
tattoos *noun*
a permanent picture or design printed on someone's skin, using needles filled with coloured ink.

tax
taxes *noun*
money that people have to pay to a government, which is used to provide public services.
tax *verb*

taxi
taxis *noun*
a car that you can hire to travel in by paying the driver money (see **car** on page 39).
■ say **tak**-see

tea
noun
a drink made by pouring boiling water onto the chopped, dried leaves of the tea plant.

***tea** plant leaves*

*cup of **tea***

teach
teaches teaching taught *verb*
to help someone learn about a subject or learn a skill.
*He has **taught** history for three years.*

teacup
teacups *noun*
a cup used for drinking tea.

team
teams *noun*
a group of people who work or play sports together.

*American football **team***

teapot
teapots *noun*
a container with a spout, lid, and handle that is used for making and serving tea.

a b c d e f g h i j k l m n o p q r s t u v w x y z

A
B
C
D
E
F
G
H
I
J
K
L
M
N
O
P
Q
R
S
T
U
V
W
X
Y
Z

tear

tears tearing tore torn *verb*
to make a hole or split in
something by pulling hard.
■ rhymes with **care**
tear *noun*

tear

tears *noun*
a drop of salty water that
comes from your eyes when
you cry.

■ rhymes with **deer**

tease

teases teasing teased *verb*
to bother someone by saying
or doing things in a playful,
but annoying way.
*He **teased** his little sister
about her dolls.*

technology

noun
science that is put to use
in everyday life.

*A printer is an example
of **technology**.*
■ say tek-**nol**-o-jee
technological *adjective*

teenager

teenagers *noun*
a person between the ages
of 13 and 19 (see **growth**
on page 94).

telephone

telephones *noun*
an instrument that allows you to talk
to and hear people who are far away,
by means of electrical signals.
Telephone is often shortened
to phone.

telescope

telescopes *noun*
an instrument with lenses
inside it. When you look
through it distant things
appear closer and larger.

television

televisions *noun*
a piece of electrical equipment
that receives pictures and
sound that are broadcast by
a television station. Television
is often shortened to TV.

*flat screen **television***

tell

tells telling told *verb*
to put something into
words, or let someone
know something.
***Tell** me a story.*

temper

tempers *noun*
1 a mood.
*Are you in a good
temper today?*
2 an angry mood.
*She threw the book across
the room in a **temper**.*

temperature

temperatures *noun*
a measurement of how hot
or cold something is.

*She took the
child's **temperature**.*
■ say **temp**-ra-cher

temple

temples *noun*
a building where people
go to worship.

*Buddhist **temple***
■ say **tem**-pul

temporary

adjective
lasting for only
a short
time.

*The box was a **temporary** bed
for the cat.*
■ say **tem**-per-ra-ree
■ opposite **permanent**
temporarily *adverb*

tempt

tempts tempting tempted *verb*
to try to persuade someone to
do something that they wouldn't
usually do or shouldn't do.
*Can I **tempt** you to take
another slice of cake?*
■ say **temt**
temptation *noun*

tendency

tendencies *noun*
the way that a person or thing
usually or often behaves.
*She has a **tendency** to be late.*
tend *verb*

tender

adjective
1 easy to chew or cut.
*A **tender** piece of steak.*
2 feeling sore when touched.

*The cat had a **tender** paw
after the accident.*
3 gentle and loving.
*He gave his baby
a **tender** smile.*
tenderly *adverb*

tennis

noun
a game that is played with a
racket and ball on a court
divided by a net. The players
try to hit the ball over the net
in a way that makes it hard for
their opponent to return
it (see **sport** on page 197).

tennis court

tense

adjective
1 nervous.
2 stretched tight.
Tense muscles.
■ opposite **relaxed**

tense

noun

a form of a verb that shows whether the action is taking place in the past, present, or future.

tent

tents *noun*

a portable shelter made of waterproof material stretched over a frame of poles.

term

terms *noun*

one of the periods of time during a year when a school or university is open for teaching.

terminal

terminals *noun*

a building at the end of a travel route where passengers arrive and depart.

terrible

adjective

very bad or unpleasant.
*It was a **terrible** day.*

terrify

terrifies terrifying terrified *verb*

to frighten very badly.

*Heights **terrified** him.*

territory

territories *noun*

an area of land that is controlled by a country's laws or lived in by an animal.
*The pride of lions never left their own **territory**.*

■ say **ter**-ri-tree

terror

noun

great fear.

terrorist

terrorists *noun*

a person who uses, or threatens to use, violence to force people to do something, usually for a political cause.
terrorism *noun*
terrorize *verb*

test

tests testing tested *verb*

to try something out.

*She **tested** the liquid to see if it was an acid.*
test *noun*

text

noun

the words of something written or printed.

text message

noun

a written message sent between mobile phones.

textile

textiles *noun*

a cloth or fabric made by weaving or knitting.

texture

textures *noun*

the way something feels when you touch it.

*Sandpaper has a rough **texture**.*
■ say **tex**-cher

thank

thanks thanking thanked *verb*

to say that you are grateful for something.
*They **thanked** him for their presents.*
thank you *interjection*

thaw

thaws thawing thawed *verb*

to melt or to make something melt.

*The snow started to **thaw** in the sunshine.*
thaw *noun*

theatre

theatres *noun*

a building where plays and shows are performed.
■ say **thee**-a-ter

theft

thefts *noun*

the act of stealing.

*The **theft** took place in the middle of the day.*

theme

themes *noun*

a main subject, idea, or topic.

*The **theme** of the fancy dress party was fairies.*

theory

theories *noun*

an idea about how or why something happens.
*She tested her **theory** with scientific experiments.*
■ say **thee**-er-ee

thermometer

thermometers *noun*

a device that measures temperature.
■ say thur-**mom**-it-er

*wall **thermometer***

a b c d e f g h i j k l m n o p q r s t u v w x y z

A
B
C
D
E
F
G
H
I
J
K
L
M
N
O
P
Q
R
S
T
U
V
W
X
Y
Z

thesaurus

thesauruses or **thesauri** noun
a book that groups
words that have similar
meanings together.
■ say thi-**saw**-rus

thick

adjective
1 large in width
or depth.

thick candle

2 packed closely together.
A *thick* forest.
■ opposite **thin**
3 having a certain
measurement in
width or depth.
*The plank was three
centimetres thick.*
■ comparisons **thicker thickest**

thief

thieves noun
a person who steals things.
■ rhymes with **beef**

thigh

thighs noun
the part of your leg
between your knee
and your hip.

thigh

■ rhymes with **sky**

thimble

thimbles noun
a small, hard covering worn
on the end of your finger
when you are sewing.
The thimble protects your
finger and helps you push
the needle through the fabric.

thin

adjective
1 small in width
or depth.

thin candle

2 hardly covered.
A *thin* layer of snow covered
the ground.
■ opposite **thick**
3 not having much fat.
A *thin* man.
■ opposite **fat**
■ comparisons **thinner thinnest**

thing

things noun
1 an object that is not alive.
2 an idea or an action.
*There are four things I want
to do this evening.*

think

**thinks thinking
thought** verb
to use your
mind to create
ideas or opinions.

*She thought about what she
could eat for lunch.*

thirsty

adjective
needing something
to drink.

*He was very thirsty after
playing with his friends.*
■ comparisons **thirstier thirstiest**

thistle

thistles noun
a wild plant with prickly
leaves and purple, white,
or yellow flowers.

thorn

thorns noun
a sharp spike
on the stem
of a plant.

thorn

thorough

adjective
complete in every way.
*He had a thorough search
for his book.*
■ say **thur**-er
thoroughly adverb

thought

thoughts noun
an idea or opinion that you
have been thinking about.
■ say **thort**

thoughtful

adjective
caring about other
people's feelings
and needs.

*It was thoughtful of her
to help him.*
■ say **thort**-ful
■ opposite **thoughtless**

thread

threads noun
a thin yarn such as
cotton or silk, that is
used for sewing.
■ say **thred**

*sewing
thread*

*embroidery
thread*

thread

threads threading threaded
verb
to pass a length of thread
or rope through a hole
in something.

threading beads onto a string

threat

threats noun
a warning that something
may happen.
*There's a threat of rain
in the air.*
■ say **thret**
threaten verb

thrill

thrills noun
an excited feeling.
*It was a real thrill to ride
on the roller coaster.*
thrilling adjective

throat

throats noun
the tube that leads from your
mouth, through your neck,
to your stomach and lungs.
■ say **throwt**

throne

thrones noun
a special chair used by a
ruler of a country or a region.

through
preposition
from one side or end
to the other.
*She drove **through** the tunnel.*
■ say **throo**

throw
**throws throwing threw
thrown** *verb*
to send something out
of your hand and through
the air forcefully.

thud
thuds *noun*
a dull sound made
when a heavy object
falls on something.
*The book dropped to the
floor with a **thud**.*

thumb
thumbs *noun*
the short, thick finger set
apart from your other fingers
at the side of
your hand.

thumb

■ say **thum**

thunder
noun
a loud, rumbling sound that
comes after a flash of lightning
during a storm.

thunderstorm
thunderstorms *noun*
a storm that has thunder
and lightning.

tick
ticks *noun*
1 a written mark that
shows that something
is correct, or has been chosen.
2 a clicking sound made
by a clock.
tick *verb*

ticket
tickets *noun*
a piece of paper that shows
that you have paid to do
something, such as travel
by public transport
or go into
a cinema.

tickle
tickles tickling tickled *verb*
to touch someone's skin
lightly, making them laugh
or squirm.

tide
tides *noun*
the regular change in the level
of the sea that happens twice
a day.

*The **tide** is out.*

tidy
**tidies tidying
tidied** *verb*
to put in order.

*He **tidied** his room.*

tie
ties tying tied *verb*
1 to fasten something
with a knot or bow.

*She **tied** a ribbon in her hair.*
2 to score the same number
of points as someone else
in a contest.
*They **tied** for first place.*
tie *noun*

tie
ties *noun*
a thin strip of fabric worn
around the neck and knotted
under the collar of a shirt.

tiger
tigers *noun*
a large, wild mammal that is
part of the cat family. Tigers
live in many regions of Asia,
from tropical forests to cold
plains. They hunt at
night for their food.

tight
adjective
fitting closely.
*A **tight** fit.*
■ say **tite**
■ comparisons **tighter tightest**
■ opposite **loose**
tighten *verb*
tightly *adverb*

tightrope
tightropes *noun*
a rope stretched high above
the ground that acrobats
balance on.

tile
tiles *noun*
a thin piece of decorated
baked clay or other
material that is used as
a wall or floor covering.

till
tills *noun*
a machine used in shops,
restaurants, and businesses
that adds up your bill and
stores the money that you
give in payment.

tilt
tilts tilting tilted *verb*
to move or be moved into
a sloping or leaning position.
*The huge pile of books
tilted dangerously.*

timber
noun
cut wood that is used for
building and making things.

a b c d e f g h i j k l m n o p q r s t u v w x y z

A B C D E F G H I J K L M N O P Q R S **T** U V W X Y Z

time

times *noun*

1 all of the past, present, and future. Time is measured in periods such as centuries, years, months, weeks, days, and hours.

2 a particular point in the day. *What's the time?*

3 a period in the past, present, or future. *In Roman times, many roads were built throughout Europe.*

4 an occasion or event. *I go swimming three times a week.*

Telling the time

minute hand

23 24 13
22 12 14
21 11 1 15
20 10 2 16
19 9 3 17
18 8 4
7 5
6

hour hand

second hand

24-hour clock

o'clock

quarter past

half past

quarter to

Time-measuring devices

winder

Roman numerals

pocket watch

timing button

stopwatch

strap

battery

back view

front view

hours   minutes   seconds

10:29:08

date display

Liquid Crystal Display (LCD)

digital alarm clock

nurse's watch

wristwatch

clock case

dial

cogs

front view

winding key

back view

carriage clock

Months of the year

January
February
March
April
May
June
July
August
September
October
November
December

month

calendar

date

Time periods

past   present   future

Days of the week

MONDAY   FRIDAY

TUESDAY   SATURDAY

WEDNESDAY   SUNDAY

THURSDAY

day

diary

Monday
Tuesday
Wednesday
Thursday
Friday
Saturday
Sunday

timetable
timetables *noun*
a chart that shows the times when events should happen, or when jobs should be done.

They checked the **timetable** *to find out when the train left.*

timid
adjective
easily frightened or shy.
The bird was very **timid** *and flew away when I moved.*
timidly *adverb*

tin
tins *noun*
1 a light, soft, silvery metal.

tin ore   *tin can*

2 a metal container for putting things in or for preserving food.

tingle
tingles tingling tingled *verb*
to have a slight stinging feeling in a part of your body.
Fizzy drinks make my mouth **tingle**.

tinkle
tinkles tinkling tinkled *verb*
to make a light, ringing sound.
The bells **tinkled** *as the sleigh moved along.*

tiny
adjective
very small.
■ comparisons **tinier tiniest**

tip
tips tipping tipped *verb*
1 to move something so that it is not upright.
2 to turn something over so that the contents fall out.
She **tipped** *the dirty water out of the bucket.*

tip
tips *noun*
1 the narrow, pointed end of something.

touching the **tip** *of his nose*
2 a helpful hint or piece of useful information.
Do you have any **tips** *for getting rid of stains?*
3 a small, extra gift of money, given in return for a service.
I left the waiter a **tip**.
4 a place where rubbish is dumped.

tiptoe
tiptoes tiptoeing tiptoed *verb*
to walk slowly and quietly on your toes.

tired
adjective
feeling that you would like to sleep or rest.
She felt **tired** *after working in the garden all day.*

tissue
tissues *noun*
1 a thin, soft paper used for wiping or for wrapping things.

2 a material that makes up a part of a living thing.
Brain **tissue**.
■ say **tish**-yoo

title
titles *noun*
1 the name of a creative piece of work such as a book, film, or painting.
2 the part of someone's name that shows their rank or job.
"Dr", "Mrs", and "Lord" are all titles.
■ say **tie**-tul

toad
toads *noun*
an insect-eating amphibian with rough, dry skin that usually lives on land. Toads move along with short hops. They hibernate in winter.

green **toad**

toadstool
toadstools *noun*
a poisonous fungus with an umbrella-shaped top.

toast
noun
1 bread that is grilled on both sides until it is crisp and brown.
2 the action of wishing someone well by raising your glass and drinking.
Let's drink a **toast** *to the bride and groom.*
toast *verb*

tobacco
noun
a plant whose leaves are dried and used in cigarettes and pipes.

toboggan
toboggans *noun*
a flat sledge that is used for sliding down slopes.

today
adverb
on this day.
I'm going to the zoo **today**.
today *noun*

toddler
toddlers *noun*
a young child who is learning or has just learnt to walk (see **growth** on page 94).

toe
toes *noun*
one of the five separate parts at the end of your foot.

toe

toffee
toffees *noun*
a chewy sweet made from sugar and butter.

together
adverb
with each other.
Shall we go **together**?

toilet
toilets *noun*
1 a bowl connected to a drain that can be flushed with water. People use toilets to get rid of body waste.
2 a room with a toilet.

a b c d e f g h i j k l m n o p q r s t u v w x y z

A B C D E F G H I J K L M N O P Q R S T U V W X Y Z

told
*from the verb **to tell***
*She **told** her friends what she had done at the weekend.*

tomato
tomatoes *noun*
a soft, juicy, red fruit that can be eaten raw in salads or cooked (see **fruit** on page 85).

*ripe beef **tomato***

tomorrow
adverb
on the day after today.
*I'm going on holiday **tomorrow**.*
tomorrow *noun*

tone
tones *noun*
the quality of a sound or a voice.
*He spoke in a low **tone**.*
■ rhymes with **own**

tongue
tongues *noun*
a flexible flap of muscle in your mouth that you use to eat, taste, and speak.

tongue

■ say **tung**

tonight
adverb
on the evening and night of the present day.
*Let's go to the concert **tonight**.*
tonight *noun*

tonsil
tonsils *noun*
one of two small lumps of tissue at the back of your throat.

took
*from the verb **to take***
*He **took** the packet out of the cupboard.*

tool
tools *noun*
a piece of equipment that helps you do a job.

***tool** box*

saw
screwdriver
hammer

tooth
teeth *noun*
1 one of the hard, white, bone-like structures inside your mouth, which you use for biting and chewing.

tooth

2 one of the pointed parts on an object such as a saw or a comb.

comb

tooth

toothbrush
toothbrushes *noun*
a small brush with a long handle that you use for cleaning your teeth.

top
tops *noun*
1 the highest point of something.

*The candle was on **top** of the cupcake.*
■ opposite **bottom**
2 a lid.

top

3 a spinning toy.
4 a piece of clothing for the upper part of your body.

*pyjama **top***

topic
topics *noun*
a subject that is spoken or written about.
*The fire was the main **topic** of conversation for weeks.*

topple
topples toppling toppled *verb*
to fall over.
*The dominoes **toppled** over.*

torch
torches *noun*
a portable lamp powered by a battery and small enough to be held in the hand.

tore
*from the verb **to tear***
*She **tore** her sleeve on a nail.*

tornado
tornadoes or **tornados** *noun*
a violent, whirling wind that causes great damage to the land and buildings.

■ say tor-**nay**-doh

tortoise
tortoises *noun*
a slow-moving reptile with a hard shell. Tortoises live in hot regions. They eat grass and other plants and can live a long time (see **reptile** on page 168).
■ say **tort**-tus

toss
tosses tossing tossed *verb*
1 to throw into the air lightly and carelessly.
*We **tossed** the ball around before the game.*
2 to throw a coin and guess which side will face upwards in order to decide something.
*We **tossed** a coin to see who should have the first turn.*
toss *noun*

total
totals *noun*
the entire amount of everything added together.
*The **total** of 2, 3, and 4 is 9.*
- say **toe**-tal

total
adjective
complete.
***Total** darkness.*

toucan
toucans *noun*
a colourful bird with a large beak that lives in the rainforests of South America. Toucans nest in holes in trees and feed on fruit, insects, small lizards, and eggs.
- say **too**-can

touch
touches touching touched
verb
to put your hand or another part of your body on something.

*Can you **touch** the floor with your hands, while keeping your legs straight?*
- say **tuch**
touch *noun*

tough
adjective
1 strong and not easy to break or damage.

*Crash helmets are made of **tough** plastic.*
- opposite **weak**
2 very difficult.
*A **tough** problem.*
- opposite **easy**
- say **tuff**
- comparisons **tougher toughest**

tour
tours *noun*
a journey that takes you to see several places.
*We went on a sightseeing **tour** of the city.*
- rhymes with **poor**

tourist
tourists *noun*
a person who travels and visits places for pleasure.

tournament
tournaments *noun*
a series of contests or matches in a sport or game.
*A chess **tournament**.*

tow
tows towing towed *verb* to pull something along behind.
- say **toe**

towards
preposition
in the direction of.

*The horse and rider walked **towards** her.*

towel
towels *noun*
a piece of soft, thick cloth or paper that is used for drying things.

tower
towers *noun*
a tall, narrow structure.
*The Eiffel **Tower**.*
- rhymes with **our**

town
towns *noun*
a place with houses and other buildings, where people live, work, and shop. A town is smaller than a city but larger than a village.

toy
toys *noun*
an object to play with.

jack-in-the-box

*The truck **towed** the car to the garage.*

trace
traces tracing traced *verb*
1 to copy a picture by placing a sheet of thin paper over it and drawing around the outline.

*She **traced** the picture of a tiger from a book.*
2 to follow or discover something by observing marks or clues.
*She **traced** her family's history back three centuries.*

trace
traces *noun*
a small mark or track left behind by something.
*There were **traces** of a fire in the cave.*

track
tracks *noun*
1 a mark or marks left by someone or something that is moving.

*The cars left tyre **tracks** in the sand.*
2 a path or rough road.
*They drove the truck up a bumpy **track**.*
3 a course used for races.
*They did four laps around the running **track**.*
4 rails laid on the ground for trains to run on.

a b c d e f g h i j k l m n o p q r s t u v w x y z

A B C D E F G H I J K L M N O P Q R S T U V W X Y Z

tractor

tractors *noun*
a farm vehicle with large wheels that is used for pulling heavy loads or machinery over rough ground.

trade

trades *noun*
a business.
The tourist trade.

tradition

traditions *noun*
a special event, belief, or way of doing something that has continued in the same way for many years.
It is a tradition to celebrate the New Year with a party.
■ say tra-**dish**-un
traditional *adjective*

traffic

noun
vehicles, ships, or aircraft moving along a route.

There was a lot of traffic on the bridge.

tragedy

tragedies *noun*
1 a very sad and unfortunate event.
The train crash was a terrible tragedy.
2 a play with a sad ending.
Shakespeare's Romeo and Juliet is a tragedy.
■ say traj-e-dee

tragic

adjective
bringing great sadness.
A tragic accident.
■ say tra-jik
tragically *adverb*

trail

trails trailing trailed *verb*
1 to drag something along behind or let something hang loosely.

He trailed his toy train behind him.
2 to walk or move slowly behind someone.
The children trailed along behind their mother.

trail

trails *noun*
1 a path or track.
A nature trail.
2 a track, scent, or other sign left by something that has passed by.

trailer

trailers *noun*
a small vehicle or container that can be towed behind a car, lorry, or tractor.

trailer

train

trains *noun*
a railway engine that pulls carriages or trucks behind it.

train

trains training trained *verb*
1 to practise sports skills or do exercises to get fit, often for an event.
She trains for three hours a day.
2 to teach or to learn a skill.
He trained his dog to sit.
training *noun*

traitor

traitors *noun*
a person who turns against his or her country or friends by helping an enemy.

trample

tramples trampling trampled *verb*
to crush something by stepping on it.

The dog trampled all over the flowers.

trampoline

trampolines *noun*
a piece of gymnastic equipment made of strong fabric and attached to a frame by springs.

■ say tram-po-leen

trance

trances *noun*
a kind of sleep, or a dazed state, when you are not completely conscious.
■ say trahns

transfer

transfers transferring transferred *verb*
to move something from one person or place to another.
He transferred his money to a savings account.

translate

translates translating translated *verb*
to turn words in one language into words of another language.
She translated the French poem into English.

transparent

adjective
able to be seen through.

This glass jug is transparent.
■ say trans-**pa**-rent

transplant

transplants *noun*
an operation to move an organ or tissue from one person or part of the body to another.
A heart transplant.

transport

noun

a way of carrying goods or people from one place to another. Different methods of transport are used to travel on land, on water, or in the air.

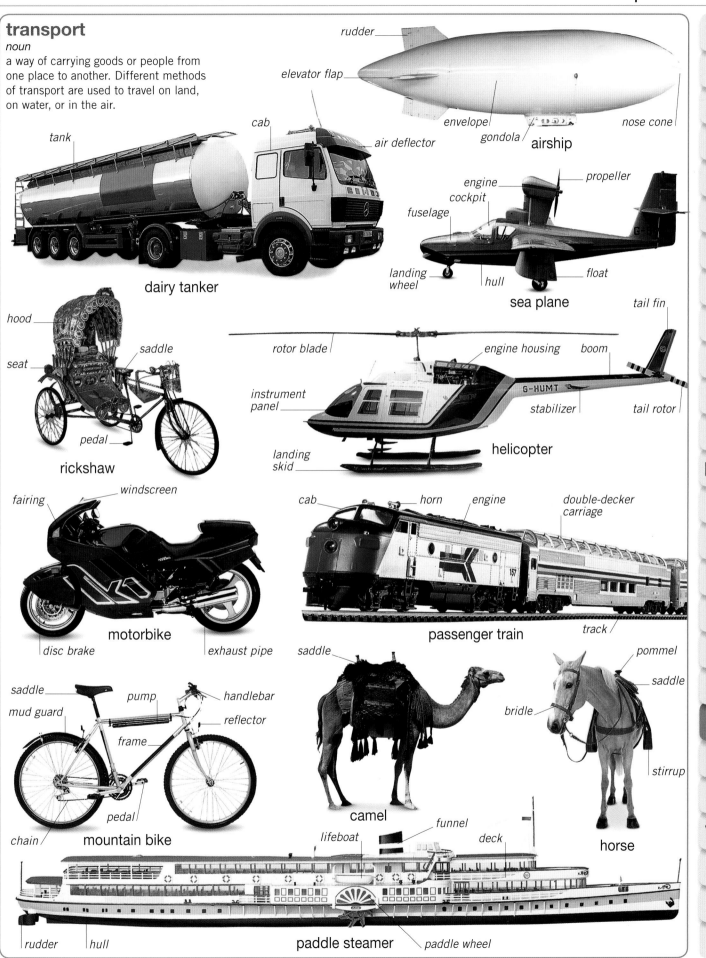

airship
rudder, elevator flap, envelope, gondola, nose cone

dairy tanker
tank, cab, air deflector

sea plane
engine, cockpit, propeller, fuselage, landing wheel, hull, float

rickshaw
hood, seat, saddle, pedal

helicopter
rotor blade, engine housing, boom, tail fin, instrument panel, stabilizer, tail rotor, landing skid

motorbike
fairing, windscreen, disc brake, exhaust pipe

passenger train
cab, horn, engine, double-decker carriage, track

mountain bike
saddle, pump, handlebar, mud guard, reflector, frame, pedal, chain

camel
saddle

horse
pommel, saddle, bridle, stirrup

paddle steamer
funnel, lifeboat, deck, rudder, hull, paddle wheel

a
b
c
d
e
f
g
h
i
j
k
l
m
n
o
p
q
r
s
t
u
v
w
x
y
z

221

A B C D E F G H I J K L M N O P Q R S T U V W X Y Z

transport
transports transporting transported *verb*
to carry people or things from one place to another.

*The truck **transported** the timber.*
transportation *noun*

trap
traps trapping trapped *verb*
to catch an animal or person and hold them in some way so that they cannot get away.
trap *noun*

trapdoor
trapdoors *noun*
a small door cut into a floor, on a stage, or in the ceiling.

trapeze
trapezes *noun*
a high swing used by acrobats for performing stunts.

trash
noun
rubbish, or something that is worthless or useless.

traumatic
adjective
upsetting enough to have a long-lasting effect on someone.
*Giving evidence in the trial was very **traumatic**.*
■ say **traw**-ma-tik
trauma *noun*

travel
travels travelling travelled *verb*
to go from one place to another.

*We **travelled** around the lakes and mountains on holiday.*
travel *noun*

trawler
trawlers *noun*
a boat that is used to catch fish by dragging a large net behind it along the bottom of the sea.

tray
trays *noun*
a flat board, often with a rim, that is used for carrying food and drinks.

treacherous
adjective
very dangerous.

*The sea can be **treacherous** for a small boat.*
■ say **trech**-er-us

tread
treads *noun*
the raised part of a tyre.
■ say **tred**

tread

tread
treads treading trod trodden *verb*
to put your foot on something.

*He **trod** on a sharp toy.*

treason
noun
the act of being a traitor to your country by trying to destroy the government or the ruler, or by helping the enemy during a war.
■ say **tree**-zun

treasure
treasures *noun*
a large amount of gold, jewels, or other valuable things.

(treasure chest)

■ say **tre**-zhur

treasurer
treasurers *noun*
a person who looks after the money and accounts of a government, a club, or a company.

treat
treats *noun*
a special thing that gives someone pleasure.

*The ice-cream was a nice **treat**.*
■ say **treet**

treat
treats treating treated *verb*
1 to behave in a certain way towards people, animals, or things.
*She **treats** her pet hamster very well.*
2 to try to make someone well.

*She **treated** the cut on his head.*
treatment *noun*

treaty
treaties *noun*
an agreement made between countries.

*signing a peace **treaty***

tree

trees *noun*
a tall plant with branches, leaves, and a main stem called a trunk. Trees are either deciduous or evergreen.

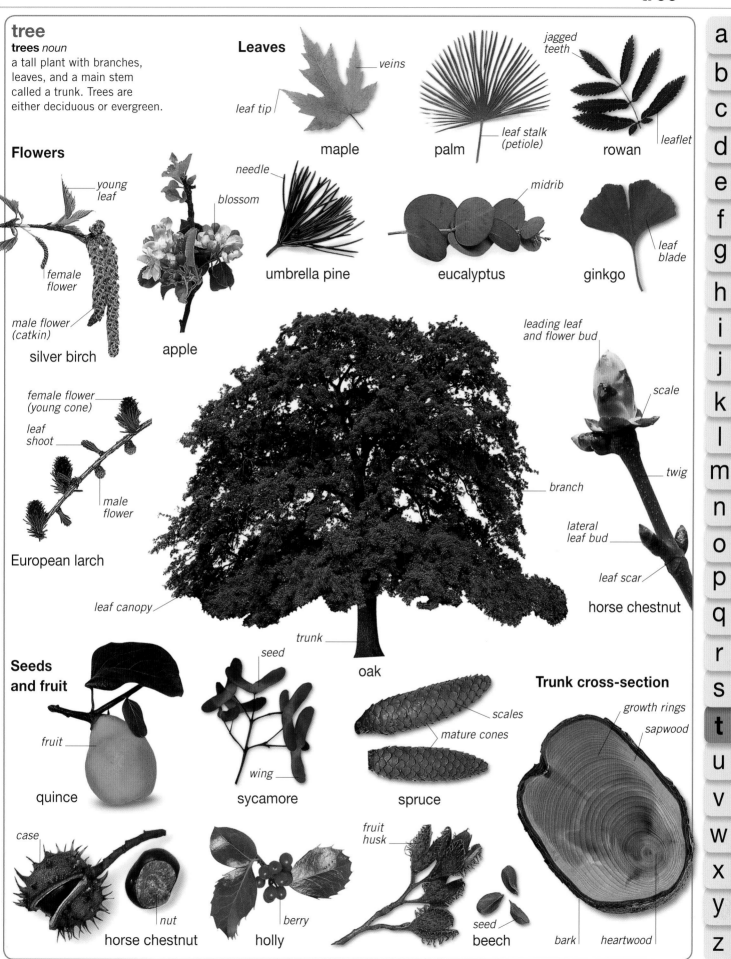

Leaves

veins

leaf tip

maple

jagged teeth

leaf stalk (petiole)

palm

leaflet

rowan

needle

umbrella pine

midrib

eucalyptus

leaf blade

ginkgo

Flowers

young leaf

blossom

female flower

male flower (catkin)

silver birch

apple

female flower (young cone)

leaf shoot

male flower

European larch

leading leaf and flower bud

scale

twig

lateral leaf bud

leaf scar

horse chestnut

branch

leaf canopy

trunk

oak

Seeds and fruit

fruit

quince

seed

wing

sycamore

scales

mature cones

spruce

Trunk cross-section

growth rings

sapwood

case

nut

horse chestnut

berry

holly

fruit husk

seed

beech

bark

heartwood

ABCDEFGHIJKLMNOPQRSTUVWXYZ

tremble
trembles trembling trembled *verb*
to shake with fear or cold.

trial
trials *noun*
1 the legal process by which a judge and jury decide whether a person is guilty or innocent of a crime. *She is on **trial** for theft.*
2 an experiment or test to see what something is like or to see if it works. *The new sports car passed its **trials** successfully.*
■ say **try**-al

triangle
triangles *noun*
1 a shape with three sides (see **shape** on page 182).
triangular *adjective*
2 a musical instrument. A triangle is played by hitting one of the metal sides with a small metal rod.

trick
tricks *noun*
1 a skilful action that is done to entertain someone.

*a magic **trick***
2 something done to deceive someone.
trick *verb*

trickle
trickles trickling trickled *verb*
to flow very slowly. *The raindrops **trickled** down the window.*

tricycle
tricycles *noun*
a vehicle with three wheels that is moved by turning the pedals around, like a bicycle.

*child's **tricycle***
■ say **try**-sik-ul

trim
trims trimming trimmed *verb*
to cut the edges or ends off something, such as hair, in order to make it neat.

*The hairdresser **trimmed** his hair.*

trip
trips tripping tripped *verb*
to stumble and fall. *I **tripped** over the book that she'd left on the floor.*

trip
trips *noun*
a journey. *We went on a school **trip** to the museum.*

tripod
tripods *noun*
a frame with three legs that is used as a support for a camera.

■ say **try**-pod

triumph
triumphs *noun*
a great success. *Winning the race was a **triumph**.*
■ say **try**-umf
triumphant *adjective*

trod
*from the verb **to tread*** *She **trod** in a puddle and splashed her clothes.*

trolley
trolleys *noun*
a small cart on wheels that is used for carrying things. *A supermarket **trolley**.*

trombone
trombones *noun*
a large, brass musical instrument, played by blowing through a mouthpiece. The notes are produced by sliding a long, bent tube backwards and forwards.

*tenor **trombone***

trophy
trophies *noun*
a cup, medal, or other prize that is given to the winner of a contest.

*tennis **trophy***
■ say **trow**-fee

tropical
adjective
from the hot, wet area of the world near the equator. ***Tropical** fruit.*

trot
trots trotting trotted *verb*
to move the way a horse does when it is walking fast. One of the horse's front hooves and the opposite back hoof are on the ground at the same time.

trot *noun*

trouble
troubles *noun*
a situation or problem that is worrying or difficult. *If you smash that window, you'll be in **trouble**!*
■ say **trub**-ul

trough
troughs *noun*
a narrow, open container for animals to eat or drink from.
■ say **trof**

trousers
noun
a piece of clothing that you wear on your legs.

224

trout
trout *noun*
a type of edible fish that is part of the same family as the salmon. Most trout live in fresh water, but some species migrate to the sea after laying their eggs. They feed on insects, small fish, and shrimps.

rainbow **trout**

trowel
trowels *noun*
a hand tool like a small spade. Curved trowels are used for gardening. Flat ones are used for spreading plaster or cement.

gardening **trowel**

■ rhymes with **owl**

truce
truces *noun*
an agreement to stop fighting for a short time.
The armies called a **truce**.

■ rhymes with **noose**

truck
trucks *noun*
a large vehicle used for carrying goods from one place to another.

trudge
trudges trudging trudged *verb*
to walk in a tired way.

They **trudged** *home through the snow.*

true
adjective
real and accurate.
A **true** *story.*

■ opposite **false**

trumpet
trumpets *noun*
a small, brass musical instrument, made of a long, curved, narrow tube with an end like a funnel. Notes are produced by pressing valves down and blowing through a mouthpiece.

valve

trunk
trunks *noun*
1 the main stem of a tree (see **tree** on page 223).
2 the main part of the body of a person or animal, not including the head, arms, and legs.

trunk

3 the long nose of an elephant (see **mammal** on page 124).
4 a large box with a hinged lid, used for storing things.

trust
trusts trusting trusted *verb*
to believe that someone or something is honest and reliable.
I **trusted** *my friend not to give away the secret.*
trust *noun*
trustworthy *adjective*

truth
noun
something that is true.
Do you always tell the **truth***?*

■ say **trooth**

try
tries trying tried *verb*
1 to make an effort to do something.
He **tried** *to climb up the tree.*
2 to test something to see if it works, or to put something on to see if it fits.

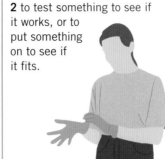

She **tried** *on the gloves.*
3 to decide in a trial, within a court of law, whether someone is innocent or guilty of a crime.
The court **tried** *him for theft.*

T-shirt
T-shirts *noun*
a shirt made from knitted cotton with short sleeves and no collar.

tsunami
tsunami or **tsunamis** *noun*
a very large sea wave caused by an earthquake.

tub
tubs *noun*
a rounded, open container that is used to store things or wash things.

tube
tubes *noun*
1 a long, hollow pipe.
A cardboard **tube***.*
2 a long, narrow container made of plastic or thin metal. The contents are removed by squeezing.

tube *of toothpaste*

tuck
tucks tucking tucked *verb*
1 to fold or push into place.

Tuck *your shirt into your trousers.*
2 to cover up in a snug way.
I like being **tucked** *up in bed.*

tuft
tufts *noun*
a bunch of grass, threads, hair, or feathers that grows or is tied closely together.

tug
tugs tugging tugged *verb*
to give something a quick, hard pull.
My sister **tugged** *at my sleeve.*

tulip
tulips *noun*
a plant with a large, cup-shaped flower that grows from a bulb.
■ say **tyoo**-lip

tumble
tumbles tumbling tumbled *verb*
to fall and roll over.
She **tumbled** *down the hill.*

tuna
tuna or **tunas** *noun*
a large, edible sea fish. Tuna feed on squid and other fish. They are fast swimmers and migrate long distances every year.
■ say **tyoo**-na

a b c d e f g h i j k l m n o p q r s t u v w x y z

A B C D E F G H I J K L M N O P Q R S T U V W X Y Z

tune
tunes noun
a series of musical notes put together in a certain order to form a melody.
He sang a song and I played the tune on the piano.

tunnel
tunnels noun
an underground passage.

turban
turbans noun
a head covering consisting of a long strip of cloth wrapped around the head, worn especially by Muslim and Sikh men.

turkey
turkeys noun
a large bird that lives wild in the forests of North America. Turkeys feed on acorns, seeds, berries, and insects. Turkeys are reared on farms for their meat in many parts of the world.

turn
turns turning turned verb
1 to go around.
The watch hands turn clockwise.
2 to change direction.
He turned to see what was happening behind him.
3 to become.
His fingers turned blue with the cold.

turn
turns noun
a chance or duty that comes to each of a number of people in order.
It's your turn to wash up.

turnip
turnips noun
a type of plant with a round root, which is eaten as a vegetable.

turquoise
noun
1 a green-blue stone that is often used in jewellery.

2 the colour of the stone turquoise.
■ say **ter-kwoyz**

turtle
turtles noun
a reptile that is part of the same family as the tortoise. Turtles live in water and feed on plants and small animals. Some turtles lay their eggs on land.

green
turtle

tusk
tusks noun
a long, pointed tooth that sticks out of the mouth of certain animals (see **mammal** on page 124).

twig
twigs noun
a small branch of a tree or shrub (see **tree** on page 223).

twin
twins noun
1 one of a pair of children or animals born to their mother at the same time.
Identical twins.
2 one of two things that are exactly the same.
twin adjective

twinkle
twinkles twinkling twinkled verb
to shine with small flashes of light.
The stars twinkled in the sky.

twirl
twirls twirling twirled verb
to spin in a quick, light way.

She twirled around to show them her new skirt.

twist
twists twisting twisted verb
to turn or wind something.

She twisted her head around.

type
types typing typed verb
to write using the letter and number keys on a typewriter or other keyboard.
■ say **tipe**

type
types noun
1 a group of people or things that are alike in some way.
The shop sold two types of boots.
2 printed letters.
This book has small type.

typewriter
typewriters noun
a machine with a keyboard, used for printing letters and numbers on paper.

typical
adjective
being a good example of something, or showing all its usual qualities.
They lived in a typical city street.
■ say **tip-i-kul**
typically adverb

Uu

ugly
adjective
unpleasant to look at.
■ say **ug**-lee
ugliness *noun*

ulcer
ulcers *noun*
a sore patch on your skin
or in your stomach.
■ say **ul**-ser

umbrella
umbrellas *noun*
a covered frame, held up
by a stick that is used to
protect a person from the
rain, or as a shade from
the Sun. Umbrella frames
are covered with cloth or
plastic and can be folded
up when not in use.

umpire
umpires *noun*
someone who makes sure
that players follow the rules
of a game or sport.
umpire *verb*

unanimous
adjective
agreed by everyone.
*The leader was elected
by a **unanimous** vote.*
■ say yoo-**nan**-i-mus

uncle
uncles *noun*
the brother of someone's
parent, or their
aunt's husband.

uncomfortable
adjective
1 not able to relax.

*The pregnant woman
felt **uncomfortable**.*
2 causing an unpleasant
feeling or slight pain.
***Uncomfortable** shoes.*
■ opposite **comfortable**

unconscious
adjective
1 not able to think and
feel, possibly because of
an illness or accident.
*The falling brick knocked
him **unconscious**.*
2 done without thinking.
*He has an **unconscious**
habit of scratching
his chin.*
■ say un-**kon**-shus
■ opposite **conscious**

uncover
**uncovers uncovering
uncovered** *verb*
to remove
the cover,
unwrap,
or reveal
something.

*The archaeologists **uncovered**
a Roman mosaic.*

under
preposition
below or
beneath
something,
or to a
lower place.

*She is holding
the ball **under**
her arm.*

undercover
adjective
done in secret to
obtain information.
*The police were working on
an **undercover** investigation.*

underdone
adjective
not cooked for long enough.

underground
adjective
below the ground.

*an **underground** cave*
underground *adverb*

underline
**underlines underlining
underlined** *verb*
to draw a line under
something, usually to
stress it or to show
that it is important.

You <u>must</u> reply.

underneath
preposition
below something,
or in a
lower place.

*The cat is **underneath**
the chair.*
underneath *adverb*

understand
**understands understanding
understood** *verb*
to know what
something means.
*Did you **understand**
the question?*

understudy
understudies *noun*
a person who learns a part
in a play or performance so
that he or she can take over if
the usual actor cannot perform.
understudy *verb*

underwater
adjective
found under the surface
of the water, or used under
the surface of the water.

*The diver swam
among the **underwater**
plants and animals.*
underwater *adverb*

a b c d e f g h i j k l m n o p q r s t u v w x y z

underwear

noun

the clothes that you wear next to your skin and under your other clothes.

vest ____

pants ____

undo

undoes undoing undid undone *verb*

to unfasten or untie.

undoing a knot in a rope

■ say un-**doo**

undress

undresses undressing undressed *verb*

to take clothes off.

■ opposite **dress**

uneasy

adjective

not feeling comfortable or happy.

She felt uneasy about leaving the door unlocked.

uneasily *adverb*

---

unemployed

adjective

without a job.

He's been unemployed for almost a year.

■ opposite **employed**

unemployment *noun*

uneven

adjective

not smooth or level.

The road had a very uneven surface.

■ opposite **even**

unevenly *adverb*

unexpected

adjective

surprising, or happening when you do not think it will.

The unexpected rain made everyone leave the beach.

■ opposite **expected**

unexpectedly *adverb*

unfair

adjective

not right or honest.

That's unfair – you've got more than me!

■ opposite **fair**

---

unfortunate

adjective

having or bringing bad luck.

Unfortunately, she sprained her ankle.

■ opposite **fortunate**

unfortunately *adverb*

unhappy

adjective

sad or miserable.

She felt unhappy when she failed the exam.

■ opposite **happy**

unhealthy

adjective

1 not well or not fit.

You look unhealthy.

2 bad for your health.

It's unhealthy to eat snacks all the time.

■ say un-**hel**-thee

■ opposite **healthy**

unicorn

unicorns *noun*

an imaginary animal in myths and fairy tales. A unicorn is like a horse, but has a long, spiralled horn on its forehead.

■ say **yoo**-ni-korn

unicycle

unicycles *noun*

a machine for riding on, with pedals, a saddle, and one wheel. Unicycles are sometimes used for performing acrobatic tricks.

■ say **yoo**-ni-sye-kul

---

uniform

uniforms *noun*

special clothes worn by members of a group to show that they belong to that group. Many school pupils and members of the armed forces wear uniforms.

19th-century army general's uniform

■ say **yoo**-ni-form

union

unions *noun*

1 two or more people, places, or things that are joined together to become one. *Russia was once a part of the Union of Soviet Socialist Republics.*

2 a group of workers that join together to take care of the welfare of employees.

■ say **yoo**-nee-un

unique

adjective

being the only one of its kind. *Every snowflake is unique.*

■ say yoo-**neek**

unit

units *noun*

1 a single part of something. *A kitchen unit.*

2 a fixed amount used as a standard by which other things are measured. *A metre is a unit of length.*

unite

unites uniting united *verb*

to join together or to do something together. *The towns united in their fight against the factory's pollution.*

■ say **yoo**-nite

universe

noun
all of space, and everything that exists in it. The universe includes Earth, the other planets, and all the stars.

The Solar System

Mercury

Venus

Earth

Mars

Satellites

solar panel

dish antenna

European Communications Satellite 1 (ECS 1)

command antenna

solar panel

Landsat

Space exploration

antenna

magnetic sensor

television camera

solar panel

star detector

dish antenna

Mariner 10

flap door

main mirror casing

small mirror casing

solar panel

antenna

Hubble Space Telescope

Spacecraft

engine nozzle

antenna

heat shield

Apollo Service Module

Apollo Command Module

Apollo Lunar Module

docking window

manoeuvring engines

landing leg

foot pad

hatch

engine nozzle

upper part of the *Saturn V* rocket

ring

Jupiter

power supply

radio antenna

extendable boom

dish antenna

television camera

Voyager space probe

rudder and speed brake

flight deck windscreen

fin   fuselage

NASA United States

heat-shield tiles

wing

main engine nozzle

Space Shuttle

ringlets

Saturn

Uranus

rings

Neptune

rings

antenna

solar panel

docking module

unmanned cargo craft

main module

Mir space station

Soyuz TM spacecraft

solar panel

a b c d e f g h i j k l m n o p q r s t u v w x y z

A
B
C
D
E
F
G
H
I
J
K
L
M
N
O
P
Q
R
S
T
U
V
W
X
Y
Z

university

universities *noun*
a place where students go for
the highest level of education.

*They received their degrees
after studying at **university**.*
- say yoo-nee-**vur**-si-tee

unkind

adjective
cruel or not caring.

*They were being very **unkind**
to him.*
- opposite **kind**

unknown

adjective
never seen or heard of.
*Motorways were **unknown**
in the 19th century.*
- say un-**noen**

unlikely

adjective
not probable.
*An **unlikely** story.*
- opposite **likely**

unload

unloads unloading unloaded
verb
to take things out of a vehicle
or container.

*He **unloaded** the shopping
from the trolley.*
- opposite **load**

unlock

unlocks unlocking unlocked
verb
to open something
by undoing a lock.

*He **unlocked** his bicycle.*
- opposite **lock**

unlucky

adjective
having bad luck, or bringing
bad luck.
*It's thought to be **unlucky**
to walk under ladders.*
- comparisons **unluckier unluckiest**
- opposite **lucky**

unnecessary

adjective
not needed.
*It's **unnecessary** to wear a
coat in very hot weather.*
- say un-**nes**-i-sair-ee
- opposite **necessary**

unoccupied

adjective
vacant, or not being used.

*The house had been
unoccupied for months.*
- opposite **occupied**

unorganized

adjective
with no order or plan.
*The trip was
very **unorganized**.*
- opposite **organized**

unpack

unpacks unpacking unpacked *verb*
to take things out of a container.

*unpacking a
suitcase*
- opposite **pack**

unpleasant

adjective
not pleasing, or not nice.
*An **unpleasant** smell.*
- opposite **pleasant**

unscrew

**unscrews unscrewing
unscrewed** *verb*
to loosen by turning,
or to undo screws.

*He **unscrewed**
the cap
from the bottle.*

untidy

adjective
in a mess.
*Her room was always **untidy**.*
- say un-**tie**-dee
- opposite **tidy**

untie

unties untying untied *verb*
to undo something that
is knotted, such as rope
or thread.

*His shoelaces were **untied**.*
- opposite **tie**

until

preposition
up to the time of.
*We were awake **until** midnight.*

untrue

adjective
false or not based on facts.
*The story about the two-tailed
dog was **untrue**.*
- opposite **true**

unused

adjective
not in use or never used.
*An **unused** notebook.*
- say un-**yoozd**
- opposite **used**

unusual

adjective
rare or not ordinary.

*a very **unusual** guitar*
- say un-**yoo**-zhoo-al

unwell

adjective
ill or sick.
*When I had flu, I felt **unwell**
for days.*
- opposite **well**

unwrap
**unwraps unwrapping
unwrapped** verb
to take the wrapping or
covering off something.

She **unwrapped** her present.
- say un-**rap**
- opposite **wrap**

up
preposition
towards a higher position.
I walked **up** the hill to
the house at the top.
- opposite **down**

up
adverb
to or in a higher position.
Stand **up**!
- opposite **down**

upright
adverb
sitting or standing up straight
rather than bent over.

The dog stood
upright on its
hind legs.
- say **up**-rite
upright adjective

uproar
noun
a state of noisy activity.
The crowd was in an **uproar**.

upset
upsets upsetting upset verb
1 to make someone sad
or anxious.
The accident **upset** him.
2 to knock something over.
The cat **upset** the vase
of flowers.
upset adjective

upside-down
adverb
with the top part
underneath,
or turned the
wrong way up.

He hung **upside-down** from
the bar.
upside-down adjective

upstairs
adverb
to or on an upper storey.

The lights are on **upstairs**.
- opposite **downstairs**
upstairs adjective

upwards
adverb
towards
a higher
position.

The hot-air balloon
floated **upwards**.
- opposite **downwards**

uranium
noun
a silvery white,
radioactive
metal used
for producing
nuclear energy.

- say yoo-**ray**-nee-um

urge
urges urging urged verb
to try to persuade
someone to do something.
He **urged** them to be careful
when playing by the river.
- say urj

urge
urges noun
a powerful feeling that makes
you want to do something.
A sudden **urge** to sneeze.

urgent
adjective
needing immediate action
or attention.
An **urgent** message.
- say **ur**-jent
urgently adverb

urine
noun
liquid waste from the body.
- say **yoor**-rin

use
uses using used verb
to put something into action.

The cat **uses** a cat flap
to come in and go out
of the house.
- say **yooz**

use
uses noun
1 the value
of something
for a certain
purpose.

This penknife has many **uses**.
2 the state of being used.
Steam trains are still in
use in some areas.
- say **yoos**

useful
adjective
able to be used for all
sorts of tasks, or good for
a certain task.

This gadget is **useful**
for unscrewing lids.
- say **yoose**-ful
- opposite **useless**
usefully adverb

usual
adjective
most often done or seen.
I left work at the **usual** time.
- say **yoo**-zhoo-al
usually adverb

utensil
utensils noun
a tool used for a particular
job, especially one used in
the kitchen.

A whisk is a kitchen **utensil**.
- say yoo-**ten**-sil

a
b
c
d
e
f
g
h
i
j
k
l
m
n
o
p
q
r
s
t
u
v
w
x
y
z

Vv

vacant
adjective
empty or not used.
*She parked in the **vacant** space.*
- say **vay**-kant

vaccination
vaccinations *noun*
an injection of a substance
called a vaccine that
stops you from getting
a particular disease.

- say vak-si-**nay**-shun

vacuum
vacuums *noun*
a space from which all,
or almost all, of the air
has been removed.
- say **vak**-yoom

vacuum cleaner
vacuum cleaners *noun*
a machine that cleans
by sucking up dirt.

vacuum flask
vacuum flasks *noun*
a container used for
keeping liquids hot
or cold. Flasks
have double
walls with
a vacuum
between them.

vague
adjective
not clear or not definite.
*A **vague** idea.*
- say **vayg**
vaguely *adverb*

vain
adjective
1 too proud of what you can
do, what you look like, or
what you own.
*Vain people look in the
mirror all the time.*
- comparisons **vainer vainest**
2 unsuccessful.
*They made a **vain** attempt
to put out the fire.*
vainly *adverb*

valley
valleys *noun*
an area of low land between
hills, often with a river or
stream flowing through it.

valuable
adjective
1 precious, or
worth a lot
of money.

*This **valuable** Chinese
ornament once belonged
to an emperor.*
2 useful or worthwhile.
***Valuable** help.*
- say **val**-yoo-bul
- opposite **worthless**
value *noun*

van
vans *noun*
a covered vehicle that is
smaller than a lorry and
is used for carrying goods.

vandal
vandals *noun*
a person who deliberately
damages things.
vandalize *verb*

vanilla
noun
a sweet food flavouring
made from the pods of
a tropical orchid, also
called vanilla.

vanilla pods

vanish
vanishes vanishing vanished
verb
to disappear suddenly.
*The magician waved his
wand and the rabbit **vanished**.*

vapour
vapours *noun*
1 the gas that certain liquids
or solids give off when they
are heated.
2 steam, mist, or smoke
in the air.
- say **vay**-pur

variety
varieties *noun*
1 change or difference.
*It is important to have
variety in your work,
or you will be bored.*
2 a selection of
different things.
*The shop had a **variety**
of mugs for sale.*
3 a particular type.
*What **variety** of fruit is that?*
- say va-**rye**-e-tee

various
adjective
of several different kinds.
*I bought **various** things
when I went shopping.*
- say **vair**-ee-us

varnish
varnishes *noun*
a type of clear paint that
makes a surface tough
and shiny when it is dry.

*wood **varnish***
varnish *verb*

vase
vases *noun*
a jar used as an ornament
for displaying flowers.

- say **varz**

vegetable

vegetables *noun*
a plant, or part of a plant, that is grown for food. Vegetables contain vitamins and minerals that keep us healthy.
■ say **vej**-tab-bul

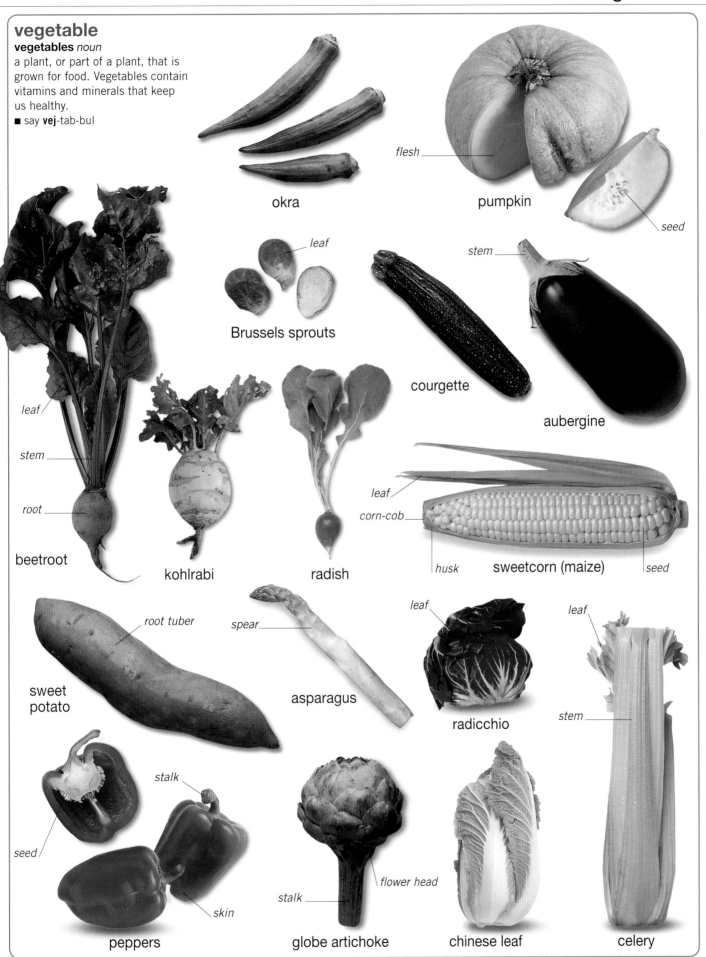

okra

pumpkin

flesh

seed

leaf

Brussels sprouts

stem

courgette

aubergine

leaf

stem

root

beetroot

kohlrabi

radish

leaf

corn-cob

husk   sweetcorn (maize)   *seed*

root tuber

spear

sweet potato

asparagus

leaf

radicchio

leaf

stem

celery

stalk

seed

peppers

skin

stalk

flower head

globe artichoke

chinese leaf

vegetarian
vegetarians noun
someone who does not eat meat or fish.
■ say vej-it-**tair**-ree-an

vehicle
vehicles noun
something that is used to transport people or things on land, in the air, or in space.

■ say **vee**-i-kul

veil
veils noun
a covering for the face or head that is made of thin fabric.

■ rhymes with **pale**

vein
veins noun
1 any one of the tubes that carries blood from other parts of the body to the heart. The vena cava is the major vein in the body.

vena cava

2 one of the fine tubes in a leaf or in an insect's wings.

vein

■ say **vane**

velvet
noun
a type of fabric covered in short, soft fibres.

velvet adjective

ventriloquist
ventriloquists noun
a person who can speak without moving his or her lips. Most ventriloquists use dolls and make it seem as if the doll is talking.

■ say ven-**tril**-o-kwist

verb
verbs noun
a word that describes what a person or thing is doing. A sentence usually needs a verb in order to make sense.

verse
verses noun
1 a section of a poem or song.
2 a general name for poetry.
*He wrote a book of **verse**.*

version
versions noun
A different kind or form of the same thing.
*I like this **version** of the story.*

vertical
adjective
standing straight up, at right angles to the horizon.

*a **vertical** line*

very
adverb
extremely, or by a great amount.
*This book is **very** long.*

vessel
vessels noun
1 a craft that is used for transport by water, usually anything larger than a boat.

2 a container in which liquid can be kept.
*Bring the mixture to the boil in a heat-proof **vessel**.*
■ say **ves**-ul

vest
vests noun
a piece of underwear worn on the top half of the body.

vet
vets noun
a person who is trained to treat sick animals. Vet is short for veterinary surgeon.

vibrate
vibrates vibrating vibrated
verb
to make tiny, rapid, shaking movements.
*The drill **vibrated** noisily.*
■ say vye-**brate**
vibration noun

vicious
adjective
likely to hurt people or things.
*A **vicious** dog attacked him.*
■ say **vish**-us

victim
victims noun
a person who has been harmed or killed by something or someone.
*The **victim** of an accident.*

victory
victories noun
success in a contest or battle.

*The athlete was thrilled with her **victory**.*
■ say vik-**tree**

view
views noun
1 everything that you can see from a certain place.

*There was a good **view** of the city from the window.*
2 an opinion.
*In my **view**, more people ought to travel by train.*
■ say **vyoo**

village
villages noun
a community in the country that is smaller than a town.

vinegar
noun
a sour liquid used to flavour or preserve food.

■ say **vin**-i-ger

vintage
adjective
old and of good quality (see **car** on page 39).

violent
adjective
using strong and damaging force.
The **violent** storm threw cars across the street.
violence noun
violently adverb

violin
violins noun
a wooden musical instrument with four strings. The violin's body is held below the chin and played with a bow.

bow

violin

virus
viruses noun
a type of germ that causes a disease such as flu.
■ say **vye**-rus

visible
adjective
able to be seen.
The mountain was **visible** for miles.
■ opposite **invisible**

visit
visits visiting visited verb
to go to see a person or a place.

They went to **visit** him in hospital.
visit noun

vitamin
vitamins noun
one of a group of natural substances found in foods that we need to eat to keep healthy.

pepper

parsley

foods containing **vitamin** C

vocabulary
vocabularies noun
1 all the words in a language.
2 all the words that are known and used by a person.
■ say vo-**kab**-yoo-la-ree

voice
voices noun
the sound that comes out of your mouth when you speak or sing.
He's lost his **voice**.
■ say **voys**

volcano
volcanoes noun
a mountain that is created by lava from inside Earth. Volcanoes sometimes erupt, sending lava and ash down onto the surrounding country.
volcanic adjective

volume
volumes noun
1 a book, usually one of a series.

the fourth **volume** of an encyclopedia
2 the amount of space inside something, or the amount of space that something fills.

This jug has a **volume** of one litre.
3 an amount.
This road has a huge **volume** of traffic travelling along it.
4 the loudness of a sound.
Can you turn up the **volume** on the television?

volunteer
volunteers noun
a person who offers to do something without being told or paid to do it.
volunteer verb

vomit
vomits vomiting vomited verb
to throw up the contents of your stomach.
vomit noun

vote
votes voting voted verb
to show your choice or opinion by putting up your hand or by marking a name on a piece of paper with a cross.

He **voted** for the candidate by putting a cross on the paper.
vote noun

vow
vows noun
a solemn promise.
vow verb
■ rhymes with **how**

vowel
vowels noun
a sound represented by the letters a, e, i, o, or u (see **alphabet** on page 16).
■ rhymes with **owl**

vulture
vultures noun
a large bird of prey that feeds on dead animals. Vultures have a good sense of smell and good eyesight. Their feet are adapted for walking rather than holding onto branches.

Egyptian **vulture**

a b c d e f g h i j k l m n o p q r s t u v w x y z

wade
wades wading waded *verb*
to walk through water.
We waded across the stream.

wafer
wafers *noun*
a thin, crisp biscuit that is
often eaten with ice-cream.
- say **way**-fer

waffle
waffles *noun*
a crisp, thick pancake with
squares pressed into it.
Waffles are made from
eggs and flour.

- say **wof**-ul

wage
wages *noun*
the money paid to someone
in return for work.
*He collected his wages
every Friday.*
- say **wayj**

wagon
wagons *noun*
a vehicle with
four wheels
used for
transporting
heavy loads.
A wagon can
be pulled by a
train or a horse.

waist
waists *noun*
the narrower part of your
body between your chest
and your hips.

waist

wait
waits waiting waited *verb*
to stay in a place or delay
doing something until
a certain event happens.
Wait for me!
wait *noun*

waiter / waitress
waiters / waitresses *noun*
someone whose job it is
to serve you with a meal.
- **waiter** is male and **waitress**
is female.

wake
wakes waking woke woken
verb
to stop sleeping or to stop
someone else from sleeping.
*I woke up very early
this morning.*
awake *adjective*

walk
walks walking walked *verb*
to move along on foot.
- say **wawk**
walk *noun*

walker
walkers *noun*
a person who takes long walks
for exercise and pleasure.

wall
walls *noun*
a vertical surface made
of stone, brick, or another
material. Walls are used
to enclose a space or to form
the outside structure and
inside divisions of a building.

*There was a high wall around
the garden.*

wallaby
wallabies *noun*
a plant-eating marsupial
from Australia that looks
like a small kangaroo.
- say **wol**-a-bee

wallet
wallets *noun*
a small, soft case for
carrying money.
- say **wol**-it

walrus
walruses *noun*
a very large sea mammal that
lives on the ice in the Arctic
and hunts for its food in
the icy waters. Walruses have
very tough skin and whiskers.
They have a thick layer of fat
called blubber to keep them
warm instead of fur.

wand
wands *noun*
a long, slender stick
used for performing
magic tricks.
In fairy tales,
wands are used
for casting
magic spells.

- say **wond**

wander
**wanders wandering
wandered** *verb*
to go from place to place
without any real purpose
or destination.
*My friends love to wander
around the shops.*
- say **won**-der

want
wants wanting wanted *verb*
1 to wish to have or
do something.
*I want a puppy for
my birthday.*
2 to need or require something.
Do you want any help?

war
wars *noun*
a period of fighting between
countries or groups of people.
- say **wore**

wardrobe
wardrobes *noun*
1 a cupboard for clothing.
2 a collection of clothes.
*A winter **wardrobe**.*
■ say **wore**-drobe

warehouse
warehouses *noun*
a large building used for storing goods.

warm
adjective
1 having a temperature that is between cool and hot.

*The hot water bottle felt nice and **warm**.*
2 friendly and kind.
*She gave us a **warm** welcome.*
■ comparisons **warmer warmest**
■ opposite **cool**
warmth *noun*

warn
warns warning warned *verb*
to tell or signal to someone that there may be a problem or danger ahead.

*The sign **warned** people not to swim in that area.*
■ say **worn**
warning *noun*

warship
warships *noun*
a ship armed with weapons that is used during a war.

wash
washes washing washed *verb*
to clean yourself or something else with water and soap.
wash *noun*

wasp
wasps *noun*
a type of flying insect that can sting. A wasp uses its sting to defend itself and to catch other insects for food.
■ say **wosp**

waste
wastes wasting wasted *verb*
1 to use more of something than you really need or want.
*Don't **waste** electricity!*
2 to fail to use something.
*They **wasted** their chance to win the match.*
waste *noun*

watch
watches watching watched *verb*
to look at and pay attention to someone or something for a time.

watching TV

watch
watches *noun*
a small instrument for telling the time, usually worn on the wrist (see **time** on page 216).

water

water
noun
a clear liquid that falls as rain and forms streams, rivers, lakes, and oceans.
■ say **wor**-ter

water
waters watering watered *verb*
to supply with water.
*Will you **water** my plants while I'm away?*

water cycle
noun
the process by which water travels around Earth and its atmosphere. Water from rivers and oceans evaporates into the air, where it gathers to form clouds. The water then falls as rain to fill the rivers and oceans.

waterfall
waterfalls *noun*
a place where a river falls over a steep cliff.

watermelon
watermelons *noun*
a large, juicy type of melon with green skin. The flesh is red and contains black seeds.

waterproof
adjective
not allowing water to pass through it.

*a **waterproof** coat*

watt
watts *noun*
a unit for measuring electrical power.
*A 100-**watt** light bulb.*
■ say **wot**

wave
waves *noun*
1 a moving ridge on the surface of a liquid.

2 a vibration of sound or light that travels through the air and moves in a similar way to a wave in liquid.

wave
waves waving waved *verb*
1 to signal to someone by moving your hand or an object from side to side.

*She **waved** goodbye as the ship sailed away.*
wave *noun*
2 to move backwards and forwards.
*The branches **waved** in the strong wind.*

wax
waxes *noun*
a solid, oily substance that melts when it is heated. Wax is used to make many things, including furniture polish and candles.

a b c d e f g h i j k l m n o p q r s t u v w x y z

A
B
C
D
E
F
G
H
I
J
K
L
M
N
O
P
Q
R
S
T
U
V
W
X
Y
Z

way

ways noun
1 a direction or route.

The sign showed the way to the village.
2 a method.
What is the right way to use a video camera?
3 a manner of behaving.
She stared at him in a very rude way.

weak

adjective
having little strength or power.

Baby birds are very weak when they are born.
■ comparisons **weaker weakest**
■ opposite **strong**
weakness noun

wealthy

adjective
having a lot of money or possessions.
The inventor sold his idea and became very wealthy.
■ say **wel**-thee
■ comparisons **wealthier wealthiest**
wealth noun

weapon

weapons noun
a tool that can be used to hurt someone.

In the past, swords were used as weapons.
■ say **wep**-on

wear

wears wearing wore worn verb
to have on, or covering your body.

He is wearing a South American cowboy outfit.
■ say **ware**

weary

adjective
very tired.

The firefighter was weary after putting out the fire.
■ say **weer**-ree
■ comparisons **wearier weariest**
weariness noun

weather

noun
the condition of the atmosphere at a certain place and time, such as the air temperature and whether or not it is raining.

a weather map
■ say **weth**-ur

weathered

adjective
having changed shape or colour due to the effects of the Sun, wind, or rain.
Weathered rock.

weave

weaves weaving wove woven verb
1 to pass threads over and under one another to make cloth.

He is weaving a mat out of wool.
woven adjective
2 to move in and out between objects.
The river weaves its way around the hills and down to the sea.

web

webs noun
1 a fine net of sticky threads made by a spider to trap flies.
2 a collection of pages linked electronically via the internet.

wedding

weddings noun
an occasion when two people get married.

weed

weeds noun
a wild plant that grows where it is not wanted.

Burdock is a common weed.

week

weeks noun
a period of seven days.

weekend

weekends noun
Saturday and Sunday, the days when many people do not go to school or work.

weep

weeps weeping wept verb
to show you are unhappy by crying.

weigh

weighs weighing weighed verb
1 to measure how heavy something is.

He weighed some beans.
2 to have a certain weight.
The package weighed half a kilo.
■ say **way**

weight

weights noun
1 the measurement of how heavy something is.
2 a piece of metal with a known heaviness, used with weighing scales to work out how much something weighs.
■ say **wayt**

weird
adjective
strange and mysterious.

*The tree had a **weird** shape.*
- say **weerd**
- comparisons **weirder weirdest**

welcome
welcomes welcoming welcomed *verb*
to show someone that you are glad they have come.
*He went to the door to **welcome** his guests.*
welcoming *adjective*

welfare
noun
a person's health, happiness, and comfort.
*A headteacher has to consider the **welfare** of the pupils.*

well
wells *noun*
a deep hole made in the ground to obtain water, gas, or oil.

well
adjective
in good health.
*Are you **well** today?*

well
adverb
1 in a good or suitable way.
*He behaved very **well**.*
2 thoroughly.
*Water the plants **well**.*

went
from the verb **to go**
*I **went** to the shops to buy some food.*

wept
from the verb **to weep**
*He **wept** when his dog died.*

west
noun
one of the four main compass directions. West is the direction in which the Sun sets.

north
west east
western
adjective
south

western
westerns *noun*
a film about cowboys and other people living in the western USA, usually during the 19th century.

wet
adjective
1 covered or soaked with water.

2 rainy.
Wet weather.
3 not yet dry.
Wet paint.
- comparisons **wetter wettest**
- opposite **dry**

whale
whales *noun*
a very large sea mammal with a breathing hole in the top of its head. Whales eat fish or tiny water animals (see **mammal** on page 124).

*sperm **whale***

what
adjective
which thing or which kind.
***What** is your favourite colour?*
- say **wot**

wheat
noun
a type of cereal that is grown on farms. The grains from wheat are used for making flour.

*durum **wheat***

- say **weet**

wheel
wheels *noun*
a circular object that turns around a fixed, central point. Most land vehicles move on wheels (see **car** on page 39 and **transport** on page 221).

wheelbarrow
wheelbarrows *noun*
a small cart with one wheel at the front, used for pushing heavy loads by hand.

wheelchair
wheelchairs *noun*
a chair with wheels. People use wheelchairs to move from place to place if they have difficulty in walking.

when
adverb
at what time.
***When** did you arrive?*

where
adverb
at, in, or to what place.
***Where** are you going?*

which
adjective
what particular thing or things out of a selection.
***Which** car is yours?*

whine
whines whining whined *verb*
1 to make a long, high cry.
*Dogs **whine**.*
2 to complain unnecessarily.
*The toddler **whined** about going to bed.*

whip
whips *noun*
a rope or strip of leather that is attached to a handle and is used for urging animals to do something.

*a cowboy's
whip*

a
b
c
d
e
f
g
h
i
j
k
l
m
n
o
p
q
r
s
t
u
v
w
x
y
z

A B C D E F G H I J K L M N O P Q R S T U V W X Y Z

whirl

whirls whirling whirled *verb*
to turn yourself or an object around quickly.

*He **whirled** the lasso around his head.*

whirlwind

whirlwinds *noun*
a very strong wind that blows in spirals, causing great damage.

whisk

whisks whisking whisked *verb*
1 to move quickly and lightly.
*She **whisked** the child out of the way of the bike.*
2 to beat a mixture lightly and quickly.

***Whisk** the egg whites until they are stiff.*

whisker

whiskers *noun*
one of the stiff hairs that grows near the mouth of certain animals (see **mammal** on page 124 and **pet** on page 148).

whisper

whispers whispering whispered *verb*
to speak in a very quiet voice.

*She **whispered** her secret into his ear.*
whisper *noun*

whistle

whistles whistling whistled *verb*
to make a high, shrill sound by blowing air through your lips.

■ say **wis**-ul

whistle

whistles *noun*
a device that you blow into to make high, shrill sounds.

white

noun
a colour.

whizz

whizzes whizzing whizzed *verb*
to move along very fast.

whole

adjective
complete, or with nothing missing.

*They bought a **whole** quiche for the party.*
■ say **hole**
whole *noun*

why

adverb
for what reason.
***Why** did you go?*

wicked

adjective
behaving in a bad way on purpose.
*A **wicked** person.*
wickedness *noun*

wide

adjective
1 being a large size, or long distance, from one side to the other.

*a **wide** river*
■ comparisons **wider widest**
■ opposite **narrow**
2 having a certain measurement from one side to the other.
*The carpet is one metre **wide**.*
wide *adverb*
width *noun*

widow / widower

widows / widowers *noun*
a person whose husband or wife has died.
■ **widow** is female and **widower** is male.

wife

wives *noun*
a married woman.
■ opposite **husband**

wig

wigs *noun*
a false covering of hair for the head (see **costume** on page 51).

wild

adjective
1 in a natural environment, or not controlled by people.

*Meadowsweet is a **wild** flower.*
2 uncontrolled, violent, or crazy.
*The children went **wild** in the theme park.*
■ rhymes with **child**
■ comparisons **wilder wildest**

wilderness

wildernesses *noun*
a wild area of land where no one lives.
■ say **wil**-der-ness

will

verb
a word used to show that the action of a verb is happening in the future.
*I **will** go out this afternoon.*
■ opposite **will not** or **won't**
■ always used with another verb

will

wills *noun*

1 the power to choose and control your own actions. *She forced me to do it against my will.*

2 a document containing instructions about what should happen to a person's possessions after his or her death.

3 determination. *She had the will to win.*

willing

adjective

in agreement with something that you are asked to do. *Are you willing to help in the garden?*

win

wins winning won *verb*

to come first in a game or competition.

She was very pleased when she won the game.

■ opposite **lose**

wind

winds *noun*

a current of air.

The wind blew her umbrella inside-out.

■ rhymes with **sinned**

windy *adjective*

wind

winds winding wound *verb*

1 to twist or coil something up.

He wound the clock.

2 to turn in a curving way. *They could see the car winding its way up the hill.*

■ rhymes with **find**

windmill

windmills *noun*

a building with large sails, which uses wind power to turn a machine that grinds grain, pumps water, or makes electricity.

window

windows *noun*

an opening in a building or vehicle that lets in light and air, often covered with glass.

wine

noun

an alcoholic drink made from the juice of grapes.

wing

wings *noun*

1 one of the parts of a bird, insect, or bat that is used for flying (see **bird** on page 28, **insect** on page 108, and **mammal** on page 124).

2 one of the large, flat parts on each side of an aeroplane that acts in a similar way to a bird's wings (see **transport** on page 221).

wink

winks winking winked *verb*

to open and close one eye briefly as a signal to another person.

winter

noun

the coldest season of the year. Winter comes between autumn and spring.

wipe

wipes wiping wiped *verb*

to clean or dry something by rubbing.

He wiped the mirror's surface with a duster.

wire

wires *noun*

a long, thin, metal thread that can be bent. Wires can be used to carry electrical power.

copper wire

wise

adjective

having a lot of knowledge and experience. *The wise old lady gave me good advice.*

■ say **wize**

■ comparisons **wiser wisest**

■ opposite **foolish**

wish

wishes wishing wished *verb*

to feel or say that you want something. *I wish I owned a car.*

wish *noun*

witch

witches *noun*

a woman who practises magic.

wither

withers withering withered *verb*

to become dry.

Their plant withered while they were away on holiday.

without

preposition

not having or not using.

She liked to walk without her shoes.

witness

witnesses *noun*

a person who sees an event happen. *Three witnesses saw him stealing the car.*

witness *verb*

wizard

wizards *noun*

a man who practises magic.

a b c d e f g h i j k l m n o p q r s t u v **w** x y z

A B C D E F G H I J K L M N O P Q R S T U V W X Y Z

wobble
wobbles wobbling wobbled
verb
to move unsteadily.

*She **wobbled** on
her ice-skates.*

woke
from the verb to wake
*He **woke** her very early.*

wolf
wolves *noun*
a wild mammal that is part
of the dog family and lives
in cold regions. Wolves live in
packs and hunt other animals
for food.

woman
women *noun*
an adult human female.
■ say **wum**-an

wombat
wombats *noun*
a marsupial that lives in
Australia. A wombat looks
like a small bear and lives
underground, eating leaves,
roots, and bark.

won
from the verb to win
*We **won** the match.*
■ say **wun**

wonder
noun
a feeling caused by
an extraordinary or
amazing thing.
*They looked in **wonder** at
the bright lights in the sky.*
■ say **wun**-der

wonder
**wonders wondering
wondered** *verb*
to question or think about
something in a curious or
doubtful way.
*I **wonder** how she managed
to arrive first?*

wonderful
adjective
amazing or extraordinary.
*A **wonderful** idea.*
■ say **wun**-der-ful

wood
noun
1 the hard material from
a tree's trunk or branches
used to make furniture and
objects or to burn for fuel.

*The child's toy train is
made of **wood**.*
wooden *adjective*
2 a group of trees
growing together.

woodwind
instrument
woodwind instruments
noun
one of a group of
musical instruments
that is played by
blowing. Some,
such as the
clarinet, are made
from wood while
others, such as
the flute, are
made from metal.

alto clarinet

wool
noun
the soft hair of sheep and some
other animals, which can be
used to make cloth, clothes,
carpets, and blankets.

*sheep's **wool**   ball of **wool***

woollen
adjective
made from wool.

woollen hat

word
words *noun*
1 a sound or group of sounds
that stands for an idea,
an object, or an action.
2 the group of letters you use
to write down these sounds.

word processing
verb
writing, correcting, and storing
documents electronically.

wore
from the verb to wear
*He **wore** a yellow T-shirt.*

work
works working worked *verb*
1 to use effort to do something.
*I **worked** hard when I painted
the house.*
2 to do a job or task.
*My father **works** in a factory.*
work *noun*
3 to operate efficiently.

*This washing machine is not
working properly.*

world
noun
the planet Earth and all the
people and things on it.

worm
worms *noun*
a small animal with a soft body
and no legs or backbone.

*earth**worm***

worry
worries worrying worried *verb*
to feel anxious.
*I am **worried** about my exams.*
■ say **wur**-ee
worry *noun*

worse
*from the adjective **bad***
very bad.
*Last week's weather was bad,
but today, it is **worse**.*

worship

worships worshipping worshipped *verb*
to respect and love, usually in a religious way.

*She **worshipped** Buddha at the shrine.*

worst

from the adjective **bad**
extremely bad.
*This is the **worst** storm I've ever seen.*

worth

adjective
having a value.

*The crown was **worth** a lot of money.*

worthless

adjective
having little or no value.
*He found an old vase, but it turned out to be **worthless**.*

would

verb
1 a word used to talk about an action that depends on something else.
*I **would** go to the park, but I have to wait here.*
2 a word used to ask for something.
***Would** you like some tea?*
■ rhymes with **good**
■ opposite **would not** or **wouldn't**
■ always used with another verb

wound

wounds *noun*
an injury to the body where the skin is torn or cut in some way.

*She put a dressing on the **wound**.*
■ say **woond**
wound *verb*

wound

from the verb **to wind**
*He **wound** the string round the parcel.*
■ rhymes with **sound**

wove

from the verb **to weave**
*She **wove** the wool into cloth.*
■ rhymes with **stove**

wrap

wraps wrapping wrapped *verb*
to fold paper or fabric around something.

*He **wrapped** the present.*
■ say **rap**

wrapper

wrappers *noun*
a piece of paper, plastic, or foil that is used to cover something you buy.

*sweets in their **wrappers***

■ say **rap**-er

wreath

wreaths *noun*
a decoration made from flowers, leaves, or branches tied together in a circle.

■ say **reeth**

wreck

wrecks wrecking wrecked *verb*
to destroy or ruin.

*The house was **wrecked** by the fire.*
■ say **rek**

wrestle

wrestles wrestling wrestled *verb*
to struggle with someone and try to force him or her to the ground.
■ say **res**-ul

wriggle

wriggles wriggling wriggled *verb*
to twist and turn from side to side.
■ say **rig**-ul

wring

wrings wringing wrung *verb*
to twist something hard using both hands.
■ say **ring**

*He **wrung** the water out of the cloth.*

wrinkle

wrinkles *noun*
a small crease or fold in skin or fabric.
■ say **ring**-kul

wrist

wrists *noun*
the joint between your hand and your arm.

wrist

■ say **rist**

write

writes writing wrote written *verb*
1 to form letters and words on a surface.
2 to create something, such as a letter, by using words.
*I **wrote** to my sister last week.*
■ say **rite**

wrong

adjective
1 not correct.
*The **wrong** answer.*
2 bad.
*It's **wrong** to steal.*
■ say **rong**
■ opposite **right**

Xx

X-ray
X-rays *noun*
a special photograph that shows your bones and other parts that are inside your body.

chest **X-ray**

X-ray *verb*

xylophone
xylophones *noun*
a musical instrument with wooden bars on a frame. Each bar produces a different note when it is struck.

■ say **zye**-le-fown

Yy

yacht
yachts *noun*
a small ship with a sail that is usually used for racing or pleasure, rather than for transporting goods or passengers.

■ say **yot**

yak
yaks *noun*
a wild ox with long hair and horns that lives in the mountains of central Asia. Yaks eat grass and are often used by people as a source of food or for carrying loads.

yap
yaps yapping yapped *verb*
to bark in a shrill way.

yard
yards *noun*
an outdoor area near a building, enclosed by a fence or a wall.

yarn
yarns *noun*
wool, cotton, or another material spun into a thread for knitting or weaving.

yawn
yawns yawning yawned *verb*
to open your mouth and breathe in deeply, usually because you are tired or bored.

■ rhymes with **corn**
yawn *noun*

year
years *noun*
a period of 12 months. A year is the time that it takes Earth to travel once around the Sun.
yearly *adverb*

yeast
noun
a yellow-brown substance made up of tiny fungi. Yeast is used in bread and cakes to help them rise with air.

dried **yeast**   fresh **yeast**

yell
yells yelling yelled *verb*
to shout or scream loudly.

*The annoyed man **yelled** at the person on the phone.*
yell *noun*

yellow
noun
a colour.

yesterday
adverb
on the day before today.
*I went to the zoo **yesterday**.*
yesterday *noun*

A B C D E F G H I J K L M N O P Q R S T U V W **X** **Y** Z

yet
adverb
up to the present time.
*The letter hasn't arrived **yet**.*

yoga
noun
a system of exercises and deep breathing, aimed at making a person healthy and relaxed in mind and body.
- say **yo**-ga

yoghurt
yoghurts *noun*
a sour food made by adding bacteria to milk.
- say **yog**-urt
- also spelt **yogurt**

yoke
yokes *noun*
a wooden frame that fits over the shoulders of two oxen or other work animals so that they can pull a load. The yoke keeps the animals together.

yolk
yolks *noun*
the yellow part of an egg.

yolk

- say **yoke**

young
adjective
in the early part of life.

*The grandmother held the **young** child in her arms.*
- say **yung**
- comparisons **younger youngest**
- opposite **old**

youth
noun
1 the state of being young.
*In my **youth**, I had dark hair.*
2 young people in general.
*A place for the **youth** of the town to meet.*
3 a young man or boy.
- say **yooth**

yo-yo
yo-yos *noun*
a toy that spins up and down on a string.

zebra
zebras *noun*
a striped African mammal that is part of the horse family. Zebras live in herds on open plains and eat grass and shrubs.

zero
zeros *noun*
nothing or none.

zigzag
zigzags *noun*
a line with a series of sharp turns and angles in it.
*The blanket had a **zigzag** design.*
zigzag *verb*

zinc
noun
a blue-white, brittle metal.

zip
zips *noun*
a device with two rows of teeth that can be opened and closed. Zips are used to fasten clothing or bags.

zip *verb*

zodiac
noun
the 12 sections into which astrologers divide the sky. Each part is represented by a sign.
- say **zoe**-dee-ak

zone
zones *noun*
an area that is divided off for a particular purpose.
*A no-parking **zone**.*

zoo
zoos *noun*
a place where people can observe and learn about animals.

zoom
zooms zooming zoomed *verb*
to move very fast.

*The two motorbikes **zoomed** past me.*

Abbreviations

An abbreviation is a short form of a word or phrase. Some abbreviations are made by just shortening a word. For example, **ad** is short for **advertisement**, and **max** is short for **maximum**. Other abbreviations, such as **CD** for **compact disc**, are made from the first letters of the words that they stand for. On this double page you will find a useful alphabetical list of common abbreviations.

ac alternating current (An electrical current that travels first in one direction, then in another.)

ad advertisement

AD in the year of our Lord (From the Latin *anno Domini*. Used in dates to count the year after the birth of Jesus Christ, eg, AD 400.) *See* CE

AIDS Acquired Immune Deficiency Syndrome (A disease that makes a person unable to fight illnesses.)

am before noon (From the Latin *ante meridiem*. Used with times, eg, 9 am.)

anon anonymous

approx approximately

asap as soon as possible

Ave avenue

b born

BA Bachelor of Arts (A title given to someone who has an arts degree.)

BC Before Christ (Used in dates to count the years before the birth of Jesus Christ, eg, 30 BC.)

BCE Before Common Era. (Used as an alternative to Before Christ or BC). *See* BC

BSc Bachelor of Science (A title given to someone who has a science degree.)

BST British Summer Time (The time used in Britain during the summer.)

C Celsius or Centigrade

c about (From the Latin *circa*. Used with uncertain dates.)

CD compact disc

CE Common Era (Used as an alternative to *anno Domini* or AD). *See* AD

CIA Central Intelligence Agency (A US government agency that deals with spies and secrets that are important to the country.)

CID Criminal Investigation Department (A part of the police force that deals with serious crimes.)

cm centimetre

Co Company (Used after the names of some companies.)

c/o care of

cont continued

d died

dc direct current (An electrical current that travels in only one direction.)

dept department

DIY do-it-yourself (Used to describe repairs and decorating that people do to their own homes.)

DJ disc jockey

Dr doctor

DVD digital versatile/video disc

E east

e-book electronic book

EAL English as an additional language.

EFL English as a foreign language

eg for example (From the Latin *exempli gratia*.)

email electronic mail

ESP extra-sensory perception (An ability some people are said to have, which makes them aware of things without using their senses.)

etc and all the rest (From the Latin *et cetera*.)

F Fahrenheit

FBI Federal Bureau of Investigation (An agency of the American Department of Justice.)

flu influenza

ft foot

g gram

GB Great Britain

GMT Greenwich Mean Time (The time used in Britain during the winter, and from which time all around the world is measured.)

GP general practitioner (The title given to a doctor who works in a surgery, rather than in a hospital.)

HD high definition

HGV heavy goods vehicle

HIV Human Immunodeficiency Virus (The virus that causes AIDS.)

HM His or Her Majesty

HMS His or Her Majesty's Ship

hp horse power

HP hire-purchase (A way of buying goods by paying in instalments.)

HQ headquarters

HRH His or Her Royal Highness

ICT Information and Communication Technology

ID identification

ie that is (From the Latin *id est*.)

in inch

Inc Incorporated (Used in the names of some US companies.)

Inst Institute

IOU I owe you

IQ intelligence quotient (A test score that claims to measure a person's intelligence.)

IVF in vitro fertilization (a medical technique where a woman's eggs are fertilized outside the womb.)

Jr junior

kg kilogram

km kilometre

kph kilometres per hour

l litre

lab laboratory

lb pound (in weight)
(From the Latin *libra*.)

LCD liquid crystal display

LED light-emitting diode

LP long-playing record

Ltd Limited
(Used after the names of some British companies.)

m metre or mile

MA Master of Arts
(A title given to someone with a BA, who completes a higher arts degree.)

max maximum

MD Doctor of Medicine
(From the Latin *Medicinae Doctor*.)

memo memorandum
(A message to remind someone about something.)

MI5 Military Intelligence 5
(The British government organization that deals with spies and secrets that are important to the country.)

min minimum

misc miscellaneous

Miss Mistress
(A title that goes before an unmarried woman's name.)

mm millimetre

MP Member of Parliament

mpg miles per gallon

mph miles per hour

mp3 MPEG (Moving Pictures Expert Group) 1 audio layer 3
(A type of digital computer file used to store music.)

Mr Mister
(A title that goes before a man's name.)

Mrs Mistress
(A title that goes before a married woman's name.)

Ms (A title for a married or an unmarried woman.)

MSc Master of Sciences
(A title given to someone with a BSc, who completes a higher science degree.)

Mt mount or mountain

N north

NASA National Aeronautics and Space Administration

NATO North Atlantic Treaty Organization
(A military group of countries including the USA and much of western Europe.)

NB take notice
(From the Latin *nota bene*.)

NE north east

NHS National Health Service

no number
(From the Italian *numero*.)

NW north west

OK all correct

oz ounce

p page

PC police constable or personal computer

PE physical education

PhD Doctor of Philosophy
(A title given to someone who has studied a subject to an advanced level at university.)

PLC Public Limited Company

pm after noon
(From the Latin *post meridiem*. Used with times, eg 3 pm.)

PO Post Office

POW prisoner of war

pp on behalf of
(From the Latin *per procurationem*.)

PR public relations

pro professional

Prof professor

PS postscript
(From the Latin *post scriptem*. An extra note written at the end of something, such as a letter.)

PTA Parent Teacher Association

PTO please turn over

RAM random-access memory
(The part of the memory in a computer that you use to work on.)

Rd road

ref referee

Revd Reverend

RIP rest in peace
(From the Latin *requiescat in pace*. Often written on a grave.)

ROM read-only memory
(The part of the memory in a computer that stores permanent information, which cannot be altered.)

rpm revolutions per minute
(The measurement of how fast records and other things turn.)

RSVP please reply
(From the French *répondez s'il vous plaît*. Used on an invitation to a party, wedding, or other event.)

S south

sci-fi science fiction

SE south east

Soc Society

sq square

Sr senior

St Saint or street

SW south west

tel telephone

temp temporary

3-D three-dimensional
(Having height, width, and depth.)

TV television

UFO unidentified flying object

UK United Kingdom

UN United Nations

Unesco United Nations Educational, Scientific, and Cultural Organization

Unicef United Nations Children's Fund
(Formerly UN International Children's Emergency Fund.)

US or **USA** United States of America

UV ultraviolet

V against
(From the Latin *versus*.)

VAT value-added tax

VDU visual display unit

VIP very important person

W west

WHO World Health Organization

www world wide web

yd yard

Spelling guide

If you are having trouble finding a word in the dictionary, it may be because you are looking under the wrong spelling. There can be many different ways of spelling the same sound. Letters sometimes make a different sound to the usual. They may even be completely silent, like the **k** in **kneel**, or the **g** in **gnat**. The spelling guide below will help you to work out the correct spelling of difficult words.

Sound	As in	Other ways to spell this sound
a (say **air**)	hair	care, wear, there, their, prayer
a (say **ay**)	cake	rain, straight, break, veil, bouquet, obey, hay
a (say **ar**)	father	heart, calm, clerk
ch	chin	catch, question
e	ten	any, said, friend, bury, head, leopard
e (say **ee**)	me	meet, seat, key, quay, machine, field, city
f	fall	laugh, telephone
g	get	ghost, guess
h	help	whole
i	fit	damage, pretty, women, busy, build, myth
i (say **eye**)	ice	height, eye, sigh, buy, fly, dye
j	jump	trudge, soldier, adjective, magic
k	kiss	come, anchor, sack, biscuit, walk, unique
l	leg	island
m	miss	comb
n	nose	gnat, kneel, pneumonia
o	not	swan, cauliflower, knowledge
o (say **oh**)	go	sew, though, boat, brooch, slow
o (say **or**)	sort	autumn, awful, broad, ought
o (say **ow**)	now	out, bough
o (say **oy**)	boy	boil
oo	zoom	threw, move, shoe, soup, through, blue, fruit, queue
qu (say **kw**)	quite	choir
r	red	rhyme, wrong
s	saw	cell, psychology, science
s (say **zh**)	pleasure	mirage, confusion
sh	she	ocean, machine, special, sure, conscience, expansion, nation
t	top	debt, bought
u	up	son, does, flood, double
u	pull	woman, wool, would
u (say **ur**)	fur	germ, heard, bird, worm, journey
v	very	of
w	wish	what
y	yard	use, onion
z	zebra	busy, scissors, xylophone

Word building

The charts on this page show how you can take one word and build a new one from it by adding a group of letters called a prefix or a suffix. Prefixes, such as **dis-**, **un-**, or **mis-**, are joined to the front of a word. They are often used to change a word to its opposite. For example, adding the prefix **in-** turns **visible** into **invisible**. Suffixes, such as **-ful**, **-ism**, or **-ment**, are joined to the end of a word. They are often used to change a word from one part of speech to another. For example, adding the suffix **-er** turns the verb **teach** into the noun **teacher**. These charts show some common prefixes and suffixes.

Prefixes

Prefix	Meaning	Example	Prefix	Meaning	Example
anti-	against	antiseptic	non-	makes the opposite	non-fiction
dis-	makes the opposite	disagree	post-	after	postwar
ex-	out of, or from	export	pre-	before	prehistoric
ex-	former	ex-president	re-	again	replace
in-	makes the opposite	independent	sub-	under	submarine
inter-	between	international	super-	above, or more than	superhuman
mis-	makes the opposite	misfortune	trans-	across	transplant
multi-	many	multicoloured	un-	makes the opposite	unpleasant

Suffixes

Suffixes that make nouns

Suffix	Meaning	Example
-age	a result	wreckage
-ance	an action or state	importance
-ant	a person	assistant
-ee	a person	referee
-ence	an action or state	difference
-er/-or	a person	teacher
-ery	a type or place of work	bakery
-ess	makes a feminine form	waitress
-ful	as much as will fill	spoonful
-ing	an action or result	painting
-ion	a process, state, or result	decoration
-ism	a belief or condition	Judaism
-ist	a person	florist
-ment	an action or state	measurement
-ness	a quality or state	happiness

Suffixes that make adjectives

Suffix	Meaning	Example
-able	able to be	inflatable
-en	made of	woollen
-ful	full of	beautiful
-ible	ability	flexible
-ish	a little	greenish
-less	without	careless
-like	similar to, like	lifelike
-ous	full of	joyous
-some	a tendency to	quarrelsome

Suffixes that make adverbs

Suffix	Meaning	Example
-ly	in a manner	quickly
-ward(s)	shows direction	forwards
-ways	shows direction	sideways

Facts and figures

Metric measures

Length
10 millimetres = 1 centimetre
100 centimetres = 1 metre
1,000 metres = 1 kilometre

Area
10,000 square centimetres =
1 square metre
1,000,000 square metres =
1 square kilometre

Weight
1,000 grams = 1 kilogram
1,000 kilograms = 1 tonne

Volume
10 millilitres = 1 centilitre
10 centilitres = 1 decilitre
10 decilitres = 1 litre

Imperial measures

Length
12 inches = 1 foot
3 feet = 1 yard
1,760 yards = 1 mile

Area
144 square inches = 1 square foot
9 square feet = 1 square yard
4,840 square yards = 1 acre
640 acres = 1 square mile

Weight
16 ounces = 1 pound
14 pounds = 1 stone
112 pounds = 1 hundredweight
20 hundredweight = 1 ton

Volume
20 fluid ounces = 1 pint
8 pints = 1 gallon

Temperatures

Degrees Centigrade / Celsius
Boiling point of water   100°C
Freezing point of water   0°C
Normal body temperature   37°C

Degrees Fahrenheit
Boiling point of water   212°F
Freezing point of water   32°F
Normal body temperature   98.6°F

To convert Centigrade to Fahrenheit:
multiply by 9, divide by 5, and
add 32. (eg: **20°C** × 9 = 180;
180 ÷ 5 = 36; 36 + 32 = **68°F**)

To convert Fahrenheit to Centigrade:
subtract 32, multiply by 5, and
divide by 9.

UK holidays

Date	Bank Holiday	England	Scotland	Wales	Northern Ireland
1st January	New Year's Day	✓	✓	✓	✓
2nd January	2nd January		✓		
17th March	St Patrick's Day				✓
Variable	Good Friday	✓	✓	✓	✓
Variable	Easter Monday	✓		✓	✓
First Monday in May	May Day	✓	✓	✓	✓
Last Monday in May	Spring Bank Holiday	✓	✓	✓	✓
12th July	The Twelfth				✓
First Monday in August	Summer Bank Holiday		✓		
Last Monday in August	Late Summer Bank Holiday	✓		✓	✓
30th November	St Andrew's Day		✓		
25th December	Christmas Day	✓	✓	✓	✓
26th December	Boxing Day	✓	✓	✓	✓

Cardinal numbers		Ordinal numbers		Roman numerals	
1	one	1st	first	1	I
2	two	2nd	second	2	II
3	three	3rd	third	3	III
4	four	4th	fourth	4	IV
5	five	5th	fifth	5	V
6	six	6th	sixth	6	VI
7	seven	7th	seventh	7	VII
8	eight	8th	eighth	8	VIII
9	nine	9th	ninth	9	IX
10	ten	10th	tenth	10	X
11	eleven	11th	eleventh	11	XI
12	twelve	12th	twelfth	12	XII
13	thirteen	13th	thirteenth	13	XIII
14	fourteen	14th	fourteenth	14	XIV
15	fifteen	15th	fifteenth	15	XV
16	sixteen	16th	sixteenth	16	XVI
17	seventeen	17th	seventeenth	17	XVII
18	eighteen	18th	eighteenth	18	XVIII
19	nineteen	19th	nineteenth	19	XIX
20	twenty	20th	twentieth	20	XX
21	twenty-one	21st	twenty-first	21	XXI
30	thirty	30th	thirtieth	30	XXX
40	forty	40th	fortieth	40	XL
50	fifty	50th	fiftieth	50	L
60	sixty	60th	sixtieth	60	LX
70	seventy	70th	seventieth	70	LXX
80	eighty	80th	eightieth	80	LXXX
90	ninety	90th	ninetieth	90	XC
100	one hundred	100th	one hundredth	100	C
500	five hundred	500th	five hundredth	500	D
1,000	one thousand	1,000th	one thousandth	1,000	M

Symbols and punctuation marks

+	plus	%	per cent	&	and	?	question mark
−	minus	°	degree	@	at	!	exclamation mark
×	multiply	√	square root	©	copyright	−	dash
÷	divide	π	pi	.	full stop	*	asterisk
=	equals	£	pound	,	comma	( )	brackets
>	greater than	$	dollar	;	semi-colon	" "	speech marks
<	less than	€	euro	:	colon	'	apostrophe

a
b
c
d
e
f
g
h
i
j
k
l
m
n
o
p
q
r
s
t
u
v
w
x
y
z

Countries of the world

On the next four pages is a list of the world's countries, arranged in alphabetical order. Under each country's name are its capital city, the name of the people who live there, and its currency. When a country has two capital cities, they are both listed. If there is a common abbreviation or symbol for the currency, such as **$** for **dollar**, this is shown in brackets after the name of the currency.

Afghanistan
Capital city: Kabul
People: Afghans
Currency: Afghani (AF)

Albania
Capital city: Tirana
People: Albanians
Currency: Lek

Algeria
Capital city: Algiers
People: Algerians
Currency: Algerian Dinar (DA)

Andorra
Capital city: Andorra la Vella
People: Andorrans
Currency: Euro (€)

Angola
Capital city: Luanda
People: Angolans
Currency: Readjusted Kwanza (Kz)

Antigua & Barbuda
Capital city: St John's
People: Antiguans
Currency: East Caribbean Dollar

Argentina
Capital city: Buenos Aires
People: Argentinians
Currency: New Argentine Peso

Armenia
Capital city: Yerevan
People: Armenians
Currency: Dram

Australia
Capital city: Canberra
People: Australians
Currency: Australian Dollar (AU$)

Austria
Capital city: Vienna
People: Austrians
Currency: Euro (€)

Azerbaijan
Capital city: Baku
People: Azerbaijanis
Currency: New Manat

Bahamas
Capital city: Nassau
People: Bahamians
Currency: Bahamian Dollar

Bahrain
Capital city: Manama
People: Bahrainis
Currency: Bahraini Dinar

Bangladesh
Capital city: Dhaka
People: Bangladeshis
Currency: Taka (Tk)

Barbados
Capital city: Bridgetown
People: Barbadians
Currency: Barbados Dollar

Belarus
Capital city: Minsk
People: Belarusians
Currency: Belarussian Rouble

Belgium
Capital city: Brussels
People: Belgians
Currency: Euro (€)

Belize
Capital city: Belmopan
People: Belizeans
Currency: Belizean Dollar

Benin
Capital city: Porto-Novo
People: Beninese
Currency: CFA Franc*

Bhutan
Capital city: Thimphu
People: Bhutanese
Currency: Ngultrum (Nu)

Bolivia
Capital city: La Paz, Sucre
People: Bolivians
Currency: Boliviano (B)

Bosnia & Herzegovina
Capital city: Sarajevo
People: Bosnians
Currency: Marka

Botswana
Capital city: Gaborone
People: Batswana (singular Motswana)
Currency: Pula (P)

Brazil
Capital city: Brasília
People: Brazilians
Currency: Real

Brunei
Capital city: Bandar Seri Begawan
People: Bruneians
Currency: Brunei Dollar

Bulgaria
Capital city: Sofia
People: Bulgarians
Currency: Lev

Burkina
Capital city: Ouagadougou
People: Burkinabé
Currency: CFA Franc*

Burma (Myanmar)
Capital city: Nay Pyi Taw
People: Burmese
Currency: Kyat (K)

Burundi
Capital city: Bujumbura
People: Burundians
Currency: Burundi Franc

Cambodia
Capital city: Phnom Penh
People: Cambodians
Currency: Riel

Cameroon
Capital city: Yaoundé
People: Cameroonians
Currency: CFA Franc*

Canada
Capital city: Ottawa
People: Canadians
Currency: Canadian Dollar (C$)

Cape Verde
Capital city: Praia
People: Cape Verdeans
Currency: Cape Verde Escudo

Central African Republic
Capital city: Bangui
People: Central Africans
Currency: CFA Franc*

Chad
Capital city: N'Djamena
People: Chadians
Currency: CFA Franc*

Chile
Capital city: Santiago
People: Chileans
Currency: Chilean Peso

China
Capital city: Beijing
People: Chinese
Currency: Renminbi (known as Yuan)

Colombia
Capital city: Bogotá
People: Colombians
Currency: Colombian Peso

Comoros
Capital city: Moroni
People: Comorans
Currency: Comoros Franc

Congo
Capital city: Brazzaville
People: Congolese
Currency: CFA Franc*

Congo, Democratic Republic
Capital city: Kinshasa
People: Congolese
Currency: Congolese Franc

Costa Rica
Capital city: San José
People: Costa Ricans
Currency: Costa Rican Colón (¢)

Croatia
Capital city: Zagreb
People: Croatians
Currency: Kuna

Cuba
Capital city: Havana
People: Cubans
Currency: Cuban Peso

Cyprus
Capital city: Nicosia
People: Cypriots
Currency: Euro (€)
(Turkish Lira in
Northern Cyprus)

Czech Republic
Capital city: Prague
People: Czechs
Currency: Czech
Koruna

Denmark
Capital city: Copenhagen
People: Danes
Currency: Danish Krone

Djibouti
Capital city: Djibouti
People: Djiboutians
Currency: Djibouti Franc

Dominica
Capital city: Roseau
People: Dominicans
Currency: East Caribbean
Dollar

Dominican Republic
Capital city: Santo Domingo
People: Dominicans
Currency: Dominican
Republic Peso

East Timor
Capital city: Dili
People: East Timorese
Currency: US Dollar ($)

Ecuador
Capital city: Quito
People: Ecuadoreans
Currency: US Dollar ($)

Egypt
Capital city: Cairo
People: Egyptians
Currency: Egyptian Pound

El Salvador
Capital city: San Salvador
People: Salvadorans
Currency: Salvadorean
Colón (¢), US dollar ($)

Equatorial Guinea
Capital city: Malabo
People: Equatorial Guineans
or Equatoguineans
Currency: CFA Franc*

Eritrea
Capital city: Asmara
People: Eritreans
Currency: Nakfa

Estonia
Capital city: Tallinn
People: Estonians
Currency: Euro (€)

Ethiopia
Capital city: Addis Ababa
People: Ethiopians
Currency: Ethiopian
Birr (Br)

Fiji
Capital city: Suva
People: Fijians
Currency: Fiji Dollar

Finland
Capital city: Helsinki
People: Finns
Currency: Euro (€)

France
Capital city: Paris
People: French
Currency: Euro (€)

Gabon
Capital city: Libreville
People: Gabonese
Currency: CFA Franc*

Gambia
Capital city: Banjul
People: Gambians
Currency: Dalasi (D)

Georgia
Capital city: Tbilisi
People: Georgians
Currency: Lari

Germany
Capital city: Berlin
People: Germans
Currency: Euro (€)

Ghana
Capital city: Accra
People: Ghanaians
Currency: Cedi

Greece
Capital city: Athens
People: Greeks
Currency: Euro (€)

Grenada
Capital city: St George's
People: Grenadians
Currency: East Caribbean
Dollar

Guatemala
Capital city: Guatemala City
People: Guatemalans
Currency: Quetzal (Q)

Guinea
Capital city: Conakry
People: Guineans
Currency: Guinea Franc

Guinea-Bissau
Capital city: Bissau
People: Guinea-Bissauans
Currency: CFA Franc*

Guyana
Capital city: Georgetown
People: Guyanese
Currency: Guyanese Dollar

Haiti
Capital city: Port-au-Prince
People: Haitians
Currency: Gourde (G)

Honduras
Capital city: Tegucigalpa
People: Hondurans
Currency: Lempira (L)

Hungary
Capital city: Budapest
People: Hungarians
Currency: Forint (Ft)

Iceland
Capital city: Reykjavik
People: Icelanders
Currency: Icelandic Krona

India
Capital city: New Delhi
People: Indians
Currency: Indian Rupee (₹)

Indonesia
Capital city: Jakarta
People: Indonesians
Currency: Rupiah (Rp)

Iran
Capital city: Tehran
People: Iranians
Currency: Iranian Rial

Iraq
Capital city: Baghdad
People: Iraqis
Currency: New Iraqi
Dinar (ID)

Ireland
Capital city: Dublin
People: Irish
Currency: Euro (€)

Israel
Capital city: Jerusalem
People: Israelis
Currency: Shekel

Italy
Capital city: Rome
People: Italians
Currency: Euro (€)

Ivory Coast
Capital city: Yamoussoukro
People: Ivoirians
Currency: CFA Franc*

Jamaica
Capital city: Kingston
People: Jamaicans
Currency: Jamaican Dollar

Japan
Capital city: Tokyo
People: Japanese
Currency: Yen (Y)

Jordan
Capital city: Amman
People: Jordanians
Currency: Jordanian Dinar

Kazakhstan
Capital city: Astana
People: Kazakhstanis
Currency: Tenge

Kenya
Capital city: Nairobi
People: Kenyans
Currency: Kenyan Shilling

Kiribati
Capital city: Tarawa Atoll
People: I-Kiribatis
Currency: Australian
Dollar (AU$)

Kosovo (disputed)
Capital city: Pristina
People: Kosovars
or Kosovacs
Currency: Euro (€)

Kuwait
Capital city: Kuwait City
People: Kuwaitis
Currency: Kuwaiti Dinar

Kyrgyzstan
Capital city: Bishkek
People: Kyrgyz
Currency: Som

A
B
C
D
E
F
G
H
I
J
K
L
M
N
O
P
Q
R
S
T
U
V
W
X
Y
Z

Laos
Capital city: Vientiane
People: Laotians or Laos
Currency: New Kip (KN)

Latvia
Capital city: Riga
People: Latvians
Currency: Lats

Lebanon
Capital city: Beirut
People: Lebanese
Currency: Lebanese
Pound (£L)

Lesotho
Capital city: Maseru
People: Basotho (singular
Mosotho)
Currency: Loti (M)

Liberia
Capital city: Monrovia
People: Liberians
Currency: Liberian Dollar

Libya
Capital city: Tripoli
People: Libyans
Currency: Libyan Dinar

Liechtenstein
Capital city: Vaduz
People: Liechtensteiners
Currency: Swiss Franc

Lithuania
Capital city: Vilnius
People: Lithuanians
Currency: Litas

Luxembourg
Capital city: Luxembourg-Ville
People: Luxembourgers
Currency: Euro (€)

Macedonia
Capital city: Skopje
People: Macedonians
Currency: Macedonian Denar

Madagascar
Capital city: Antananarivo
People: Malagasy
Currency: Ariary

Malawi
Capital city: Lilongwe
People: Malawians
Currency: Malawi Kwacha

Malaysia
Capital city: Kuala Lumpur,
Putrajaya
People: Malaysians
Currency: Ringgit

Maldives
Capital city: Male
People: Maldivians
Currency: Rufiyaa

Mali
Capital city: Bamako
People: Malians
Currency: CFA Franc*

Malta
Capital city: Valletta
People: Maltese
Currency: Euro (€)

Marshall Islands
Capital city: Majuro
People: Marshallese
Currency: US Dollar ($)

Mauritania
Capital city: Nouakchott
People: Mauritanians
Currency: Ouguiya (UM)

Mauritius
Capital city: Port Louis
People: Mauritians
Currency: Mauritian Rupee
(Mau Rs)

Mexico
Capital city: Mexico City
People: Mexicans
Currency: Mexican Peso

Micronesia
Capital city: Palikir
(Pohnpei Island)
People: Micronesians
Currency: US Dollar ($)

Moldova
Capital city: Chisinau
People: Moldovans
Currency: Moldovan Leu

Monaco
Capital city: Monaco-Ville
People: Monégasques or
Monacans
Currency: Euro (€)

Mongolia
Capital city: Ulan Bator
People: Mongolians
Currency: Tugrik

Montenegro
Capital city: Podgorica
People: Montenegrins
Currency: Euro (€)

Morocco
Capital city: Rabat
People: Moroccans
Currency: Moroccan Dirham (DH)

Mozambique
Capital city: Maputo
People: Mozambicans
Currency: New Metical (Mt)

Namibia
Capital city: Windhoek
People: Namibians
Currency: Namibian Dollar

Nauru
Capital city: Yaren District
People: Nauruans
Currency: Australian Dollar
(AU$)

Nepal
Capital city: Kathmandu
People: Nepalese
Currency: Nepalese Rupee

Netherlands
Capital city: Amsterdam
Seat of government: The Hague
People: Dutch
Currency: Euro (€)

New Zealand
Capital city: Wellington
People: New Zealanders
Currency: New Zealand Dollar
(NZ$)

Nicaragua
Capital city: Managua
People: Nicaraguans
Currency: New Córdoba

Niger
Capital city: Niamey
People: Nigeriens
Currency: CFA Franc*

Nigeria
Capital city: Abuja
People: Nigerians
Currency: Naira (N)

North Korea
Capital city: Pyongyang
People: North Koreans
Currency: North Korean Won

Norway
Capital city: Oslo
People: Norwegians
Currency: Norwegian Krone

Oman
Capital city: Muscat
People: Omanis
Currency: Omani Rial

Pakistan
Capital city: Islamabad
People: Pakistanis
Currency: Pakistani Rupee

Palau
Capital city: Melekeok
People: Palauans
Currency: US Dollar ($)

Panama
Capital city: Panama City
People: Panamanians
Currency: Balboa (B)

Papua New Guinea
Capital city: Port Moresby
People: Papua New Guineans
Currency: Kina (K)

Paraguay
Capital city: Asunción
People: Paraguayans
Currency: Guaraní (G)

Peru
Capital city: Lima
People: Peruvians
Currency: New Sol (NS)

Philippines
Capital city: Manila
People: Filipinos
Currency: Philippine Peso

Poland
Capital city: Warsaw
People: Poles
Currency: Zloty (Zl)

Portugal
Capital city: Lisbon
People: Portuguese
Currency: Euro (€)

Qatar
Capital city: Doha
People: Qataris
Currency: Qatar Riyal

Romania
Capital city: Bucharest
People: Romanians
Currency: New Romanian
Leu (lei)

Russian Federation
Capital city: Moscow
People: Russians
Currency: Russian Rouble

Rwanda
Capital city: Kigali
People: Rwandans
Currency: Rwanda Franc

Saint Kitts & Nevis
Capital city: Basseterre
People: Kittitians,
Nevisians
Currency: East
Caribbean Dollar

Saint Lucia
Capital city: Castries
People: Saint Lucians
Currency: East Caribbean Dollar

Saint Vincent & the Grenadines
Capital city: Kingstown
People: Vincentians
Currency: East Caribbean Dollar

Samoa
Capital city: Apia
People: Samoans
Currency: Tala

San Marino
Capital city: San Marino
People: Sammarinese
Currency: Euro (€)

São Tomé & Príncipe
Capital city: São Tomé
People: São Tomeans
Currency: Dobra

Saudi Arabia
Capital city: Riyadh
People: Saudi Arabians
Currency: Saudi Riyal

Senegal
Capital city: Dakar
People: Senegalese
Currency: CFA Franc*

Serbia
Capital city: Belgrade
People: Serbs
Currency: Serbian Dinar

Seychelles
Capital city: Victoria
People: Seychellois
Currency: Seychelles Rupee

Sierra Leone
Capital city: Freetown
People: Sierra Leoneans
Currency: Leone (Le)

Singapore
Capital city: Singapore
People: Singaporeans
Currency: Singapore Dollar (S$)

Slovakia
Capital city: Bratislava
People: Slovakians
Currency: Euro (€)

Slovenia
Capital city: Ljubljana
People: Slovenians
Currency: Euro (€)

Solomon Islands
Capital city: Honiara
People: Solomon Islanders
Currency: Solomon Islands Dollar

Somalia
Capital city: Mogadishu
People: Somalis
Currency: Somali Shilin

South Africa
Capital city: Pretoria, Cape Town, Bloemfontein
People: South Africans
Currency: Rand (R)

South Korea
Capital city: Seoul, Sejong City
People: South Koreans
Currency: South Korean Won

South Sudan
Capital city: Juba
People: South Sudanese
Currency: South Sudanese Pound (SSP)

Spain
Capital city: Madrid
People: Spaniards
Currency: Euro (€)

Sri Lanka
Capital city: Colombo, Sri Jayawardenapura Kotte
People: Sri Lankans
Currency: Sri Lanka Rupee (SL Rs)

Sudan
Capital city: Khartoum
People: Sudanese
Currency: New Sudanese Pound or Dinar

Surinam
Capital city: Paramaribo
People: Surinamers
Currency: Surinamese Dollar

Swaziland
Capital city: Mbabane
People: Swazis
Currency: Lilangeni (E)

Sweden
Capital city: Stockholm
People: Swedes
Currency: Swedish Krona

Switzerland
Capital city: Bern
People: Swiss
Currency: Swiss Franc

Syria
Capital city: Damascus
People: Syrians
Currency: Syrian Pound

Tajikistan
Capital city: Dushanbe
People: Tajiks
Currency: Somoni

Tanzania
Capital city: Dodoma
People: Tanzanians
Currency: Tanzanian Shilling (TSh)

Thailand
Capital city: Bangkok
People: Thais
Currency: Baht (B)

Togo
Capital city: Lomé
People: Togolese
Currency: CFA Franc*

Tonga
Capital city: Nuku'alofa
People: Tongans
Currency: Pa'anga (Tongan Dollar)

Trinidad & Tobago
Capital city: Port-of-Spain
People: Trinidadians, Tobagonians
Currency: Trinidad and Tobago Dollar

Tunisia
Capital city: Tunis
People: Tunisians
Currency: Tunisian Dinar

Turkey
Capital city: Ankara
People: Turks
Currency: New Turkish Lira

Turkmenistan
Capital city: Ashgabat
People: Turkmens
Currency: New Manat

Tuvalu
Capital city: Fongafale (Funafuti Atoll)
People: Tuvaluans
Currency: Australian Dollar and Tuvaluan Dollar

Uganda
Capital city: Kampala
People: Ugandans
Currency: New Uganda Shilling

Ukraine
Capital city: Kiev
People: Ukrainians
Currency: Hryvna

United Arab Emirates
Capital city: Abu Dhabi
People: Emiratis
Currency: UAE Dirham

United Kingdom
Capital city: London
People: British
Currency: Pound Sterling (£)

United States of America
Capital city: Washington DC
People: Americans
Currency: US Dollar ($)

Uruguay
Capital city: Montevideo
People: Uruguayans
Currency: Uruguayan Peso

Uzbekistan
Capital city: Tashkent
People: Uzbekistanis
Currency: Som

Vanuatu
Capital city: Port Vila
People: Ni-Vanuatu
Currency: Vatu

Vatican City
Capital city: Vatican City
People: Citizens of the Vatican
Currency: Euro (€)

Venezuela
Capital city: Caracas
People: Venezuelans
Currency: Bolívar Fuerte (Bs)

Vietnam
Capital city: Hanoi
People: Vietnamese
Currency: Dông (D)

Yemen
Capital city: Sana
People: Yemenis
Currency: Yemeni Rial

Zambia
Capital city: Lusaka
People: Zambians
Currency: Zambian Kwacha (K)

Zimbabwe
Capital city: Harare
People: Zimbabweans
Currency: Zimbabwe Dollar (Z$) (suspended in 2009)

* The **CFA Franc** is used in a number of French-speaking African countries. CFA stands for "Communauté Financière Africaine".

a b c d e f g h i j k l m n o p q r s t u v w x y z

Acknowledgements

Dorling Kindersley would like to thank the following people for their help in the production of this book:

Additional design assistance
Bronwen Davies, Susan Downing, Karen Fielding, David Gillingwater, Tim Lewis, Sharon Peters, Peter Radcliffe, Sarah Scrutton, Hans Verkroost, Martin Wilson, Tanvi Sahu, Vidit Vashisht

Additional editorial assistance
Bharti Bedi, Carron Brown, Monica Byles, Helen Drew, Matilda Gollon, Stella Love, Priyanka Naib, Ishani Nandi, Sonia Yooshing

Picture research
Kathleen Collier, Catherine O'Rourke, Lucy Pringle, Jenny Rayner, Joanna Thomas

Additional illustrations
Janos Marffy, Liz Roberts

Additional photography
Simon Battensby, Paul Bricknell, Geoff Brightling, Jane Burton, Peter Chadwick, Matthew Chattle, Gordon Clayton, M. Crockett, Geoff Dann, Tom Dobbie, Philip Dowell, Michael Dunning, Andreas von Einsiedel, Jo Foord, Philip Gatward, Mike Good, Christi Graham, Frank Greenaway, Peter Hayman, Stephen Hayward, Alan Hills, Jacqui Hurst, Colin Keates, Gary Kevin, Dave King, Bob Langrish, Cyril Laubscher, Bill Ling, Liz McAulay, Andrew McRobb, Diana Miller, Graham Miller, Ray Moller, David Murray, Jack Nicholls, Martin Norris, Ian O'Leary, Stephen Oliver, Daniel Pangbourne, Roger Phillips, Martin Plomer, Laurence Pordes, Susanna Price, Dave Rudkin, Karl Shone, Steve Shott, James Stevenson, Clive Streeter, Harry Taylor, Kim Taylor, David Ward, Matthew Ward. Philip Dowell © 1990 and 1991 page 90 goat and kid; page 111 jaguar; page 118 leopard; page 183 sheep. Jerry Young © 1990 and 1991 page 168 rattlesnake, flying gecko, milkshake, today lizard, starred tortoise, and leopard gecko; page 217 green toad; page 242 wolf.

Models
Shiran Abay, Di Anguige, Sarah Ashun, Oliver Barber, Lindsey Bender, Marvin Campbell, Louis Chan, Puishan Chan, Danny Cole, Andy Crawford, Ebu Djemal, Helen Drew, Andrea East, Josey Edwards, David Gillingwater, Emily Gorton, Julia Gorton, Kashi Gorton, Steve Gorton, Sheena Haria, Laura Hobbs, Paul Holden, Marcus James, Stella Love, Naomi McLean, Rachael Malicki, Jamie May, Ryan Munroe, Emily Parsons, Jade Reading, Jonathon Reed, Tim Ridley, Matthew Saunders, Sarah Scrutton, Silpa Shah, Lee Simmons, Cheryl Telfer, Nicola Tuxworth, Aubrey Weiner, Martin Wilson, David York.

Additional acknowledgements
Anatomical models on pages 20, 98, 114, 120, 122, 202 and 232 supplied by Somso Modelle, Coburg, Germany.
Chest page 43, chest of drawers page 65, and fan page 75 loaned by Gore Booker, Covent Garden, London; drum page 67 loaned by Foote's Musical Instruments, London; leotard page 118 loaned by Porselli, Covent Garden, London; cup page 55 loaned by Whittard, Covent Garden, London; chess set page 43 loaned by the British Museum Shop, London.
Thanks to Clark Denmark at the Centre for Deaf Studies, Bristol University for advice.
Thanks also to the BCP contributors: Gemma Casajuana (Conversion manager), Miguel Cunha (Conversion coordinator), Colleen Dixon (Conversion DTP), Marc Staples (Conversion DTP).

Picture agency credits
KEY: a-above; b-below/bottom; c-centre; f-far; l-left; r-right; t-top.

The publisher would like to thank the following for their kind permission to reproduce their photographs:

Alamy Images 180tc; Noam Armonn 119cla, Comstock Images 141bl; Jupiterimages/Pixland 139cb; Alexander Shalamov 88cra; Hugh Threlfall 48ca. **Ayrton Metals Ltd and The Platinum Advisory Centre** 112car, 112cbfr. **Beaulieu Motor Museum** 39cla, 222tr. **Kremlin Museums, Moscow** 54tl. **British Museum** 35tfl, 99bfr, 112ca. **British Museum/Museum of Mankind** 221cafl. **John Bulmer** 224tr. **Christies's Images** 9cbl, 131cbr. **The Coleman Company** 38tfr; Bruce Coleman Limited/Erwin and Peggy Bauer 226bfl; John Cancalosi 179tfl; Peter Davey 42cafr, 211cra; P. Evans 18cr; Christer Fredriksson 22car; Frans Lanting 70tl; Luiz Claudio Marigo 124tc; William S. Paton 104bfl; Eckart Pott 166br; Andy Purcell 8bfl, 142car; Hans Reinhard 6c, 7tl, 25bfr, 58cfl, 70cla, 163bc; Dr Frjeder Sauer 147bfr; Konrad Wothe 97tr. **Corbis** Theo Allofs 66ftr; Andrea Rugg Photography/Beateworks 115cla; Atlantide Phototravel 25cl, 103tl, 169crb; Sayre Berman 234c; Bilderbuch/Design Pics 169bl; B. Bird/Zefa 211fcrb; Christophe Boisvieux 22ftl; Ron Chapple 171crb; Mike Chew 20cra; Philip Coblentz/Brand X 176clb; Wolfgang Deuter/Zefa 153br; Dex Image 199fcr; ER Productions 174clb; Warren Faidley 104bc; First/Zefa 45fcra; Mike Grandmaison 176cr; John Harper 46fbl; Ian Hodgson/Reuters 203fbr; Jose Luis Pelaez, Inc. 186cl; Robert Llewellyn 141cla; John Lund 222bl; Lawrence Manning 232fbl; Robert Marien 226fcla; Kevin Mason/Loop Images 91ftr; MM Productions 150cr; Moodboard 132fclb, 185cla, 212fcl; David Muench 91tr; Ron Nickel/Design Pics 24tl; Richard T. Nowitz 220fclb; Owaki - Kulla 130tr; Carl Purcell 171fcla; Radius Images 227fbr; Jose Fuste Raga 162br; Eddy Risch/EPA 73ftl; Bill Ross/Corbis Outline 139tr; Charles E. Rotkin 165fbr; Galen Rowell 119cr; Kevin Schafer 235tr; Terraqua Images 69cra; Thinkstock 190ftl, Stefano Torrione/Hemis 139fclb; Visuals Unlimited 228fcrb; R. Wallace/Stock Photos/zefa 71fcra; Weatherstock 215tl; P. Wilson/Zefa 237fcra; Jim Zuckerman 241cl. **DK Images** 4hoplites 193tc; American Police Hall of Fame and Museum 41clb; Aven Armand 199bc; Boott Cotton Mills Museum, Lowell, Massachusetts 192cb; Peter Bull 136cla; Jerry Young 15ftr; Cavernas Del Rio Camuy 199crb; City Clocks, London 60clb; Dartington Crystal 86bc (furnace); Raj Dashi 20bc, 33tr, 98bc, 98bc (Body); 114tr, 121cla, 121ca, 132cra, 202tc, 234bl; Neil Fletcher 149tr; Lee Foster 77cra; Jon Hughes 73tr; Sloans & Kenyon/Judith Miller 122bc; Kitten courtesy of Betty 88c; NASA 68fcra, 172ftl; Medimation 19cl, 122crb; Natural History Museum, London 17br; Rough Guides 17tc, 24cr (Baseball), 27cla, 38cb, 40, 40ca, 53cra, 57cl, 67tc (dune), 70cb, 73cla, 82bc, 86bc, 89ca, 96cl, 100tl, 103clb, 120tr, 121cr, 135c, 140tl, 144bc (parachute); 145cr, 150ca, 150clb, 159clb, 162clb, 173tc, 173ca, 174crb, 175cla, 176crb, 190cra, 199fcrb, 203bc, 208fclb, 228ca; The Science Museum, London 43br; Sedgwick Museum of Geology, Cambridge 156cb; Wallace Collection, London 238b; Woolley and Wallis/Judith Miller 43crb. **Massey Ferguson** 152bfr. **Ermine Street Guard** 195cbl. **Dreamstime.com** Alysta 245bl; Nagy-bagoly Ilona 220crb; Alexey Bazykin 239tl; William Berry 154cb; Tomasz Bidermann 81c; Andrew Buckin 105c; Buurserstraat386 241bl; Patricia Cale 83bc (fork); Andras Csontos 14crb; Greg Da Silva 52cr; Dragoneye 89br; Eslivanova 123c; Sonya Etchison 231bc; Exinocactus 106tc; Paul Fleet 239bl; Gabivali 167crb; Ben Goode 36cra; Gors4730 39cra; Gow927 158clb; Intst 129tc; Eric Isselee 54br; Kasiap 86cra (armchair); Kurhan 152crb; Paul Lemke 72br; Luchschen 92fcrb; Lussoadv 82cr; Magomed Magomedagaev 55bc; Steven Melanson 75crb; Monkey Business Images 98bl, 207br; Myszolow 215cra; Kutt Niinepuu 231cbb; Richmond Paul Ruiz 176tc; Petesalo utos 13tr; Alexander Podshivalov 204br; Sergei Razvodovskij 83bc; Andres Rodriguez 230tl; Rozaliya 228cb; Sabphoto 138clb; Saintho 21ca; Yury Shirokov 158bc; Sommersby 154crb; Sergey Sukhorukov 150c; Talim 163c; Tobkatrina 55cb; Maksim Toome 39bl; Eddie Toro 222clb; Eugeny Trembach 105cla; Sandra Van Der Steen 142cl; Victoo 81bc; Amy Walters 179bc; Yael Weiss 40tc; Am Wu 84crb; Xjjx 64cra; Ys1982 32ca; Zirconicusso 155cra; Zuperpups 213tr; Peter Zurek 78cl; **Fotolia**: Anatoliy Babiy / bloomua 177crb; jamalludin din 115cl; Christopher Dodge 39c; Lev Dolgatsjov 94fbl; 107fclb; dundanim 68tc; Yong Hian Lim 144c; Eric Isselee 18crb, 72bl; Ivan Polushkin 111fcrb; shama65 69c; TimurD 67crb; Vadim Yerofeyev 92cb. **Getty Images** Altrendo Travel 235ftl; Blue Jean Images 145crb; Image Bank/Tim Graham 160fcrb; Daryl Benson 215bl; Alistair Berg 181fcrb; Philippe Bourseiller 232bl; Rosemary Calvert 218fcla; Gabriel M. Covian 227br; Andy Crawford 113cra; Dex Image/Luxe Party 125fbl; Digital Vision/Robert Glusic 116cra; Digital Vision/Steve Wisbauer 118cr; Digital Vision/VisionsofAmerica/Joe Sohm 45tl; Sergio Dionisio 34bl; EschCollection 234fbr; David Evans 240crb; Don Farrall 218fcra; Stephen Ferry/Liaison 62tr; James Forte 198bl; Jill Fromer 200cla; Yasuhide Fumoto 212clb; Gallo Images/Travel Ink 125fbr; Glowimages 20ftl; Gorilla Creative Images/Harri Tahvanainen 136clb; Gavin Gough 200ftr; Frank Greenaway 171br; Iconica/2008 ML Harris Photography 41cla; Iconica/Caroline von Tuempling 95fcr; Image Bank/Sasha Weleber 101crb; Mathew Imaging/WireImage 21fbr; Jill Fromer/iStock Exclusive 85cl (Pomegranates); Seth Joel 195cbl; Taylor S. Kennedy 206fcra; Pornchai Kittiwongsakul/AFP 14cr; Darryl Leniuk 165fcra; Lonely Planet Images/Lee Foster 23br; Lonely Planet Images/Peter Hendrie 110ftr; David Madison 174cla; Ethan Miller 38fcra; Mr. Sunshine 202clb; National Geographic/David Evans 59fclb; National Geographic/Paul Nicklen 107fcr; Mark Nolan 42ftl; Thomas Northcut 224tr; Per-Anders Pettersson 113fcr; PhotoAlto/Matthieu Spohn 127bl; Photodisc 88bc, 111bl, 193fcrb; Photodisc/Jeff Maloney 114fbl; Photodisc/Kim Carson 25fcrb; Photodisc/Paul Burns 103fcla; Photographer's Choice/Michael Rosenfeld 37clb; Joshua Ets-Hokin/Photodisc 54tc; Bryan Mullennix/Photodisc 149clb; C Squared Studios 219clb; Photographer's Choice/Simeone Huber/Slow Images 40ftl; Photographer's Choice/Tom Walker 144bl; Photographer's Choice/Travelpix Ltd 60br; Photographer's Choice RR/Fry Design Ltd 146tr; Photographer's Choice RR/Geoff Du Feu 50fcr; Photonica/Silvia Otte 62fclb; Andrea Pistolesi 212crb; Mike Powell 203crb; Robert Harding World Imagery/Christian Kober 169cla; Lew Robertson 150cra; Rubberball Productions 88bl; Rubberball Productions/Mike Kemp 111cla; Pete Ryan 163cr; David Sanger 242clb; Science Faction/Jim Reed 96fbl; Zack Seckler 203fcrb; Erik Simonsen 175br; Check Six 211ftl; Stockbyte 12ftr; Stone/Kevin Cooley 34cr; Stone/Oliver Benn/Royal Philharmonic Orchestra 142tl; Stone/Rex Butcher 157br; Stone/Roger Tully 64fcla; Taxi/Francesco Bittichesu 154fclb; Taxi/Jasper White/jasper@jasperwhite.co.uk 88fbl; Tetra Images 207tl; Alan Thornton 166fcrb; Travel Ink 166cl; Slaven Vlasic 130fcrb; Gary Wade 201cla; Gordon Wiltsie 196clb, 206clb; Yashoda 43fcra. **Greenwich Maritime Museum** 31tr, 31tl, 31cr, 31car, 109cl. **Jupiterimages** Fancy/HBSS 76cla; **Alan Buckingham (c) Dorling Kindersley**. **Robert Harding Picture Library**/G and P Corrigan 131tl. **Michael Holford** 112cal. **The Image Bank**/Gary Cralli 24cbr; Gary Gay 103tr; Alvis Upitis 23tfr. **NASA** 21fcla, 68 cafr, 172 tfl; JPL-Caltech/UCLA 47cra. **National Museum of Denmark, Copenhagen** 112tl. **Natural History Photographic Agency**/Peter Johnson 100cl; Norbert Wu 111tfr. **Nature Photographers Ltd**/David Hutton 115bfr. **Oxford Scientific Films** 76bfr. **Pearson Asset Library** Jon Barlow 23crb, 83tl, 88crb, 93cra, 94bc, 94bfr, 110cla, 136clb, 180tr, 192cb; Gareth Boden 50c, 55clb, 84clb, 95cb, 103crb, 124tr, 128bc, 130cr, 158cb, 187tr, 228tc; Jörg Carstensen 42crb, 94b, 134ca, 205cra; Joey Chan 90tc; Trevor Clifford 14ca, 15bc, 27cb, 46tc, 58ca, 73cra, 234cr; Stuart Cox 154crb (portrait); Handan Erek 170tc; Rob Judges 147crb; Cheuk-king Lo 44crb, 92crb, 137cl, 213br; Terry Leung 89, 152bl; MindStudio 194tc; David Sanderson 81cra; Jules Selmes 73cl, 76bc, 87bc, 94bl, 116cra, 158crb, 160cl, 199cb, 214crb; Studio 8 15tc, 19clb, 87tc, 87c, 127cb, 129cla, 138bc, 158ca, 159cla, 161cra; Tudor Photography 49tr, 120tl, 162tl, 230cla, 234bc; Coleman Yuen 23cl, 46cla, 47cla, 56cra, 76clb, 107clb, 111crb, 147tl, 174crb (sign board), 185cb, 187crb, 210tr. **The Pitt Rivers Museum** 183cbr. **Photolibrary** Stockbroker 159cra; Digital Vision / Dougal Waters 59tr. **PunchStock** Photodisc 243cl. **Quadrant** 220br. **Rough Guides** 192 bl. **Rough Guides**/Alex Robinson 208 bfl. **Science Photo Library** 224cal/John Burbridge 80cbfr; CNRI 83cbfr; Peter Menzel 162cbr; Astrid and Hanns-Frieder Michler 245crb (zinc); Jim Selby 232cfl; US Department of Energy 231tr. **Tony Stone Images** 120cbfl, 244bfl/Tim Beddow 226cfl; Dave Bjorn 207tc. **Thistle Quilters/The Quilter's Guild** 161cafr. **Warwick Castle** 5br. **The Worshipful Company of Goldsmiths**/Andrew Grima 131cl. **Rollin Verlinde** 131cl, 137ca.

Every effort has been made to trace the copyright holders. Dorling Kindersley apologizes for any unintentional omissions and would be pleased, in such cases, to add an acknowledgement in future editions.

All other images © Dorling Kindersley
For further information see: www.dkimages.com